# IT'S TIME THE TALE WERE TOLD

## A PEOPLE'S HISTORY OF THE SMITHS

# IT'S TIME THE TALE WERE TOLD

# A PEOPLE'S HISTORY OF THE SMITHS

## IAIN KEY & RICHARD HOUGHTON

First published in Great Britain 2019
This edition published by Spenwood Books Ltd 2026

Spenwood Books Ltd
1 Totnes Road
Manchester
M21 8XF



A CIP record for this book is available from the British Library.

ISBN 978-1-915858-28-3
All other image copyrights: as captioned
In the event of copyright query please contact richard@spenwoodbooks.com

Cover design: Michelle Hickman & Bruce Graham
Design: Bruce Graham, The Night Owl
Copyediting & Proofreading: Elizabeth Dodgson & Jade Barnes
Picture Editor: Jade Barnes

For the last 20 years I've lived in Stretford, surrounded by Smiths lore. Ten minutes from the Iron Bridge, a few more from Morrissey's former home on Kings Road, as well as down the road from the gone but not forgotten El Patio. My local, and favourite record shop, Fountain Records, was previously called Reel Around The Fountain, named after the song of the same name, which itself was inspired by the water feature in Stretford Arndale (until its removal at some point in the late 1980s).

Like many, my first introduction to The Smiths was via *Top Of The Pops*, the weird bloke with… I'm not sure. Was it waving the gladioli, the flowers in the back pocket or the hearing aid? The memory cheats but the conversation on the school bus the following morning still seems real: 'Did you see that band?'

As I was a *Smash Hits*-reading teen, living in a Worcestershire village, with limited funds and access to record shops, I was reliant on the likes of the Top 40 and my trusty handed-down cassette player to tape what I could. It would be a year or so before I discovered John Peel but, by early 1985, I'd managed to get a friend to record the debut album and *Hatful Of Hollow* onto a C90 cassette (omitting the last few tracks due to timing reasons).

Come 1986, we had moved back to Manchester and I was buying singles, reading the music press and obsessed by the 'indie scene' although still slightly too young to go to gigs on my own. *The Queen Is Dead* was released a couple of weeks after I'd completed my O levels and accompanied me that summer as I attended various interviews for jobs, eventually ending up on a Youth Training Scheme in the Taxation Department at the Co-operative Wholesale Society, surrounded by a number of colleagues who seemed to be from a bygone age and the perfect material for Morrissey's dry and witty lyrics.

The following year I bought Strangeways, *Here We Come* on the day of release whilst en route to a date with a girl in Longsight. It didn't last more than an hour; she wasn't a fan and thought I was weird for liking them. My wish to see them in concert had been scuppered by the fact they'd already split up, meaning my only experiences of hearing the band live at that time were limited to a few B-sides, the Piccadilly Radio broadcast of their set from 1986's The Festival of The Tenth Summer (weirdly, almost a year later in 1987) and the arrival of *Rank*.

Thankfully there are many bootlegs, from the earliest of days, which have soundtracked my work on this book. It's been a pleasure and a privilege interviewing fans and compiling their memories for *It's Time The Tale Were Told*, with contributions from across the globe.

I hope you enjoy it.

IAIN KEY

## ACKNOWLEDGEMENTS

Iain Key and Richard Houghton would like to thank the following: Simon Wolstencroft, whose memoir *You Can Drum But You Can't Hide* is a must read for any Smiths fan; Lee Thacker, illustrator extraordinaire, whose Peel inspired book on the Festive Fifty is available at http://www.lulu.com/shop/lee-thacker/the-festive-fiftyan-illustrated-memoir/paperback/product-11605351.html

For permission to quote from their publications or blogs: Karren Ablaze, *The City is Ablaze*; Martin Whitehead, *The Underground*; Stuart Edwards, blackcountryrock.co/2015/0522/with-love-frommanchester; photographer Mike Powell, michaelpowell.com; Colm O'Callaghan, *The Blackpool Sentinel*, https://theblackpoolsentinel.wordpress.com/2017/08/04/the-smiths-in-cork-1984/; the late Peter Smith, https://vintagerock.wordpress.com/2014/03/30/redwedge-tour-newcastle-cityhall-31st-january-1986/ and his daughter Laura; Neil Ward, UEA Vice-Chancellor, 'The Smiths 14 February 1984: a belated review'; Brian Bilston for 'Could Have Been a Poet'; Dave Haslam for the edited extract from *Sonic Youth Slept On My Floor* (Constable, 2018); Dave Scott aka @arghkid for Colpo di Fulmine: The Thunderbolt; Keeley Moss; Tim Baigent (https://www.palooka5.co.uk); James Reid-Sinclair (https://www.instagram.com/jamesboyrecords/); Peter Martin, for his stories and many photos; the following Facebook page administrators for their kind support for and promotion of the appeal for Smiths fans to get in touch: Ben Darnton from Guildford Past and Present; Aberdeen Music; Paul from Decade 77-87 – A Grown Up Disco; Davie Kirk from The Westway Kilmarnock Music Society; Nick Boldock from Hull Music Archive; Matthew Norman and Manchester Digital Music Archive, www.mdmarchive.co.uk; James Bruce from Colchester Music; Luke Gilligan from Classic Dublin Gigs; William Wycherley (@MorrisseyIndeed).

### IAIN KEY

I would like to thank: Richard, for allowing me the opportunity to work on this project; Brian Bilston for the brilliant 'Could Have Been A Poet'; Michelle Hickman for her Smiths image; and Bruce Graham, for his work on the design; my son, Mckenzi, of whom I'm eternally proud as he gets ready to start his 'University' life; Paul, my best mate who has always encouraged my love of music and writing; my siblings, Barbara, Andy and Cathy, on account of being my family; Debs, Jason and Cat – working in Telecoms will always be more exciting than writing books, honestly; John, Nigel, Audrey, Wayne, Ged, Nathan, Naomi, Mel and everyone at Louder Than War; Guy and Mags, whose love of The Smiths knows no bounds; Nigel Young at Fountain Records for feeding my vinyl addiction; Carolyn Bernier, Natalie Golden, Justin Jelly, Dave Deamer, Billy Burns, Dan

James and Rob Smart, all for many years of friendship. And my fiancée Gillian Marie Rimmer, for whom there will always be a light that will never go out.

## RICHARD HOUGHTON

I would like to thank: Lou Duffy-Howard and Jeremy Kidd of The Red Guitars (https://www.redguitars.co.uk/); Billy Bragg; Roger Denton, for his loan of Johnny Marr's *Set The Boy Free* and for the early and relentless exposure to The Smiths; Sharon Watters, Steve Catterall, Joseph Kelly, Martin Mullaney, Ken Sweeney, Gavin Underhill, Dave Stan, David Manning, Peter Lindsey-Jones, Anthony Jackson, Brian Parkyn and Nuan Butcherd and Sam O'Daniel of yourolderbrother.com; Neil Cossar and Liz Sanchez for publishing the first edition of this book; Steven Wright; Bruce Graham for his design skills; Bill Houghton for undertaking the additional domestic duties that enabled me to get this book finished first time around (and for passing his degree); and Kate Sullivan for the peace, love and understanding.

If you have a memory of a Smiths show, a solo Morrissey show, or of any other act from the last 50 years we'd love to hear about it at iwasatthatgig@gmail.com.

**Could Have Been a Poet**

It's time the tale were told

of how you took a boy into your fold

and opened his eyes

for a maximum recommended retail price of £3.99

Oh, how I loved the way you would sing a line

and then repeat it

Yes, I loved the way you would sing a line

and then repeat it


Good times for loose change

and for what I was about to receive –

sixteen songs and a gatefold sleeve –

I was truly grateful

You filled in the hollows of those hateful days

of nothing much in particular

And those guitars! Heavens knows I swooned

like a lovelorn Caligula


Oh, the melancholic afternoons

we would spend in my room

you spinning round

me with your words in my hands

I think you helped me get through my exams,

and unhampered life's complexities

There's more to it than textbooks, you know

there's so much more

I would rather not go back

to those old days anymore

But even now I can remember the length of each track –

*Still Ill*, three minutes thirty-four,

*Accept Yourself*, four minutes two –

it was not like any other love

I decree it was really something

I'm still more than fond of you


Yes, it was really something

and I'm still more than fond of you


*Brian Bilston*

*Image: (Stephen Wright)*

# THE VINE

## 1981, SALE, MANCHESTER, UK

### SIMON WOLSTENCROFT

I had a brief association with The Smiths, for better or worse! I was in a band with Ian Brown and John Squire. We would drink together in a pub called The Vine in Sale, a suburb of Manchester. Ian then went travelling around Europe before he and John became the Stone Roses. A mutual friend of Johnny Marr said that Johnny was looking for a drummer to start a new band, so I agreed to meet him in The Vine one night. Sure enough, he came along. And he was very, very cocksure. I got to meet Johnny and he looked fantastic, with what he was wearing and his haircut. He was such a hustler. And he was such a funny guy, very quick-witted. He doesn't suffer fools.

We started to hang out at Andy Rourke's dad's house, in Sale, and started a band.

Andy's dad was always away on business so Andy and his three brothers often had the run of the house. Their mother wasn't with them anymore. It became a bit of a den of iniquity. We were listening to a lot of music and talking about forming this group called Freak Party – why Johnny chose that name I don't know – and me, Andy and Johnny started rehearsing at the house. Then we got a rehearsal room in the cellar of a carpet shop in Sale and then we started rehearsing in Ancoats. This was 1981, going into 1982.

We were all taking drugs – Andy and I more than Johnny – and all got arrested in the studio as we were auditioning singers for Freak Party. Johnny got arrested, fined and prosecuted and said to us, 'I can't hang around with you guys anymore because I'm going to get into trouble.' We didn't see him for two or three months. He moved out from Andy's, where he'd been sleeping in Andy's dad's bed with

*Above: The Vine pub in Sale, Greater Manchester is where the seeds of The Smiths were sown*

*Top: Simon Wolstencroft was Johnny Marr's first choice for drummer with The Smiths*

his girlfriend, Angie, and Andy and I carried on without him.

# DECIBEL STUDIOS

## 1981, ANCOATS, MANCHESTER, UK

### JAN DZARAN

Decibel Studios was located on the third floor of the largely empty Beehive Mill in Ancoats, Manchester. (The mill was quite dilapidated at the time and probably a death trap, but you don't think about that when you're young and having fun.)

In 1980 I secured a job there as an assistant studio engineer. I didn't know that much about studio recording, having only done live work, but I was friends with Jon Hurst, who was for a while the main engineer at Decibel, so perhaps he thought I showed promise. I was eager to learn. Studio owner Philippe Delcloque took charge of the more prestigious sessions, but left Jon and I to record the regular bands and run the place.

We had many unofficial recording sessions there, inviting friends in for late night sessions. This was okay as I was paid in studio time rather than money, so we got away with a lot. The studio also had rehearsal rooms, and Johnny Marr and Andy Rourke, who I already knew, were regular visitors. Back then, most musicians knew one another, or had at least met, and it's largely the same today. Manchester, though a city, is culturally more like a village.

One day in 1981 Johnny, Andy and Simon (Wolstencroft) turned up to record something. I can't remember if another engineer recorded the band (it may have been me) but I certainly did the mixes. The band were recorded live, in one take, and there were no overdubs or drop-ins.

I spent some time processing Johnny's guitar through reverbs and EQs on mixdown, bouncing it back and forth more or less to see how wild and extreme I could make it.

I also applied the same extreme process to the bass. I was working with an Otari eight track on one-inch, through a TAC desk, with quarter-inch mixes made on a Revox B77. It was a complete experiment on my part, and I must have done at least half a dozen mixes.

The whole track, an instrumental which I think was improvised, sounded, raw, wild and somewhat Dionysian. Johnny was very pleased with the result, and asked for the wildest mix, but Simon wasn't happy as the kick wasn't strong enough. A fault on my part as I had got somewhat lost in the guitar and bass. (I offered him some lame-arsed excuse at the time which I apologise for here.)

### SIMON WOLSTENCROFT

We tried to audition three or four different singers but the final straw was the arrest of us all by the Serious Crime Squad in the studio. Johnny leaving finished Freak Party off.

### RICHARD SINGLETON

I used to rehearse at Spirit Studios on Tariff Street with my band The Still. I remember our original member Dale Hibbert telling me he'd joined a new band called The Smiths with a guy called Morrissey, and Mike Joyce who I knew from his Hoax days. My thoughts were, 'Another band with a rubbish name who will go nowhere.'

The Still are now a covers band who do Smiths songs.

### SIMON WOLSTENCROFT

Two or three months later, Johnny rang me out of the blue to say, 'I've met this guy, Stephen Morrissey. We've started a new band called The Smiths and we want you as the drummer.' My head wasn't really in a good place at the time with the drugs and everything, so I said, 'Oh, I don't know about that, Johnny.'

He said, 'Come on, please give it a go at least. We're doing a demo recording at Decibel Studios.' The studio owner was away in Paris on business and Johnny said, 'We've got the studio for nothing.'

I went along. Andy Rourke hadn't been asked to join the band. The engineer Dale (Hibbert), who had the key to the studio, was playing bass. It was me on drums, Johnny on guitar and Morrissey came along. But I didn't like the cut of his jib. He was what back in the day the *NME* was calling a shoe-gazer. I didn't like his style.

*Funky Si at Salford Lads Club (Richard Houghton)*

Because we'd been listening to jazz-funk and Grace Jones and Earth, Wind & Fire round at Andy's for the last six months, we wanted the band to sound a bit like that. Freak Party were very similar to A Certain Ratio. We were listening to the album *Sextet* over and over again with Andy playing all the bass lines off it and Johnny doing that Nile Rodgers-style guitar. I was hoping the band would sound like this when Morrissey came. But, of course, that wasn't to be.

There were a couple of songs recorded, including 'Suffer Little Children' about the Moors Murders, which was very morose and I just thought, 'Ugh, what is this?' So when Johnny told me the band was called The Smiths, I said, 'It's a shit name.' It was very plain and boring. People had exotic-sounding names like Freak Party or Depeche Mode.

We did the two tracks and I didn't really like it, so I said, 'Thanks Johnny, but I don't really want to do it.' According to Johnny in his book, he was offering me big bags of weed to do the gig, but I don't remember that. I just wasn't really interested at all. I said 'no' and that was basically the last time I played with them.

Another reason I didn't want to join The Smiths was because Andy had not been asked to play bass from the very beginning. I knew Andy was a better bass player than Dale.

If Andy had been in the band right from the word go, it might have all been different. It might have been me with a big mansion in Cheshire. But it just wasn't to be. They asked Andy to join pretty soon after that.

Andy was my best mate and I was absolutely gutted and sank into a bit of a depression, self-medicating with the drugs. It was a pretty bad time really. Within about six months to a year, they were riding high. The next thing you know they're on *Top of the Pops*. I learned to like them. With 'What Difference Does it Make?' I thought, 'Wow, this is pretty good, this one.' That was the first one that stood out for me. 'Hand in Glove' was a bit too indie and shambling for my liking.

I did used to go and see them on the early tours. One gig that stands out is at Cannock, in a marquee in Staffordshire. It was a very threatening atmosphere. I think they'd been in the paper already about the Moors Murders. And there was the association of Morrissey flailing flowers about. There weren't many people there but it was quite scary to be there, with all these little locals hanging about outside the marquee and looking very threatening.

I remember Brixton Fridge. That night, Seymour Stein from Columbia/Warner Brothers had flown over on Concorde just to see The Smiths. He was dressed up in this white flowing shirt with white trousers and white shoes. He looked like he had a lot of money, which of course he did! But Mike Joyce made a couple of cock-ups on the drums that night. I drove Andy back home because I had driven down in my car and, for a minute, I thought I was going to get back in the band because Mike kept making these mistakes, which wouldn't have been very fair on Mike. Andy and Johnny were trying to get me back in the band. But Joe Moss, the manager at the time, knew my history for dabbling in drugs and said, 'Whoa, whoa, whoa, we'd better not rock the boat at this stage'. Andy was having his own problems of course.

By the morning time, we'd had an official statement off Joe Moss saying, 'We're going to stick with Mike' and that was the end of that.

Morrissey's a very charming guy. He didn't actually look me in the face during the recording. But he'd see me at the gigs and he'd say, 'Hello Simon. How are you? Lovely to see you.'

The Free Trade Hall in March 1984 is another gig I remember. I

went to pick Morrissey and Sandie
Shaw up off the train from London.
They were going straight to the gig.
Johnny must have said, 'Do you
mind picking him up in case he gets
lost?' I had a Triumph Dolomite.
Sandie got in the back and
Morrissey sat in the front. He was
stroking the fake walnut dashboard
and he said, 'This is a lovely car,
Simon.' That was a good night.

By 1986, I'm in The Fall and
we played the Festival of the
Tenth Summer at the G-Mex in
Manchester, which was packed out.
The Smiths were on, as well as New
Order, Orchestral Manoeuvres
in the Dark, A Certain Ratio and
others. One of my best memories
is watching them there, with
Morrissey waving the placard
'The Queen Is Dead' about on
stage, to an ecstatic crowd. They
just sounded so powerful, partly
because of Johnny who is the finest
guitarist of my generation.

Johnny asked me if Craig
Gannon would join The Smiths
when they wanted to double up
and have two guitarists when they
went to America. So I feel I was
responsible for him getting the gig
with The Smiths.

I was in and around the
entourage right throughout the
career of the band. I was there the
night Andy got fired, after he got
arrested. I remember the characters
around the band, and the road
crew going for sneaky McDonalds
like naughty children so Morrissey
wouldn't find out. Johnny bought
into vegetarianism very early on in
the band.

I'm still friends with Andy. I've
been over to New York a couple
of times to see him, and he comes
over here maybe once a year so
I always hook up with him. He's
been there for over ten years now.
He's got another band.

I love Mike. He's a very, very
funny guy. I bump into him from
time to time if I'm out and about.
Going back to the Seymour Stein
night, I don't know where Mike
got to hear about that. I think I
mentioned it in my book.

I don't see Johnny a lot. I see him
mostly driving around town now in
a Bentley. When my book came out,
I bumped into Johnny and he said,
'Si, I love your book. It's brilliant.
I've read it. Thanks for saying nice
things about me.' And he returned
the favour in his book. He put
a lovely picture in, so I'm really
grateful to him for doing that.

I don't see Morrissey at all, although
people see him in the Unicorn Deli in
Chorlton when he's over here. After
The Smiths split up, in 1989 I wrote
to Morrissey asking 'Any chance of
playing drums in your solo project?'
He wrote me an amusing postcard
saying, 'My hip-swivelling days are
temporarily suspended. In the event
of a thaw, I'll give you a ring. But is
your P45 not spoken for? I thought
you were in The Fall.' Which I was.
But had he said, 'Yeah, come down
to the studio next week,' I would
probably have left The Fall and been
off like a shot, because he was a
household name by then.

I'm still playing. After The Fall
I went with Ian Brown, my old
schoolmate, for a couple of years in
1999/2000. Since then, I've been in
a few line-ups of different bands.

I could have had a mansion and
a Bentley but I've lived the dream

too. I've been in a band touring the world. I've been very lucky with the bands I've been in. I don't feel totally hard done by. I got over it when I joined The Fall, because I didn't have time to think about what The Smiths were doing. Mark E Smith always used to take the piss, because they'd made it. He used to say, 'You're not like them, Simon.'

I am a fan, definitely. It was just that first impression that changed the course of my life in that room in Ancoats. It would have all been different had I said, 'Yeah, I'll stick with the band.'

## THE RITZ

### 4 OCTOBER 1982, MANCHESTER, UK

Supporting Blue Rondo à la Turk, The Smiths' first live appearance was with a line up of Morrissey on vocals, Johnny Marr on guitar, Mike Joyce on drums and Dale Hibbert on bass. Morrissey's friend James Maker introduced the band and remained on stage throughout the performance as a dancer, apparently on a whim of Morrissey's.

James Maker: There were no instructions. I think it was generally accepted I would improvise… I was there to drink red wine, make extraneous hand gestures and keep well within the tight, chalked circle that Morrissey had drawn around me.

After the first gig Dale Hibbert was replaced by Andy Rourke.

Andy Rourke: I played my first gig in a tiny gay club called Manhattan Sound. I was very nervous. We all were. [Morrissey] had a pocket full of confetti and threw it over the audience, which none of us expected.

## MANHATTAN SOUND

### 25 JANUARY 1983, MANCHESTER, UK

### ANNE FORD

I was in my first year at university and I was a regular at the Manhattan, a basement club in Spring Gardens. Originally a cocktail/Stringfellows sort of place, with young women serving drinks dressed in tutus or something and not particularly a young persons' club, it was taken over by a chap called Peter who later bought the Rembrandt. It wasn't really a live music venue and was fairly small. There was a separate room where films were sometimes shown on a screen. There was no stage as such. Acts performed on the dance floor.

There had been a few bands on,

*Manhattan Sound advert*

promoted by a couple of lads that came into the bar. I remember the poster going up behind the bar advertising The Smiths. It was the grey/lilac one that featured 'Hand In Glove'. The thing that struck me was their name. It was so different sounding compared with Joy Division, Duran Duran, Spandau Ballet, etc. We had no idea what sort of sound to expect.

There were about 40 people there. We were close to them as it was so small. Morrissey was Morrissey and did the flailing arms thing. The sound was great and different. They felt like they would stay around a bit and I think most people there liked them although I don't recall anyone having seen or heard of them before. I saw a few other acts there; Sade, who was called Pride at the time, performed with a sax player and was sexy, understated and fab. There was a bit of a scuffle right in front of her and she stopped singing and asked them to stop.

Two or three years later, I used to hang out at Corbières and they had bands on – A Certain Ratio, Easterhouse. When that closed, we used to walk over to Pierrot, off Cross Street. Pierrot also had the occasional band on. I hung out with the Diggle brothers and Craig Gannon, who had just joined The Smiths. I remember one time, when we wanted to carry on drinking mid-week, we decided to walk over to the Man Alive club on Grosvenor Street. We walked in, they saw Craig and they started playing Smiths tunes, followed by Sandie Shaw.





## THE HAÇIENDA

### 4 FEBRUARY 1983, MANCHESTER, UK



### LYNDON MULHEARN

I first saw them with my pals in February '83 at the Haçienda and have followed them all ever since. I have met Jonny and Mike lots of times as they are both Man City fans and go to the matches. Me and my mate even had guitar

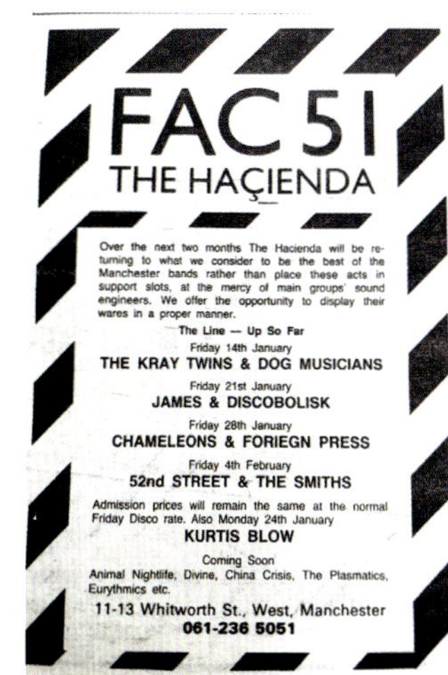



*Haçienda*

lessons off Andy and Johnny a few years back.

I only met Morrissey once, during a photo shoot by Stephen Wright in the Arndale Centre on the same day the Salford Lads Club pic was taken for *The Queen Is Dead*. But I've seen him loads of times in this country and went to see him at the Hollywood Bowl last year.

### GUY BURKE

My personal journey to Smiths fandom probably began before the band actually existed. In the very early eighties, I began frequenting The Quadrant pub in Stretford, Manchester, not far from the Morrissey family home on Kings Road. It's pretty certain that I was in there the same time as him on many occasions, but neither of us knew who the other was!

One of the people my friends and I did know however was Ivor Perry, later to join The Smiths briefly himself. We were all budding musicians, but Ivor always seemed to be a few steps ahead of us. He later formed Easterhouse who had a cult following for the first half of that decade.

I was an avid reader of *NME* and in 1982 and there was a rumbling within its pages about this new band from Manchester who were going to be huge. In early 1983, I saw them at the now legendary Haçienda gig. If there were 80 people in attendance I would probably be exaggerating, and it appeared that at least half of those were mates of the band! In a set lasting probably no more than about 40 minutes I can honestly

say I was quite underwhelmed and this bloke chucking flowers around didn't do it for me at all!

They did however leave me interested enough to buy the debut album not long afterwards and again it didn't really grab me despite a couple of good tracks. They were getting rave reviews from the likes of David 'Kid' Jensen on Radio 1 but in all honesty, I was failing to see what all the fuss was actually about!

It was the 'What Difference Does It Make' single that was my lightbulb moment and the *Hatful Of Hollow* album that sealed the deal! I never saw them live again but did buy or had bought for me many of the albums, and the rest as they say…

### DAVID MYERS

I saw their third ever gig at the Haçienda in Manchester in February 1983 and then their visit to Stoke Poly where I was a student not long after. Before all that, I bought my trousers from Johnny when he worked at X Clothes in Manchester.

## RAFTERS

### 21 FEBRUARY 1983, MANCHESTER, UK

### SIMON DAVIES

I saw them a few times. The first time was at Rafters where they supported Richard Hell. As an aspiring guitarist, I knew it was game over after seeing Johnny. I'd just got my first car, a Triumph 1500, so it was a first drive into

*Rafters ad*

town. It wouldn't start after the gig and we were helped by a policeman, who took his helmet off to have a look in the bonnet. He then noticed my mate Ted jigging around with it on his head.

### GED DUFFY

Slim, future formidable roadie, and I were asked to work at the Richard Hell and The Smiths gig at Rafters. This was the first time we had worked for the promoter Alan Wise for a while, as he had been concentrating on managing Nico.

After both bands had done their soundcheck, Alan asked Slim and I to carry about 30 chairs down from Fagin's (the venue upstairs) and set them up in front of the stage. When the audience started coming in, we were told to keep people away from the chairs. Shortly before The Smiths took to the stage, the seats were occupied by family members of the band. Parents and grandparents were all there.

Once The Smiths were on, Slim and I had to stand behind the chairs so that no one banged into the people sitting there. It was so strange as comments were being passed from the families to the stage and back from the stage to the families. 'Oh Stephen, that was wonderful,' or, 'John, I never knew you could play like that,' that kind of thing. It was like a private concert for the family. Very strange, I must say. Despite that I thought that The Smiths sounded really good and were a band to keep my eyes on.

As soon as they had finished, we had to get all the chairs back upstairs to Fagin's. I had never seen anyone do this at a gig before. Richard Hell was really good. The crowd liked him, and we spent a bit of time backstage with him. He was a top bloke.

## THE ROCK GARDEN

### 23 MARCH 1983, LONDON, UK

### PHIL MCADAM, AGE 19

Like all my favourite bands I heard them via John Peel and read about them in *NME* or *Melody Maker*. I only saw them the once and I can't remember much about it. It was around the time of 'Hand In Glove' and before the first album came out. It was their first London show.

## 'HAND IN GLOVE'

### RELEASED 13 MAY 1983

### WILLIAM SMITH

I'd spent my life cursing the name. Smith. Stout. Squat. Common

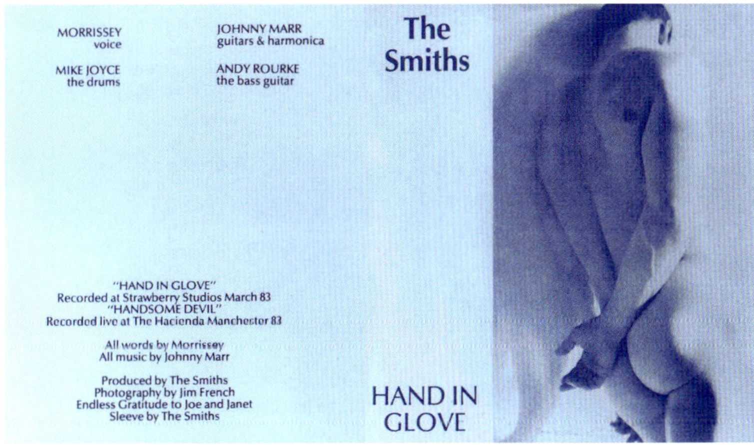

as. I imagined Patti as a long-lost aunt and Mark E as a cousin once removed. Then came The Smiths, from Manchester not New York, not a Smith amongst them. The land of Joy Division, New Order and The Fall, 200 miles north and a world away from suburban Essex, the land of Dr Feelgood, Ian Dury, Billy Bragg and my youth. My paternal grandfather, Bernard, hailed from Blackburn so I sort of identified. As resolutely northern as rain, Smiths were a breed apart.

Happily shunning the Factory production line for Rough Trade, Kings Cross, they left the north and travelled south. While frontman Morrissey doffed a lyrical cap to The Kinks and Small Faces, the wunderkind Johnny Marr paid his own tribute to the Stones and The Who. Although I'd found my generation's voice in The Jam and the Blockheads – both of whose jobs were done and gone – there was always Madness, but by 1982 they were writing songs about condoms and Morris Minors. Much as I loved the nutty boys, that joke wasn't funny anymore.

So, we were looking for a serious band with a gang like attitude, on a mission. And The Smiths were it. Having arrived almost fully formed, they resurrected the notion of the indie band as a dangerous, subversive vehicle for renegade art and ideas. As fresh and unique as they sounded in 1983, The Smiths were the latest in a long line of articulate, erudite, literary indie guitar groups. Manchester's afore-mentioned finest, along with Buzzcocks and Magazine, had all pushed the indie envelope beyond its obvious limitations in the post punk era. But The Smiths were able to redefine and reinvigorate the genre because of the singular, up front, songwriting strike partnership of Morrissey and Marr. In this pair of determined pop iconoclasts, The Smiths had two ferociously gifted craftsmen who'd dedicated their young lives to the study of art, fashion, film and literature as well as music.

The Smiths were a beacon of hope, a shining light of lovelorn levity, a lo-fi jingle jangle mourning for an age of excess. First heard on John Peel, 'Hand In Glove' was an opening rush of epic proportions, a defiant manifesto for love and loyalty, Morrissey's poetic declarations bolstered by Marr's guitar and harmonica. 'Reel Around The Fountain', the Peel session, was its stately companion piece, a sacrificial yearning and a tremulous awakening beauty. Then 'This Charming Man', the singular, siren sound of Marr's guitar heralding the arrival of Morrissey's saviour. It felt like a baptism, a conversion and a consummation in one. The ringing arpeggio chords of Marr's guitar sound like the very chimes of freedom and the perfect joyous chaperone to Morrissey's funny peculiar pitch and phrasing, betraying such naked vulnerability. 'This Charming Man' was rarely off my turntable, on constant rotation with the flip sides, 'Jeane', 'Accept Yourself' and 'Wonderful Woman'. And this was all before 1984, the eponymous debut album and *Hatful Of Hollow* – brim-full of the first five A sides, B sides and album session tracks – and still the most compelling document of The Smiths' first golden year.

More than 40 years on, I'm still aghast, still ill, still happy to be a part of the great Smith family.



## UNIVERSITY OF LONDON UNION
### 6 MAY 1983, LONDON, UK

### STEVE CATTERALL

I first saw The Smiths at ULU. I first recorded them at the Brixton Ace in June. From the end of 1984 onwards, I saw – and recorded – pretty much every Smiths show in the UK and Ireland. At the time I thought I'd take the opportunity to put down my memories of each show before I forgot them. Memory is a funny thing. Looking at those entries now, there are some I can't remember, and some I remember slightly differently. Recording the shows does give you a view, which is slightly set apart from the actual event sometimes.

The Smiths hardly varied their set list from show to show on individual tours, which meant that shows did tend to blend into one another a bit. My favourite tour was probably the Scottish tour in 1985.

I think they were at the top of their game at this period, and the tour was short enough and stopped in some out of the way places, such as the Shetland Islands, so that it never lost the initial energy.

## PEEL SESSION MAIDA VALE STUDIOS
### 18 MAY 1983, LONDON, UK

Broadcast on Radio 1's *John Peel Show* on 31 May 1983, the band went into the BBC's Maida Vale Studios and recorded their first session for legendary DJ John Peel, whose reputation for breaking bands in the UK stretched back to the sixties and acts such as Pink Floyd and T. Rex. The band recorded four tracks – 'Handsome Devil', 'Reel Around The Fountain', 'Miserable Lie' and 'What Difference Does It Make?' – and the session was broadcast five further times in the following three years. Three of the four tracks, excluding 'Miserable Lie', were later released on *Hatful of Hollow*.

## ELECTRIC BALLROOM
### 21 MAY 1983, LONDON, UK

### GREG COTMORE

Context gives meaning, if only to the writer. I left New Zealand in early 1983 to follow my English-born girlfriend to London. Fool that I was and ever so in love, I saved up my wages from a deadbeat job and

*(Manchester Music Digital Archive)*

flew over to join her in Camden Town. Looking back at the young besotted idiot that I was, I'm sure I talked myself into believing she was pleased to see me. Maybe she was, but probably not.

Arriving in London was a daunting experience: all those people, all those buildings, all that history. Moreover, it wasn't easy getting established as job opportunities in Thatcher's England were not exactly throwing themselves at me. Consequently,

I was somewhat miserly with what little money I had. Nevertheless, I still bought the *New Musical Express*, a regular read of mine since 1973. It was here that I saw an advertisement for The Fall playing at the Electric Ballroom in Camden. I don't remember noticing the name of the support band.

My girlfriend, not being a fan of The Fall, wasn't keen. Indeed, it was because of her that I had to leave The Fall's 1982 NZ Wellington gig before it ended, exiting mid-way through 'Tempo House'. I have remonstrated with myself for that stupid mistake ever since.

The idea of The Fall playing a gig within walking distance was a temptation I couldn't resist. So off I trotted to Rock On Records and bought my £3 ticket. I'm pretty sure it had the name of the support band printed on it but, again, I paid no heed.

From the distance of 36 years, the night of the gig is memorable for two reasons. First, the stink and pall of smoke; cigarettes back then were not banned at concerts. I had to wave my hands about to see the stage, never mind breathe, and my jacket reeked of smoke for weeks afterwards. Second, the support band, the name of which I had dutifully ignored until now. They were, of course, The Smiths.

In 1983, I was still waiting for the music of the eighties to happen; Duran Duran definitely were *not* the starting gun. By the end of The Smiths' short set, for me, the music of the eighties had arrived.

Due to the passage of years, my memory of the setlist is somewhat vague. I remember the relentlessness of 'What Difference Does it Make?' and 'Hand In Glove', which had just been released as their debut single. One song is deeply etched into my brain; their performance of 'Reel Around The Fountain'. I was in awe of the majesty, mystery and magnitude of attitude. In that moment, I experienced my own pre-fame Beatles or Bowie moment. I knew that, in years to come, I would get a thrilling buzz to say, 'I saw The Smiths before they were big.' I did, and still do.

When The Fall came on, it was to the strains of 'Tempo House'. The smile on my face must have been insufferable.

### PADDY SHENNAN, AGE 19

It's always a bonus when you enjoy a support band you had never previously seen or heard. I was vaguely aware of a new group from Manchester called The Smiths, possibly having seen them mentioned as the support in the gig listings in *NME*. The name would have intrigued me as my favourite band at that time – by a mile – was The Fall. Perhaps I imagined the name was a tribute – a Manchester band named in recognition of

*Paddy Shennan thought The Smiths were a tribute band to The Fall's lead singer, Mark E Smith*

Mark E Smith. I travelled from my home town of Preston to stay with a friend, Paul Platypus, who like me was an active participant in the underground cassette scene and who, like me, had compiled the Obscurist chart for *Sounds*.

This was The Smiths' seventh gig, and I recall watching their performance while sitting on the floor of the venue. Between songs I remember saying, 'Pretty good, aren't they?' I was impressed by their bright, clean sound, and their catchy songs. You could clearly hear the words, and they sounded intelligent and witty. I also recall thinking, 'That shades-wearing guitarist looks pretty cocky!' No offence, Johnny.

After the gig, Geoff Travis walked past me. Both bands, of course, were on his Rough Trade label, and Mark E Smith was later to complain about most of the company's resources being concentrated on The Smiths. Not at this point, though – The Fall were very much the bigger of the two bands. But The Smiths were beginning to make their mark. When I got home, I ordered their newly-released single, 'Hand In Glove', from Rough Trade's mail order business.

## MINERS GALA, CANNOCK PARK

### 2 JUNE 1983, CANNOCK CHASE, UK

### MICHAEL SMALLMAN

My love of music had me always on the lookout for exciting new bands. Most of my gig-going was centred on the Birmingham and Wolverhampton areas, but for favourite artists I would travel around the country. I was heavily into bands like Siouxsie and The Banshees, The Fall and Dead Kennedys, and consider myself very lucky to have seen them many times plus others such as Magazine.

The Smiths hadn't really entered my list of 'bands I must see', but they were playing in my home-town of Cannock. The Miners Gala had been taking place for many years. As a child, it was one of the highlights of the year as there was so little to do in this quiet little mining town. In 1983, I remember an advert for it in the *Cannock Advertiser*. In small print, right at the very bottom of the page, it was announced that The Smiths would be playing live at the closing of the gala. I decided to join a few friends in the beer tent to watch the show. The gig was free entry, but strategically placed collection boxes were there for anyone wanting to make a donation to the miners' cause.

When I got to the park the large marquee where the bands would be performing was about a quarter full of people who were already well on the way to becoming blotto with booze. I joined my friends, who included members of local band Balaam and the Angel, and found a place to stand. The gala had been going on all day, with guest speakers including high up officials from the miners' union. This was the year before the great miners' strike of the eighties and tensions were already running high as the threat of the closure of many of the areas surviving coal mines was ever present. A funfair was provided for children and several beer tents for the adults. A carnival queen would also have been crowned. Three bands would be providing the entertainment – A Dog Named Ego, Shambolic Climate and The Smiths.

A Dog Named Ego's set went by with little acknowledgement from the audience, who were mainly only interested in the seemingly never-ending flow of beer. Shambolic

Climate were next and it was then that I noticed the first stirrings of the trouble that was to come later. The bass player had a habit of playing with his tongue stuck out and this did not go unnoticed by some unruly audience members, who spent most of the set mimicking him, leaping around in front of the stage with their tongues hanging out. It was starting to get ugly, but as soon as the band finished their set the ringleaders were back to the bar area.

Most of the ringleaders were known to me – I used to go to school with several of them, whilst I was aware of others from local pubs. For the most part I had no problem with these people, but it became increasingly clear that the long day had induced their inner aggression and they were looking for an outlet to unleash it. The Smiths would, unfortunately, become that outlet.

The Smiths took to the stage at around 9pm. Morrissey introduced the band and The opening number, 'You've Got Everything Now'. I was immediately struck by how professional they sounded in comparison to the opening acts. As the band continued, 'Handsome Devil' was next, proudly introduced by Morrissey as 'one

side of a record we have out'.

By now the drunken louts were starting to notice the band and were drifting back towards the stage area. The next song was introduced as a question to the now very vocal gathering – 'Can you accept yourselves?' The rowdy crowd were throwing beer over each other and were getting dangerously close to the stage.

At the end of the song, Morrissey stated, 'Obviously not. Oh well, what difference does it make?' It was clear now that what the gig most needed was security – but there was none. 'Reel Around The Fountain' was next and amazingly things seemed to settle down for the duration of the song. The next track was introduced as 'a brand new song called 'Wonderful Woman', and at this point the aggression boiled over and the louts decided that their idea of fun would be to spoil the event for the few of us that wanted to watch the band.

Morrissey was ridiculed and called all manner of insulting names. The aggressors also turned on members of the audience. Despite pleas from the band to calm down, the wailing and screaming continued. The band pressed on by playing the other side of the single, 'Hand In Glove'. By now plastic glasses filled with beer were being lobbed around the marquee, aimed mainly at the audience. The band soldiered on through the song, bravely ignoring the hail of abuse aimed at them. Morrissey announced the song 'Miserable Lie' and was met with a hail of beer and homophobic abuse. After a few minutes, the band threw their arms up and abandoned the set – things had just got too dangerous for them to continue. It was quite obvious that they couldn't wait to get out of Cannock, and accompanied by a police escort they left.

It was such a shame, seeing the band perform for the first time was marred by a gathering of idiots. This was the first time The Smiths had played outside Manchester or London. After the set finished I grabbed a set list from the stage. I only wish I still had it. It showed that several more songs were due to be played, including 'I Don't Owe You Anything' and 'These Things Take Time'.

## FIGHTING COCKS

### 3 JUNE 1983, MOSELEY, BIRMINGHAM, UK

### CLIVE WHITTAKER

I can't remember whose idea it was to get into promoting. I can remember Brian Farley and I had given up with our own group and were sick of going to poorly run gigs in Birmingham. Brian – Wurz to his friends – wrote down an action plan which seemed to be pretty do-able and we started contacting venues and bands. After struggling to stop losing money elsewhere putting on bands that we liked, we fell into step and fetched up at the Fighting Cocks in the fall of '79.

We had been getting demo tapes from a small ad Wurz put in the *NME*. Most of them were dire and it really was about showcasing the local talent, so we gave ourselves up to the arms of agents and agencies. This is how we found ourselves working with

Rough Trade who really were, and probably still are, the most ethical agency looking after their roster. The local music scene was buzzing with raw and practised talent and the likes of The Nightingales, Surprises, Dangerous Girls and Crucial Music kept the venue afloat along with a collection of young people who were just starting out and a loose collective of bands that merged and demerged at alarming rates.

We named our outfit Nitelife and amongst us we designed printed and posted our print run of usually 100 posters a week. We rang the bands and agencies and tried to match the musical styles to give our young talented locals some good exposure other than to their own mates. They would fill the support slot of 8.30pm to 9pm-ish.

The pubs shut at 10.30pm at first, moving to 11pm every Friday and Saturday night, so we had to get the main band off before last orders were called. The crowds that came were many and varied. If a touring band had only a few reviews and a couple of plays by John Peel, some of the crowd would come from as far as Shrewsbury and Gloucester, the locals eschewing a lucky bet. Sometimes, if the weather was good, we would have a room full and be turning people away. It was all pot luck.

Sometimes we hit paydirt. Pairing a very young Benjamin Zephaniah with Crucial Music was fantastic, The Dancing Did with And Also The Trees was memorable, and any gig with The Nightingales and The Cravats brought in the serious moodies, like Adrian Goldberg. The Surprises and latterly The Ever Readies were always fun and good

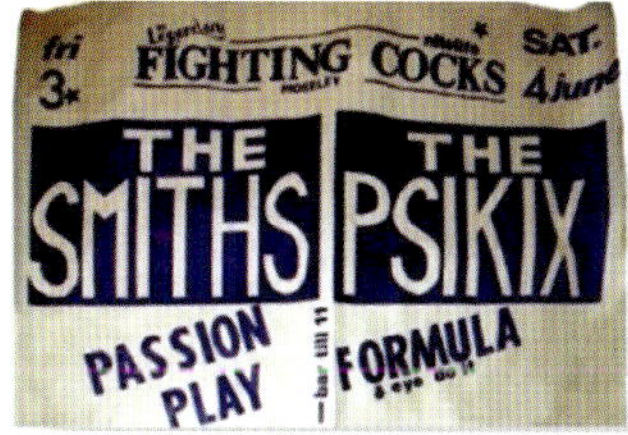

*The Smiths played the Fighting Cocks in June 1983*

for our Christmas gigs. Attila the Stockbroker brought the young *NME* scribe Steven Wells (aka Seething Wells) for some good ranting poetry. Blurt blew the house down and Sisters of Mercy ground it into the dirt, but of course our piece de resistance, little noticed by many at the time, was The Smiths on their first tour after the release of 'Hand In Glove'.

Contrary to the hazy memory of many Moseleyites – who weren't there – only 70 people turned up, which just paid the bills. This was to be one of the turning points of our journey at the Cocks, as soon after our growing band of entrepreneurs fell out and split up, closing the doors for good in the winter of '83.

### BRYAN FARLEY

My part in the Smiths' story is fairly insignificant. They had just started doing gigs outside Manchester and were signed to Rough Trade for bookings. I read a gig review in *Sounds* and decided to book them. My friend Clive and I were putting on bands, mainly pub gigs, in an upstairs room in a bog standard Mitchells and Butlers city pub called the Fighting Cocks in Moseley. We used to charge £1 entry and get loads of liggers. It's a very expensive, gentrified part of Birmingham now and the pub's still there, but unrecognisable from what it was.

Most cities have got rough areas and posh areas and King's Heath and in particular Moseley have always been very hippie-ish, very bomhemian, with lots of people in sandals and kaftans and dope smokers. There was a thriving music scene in most big cities around that time but in Birmingham it was largely ska and reggae-influenced.

There were a lot of reggae bands in Birmingham and The Specials and Selecter captured the imagination in nearby Coventry, so there was a lot of that sort of thing going on. There were a few goth bands but mainly they came from Leeds and places up north. And then there were a few indie outfits like Eyeless in Gaza and Felt and Fashion, who hovered around the fringes of the indie chart on labels like Cherry Red. Quite a lot of them were Midlands-based.

There was a large multi-occupied detached Georgian house set in grounds in Edgbaston, which has since been pulled down. Lots of musical people used to move in and out of it, people who went on to form bands like The Beat and The Au Pairs and others of that ilk from the Birmingham area. Clive lived there, so he knew quite a few people, and he and I had been pals for a while and I was really into listening to music.

'Hand In Glove' had just come out on Rough Trade and I liked the single. I think Peel had played it. I read a review in *Sounds* of a concert in Manchester and thought they sounded really interesting, so I spoke to my contact at Rough Trade booking. I'd had one or two indie bands from Rough Trade previously that we'd put on for not much money.

My contact at Rough Trade said, 'Yeah, they're looking for gigs outside of Manchester' so I booked them. I think the fee was £50. And we had to provide a case of Heineken and a large bunch of gladioli. That was the deal!

I did a recording at the time because we used to have a PA company that was really local to the pub do our sound system. Clive would hang microphones up from the rafters in the early days, and then we moved on to taping it off the mixing desk. I've got a pretty rough and ready recording of the show on an old EMI tape. But you can tell it's The Smiths.

Clive and I fitted together quite well. Clive was into the technical side of it – the PA, and the silk screen printing which he had at home which he was a master of. We used to silk screen all the posters for our gigs, a very smelly, time consuming and dirty job. We'd print about 100 posters for each gig, throw away 40 that were not right and then fly post the rest around the centre of Birmingham, only to find two nights later that they'd been covered up by the heavy mob from London who did the corporate posting for the big venues.

Clive used to enjoy the ligging and the mixing with people. I enjoyed the booking. I used to book quite a lot of 'out there' bands. We did goth bands. We did reggae bands. If somebody rang me up and said, 'You can have this lot for 200 quid', we'd have to put them in a bigger venue to try and make money. I thought The Go-Betweens were wonderful. They were signed to Rough Trade and we had them on about three times.

We had a reasonable turn out for The Smiths. The venue only held 150. I've still got the original contract somewhere. I'm pretty sure we lost money on it. They became quite sought after quite quickly. People started writing good things about them. Suddenly it made a helluva difference to Rough Trade

to have a Kylie Minogue-type act on their books as opposed to these touring indie bands who lost them shitloads of money every time they put a record out.

Mike Joyce: I remember we played in Birmingham at the Fighting Cocks very early on and there were about five people backstage. Morrissey told us, 'I don't want to be called Steve anymore, I want to be Morrissey'. So I was like, 'OK, fair enough.' After we'd done the gig we were gonna have to drive back. I didn't have my watch on, so I thought, 'I'll ask Steve the time.' But then I thought, 'No it's not Steve is it, it's Morrissey?' So, I said, 'Morrissey, what time is it?' and he said, 'It's about quarter to twelve, Joyce.'



## BRIXTON ACE

### 29 JUNE 1983, LONDON, UK

### DAVID MCLEAN

It was a converted cinema. The Smiths were sandwiched between leather-trousered goth bands The Sisters of Mercy, who were headlining, and Flesh For Lulu. An incongruous billing, but it was not unusual at the time to jumble bands up, which I liked. It's a pity it's not done today. It was still quite quiet when they came on but Morrissey seemed happy, saying something like, 'How kind of you all to abandon the pub for us.' I can only recall 'What Difference Does It Make?' from the short set they played – that and one of my friends passing out drunk mid-set – but I remember Morrissey dancing round the stage and waving those gladioli about.

## UNIVERSITY OF WARWICK

### 30 JUNE 1983, COVENTRY, UK

### SAM DEEMING

I saw one of their first gigs at Coventry College (University of Warwick). I loved them.

Morrissey had his flowers swinging around. I've got photos but they are at my ex's house.

## MIDNIGHT EXPRESS CLUB

### 1 JULY 1983, BOURNEMOUTH, UK

### MICK TARRANT

I had an indie record shop called Armadillo Records in Bournemouth which started around '75 or '76 and which came up through the whole DIY punk ethic. Quite early on I ran into Geoff Travis from Rough Trade at a record wholesalers in Harrow Road in London called Lightning Records. Geoff overheard me asking, 'Have you got a copy of such and such?' and said, 'I can help you with that.' So I went back to Rough Trade's premises with him and got whatever I was looking for and a bunch more stuff I wanted. From then on, I called there when I went on my buying trips to London and so built up a relationship with Rough Trade.

I sold a half share in the record shop to somebody who took on the running of it and started a small live music club with about 200-capacity.

Because of the Rough Trade connection I started doing quite a few of their bands, The Smiths being one of them.

By this time, they had the record label and they started a booking agency. And, as I was known to them, they started offering me bands.

I put The Smiths on in July 1983. That same month I had The Cure in there, despite them being quite a big band by that time. It was quite fortuitous that in a 200-capacity club we had two of the biggest bands of the time.

They'd only had 'Hand In Glove' out and I quite liked the guitar sound on it. I knew Johnny Marr played a Rickenbacker. I was – and still am – a big fan of The Byrds, which formed a very important part of their sound. After they sound checked, I fell into conversation with Johnny and had a drink and quite a long chat about The Byrds. He was a nice guy. Morrissey pretty much kept himself to himself.

A few in the audience were familiar with the single. They went down quite well. I think their fee was 150 or 200 quid and they didn't sell out. We got about 150 in.

## DAVID JENSEN SHOW, BBC RADIO 1

### 4 JULY 1983, LONDON, UK

Morrissey was interviewed by DJ David 'Kid' Jensen. Three tracks were recorded for the show – 'These Things Take Time', 'You've Got Everything Now' and 'Wonderful Woman.'

## HAÇIENDA

### 6 JULY 1983,
### MANCHESTER, UK

### GED DUFFY, LAVOLTA LAKOTA

We supported The Smiths at The Haçienda. We had done several gigs in small venues, and this was the first large venue that we played. We had a right laugh with Mike Joyce and Johnny Marr, but Morrissey was up his own arse. Malcolm Whitehead videoed us and when I watched it a few days later, I was shocked that we didn't sound that bad. Pete Hook generally did our live sound, but he was away with New Order in Canada, so I think the guy who owned the PA did it for us.

Morrissey used to have flowers sticking out of the arse pocket of his jeans and would throw some out into the crowd. The box of flowers was sat at the side of the stage and Glenn, one of our roadies, had cut all the heads off them. As Morrisey ran towards the stage, he stopped to grab the flowers. The look on his face as he realised! He looked at Slim, our other roadie, who was stood there with his arms folded, looked again at the flowers and was about to say something… Slim simply asked him a question, 'Anything wrong, mate?' Morrisey didn't reply and went on stage.

After the gig, Glenn told Slim that we were missing a guitar tuner and that The Smiths road crew must have taken it. Slim 'lost it' and took matters into his own hand. He had two of their road crew pinned up against the wall with a hand round the neck of each of them, whilst the third one was frantically searching for the tuner.

After a few minutes of Slim threatening to cause some serious damage to each of them, Glenn put his hand in his pocket and pulled out the tuner saying, 'I've found it.' Slim growled at all three of them and walked off. It was Glenn's idea of a joke. Slim would have hammered them if Glenn hadn't come clean. Loads of our mates including Mani were there that night and we got a good reception from them.

Tony France of my former band Stockholm Monsters also had a heated argument with Morrissey at the bar that night. I think a few home truths about his image were discussed between the two. From where I was stood, Tony was right in Morrisey's face and thought that he was about to punch him!

## NIGHT MOVES

### 9 JULY 1983, GLASGOW, UK

### JOE WHYTE, AGE 20

It's time this tale was told, dear readers. I swear I was there and all joking and Manchester Free Trade Hall punning aside, my memory remains relatively acute for the important parts of the gig. This seems to be a mostly undocumented Smiths early show and there has been some dispute online about the circumstances and attendance at it. It also seems to have been reported as the 10th July, but I suspect that's incorrect.

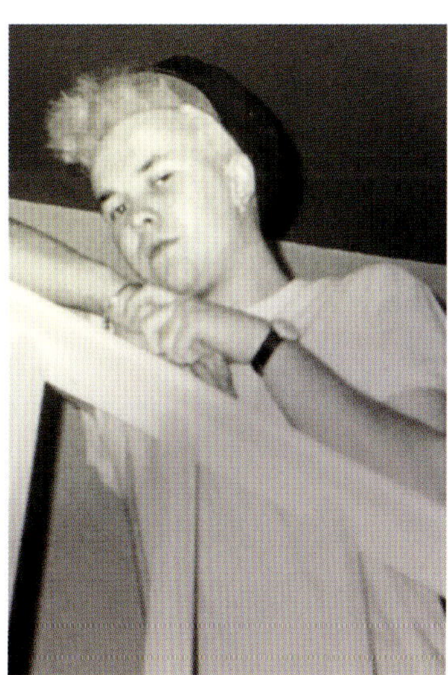

*Joe Whyte was at the Glasgow Night Moves gig that has slipped from Smiths gig history*

There's actually a guy who tells the story in a Smiths forum of how his band supported that night (and of The Smiths replacing A Certain Ratio who'd cancelled) and of how the venue was mobbed. I can confirm from memory, albeit faded, that it certainly wasn't mobbed – there would have been around 40 people there. It was a Thursday night and I'm pretty sure it was the night of the General Election.

The Smiths had been on the *John Peel Show* a few nights earlier with presumably what would have been their first Peel session; Night Moves was a venue that attracted a fair crowd most weekend nights due to owner Willie Pott's policy of booking the movers and shakers of a pretty vibrant post-punk scene and the up-and-coming acts of the day.

Remember, this was pre-internet; music news was from the *NME* and the like, via the radio and by word of mouth. The reason that The Smiths gig was so empty, apart from them being not at all well known, was that this weekend was the start of the Glasgow Fair, a trades holiday that seems to have slipped into insignificance in the modern world. At that time, the city virtually emptied for a couple of weeks as people holidayed both abroad and in the well-worn stretches and lights of Blackpool and the like.

The gig was free entry, which wasn't unusual on a Thursday at Night Moves – this was perhaps one of my reasons for being there – and, as mentioned, there were around 40 people who had climbed the three or four floors of winding stairs to the well-loved venue.

The odd thing is, being a pretty high-tech venue for the time, the DJ would always video the performances as they were projected live onto TV screens above the bar and at the sides of the venue. Most bands would leave with a copy of their show and it's pretty bizarre that a copy of this one has never been heard of, far less seen. Perhaps the DJ wasn't working that night, perhaps it wasn't filmed. Yet another mystery around a gig that seems to have pretty shadowy circumstances surrounding it. Glasgow also had a pretty avid bootlegging community and again it's odd that this one hasn't been recorded for posterity.

Johnny Marr has spoken about the gig, saying it was his first time north of the border in an interview with the *Daily Record* but his recollection of 'eleven people watching' is slightly underestimated.

The band, who I'd paid little attention to prior to this show, were tight and powerful and clearly much better musicians than much of their pre-indie/post-punk peers. I recall 'Suffer Little Children' being particularly potent as it slowed the set down for the first time. Of course, Marr's guitar playing was the focus for me – he switched between the Rickenbacker and a cream Telecaster and those water-falling arpeggios and jangling surges gave the band an edge that certainly made them stand out. The rhythm section was tight and taut; I remember Mike Joyce grinning happily from the drum riser and Andy Joyce looking pretty impassive and serious.

This next opinion is my favourite memory and just shows how one's 23-year-old self is self-righteous and opinionated and often wrong. Watching The Smiths play, with

Morrissey flailing around the stage flagellating himself with the microphone lead, I distinctly remember saying to myself, 'This band are great but they need to get shot of the singer.' The operatic falsetto parts of his singing were getting right on my nerves and his onstage fractured Romeo antics (which of course, we all grew to love) were grating on me. It was a short set, I don't recall them doing an encore, and it was mostly made up of the songs from the first album. My friend Rob Christie remembers helping the band load out via the venue lift at the end of the night and recalls Morrissey not having much to say. If only it had stayed that way!

## LYCEUM THEATRE



### 7 AUGUST 1983, LONDON, UK

### SEAN NEYLON

In the early eighties, I started going to Loughton College with two fellow Chelmsford school friends, John and Chris. It meant a free student pass for buses and trains and new friends in London where I could stay over. We were into the alternative end of alternative music – the industrial scene – and saw the likes of Cabaret Voltaire, Psychic TV, Einstürzende Neubauten and Test Dept as well as equally obscure artists like Artery and Danielle Dax. But we also liked Magazine, Echo and The Bunnymen, Bowie and The Cure. Liking similar bands was really handy – I got given the debut Bunnymen album and Bowie's *Low* by Chris (he also gave me *Heroes* but regretted it so took it back) and discovered the weird and wonderful world of Chrome

when John gave me his *Red Exposure* album. With only Peel to listen to, if we didn't hear bands we wanted to listen to on his show, we'd take a chance and buy the record we'd read about in *Melody Maker* or *NME* – not always with successful results.

We discussed going to see Howard Devoto (ex-Magazine) play at the Lyceum in London. SPK were supporting so it was all good. Myself and Chris, both still in Chelmsford (John had moved to London by now), decided that the decider would be whether or not we liked The Smiths, a band we were unfamiliar with, who were third on the bill. Peel was repeating their debut session a couple of days before. I remember the Peel session being energetic, lively and very different – almost monotone in the vocal delivery – to what we had all been listening to.

The next day Chris called me up. We agreed it was pretty good, but the decider was the words and their humour! 'I look at yours, you laugh at mine…' and, 'Let me get my hands on your mammary glands.'

The Lyceum was average-sized and had an upstairs section at the back above the main floor with a bar and seating. It wasn't packed, so we got seating at the front of this section by the railings. One of the girls we were with, Julie, had my Cure button badge on which I'd lost at college that week. 'It fell off' she said, 'so I put it on!' I got it back and I sat down with a beer chatting to my pal Sarmad, who lived in Snaresbrook with his mum (who we all fancied, *Inbetweeners*-style) and who had a big spare room we stayed in after gigs. As we talked, the background music was shattered by the sharpest, loudest sound that made us both jump. It was the opening guitar chord from The Smiths.

They were dressed like regular, slightly scruffy students and shambled about the stage. The sound was tight yet ramshackle and unfamiliar at this stage, and reminded me of a kind of modern take on rockabilly with that rhythm section. A few people danced, but not many – that sort of dance everyone did at the time, which seemed to consist of wandering about bumping gently into one another with flapping chicken arms and with hands folded in.

It's quite telling looking back that I have absolutely no recollection of seeing SPK or Howard Devoto at the Lyceum, only The Smiths.

## DINGWALLS

### 13 AUGUST 1983, NEWCASTLE-UPON-TYNE, UK

### PHIL DUNN, AGE 18

I was born in Hartlepool. I was just too young for punk but got into new wave and people who were lyrically clever – like Elvis Costello, and Difford and Tilbrook from Squeeze – and had a bit of an edge to them and something to say. When Morrissey came to the fore I was very interested in what he had to say.

'Hand In Glove' and 'This Charming Man' were the only songs I'd heard, at the alternative nights at the Gemini on a Thursday, Hartlepool's only nightclub. We were 22 miles from Newcastle but there was no train back to Hartlepool after ten past ten. But a guy called John Little had a record shop called The Other Record Shop. He sold gig tickets as part of which you got the bus up and down to Newcastle.

I got on the bus in Park Road outside the Park Hotel and almost everybody on with the exception of me was an art student from the local art college. There were a lot of faces from student night at the Gemini on the bus.

Dingwalls was a small venue and I'd already seen Orange Juice and New Order there. The Smiths didn't disappoint. It was crammed. There was a distinct buzz about the gig and the fact that they were going to be big. It was a case of 'get in to see these lads while they're playing at places like Dingwalls because they won't be playing places like this much longer.' They hadn't been on *Top of the Pops* at this stage so I didn't know what to expect. It was the first time I'd ever seen anyone chucking flowers around – and flowers sticking out of somebody's arse!

The next time I saw them was at

*Adam Sweeting's review of the Lyceum show*

**HOWARD DEVOTO/SPK/THE SMITHS**

Lyceum, London

WELL, you can always *hope*, can't yer? Fat lot of good that'll do you on a night like this.

The Smiths were in flight as I arrived, warbling into the gloom as though the indifferent crowd somehow *owed* them something. Thrumming and strumming like the Farmer's Boys, with cow dung spilling into their waders, The Smiths remained obstinately and depressingly earthbound. I headed for the sorum at the bar.

An A&R man of my acquaintance tried to convince me that SPK were part of some sort of new movement which allegedly also includes Test Department. However, it will take more than his generous offer of women and drugs to convince me that a man beating on packing cases with lengths of car bumpers and a female singer who blends the worst of Siouxsie with out-takes from Lohengrin will ever be more than an excruciating racket.

Finally, Mr Devoto and his group took the stage. Howard strove to project an off-hand bonhomie but failed miserably, leading his team into a rendition of "Way Out Of Shape" which sounded like a jaded country and western band plugging in for the fifth set of the night.

Despite loose-limbed versions of "You Never Knew Me" and "A Song From Under The Floorboards", Howard delivered little to make me disagree with Professor Worrall's hostile review of a couple of weeks back. Of his new songs, only "Rainy Season" came close to competing with the balding guru's past masterpices, and even this was scarcely show-stopping.

Dave Formula exhibited no little subtlety at his keyboards while Alan St Claire showed his guitar no quarter, but Howard seemed unable to do more than skate through the motions. Casual to the point of absent-mindedness, Devoto simply didn't seem to *care*, and by the end of the proceedings, nor did I.

The tide's gone out, Howard.

● ADAM SWEETING

Middlesbrough, which was closer to home, only six or seven miles. I remember looking at the gig listing in the *NME* and thinking, 'This guy (Morrissey) knows what he's doing because they're actually playing smaller places and going off the beaten track a little bit.'

*(Some sources suggest that The Smiths pulled out and that this gig never actually took place.)*

## GALA BALLROOM

### 19 AUGUST 1983, NORWICH, UK

### DAVE GUTTRIDGE

Having heard 'Hand in Glove' on John Peel's show, I'd bought it and written to the address on the back of the sleeve to say how much I loved it, requesting a lyric

*Dave Guttridge blagged his band a support slot with The Smiths*

*Norwich Gala ballroom (Dave Guttridge)*

*18 Yellow Roses shared a bill with The Smiths thanks to Dave Guttridge's blagging*

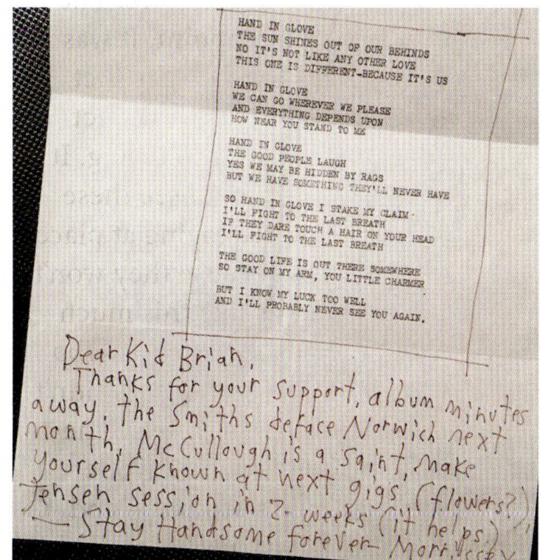


*Dave Guttridge got a note from Morrissey after he asked for a copy of the lyrics to 'Hand In Glove'*

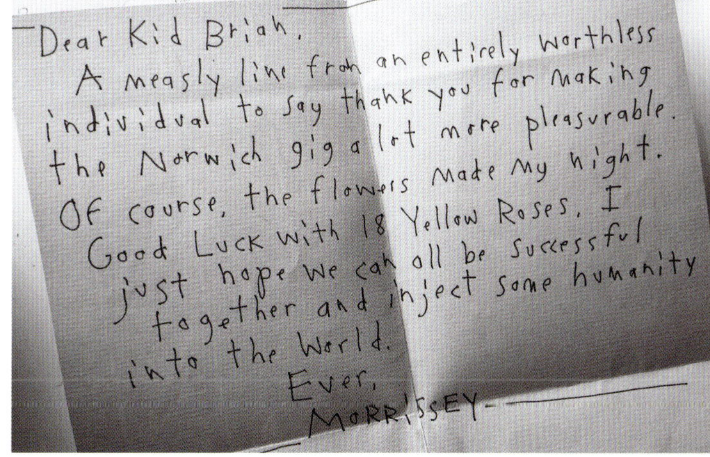


*Dave Guttridge also got a reply from Moz when he sent him a tape of the Norwich Gala Ballroom show*

Andrew Hook remembers the Gala Ballroom being only half full

Andrew Hook's ticket for the Norwich Gala Ballroom gig

sheet. I was knocked out to receive a letter back, partly handwritten by the singer and with the lyrics typed by the composer on the back of a photocopied promo picture.

I played bass in a Norwich band called 18 Yellow Roses, named after a Marty Robbins song recorded by Bobby Darin. Once I found out that The Smiths were coming to our favourite venue, my only mission was to get us the support slot. When I rang the venue manager, who didn't know me from Adam, he told me another Norwich group, The Gothic Girls, had been given the gig. Amazingly, I was able to convince him during this phone call that they were completely unsuitable and that we were the ideal act for the job. I was very close friends with The Gothic Girls, and even produced their first single, but I stand by my opinion and actions. Lo and behold we were added to the bill.

So, having been prompted by Morrissey, we turned up at the Gala for the sound check and presented him with 18 yellow roses. Not the ideal bouquet, due to the thorns. We were able to watch them set up and run through three or four songs for their soundcheck. As a Fall fan, I was delighted to be introduced to Grant Showbiz, who was their soundman. He ended up staying at our house after the gig as he wanted to visit Norwich's comic shops.

The gig was one of the most exciting and powerful I ever witnessed at the Gala, about 40 minutes of raw romanticism with an energised and enthusiastic audience in very high spirits. The encore was a second rendition of 'What Difference Does It Make?' We asked them in the dressing room about the next single release and they were sure it would be 'Reel Around the Fountain'.

After the gig, as we were packing up, Andy and Johnny took me outside to show me their new touring van, a very basic Transit-type with a load of cushions for the band to relax on. I remember being quite taken aback by a couple of the band members smoking a joint backstage. I'd led a sheltered life!

I recorded both bands sets with a Panasonic Walkman – a much better recording than the one on YouTube – and sent a cassette to Morrissey, getting another nice reply. I've still got the poster for the gig, which is apparently pretty collectible, but it'll take a fair few quid to prise it out of my hands.

### ANDREW HOOK, AGE 16

Post-punk, I wore black t-shirts, black jeans and desert boots. I'd been attending gigs sporadically for a couple of years – The Stranglers, Talk Talk, A Flock of Seagulls, Kissing The Pink. I was naïve. I was young. I had never been kissed.

I remember first hearing The Smiths at a friend's house – Steven Allen. I assume Steven's older friend, Dave Foulkes, had taped a Peel session off the radio. I recall being struck by 'Reel Around The Fountain', particularly the line about falling out of bed twice. I always thought there was a lot of humour in Morrissey's lyrics, something that the music press who wanted to brand him as a miserablist didn't often understand. There was a gig coming up. £2. Steven convinced me that we should go.

The Gala was a small venue, long since converted into a laser tag site. My memories of the venue are vague but I doubt the capacity was much over 200. I recall a low stage, situated in a corner. Myself, Steven and Dave milled about. We weren't drinkers. The venue was less than half full.

36 years later what do I remember of The Smiths? Much more than the local support band, 18 Yellow Roses, who were possibly Southern Death Cult-ish and who I never saw again. The Smiths were great. They laughed a lot. They played twelve songs. They ran out of material, reprising 'Hand In Glove' and 'Handsome Devil' as encores. There was a lot of intelligent energy. Morrissey had flowers stuffed down the back of his jeans. The music was fresh, was *now*. I was lyrically enchanted.

According to my five-star, gig-logging system of the time, I awarded this one four. On the way out I grabbed a handful of used tickets, managing to get my numbered one back, plus others that decades later I sold as memorabilia on eBay.

I was enamoured. I bought 'Hand In Glove', then 'This Charming Man' on twelve-inch. Then suddenly – at school – everyone seemed to be into The Smiths. What difference did it make? I wasn't into popularity and I could feel my love draining. Musical snobbery taking hold.

## JONTY YOUNG

Myself and Kenny Smith set off to celebrate his birthday on a Friday night out in Norwich. Somehow, we had got our hands on a bottle of Malibu, not a particular favourite

in a post-punk era but a means to an end. Our aim was simply to head to the Gala Ballroom to see an up-and-coming band from Manchester called The Smiths (no relation). The rules were the same then as they are today. Any band that has signed to Rough Trade were more than worth a listen, or in this case, a look.

The nearest pub en route to the venue was The Trowel and Hammer. We popped in for a couple of large pineapple juices, added lashings of our coconut-flavoured liqueur, and came out very drunk about 8.45pm. We then stumbled to the Gala, no more than a few hundred yards away.

Two things immediately struck us. The venue was by no means full, as it normally was on a Friday night, and it was a totally different crowd than usual with plenty of familiar faces from the flourishing Norwich music scene. Two free cans of warm Breaker later, courtesy of the management, we installed ourselves in a prime position and viewing point.

Support on the night came from the Norwich-based 18 Yellow Roses, featuring Andy Hackett on guitar, now with Edwyn Collins and country outfit The Rockingbirds, and Dave Guttridge, the John Peel Archives photographer and BBC 6 Music regular, DJ78. All I can really remember about their set is that they got a great reception from an excitable crowd and there was a trumpet involved. I knew for one thing I'd undoubtedly see them again.

As the lights dimmed for The Smiths, everyone pushed closer to the front. There seemed to be quite a buzz in the 300-strong crowd. After a few welcoming quips from Morrissey, the band launched into their first song. Some 60 seconds later, me and Kenny looked at each other and made faces of disappointment. Far too much jingly-jangly guitar for our liking.

The second song was much better. Morrissey moved to the front of the stage with a bunch of flowers (which I now know to be gladioli) waving above his head. He was joined in the audience by two girls, in matching dresses, giving out more gladioli to everyone looking their way. Me and Kenny, not quite of an age to appreciate gardening, threw ours unapologetically to the floor. This song was catchy though, especially the chorus, 'What difference does it maa-aaaa-aaake?'

By the third song they had really got going, as had the crowd and Morrissey, with his drawling vocals and lyrics, had made the stage his own. Next up was a series of what I believed to be unremarkable and slow songs. Just as I had started thinking that this lot had something, they totally lost me over the next 20 minutes or so. My firm belief was that only great bands could slip in a couple of slow songs and this was a Friday night after all. The rest of the set went in something of a blur.

For me, Johnny Marr's guitar was undoubtedly the highlight. Even at my most doubting moments, his effortless control of the strings was a joy to behold. The majority of the audience, on the other hand, absolutely loved them. They had begged for an encore and then received two. That's unheard of for a band well outside of their comfort zone with one single to their name, which they played twice.

The next day was a hangover day. I woke up mulling the night before, cursing the taste of coconut and pineapple and thought to myself, 'I wonder if The Smiths will ever make it?' Some seven months later and two more singles down, The Smiths played to a baying, sell-out crowd of 1,500 at the University of East Anglia and the rest, as they say, is history.

### ADRIAN LAST

They were the darlings of the music press at the time and played a memorable short set. It has stuck in my mind to this day, even though the music we heard that night was completely new to me. As I have never been a fan since bar the odd song, they must have been doing something right that evening!

## DAVID JENSEN SHOW, BBC RADIO 1
### 25 AUGUST 1983, LONDON, UK

Broadcast on 5 September 1983, the band were back recording for Radio 1's *David Jensen Show*. 'Accept Yourself' (later to appear on *Hatful Of Hollow*), 'I Don't Owe You Anything', 'Pretty Girls Make Graves' and Reel Around The Fountain' were taped, with the latter song then banned by the BBC and excluded from subsequent airings of the session for two years.

Broadcast on the *John Peel Show* on 21 September 1983, the band returned for their second Peel Session, recording 'This Charming Man', 'Back To The Old House', 'This Night Has Opened My Eyes' and 'Still Ill'. All four tracks were later released on *Hatful Of Hollow*.

# MOLES CLUB

## 16 SEPTEMBER 1983, BATH, UK

### MARTIN WHITEHEAD

On the strength of nothing more than their first single, I wanted to interview The Smiths for my fanzine, *The Underground*. My usual method of turning up at the venue at soundcheck time when the band might be hanging around with time to spare worked again, and I got one of the best interviews of my fanzine career.

I was struck by how unusual Morrissey's appearance was, a profile like a new moon, dominated by a pair of NHS specs. I was also impressed by how Morrissey and Johnny complemented each other in the interview. When one was lost for a word the other took over the sentence. Both were very sure about what The Smiths were about and where they were going with the band, and their respective ideas were completely in tune with each other.

Some people have suggested that Morrissey's persona is adopted, a sham personality put on for publicity. One of the reasons I idolised The Smiths, apart from sweeping away the dark cloak of goth that hung over the land at the time, was that Morrissey seemed very genuinely and earnestly to believe he was on a divine mission to regain pop's high ground. At the time I predicted The Smiths would be the most important band since The Sex Pistols and I still largely stand by that.

I've never been totally fired up by Morrissey the way I was by The Smiths, but even now the echoes of what they did are still ringing in the charts. Johnny Marr put the guitar back on the instrumental agenda for all the post C86-ers and the band flew the flag for the indies and showed the world you didn't need black wigs and flour on your face to form a band. The Clash were lording it up in America and Strummer had become the irrelevant popstar he'd previously rallied against. We had four lads from Manchester with great songs and missionary zeal. Everything that has happened subsequently seems obvious in retrospect.

Moles Club back then could hold maybe 100 people. There wasn't even room for a stage. Despite that, the club was about two-thirds empty. Barely 30 people had turned up to see the most influential and iconic band of the decade. This gave an opportunity to shoot some pictures to go with the interview.

Five months later The Smiths played to a packed-out main hall at Bristol University. I couldn't even get close to the stage, never mind the band.

## FUTURAMA FESTIVAL, QUEENS HALL

### 17 SEPTEMBER 1983, LEEDS, UK

Scheduled to play as part of an all-day line-up, and billed below The Comsat Angels, The Armoury Show and headliners The Bay City Rollers, The Smiths cancel apparently because Morrissey didn't want to appear with the Shang-a-Lang lads. The crowd were also unimpressed by Edinburgh's finest, bottling them off stage.

## GUM CLUB AT FERNANDO'S

### 23 SEPTEMBER 1983, BLACKBURN, UK

### BRIAN FOSTER

I was the promoter of this gig in Blackburn with my friend Wayne. There were daffodils and arguments that night. My mam made Morrissey an omelette because he wouldn't eat fish and chips.

### WAYNE FARNWORTH

The Gum Club was a mid-week indie disco held in a town centre pub called Fernando's Wine Bar. The night was run by myself, my then partner Jane Goetzee and our next-door neighbours – siblings Brian, Gaynor and Alma Foster.

It was a fairly short-lived venture, lasting less than a year. Brian and myself DJ'd, and Jane, Gaynor and Alma ran the door.

Brian is claiming to be the promoter, and I get a mention as 'a friend'. But I booked the band, arranged the venue and signed the contract. Brian had no involvement in booking the band.

The Gum Club was my baby. I had the idea of starting a one-off night, I thought of the name, I designed all the artwork, I went flyposting, etc., etc. All design work was done by me. Brian had a friend who did some cheap printing for us. Alma, who was a talented artist, brought amongst other things a performance artist to the bar who spent the evening doing mime for patrons.

I didn't book many bands. Some had to be cancelled at the last minute because of the bar owner's incompetence in gaining the correct licences. The three more well-known bands we booked were The Chameleons (twice), The Smiths and The Membranes. (John Robb rang me weekly to get The Membranes on. In the end, I booked them to stop him calling!)

The Smiths were offered to me by their agent, whose name I cannot recall. They called me and offered me the gig at a very good price. I signed the contract with the agent and booked the upstairs venue in the town centre.

On the day of the gig, they turned up at the venue in the late afternoon. Johnny Marr, Andy Rourke and Mike Joyce were all very friendly. Morrissey was stand-offish. After they had set up and done a sound check I took them, and their small road crew, back to my house for food.

After eating, I crammed all four Smiths into my green 1966 Morris Minor and drove them to an interview I had organised for them with Radio Lancashire on Steve Barker's *On The Wire* show. As part of the interview, I made a pair of free tickets available for a phone in competition. The winner's name was John Slater (he was from Leyland or Chorley). I remember the name because one of my best friends was also called John Slater. At first, I thought someone was winding me up.

Interview over, we drove back to my house and they all got changed for the gig. We all left my house and I locked the front door (with a lever mortice lock), got into my car and started the engine. The Smiths and road crew got into their van. We were about to drive off when suddenly I saw a figure inside my front door, banging urgently. Mike Joyce had still been in the bathroom getting ready and we almost left him behind!

The support band for the night were Blackburn band Some Now Are whose three founding members – Danny Forkin, Paul Green and Andy Mahon – were friends of mine. A pint of lager from Paul one Saturday night at the Elma Yerburgh pub in Blackburn sealed their support slot. (It's not what you know...)

The gig wasn't well attended – around 150 people in a venue with 400 capacity – but that's Blackburn for you. If I had a quid for everyone who said they were there over the following years, I would have a nice little savings pot. The Smiths were okay. They made our lighting guy Brian Cox limit his lights to only blue and green, but the band weren't brilliant at that stage.

That was one of the last gigs I promoted. As other band promoters found out, Blackburn was a difficult place to try anything new and to get people off their sofas. And if you can't entice them out with The Smiths, what's the point?

### EMILY KELLY

It was a very small venue, not packed but also not empty. Brian, who organised the event, lectured in photography at Blackburn College. He was very into the band scene and was connected to the band James. I was studying graphic design at the college, which is how I knew him. Before the gig, I was bashing the cigarette machine trying to get the fags out that I'd paid for. Johnny Marr came over and put more money in, smiled and handed me the pack of John Players Blue. (I thanked him). Morrissey was dressed in full flowery shirt mode and waving glads, which he stuck in his pockets. It was so small I was able to stand right up to the space they were playing in. It was a lovely intimate gig, with fewer than 50 people there.

### MICHAEL CLARE

I became pretty obsessed with The Smiths thanks to John Peel. The first time I saw them was in September 1983 at the Gum Club in Blackburn. (I saw The Chameleons there a week or two later.) The place was only about half full and the set was quite short. After the **gig**, my **girlfriend** and I went backstage and they were all very friendly, especially Mike. Andy Rourke had left. Morrissey said they had cut the set short as he didn't think people were enjoying it, but they were fantastic! I got some stuff signed and took a bunch of daffodils (for which the police stopped us on the way home under suspicion of nicking them from the park). Liz (Taylor), the woman who designed the first t-shirts and worked at Crazy Face, was there too and she took my address so they could send me more posters, flyers and promo stuff. It turned out it was Morrissey who sent them – I recognised his handwriting from how he'd signed a poster. Not long after the Gum Club gig, a few friends and I were in Manchester and went to stalk them at the Crazy Face offices. As we got there, Mike Joyce was just arriving, recognised us and invited us in. I think only Liz was around but we had a chat and got some more goodies.

I had a couple of deliveries in the next month or so, but then they hit the big time, the Haçienda in November (another wonderful gig, and the last time I saw them), and I never heard from him again! Soon after, I belatedly discovered The Birthday Party, The Smiths began to lose their appeal, and my life got all a bit gothy...

### JOHN ROBINSON

A friend from Brinscall was bolstering his income whilst doing 'A' levels by working Saturdays at a now closed but then long-established hardware store close to King George's Hall. He found out about some up-and-coming concerts at The Gum Club.

With him, I drove there in my mum's old Morris Marina on two occasions, firstly to see The Chameleons followed a week or so later by The Smiths. I was an apprenticed fabricator and thought The Smiths name had some association with forging (blacksmithing). Well, that was my first mistake!

It was rented out and called The Gum Club by students from Blackburn College. The building front was rendered white with artificial Georgian windows facades and the club, upstairs on the first floor, held about 150 people and had a bar on one side with the bands set up in one corner. We were listening to post-punk music such as Death Cult, Bauhaus, Spear of Destiny, Killing Joke and Echo and The Bunnymen, so image was important. We came away from The Chameleons thinking their gig and the song 'Don't Fall' to be very good.

But we left the Smiths' gig before the end as I couldn't believe the actions of the then-unknown singer with his dancing style, and the band looked pretty bland. My friend reminded me 25 years later that I shouted, 'No more!' after several songs. Shameful indeed and more than a little embarrassing knowing now what they made as a legacy. Obviously what did I – some Northern numpty from a backwater – know?

By the time I saw them again at Lancaster University in March 1984, everything had changed. They had already released two singles and a debut album, and I was amazed at what a contrast it was to the night at Blackburn. I'm fairly sure I didn't walk out on that one.

### ALAN LEWIS

I was going to be a professional trumpet player. I went to the junior school of the Royal Northern College of Music from the age of about 15. When I was 18 I got a phone call from my cousin who ran a fanzine in Blackburn. A band called Some Now Are had won a competition to record with Peter Hook from New Order. I went and did a couple of records with them at Strawberry Studios, and we recorded at Suite 16 in Rochdale. Our record 'The Truth' got five plays on Radio 1, three with Kid Jensen and two with John Peel. You can still find the seven-inch disc out there.

We ended up doing a support gig for a band called The Smiths at the Gum Club. Perhaps they were pretty well known if you read the *NME* or *Sounds,* but I didn't know who they were. I remember their long shirts and Morrissey twirling his daffodils around. I've seen conflicting accounts about the capacity. It wasn't a sell-out. I would say the venue held about 300 to 400 and that there were between 140 and 150 people in there. There were no seats. We did a couple of sets and they played after us. I have never been impressed by Morrissey and he didn't impress me that night. I didn't like the material. But I thought the guitarist was pretty good. He looked down at his fingers all of the time. I don't know if he still does. They were clearly well rehearsed and accomplished at what they did.

I got offered a place at the Royal Northern College of Music to do classical trumpet studies, but had a place to study Law at Manchester University. I wanted to play in an orchestra but you're waiting for dead man's shoes, so I took the legal route. But I kept up playing on an amateur basis and won a lot of brass band trophies and did a lot of recording. You can hear me five times every day on a TV channel somewhere as I sat in with the Black Dyke Mills Band to record the theme music for *Ground Force.* I wish I was on royalties for that!

## MOUNTFORD HALL LIVERPOOL POLYTECHNIC

### 8 OCTOBER 1983, LIVERPOOL, UK

### CATHY CASSIDY, AGE 19

I went with my boyfriend, now husband, Liam and we loved it. Liam found a pair of proper Ray Bans and I caught a thrown flower. I loved Morrissey at the time, loved the songs. I was an illustration student at the art college. It was perfect music for its time.

## BAR ONE, UNIVERSITY OF SHEFFIELD

### 17 OCTOBER 1983, SHEFFIELD, UK

### DAVID HARRINGTON

It was 'intro week' of my first year at Uni. A London lad north of Watford for the first time, I was sharing a house with seven other first years, all from the Manchester area. Music became the main topic of conversation with John Peel our collective idol. One guy had taped a session by a band called The Smiths that the rest of us hadn't heard of. Coincidentally, they were playing at the Uni that Friday evening.

Bar One wasn't exactly a music venue of note, more of a small basement student bar that I later found out even the students avoided. We turned up with low expectations together with 80 or 90 other bedraggled late teenagers. Bedraggled was the student look of the early to mid-eighties. I don't remember a support band, but I'll never forget the first few minutes of a band that looked and sounded like nothing I'd seen before. The front man not only carried a bunch of gladioli but whirled them around his head when he sang. We could hear every word he said and the melody from the guitar filled the air with a twangy, 'chang-chang' sort of sound. They were brilliant and everyone who attended that gig probably did exactly the same thing as me, which was to write multiple letters to their mates telling them of this new discovery. It was also a time when 'I saw them first' was an important part of musical appreciation.

I went on to see The Smiths several times, and they were always fantastic live. Oh, and I was lucky enough to catch Morrissey's beads when he threw them into the crowd. They were a proud possession for a couple of years until some drunken student stole them from my bedroom during a house party.

*This Charming Man*

*'Reel Around The Fountain' was planned as The Smiths second single (Jamming 1983)*

## 'THIS CHARMING MAN'

### RELEASED 31 OCTOBER 1983

Topping the UK independent charts, 'This Charming Man' was the band's first UK Top 40 single, reaching number 25.

### TRACEY DONNELLY

Somehow, back in the day you found your tribe. I found mine, a bunch of like-minded young people who hung around town and loved the same music, fashion, hairdressers, shop assistants, students, etc.

Johnny Marr was part of this gang, along with my mates Andrew and Cath Berry. Johnny worked in X Clothes, and we all knew he wanted to start a band. Me and Cath used to call him and see him in the shop each day as it was on our route home from work.

He'd keep us up to date on how he was getting on. Then one day he told us he'd thought of a name for the band: 'The Smiths'. Me and Cath weren't so sure, especially as Smiths was a brand of crisps at the time. They don't exist anymore, but The Smiths tunes will last for eternity… Shows you how wrong you can be!

Through Johnny we got to know Mike and Andy, and they were soon part of our mates group. Morrissey never really got involved though, maybe because he was that bit older which felt like a big thing back then.

It was such an exciting time. It was a buzz seeing your mates take off with their band: the *John Peel Show*, getting a record deal, 'Hand in Glove', the monumental gigs…

Then came 'This Charming Man'. I was working in a clothes shop, Stirling Cooper, on Cross Street and could see HMV on Market Street from it. The day that HMV gave the whole front window up with the covers of 'This Charming Man' remains a special memory for me. It's funny, I know the world is bigger than Manchester but at that moment I felt that they'd arrived and the rest, as they say, is history.

### DAN BURKE

My dad had great taste in music and saw The Smiths live in his youth (as well as other legendary bands of that era such as Joy Division) but he never really forced his taste onto me and my brother when we were growing up.

At the age of 13 or 14, I began to take a genuine interest in music and, having grown bored of the Red Hot Chilli Peppers, finding my own way involved raiding my dad's CD collection one rainy afternoon. One of the CDs I plucked out was The Smiths' Singles compilation. I stuck it on and by track 2 – 'This Charming Man' – I realised I was listening to music that would change my life forever. The combination of Johnny Marr's amazing guitar playing, Morrissey's exuberant singing voice and those evocative, humorous lyrics was like nothing I'd ever heard before. The Smiths instantly became my favourite band.

From there I explored their other albums and Morrissey's solo work. 25 years later, I still count The Smiths as my favourite band, and 'This Charming Man' as my all-time favourite song. Who knows how different my life might have been if my dad had tried to force them onto me before I was ready instead of letting me find my own way?

### JAMIE REID-SINCLAIR

The Smiths came along in my life at a time when I needed a new musical fix. Not just an 'isolated tune kind of fix', but the whole package. A concept! Something to properly immerse myself in. Bands did that back then. I'd experienced this before, when I was 13 and The Jam invaded my world with a life-affirming adrenalin rush. Only they disappeared in 1982, and I didn't think I could feel the same way again, until I heard twelve bars of the most outrageous guitar followed by a most singular voice asking, 'Will nature make a man of me yet?'

This was 1983, 'This Charming Man', and they had me, swooning and smitten and looking for beads to adorn my polo neck jumper. I loved them all, but as an aspiring guitarist I was always more Marr

*Tracey Donnelly at Swing in The Haçienda (Tracey Donnelly)*

*Jamie Reid-Sinclair remains a charming man*

than Morrissey, Rourke or Joyce.

My soul was sated by seeing them live and then further fed by glorious picture sleeve singles and albums that were signposts to a better life, one where disappointment could be worn like cosy cardigan armour against a World that could never understand!

A whole different vibe to The Jam, still suburban but not aspirational. This was more resigned. Grey curtain twitching days with a cold cup of tea and shattered kitchen sink dreams. I loved it. Still do. Still ill. Smiths indeed!

### IAN MOSS

The Smiths were big news, and this, their second single, was good enough to live up to the sky high expectations that were placed on their slender shoulders. It was recorded at Stockport's Strawberry Studios, and its punchy production was a cut above the sound quality of a typical independent release.

Tunesmith Johnny Marr was an excellent guitar player who was tenacious in his quest to achieve the sound he heard in his head. To that end he worked hard in the studio to create a multi-textured tapestry of guitar takes. He was aided by a rhythm section who operated wonderfully well together and were perfectly suited to the Smiths' sound.

Andy Rourke grooved on bass like Motown's James Jameson, whilst the drumming of Mike Joyce was crisp and propulsive. The singer was quick-witted and theatrical, his use of arcane language highly imaginative. His lyrics portrayed himself as a sensitive soul, somewhat out of step with the harsh modern environment. He would

create his own world, based on studied good manners, a portrayal of kindness and seemingly high principles. This record captured all of this, and The Smiths became a beacon of light to a swathe of devoted fans who bought into this image of outsider sensitivity. They invested their love and belief into the group, placing them atop a pedestal, only to be left bereft when in later years, the band's former singer and chief beneficiary of their affections, revealed himself as a sinister, deeply cynical, racially motivated bigot. In doing so, he betrayed the faith of a generation.

## POLYTECHNIC

### 10 NOVEMBER 1983, PORTSMOUTH, UK

### KATE ROSSI

I was in my late teens. They were just breaking. I went with my then boyfriend, Damien. I was there, but I was honestly so drunk I can't really remember much about it. I do remember the gladioli.

## POLYTECHNIC

### 16 NOVEMBER 1983, LEICESTER, UK

### IAN GELLING

I saw them at Leicester Poly and then at the De Montfort Hall in March 1984. They were fine gigs and Johnny Marr was marvellous. Moz is my most seen act after The Wedding Present. I've seen him walk off after a few tunes on a few occasions and I've turned up when he hasn't bothered to do so, even in the USA. I've even seen him feign death to avoid playing a cowshed of a leisure centre in Swindon. Around that there were numerous superb performances and some great nights. But Moz has pissed me off so much lately that I can't be arsed anymore.

### JOHN FEATHERSTONE

I worked with them at this gig and ended up being the lighting designer for every Smiths show from December 1983 until the very last show.

I was playing drums in garage bands in Leicester when a kid moved into the neighbourhood who had a cooler drum set than me; the same gold glitter Ludwig set that Ringo Starr played. I had a blue Premier kit – Leicester boy, Leicester drums – so it was suggested I find something else to do. Tail between legs, and after much protestation and me saying I was a better drummer (hashtag, I was), I sold my drums and bought some lights and started to light bands in and around Leicester.

I became the house lighting guy at Leicester Poly. The Smiths were one of the many, many bands who came through. You could tell how high up the bill they were because they were playing on a Wednesday night. This was before 'Hand In Glove' was even released and nobody had really heard of The Smiths. It wasn't quite the sort of situation where it was easier to introduce the members of the audience to the members of the band (because there were more people on the stage than in the audience) but it was not super-well attended.

Lo and behold, John Peel decided he was going to show up, so all of a sudden, that got a ton of attention. So they do a little Radio 1 John Peel simulcast thing (we'd call it a podcast now) and I remember this slightly scruffy, but in a cool kind of way, band member with a moptop coming off the elevator. You know how you have these people in your life that you've run into where you're just like, 'All right, this notion of a lost tribe? I get it now.' It was Johnny, and we just clicked immediately.

I was frankly bored doing band after band after band, so I'd been experimenting, near randomly picking a really narrow colour palette. I didn't know any of their music. I didn't know much about them, so for the Smiths show I was like, 'All right, what if we do this in all blue, green and white?' (I have always been a lighting designer whose tendency has been, if it doesn't look great, turn stuff off rather than turn stuff on and when in doubt, do less and let the music speak.)

After the show, it was high fives – or at least gentlemanly shaking of hands – all around. And they were like, 'We think we're taking off. We'll give you a call if we need anything.'

*Leicester Poly*

## WESTFIELD COLLEGE
### 17 NOVEMBER 1983, LONDON, UK

### PETER LINDSEY-JONES

They were booked to play the Student Union by an old friend of mine. They became famous between the booking and the gig, and the campus was swamped with Smiths fans.

### SEAN NEYLON

We must have really felt something from seeing them at the Lyceum and hearing that Peel session because a few months later we went to see them again at a gig at Westfield College. I think it was for Westfield students only, but we went anyway. This time it was just me and Chris and so began an obsession that would last the band's entire career.

In my mind it was a bright warm sunny summer's day as we queued up through the grounds to get into the hall, but the internet tells me otherwise! Everyone was happy, everyone was friendly and smiling, there was excitement in the air and a feeling of genuine anticipation. Many of the girls wore flowers and beads were everywhere. I think I've given this queuing up a rather apt 'summer of love' vibe to my memory, hence thinking it was summer, because that's certainly how it felt.

Inside it was a standard college or school hall, and I remember being surprised at just how popular they had become in such a short time. 'This Charming Man' had come out two weeks before and the buzz had begun. At one point, I saw a gladioli being flung into the crowd by Morrissey. It was heading towards me, but I couldn't free my hands from the throng in time, and it struck me on the head.

It was one of the happiest gigs I've ever been to – there was just such a buzz about what was happening. Afterwards, the band came down with a couple of what looked like crates of beer. Me and Chris had to get back to Liverpool Street to get the last train to Chelmsford, so had to make a quick decision; chat to them or get back for the train? One of us said, 'No, we'll chat to them next time.' Of course, we never did. Famous last words that we came to regret.

Even the staff got caught up in the happy atmosphere. Outside afterwards, I tried to prise open the notice board to get the gig ad – the 'Hand In Glove' poster with the time scribbled on in felt tip – as a souvenir and two of the young staff came over. I thought I was in trouble. 'Do you want the poster? Hold on I'll go and get the key.' He did and I got my souvenir. It's worth a fortune now and I've been trying to find it for the past year!

The buzz we'd felt at Westfield and the electricity between band and audience just grew as more and more people got to hear The Smiths. We'd never ever see them in such a small venue again. They were headline artists now. Another college friend, Rob, had repeatedly turned down the opportunity to come to see The Smiths. Then he heard 'This Charming Man' on the radio over breakfast and was gutted. 'I just thought they'd be another one of your noise bands like Cabaret Voltaire or something!' Now he's another Smiths convert.

### DON PERRETTA

I was there, and wrote this review for *Smash Hits* magazine at the time:

*The wonderful thing about college gigs is the sheer mixture of people who go to them. Tonight at Westfield College – a cross between a school dining hall and a gymnasium – is no exception. Standing side-by-side are trendies in long leather coats, punks in exhausted combat gear and even the odd longhaired hippie or two.*

*But all with something in common – they're all wearing flowers in their hair. You see, they've all come to see The Smiths which, of necessity nowadays, means a trip to the florist beforehand.*

*The atmosphere is very relaxed; the stage is small and bare, with a tiny PA and a mere five spots either side. It doesn't look like the setting for a band in the upper reaches of the chart, more like an amateur cabaret night in an old people's home. Still, nobody seems to mind.*

*A massive shower of carnations announces The Smiths' arrival on stage. The reaction is instantaneous – off the floor, up to the front and dance like a lunatic. The bobbing mass just below the stage laps up singer Morrissey's every gesture as he swings a huge bunch of flowers over his head, getting faster and faster until the stalks snap, sending yet another flurry of petals into the audience.*

*Johnny Marr's melodic but forceful guitar lines perfectly frame Morrissey's finely textured voice to produce pop with a delicate passion. The intention is pretty simple – vibrant, optimistic, uplifting songs; a celebration of youth, love and having fun.*

*What a night – a floral riot, the sweet smell of success hanging in the air. And I even managed to catch a flower to take home with me.*

It was a great gig. I think of it often as it was the first time I took my then girlfriend out with me on a 'working' night. She of course loved them and Morrissey in particular. She later named our cat after him. We married three years later, and we referenced that night often, even to our kids who must have got bored to death by it. Sadly, she passed away in 2010. I can't listen to The Smiths without thinking of her. So it's bittersweet. But still a great night.

## EDGE HILL COLLEGE

### 18 NOVEMBER 1983, ORMSKIRK, UK

### LOUISE BENNETT

Yes I saw The Smiths at Edge Hill in 1983. Amazing gig but I was slightly drunk!

### JEREMY KIDD, RED GUITARS VOCALIST

'I need advice, I need advice, I've got my balls trapped in a vice...' we'd croon to each other in the van as we criss-crossed Britain in

*Jeremy Kidd & Lou Harris from Red Guitars who supported The Smiths*

the wake of The Smiths during the winter of 1983 and the spring of '84. It was clear that something special was going on from our first gig supporting them at Edge Hill College in Ormskirk.

When we arrived in mid-afternoon for the soundcheck there was already a buzz about the place, and there were loads of people hanging around just trying to catch a glimpse of the headliners. I grew up obsessed with The Beatles but too young to actually participate in Beatlemania. I had to be satisfied with listening to the records and

*Edge Hill College, Ormskirk (Adam Marsh)*

watching them on telly or at the cinema. Of course, The Smiths weren't The Beatles, but there were parallels.

For me 'This Charming Man' was their 'She Loves You' and when Morrissey sang, 'Do not go to them, let them come to you, just like I do' or, 'I never had a job because I never wanted one,' I thought it was the equivalent of Lennon asking the people in the cheap seats at the Royal Variety Show to clap along and the others to 'just rattle your jewellery'. Not to mention the fact that in those days Johnny Marr was wearing a Rickenbacker and sporting a mop top.

Johnny and Steven – both great craftsmen, very skilful. And I can't say the so-called plagiarism ever bothered me. It was just the vernacular out of which they grew and above which they soared with exhilarating frequency.

I reckon I witnessed getting on for ten per cent of all the Smiths live shows, and from backstage to boot, and I have to say it was a privilege.

### LOU DUFFY-HOWARD

It was producer John Porter who introduced us to The Smiths. We recorded a John Peel session with him at Maida Vale studios in August '83 and he'd just recorded The Smiths. He spotted something in common between Hal's African guitar riffs in 'Marimba Jive' and Johnny's guitar intro in 'This Charming Man'. I couldn't hear the similarity at the time. We chatted to them and their manager back then, Joe Moss, swapping cassettes and playing a couple of gigs with them at the end of the year, one at a

college in Lancashire and one at the Electric Ballroom.

Red Guitars had a handful of singles in the Indie charts, and we were preparing to record an album for release on our own label, Self Drive. The Smiths album – produced by John Porter – was due to come out and they invited us to support them on their first UK tour, without a buy-on which was brilliant.

We played around 20 shows with them and, during the course of the tour, 'This Charming Man' hit the charts so the gigs were packed and we all had a blast. We were very different bands but got on well and it was interesting to watch them play every night and see the set develop.

One time we turned up to do our soundcheck and when they saw us, they started to jam out one of our songs, 'Heartbeat Go'. That was cool. Morrissey kept himself to himself a lot of the time but one of my daughter Christa's earliest memories is that he gave her a piece of chewing gum. She was only about three, too young to know what it was. I think she just ate it.

Both bands kept in touch with John Porter who took us to record in the legendary Matrix Studio in Bloomsbury. We went in to record some demos, and he played us an early version of 'How Soon Is Now?' he was working on. It sounded fantastic and still stands out to me as the best of their songs.

## DEREK MOIR, AGE 17

We lived in Perth, a town of 50,000 with a strong underground scene, and had been hanging with the punk/post-punk crew but felt we had missed seeing all those bands in their prime and were really passionate about making sure that we didn't miss the next wave of brilliance. We had heard 'Hand In Glove' and taped the first two Peel sessions. We read that they were playing in Ormskirk, outside Liverpool, so skived off work or college and drove down from Scotland without tickets.

Four of us set off early on the Friday. My mate had a run-down Chrysler Sunbeam – more rust than orange. We called in sick and set off early to get to Ormskirk – where the fuck was that? The car overheated once or twice but got us over the border. As we entered Ormskirk we got lost, as you did in the pre-satnav world, and stopped at a bar to ask for directions. Everyone told us that we were mad and that the gig was sold out. Nevertheless, a very kind (ie. pissed and off-duty) policeman offered to take us to the college where the gig was, despite his indicators not working. He did the old 'hands out of the window' 1932 thing as he took us to the venue and dropped us off.

They were playing in a college dining hall. The dinner ladies told us, 'Ohhh, you won't get in – it's sold out,' but sneaked us in through the dining room partition. The Red Guitars were soundchecking. The Smiths were watching it, and Grant Showbiz was doing the sound. I got the job of going up to Grant and telling him our story. He was amazed we had travelled so far. The Smiths – Johnny, Andy and Mike – were amazed as well and invited us to stay for the gig, but we had to work for it. The bar was in a separate building to the gig, so we got the job of fetching booze and fags. Great fun, especially when we were trailing these back as The Alarm were being refused entry!

We asked if we could record the gig on our boom box and they were very happy for us to do so. It was recorded from the drum riser but it's great. Our mate's family had just moved down to Ormskirk and put us up for the night. The Smiths letting us stay for the soundcheck was like Christmas!

### BANJO

Bands never came to Ormskirk, so this was something of a big deal. Actually, some bands did come to Ormskirk, and I just didn't know about it, meaning I missed a gig by Orchestral Manoeuvres In The Dark, but The Smiths was enough of an event that word spread out from the local college, where the gig was being held, to the locals.

*Sounds* journalist Garry Bushell had alleged that the B-side to 'This Charming Man', 'Handsome Devil', was endorsing paedophilia. It was bullshit from a man who was almost a polar opposite of what The Smiths stood for, but some of the mud he threw stuck.

I'd heard enough to realise that the emerging buzz about The Smiths was likely to be justified. It was quite a big gig for a band of that size, but there were no tickets left because not much else went on in Ormskirk and thanks to the media exposure resulting from the Bushell hatchet job. I decided to go anyway and see if I could bunk in somehow.

A few punks and goths from out of town had the same idea. (There always seemed to be a good number of goths in the crowd at early Smiths gigs.) We were milling around the front door and the security were trying to disperse us all. I said I was on the guest list and security asked me how I'd managed that. With a smile on my face, I told them that I was Morrisey's gladioli roadie and the show couldn't go ahead without me. Probably being quite surprised at the number of flowers that were on the stage, the security guard started laughing and, as much for my cheek as anything else, let me and a friend in for free.

Red Guitars were supporting and were quite good until the guitarist fell off the small stage and came back up again in a really bad temper, all scowls and knotted eyebrows. His mood was contagious and the set ceased to be fun. If he'd have laughed it off, I think the band would have got a better reception, but petulance is seldom entertaining to watch.

I only have snapshot memories of The Smiths, such as the high-hat pattern on 'This Night Has Opened My Eyes' and Morrissey's flower waving. But I know that the gig was great because the friend I snuck in with recorded the gig on a professional Walkman. He did this a lot and some of his recordings have become fairly well bootlegged. This recording surfaced as a CD called *Gladioli All Over*. The recordings reveal them to be tight and well-rehearsed, but with a more abrasive sound than we generally attribute to them. Maybe this explains the goth contingent.

It was enough to fully convert me to a fan and I was able to see them another five times, although the last one was the gig at Preston Guildhall where Mike Joyce threw a drumstick into the audience and someone threw it back, hitting Morrissey, which led him to depart the stage never to return.

## *TOP OF THE POPS*

### 24 NOVEMBER 1983, LONDON, UK

The Smiths appeared on the BBC TV's legendary pop programme for the first time, performing 'This Charming Man'. Forced to mime, Morrissey sang into a bouquet of gladioli. Afterwards, the band caught a train home to Manchester for a gig at the Haçienda.

### MELANIE SMITH

I met the eighteen-year-old Johnny Marr in 1982, right around the time he'd just formed a band. I didn't know then that it would be The Smiths. Manchester was buzzing with music and style, still rough around the edges but alive with possibility. The New Romantic era was in full swing, post-punk was pulsing through the city, and my friend Karen McWilliams and I would spend the odd Saturday afternoons hunting for records and clothes and posing around town.

I recall my Karen saying, 'Let's go and see my friend Johnny.' (I got the impression she was seeing him, but I think he was just a mate.) She said, 'I'll introduce you.' She knew him from going to the nightclub Pips. It didn't feel like a big deal, and although I kept a diary, I obviously didn't think at the time it was anything worth a mention. He was working at X Clothes, a trendy clothing shop, located down a small side street called Chapel Walks.

Johnny, with his long, floppy black hair, was behind the counter when we went in. He was friendly and practically gushing as he told us he'd joined a band and got a new guitar, and he brought it out from the back, showing it off. It was either a Rickenbacker or a Fender Telecaster. There was that mix of pride and excitement emitting from him.

Somehow, we ended up going for a cuppa with him. I think it was a café in a little basement. We sat there chatting, just the three of us, and it all felt perfectly ordinary at the time. I can't even recall what we talked about. I wish I could. He

*Karen McWilliams & Melanie Smith went for a cuppa with Johnny (Melanie Smith)*

may have talked about meeting Morrissey, or their first Ritz gig on 4 October 1982. Who knows? I wish my memory was better and I'd recorded it in my diary.

And possibly a year later (but it felt like months) whilst watching *Top Of The Pops*, with a new band called The Smiths playing 'This Charming Man', the very same Johnny Marr I'd had tea with was now on stage, guitar in hand. I remember shouting out, 'I know him, he works in a clothes shop in Manchester!'

That quiet, ordinary moment in a cellar café suddenly felt extraordinary. I'd been there, right at the very start, without even realising it.

Oh, and I also was also at the Patti Smith gig at Manchester Apollo in August 1978 where legend has it that Morrissey was introduced to a very young Marr by Billy Duffy (later of The Cult) whilst in the queue!

Johnny Marr: At the time, there'd been this question of whether it was cool to go on *Top Of The Pops*, probably from The Clash refusing to do it. But we were a new generation, and it felt like there were new rules… Plus, when the members of The Smiths were children, *Top Of The Pops* was one of the most important days of the week. Suddenly we found ourselves on it. Previously, we'd been synonymous with the John Peel show, and suddenly that culture was on *Top Of The Pops* – John Peel started to present it, and it was a new phase: post-punk going mainstream.

Everyone remembers the flowers Morrissey took on to the show. I'd been very aware of how powerful *Top Of The Pops* could be visually, from my childhood watching T. Rex. We'd first used gladioli onstage at the Haçienda about a year before, to counteract the all-encompassing austere aesthetic of Factory Records. People assumed it was an Oscar Wilde homage but that was a bonus. The flowers made the stage very treacherous if you were wearing moccasins, but they became emblematic, iconic. After that we tried to make every TV appearance a spectacle – Morrissey pulling off his shirt and having things written on his chest, the hearing aid.

## HAÇIENDA

### 24 NOVEMBER 1983, MANCHESTER, UK

### CHRIS PARKER

I first heard The Smiths sometime in 1983, probably on John Peel's show. They immediately felt like a very personal find – *my* band, from *my* town. Being in at the start felt important, without even knowing what it was the start of. Getting records on the day of release was always vital, if you didn't want someone else casually telling you how ace something was and, 'Haven't you heard this new band/song yet? You're not a proper fan then…'.

This was special though. 'Hand In Glove'. The sun shines out of our behinds. A naked man on the sleeve, looking half-ashamed, half-oblivious. What an introduction to everything that followed. There were rumours Morrissey had been in another group from round our way (Wythenshawe): Ed Banger and the Nosebleeds. I didn't know if that was true (Google later killed that wonderment), but even a hinted at local connection was good enough back then.

I couldn't have been, or looked less, like Morrissey if I'd tried. He was cool. I looked like a teenage Ned Flanders: long-haired, sporting Wrangler denim and sibling-cast-off corduroy, or big baggy jumpers and drainpipe jeans, or even my dad's stuff from the fifties, just to look different. But not the way he did. I'd have to change. It got me beaten up by drunk United fans some time later, but that just made me love them, and Manchester City, all the more.

Before 1983, I'd been into heavy rock (brothers) and punk (schoolmates). I'd seen Led Zeppelin, Black Sabbath, The Jam, The Damned, all before I was 18. But I'd missed out on Sore Throat and various reggae and ska bands because I was too scared to risk missing the all-nighter back from the clubs in Moss Side and having to walk all the way back to Benchill, dressed as I did. There's a big difference between defiance and idiocy.

Then John Peel happened and Factory happened and sticking to genres seemed pointless; suddenly there was just great music of all kinds, or stuff you turned off. When The Smiths arrived out of nowhere, I wasn't going to miss out again. I'd bought two tickets well in advance, proudly brandishing my pink and yellow striped Haçienda membership card, Ned portrait and all, at the box office as proof of cool entitlement, though it was clear anyone could buy them without one.

On the day, I was at the tail-end of splitting up with the girl who the second ticket was intended for. We decided to be adult about it and go together anyway, the way teenagers imagine being adult works. Besides, she loved them just as much; well, almost. Later, 'How quickly would I die, if I jumped…' reminded me of her dramatic frailty, then if not now.

That Thursday early evening was typical. You always watched *Top Of The Pops*, if only to criticise who was on. But then, there they were, in amongst a load of average other stuff, waving flowers about and singing the best song of the year. Hearing them on the radio was one thing, but seeing them on telly…I couldn't believe it, not least because I thought *Top Of The Pops* was made in London. Maybe they'd cancelled the gig? Or was it recorded? No idea, then or now. But it was a lovely taste of things, hopefully, to come.

There was no way to find out then, short of ringing the club, and we didn't have a phone. Besides, going into town was always an adventure in those days. So dressed half-rocker, half-punk, I called for the girl, and we got the bus into town, the 102 from Hall Lane in Baguley. We sat on the top deck, at the front. She'd seen *Top Of The Pops* too, so any awkwardness was warded off by the excitement of that performance and the thrill of the gig to come. No heavy words lightly thrown, just giddy chat and not-talking about tomorrow.

I remember town that evening as drizzly and cold, not icy, but grim.

Manchester often seemed like that. But Manchester then wasn't like now, not buzzing and busy and with options galore, nor was it quite the grimy seventies either. We got off near The Ritz to walk back down the road and straight away there was a sense of something. We heard the queue before we saw it. The shivers that shook us weren't from the cold. This was going to be something else. No-one complained about the wait to get in.

I was used to the girder chic of the club's insides, but it was her first time, and she thought it was fascinating and cool and brilliant. Drinks weren't cheap, so we made do with just a couple, though getting served was a chore for someone who still never catches a bartender's eye. We stood near the back and people-watched and drank and chatted, with a view of the stage over to the left and the entrance back over to the right. And we waited. You run out of things to say in the end and I – and I suspect she – just wanted the gig to get going. Sometimes bands don't turn up, do they? Surely not for a home tie?

Then James came on and were superb. We liked what we knew of them before that, but now we loved them. They lit the fuse. The singer's shocking, epileptic jarring dances, tiring just to watch, sparked a mosh of at first reluctant then embracing madness. 'Hymns From A Village'. Some people left straight after, obviously not mithered about seeing the headliners. That struck me as odd at the time, like leaving a match before the end, but people still do. 'The Smiths had better be good to outdo this, mind,' we said, half expectant, half fearful.

They were. After a long wait, when we thought they might not show up, with people around us saying they definitely wouldn't and that was why others had already left, and you looked to the people at the front for a sign that they'd seen or heard something or someone, but there was nothing to indicate one way or another. It was getting late, we were thinking about last buses and maybe a taxi, or a train and a long walk, or…

There's that split second before a band comes on, the lights are out, and there's a swell and a surge and you know something's about to happen, something you knew was going to happen anyway but that creates a sensation you never experience doing anything else in life. We felt it, looked at each other, grinned and laughed. And on they came. Can a band save a relationship? Did either of us want it saving? These things take time.

They crashed into the first song and the place went mental. Everyone sang, everyone knew the words, everyone was Morrissey. You handsome devil. There were flowers everywhere, just like the ones on *TOTP*. Apart from my mum, I didn't know anyone who knew what gladioli were, but now everyone knew. They took each single one of us and made us as one, flowers in hand, chucked or plucked from the stage and strewn and caught with glee. Not sunny sixties San

Francisco, just a rainy winter's night in eighties Manchester.

We bounced about, sang along, got close enough to get some flowers. Then slower songs brought the mood down. People swayed but sang less. They were controlling things. Or maybe they didn't have enough bouncy songs written yet. But it was a reminder. They might be young and cool and different, but they sang about pain and bad things as well as joy and not caring. Bad Manchester things, good Manchester things, all full of universal truths. You don't want that in the middle of a performance like that, but you accept it. And something else is going to happen, soon, you can feel it. They'll get us bouncing again.

They do. 'Hand in Glove'. The sun shines out of our behinds. With flowers in. Tight songs tightly played. Two encores, two song repeats. By their choice or demands from us? 'Haven't they already done this one?' 'Who cares!?' Then before you know it, it's over and the lights go up and suddenly it's just a bright warehouse full of sweaty, ecstatic, buzz-deaf kids. Children of a revolution? Nothing could be the same again now, surely. Maybe everything from now on would be always this good.

Going home, we sat on the back seat, downstairs. We didn't stop talking all the way to Baguley. About the gig, the band, the songs, the flowers she still had in her hand, bedraggled a bit now but proof that it wasn't a dream, was real, had all happened, just as we were describing. But not about us.

I dropped her off and headed for the subway under the motorway, running through it as fast as I could to the light at the end, dodging the broken glass underfoot. Liking the same band, even that band, isn't enough. All the better for her – she's got everything now. So have I and I went to see her that night. Betrayal is part of The Smiths as well, isn't it?

A few years later, I was in St Ann's Square, outside a clothes shop where my new love was browsing. Looking towards the Royal Exchange steps, a tall man was gangly, gracefully walking in the direction of the church. People around stopped. Watched. Pointed. Isn't that…? What's he doing here…? What's he doing…? Let the people stare, he really didn't care. He was just walking along. Like a normal person. Like someone who looks like Morrissey.

Whose words have become part of your own vocabulary, of how you describe and frame your life story. I was looking for a band and then I found a band. Of all the bands I've ever seen, or wanted to, they were and are number one. And I'm glad they never reformed; that Morrissey went his own way; that there were acrimony and accusations; that what remains of them is the love of a clutch of fantastic music and lyrics, no filler, nothing forced, all instantly recognisable. It's what you want from a great band. Half a lifetime later, I'm still boasting about seeing them. Pathetic really. And brilliant.

### BILL MATHER

Back in the summer of 1983, I'd made a terrible mess of my A-levels while I was at Stretford Grammar

*Bill Mather sent off a postcard to the address on the sleeve of 'Hand in Glove' (Mat Norman)*

School on Great Stone Road, and I was wondering what to do with my life. I spent a lot of time just listening to an old radio which my uncle Ernie had given me. It had a Piccadilly Radio 261 sticker attached to it.

I used to listen to John Peel and various other programmes on it. On one particular night, Peel played this song called 'Hand In Glove' by this new band called The Smiths. He said that they were going to be a very important group.

I immediately decided that I was going to go up to town to buy this record from HMV. I was served by a guy called Derek, with whom I later became good friends when I worked there some years later. Derek informed me that the band came from Manchester and 'the guitarist', as he called him, had dropped copies of the single off in the shop that day.

I bought the record and took it home. On the cover, it listed the singer as being called 'Morrissey'. The only other thing I could see was that it had 70 Portland Street as the contact details, which I found out was the address for Crazy Face Jeans. They were a well-known name and had a few shops dotted around Manchester and Stockport and were run by a guy called Joe Moss. It turned out that Joe was the Smiths' manager.

I sent off a postcard and ended up receiving items through the post from The Smiths' office. Sometime later, I realised it was Morrissey himself who had sent these things to me.

The Smiths were playing at the Haçienda on Thursday, 24 November 1983. That date will always be tattooed on my mind. The very same day, they performed their second single, 'This Charming Man', on *Top Of The Pops*, getting the train straight back to Manchester afterwards to play the Haçienda.

The Haçienda was completely overrun with people, and it was a very, very joyous night. The very next day, Morrissey had truly arrived in the nation's front rooms. My friend Mike McVeigh's sister, Anne-Marie, remembered this strange guy who was at North Trafford College on Talbot Road, Stretford. She proclaimed that he was actually called Stephen Morrissey, and from that, we found out that he lived on King's Road in Stretford.

From then on, I took The Smiths to my heart. I have followed them ever since.

### CATH COLLINS, AGE 17

I was a fan before they were on *Top Of The Pops*. Before they were big. I was going to Xaverian College in Manchester, and we used to go to the Haçienda. You know when you're all in the park and being cool? I remember having a tape recorder and somebody playing 'Hand In Glove' and I thought, 'Flipping heck' and, 'Oh, my God.' Then 'This Charming Man' came out and that Haçienda gig was a massive homecoming, because they'd been on tour. The Haçienda was absolutely rammed. It was a really brilliant gig, the best of all the gigs I've ever seen. I saw them at Glastonbury too. But I didn't see them again after that. You know when you think, 'Oh, they've gone a bit big?' It's not in a conscious way but suddenly it's outside of your own then.

In 1986, we were in the Seymour, one of those humongous old-fashioned pubs. It's not there now, but it was on the corner of Upper Chorlton Road in Manchester so about half a mile from Morrissey's childhood home. This chap who was part of the group I was sat in the pub with said, 'Do you want to come back to mine for a drink?' So we went back to his house, a council house, and he made us tea and toast. The walls were lined with gold and silver discs. He was playing us videos of Morrissey being interviewed but not just the parts that were broadcast. He had the full tape before it was edited, including Morrissey being miked up beforehand and unmiked after. It was Morrissey's dad. I was having tea and toast with Morrissey's dad!

Mike Joyce: By the third Haçienda gig I remember Interflora bringing 30 boxes of gladioli at that gig. The place just stank. By this time, we were being mobbed. The height of the stage was perfect for people to use other people as a stepping-stone to get on stage. It was absolutely insane.

## ASSEMBLY ROOMS

### 6 DECEMBER 1983, DERBY, UK

### JOHN FEATHERSTONE

About a week later the long-lost and much-missed Joe Moss called me up and said, 'Hey, we're doing an *Old Grey Whistle Test* thing in Derby. That's just up the road for you. Would you do the lighting for us?' So I was like 'sure' and I rented a bunch of lights.

The band were really just four lads from Manchester and more like a gang than a band. Mike and Andy were two lovely Manchester lads who were into playing music. But Johnny and Morrissey were very focused on the visuals, the brand and the image. Johnny and Morrissey really liked *Whistle Test* when it went out, and as they say, 'The rest is history.' Before I could even spell 'lighting designer' I was one. So I ran away and joined the circus.

I did every show from that show in Derby until the fateful show at Brixton Academy, which none of us knew was going to be the last one. We thought it was just a little bit of a coda to the end of *The Queen Is Dead* tour.

### LYNNE DICKENS, AGE 20

I saw The Smiths at the Assembly Rooms before they were really well known, performing for *The Old Grey Whistle Test*. I think it was free. My boyfriend at the time, now my husband, bought a Smiths LP and I liked them straight away. I think a lot of people who went to that gig just went because it was free. I saw them again in Nottingham for *The Queen Is Dead* tour. They were absolutely brilliant on both occasions. They really played to the crowd. I was gutted when they split up.

### THOMAS JONES

We got free tickets for the filming for *Whistle Test* and, as four lads from the sticks – well, Crewe – we didn't know much about the band except for the two singles to date and snatches we'd heard on John Peel. 'This Charming Man' had been on *Top Of The Pops* a week or so before and that was our Road to Damascus moment. Everyone at school the next day was saying, 'Did you see that?'

The Assembly Rooms were decked out in flowers and people were throwing them at the stage and each other even before the band took the stage with 'Handsome Devil', Morrissey brandishing a bunch of gladioli. The band later went on record as saying this gig was a low light for them as their hardcore Manchester fans didn't land tickets. All I know is that the whole room seemed to fall under their spell and by the time of the stage invasion, during 'You've Got Everything Now', it was beautiful pandemonium. I ended up standing a couple of feet from Johnny, next to his Fender Twin Reverb amp, and I well remember the slightly nonplussed mascaraed scowl at the chaos that was unfolding.

A particular highlight was the breakneck 'Miserable Lie'. Morrissey had been hit in the eye with a flower in the intro after 'Please stay with your own kind' and the remaining three had to count the bars and go into the fast section without any vocal cues. He returned to sing the song – with extra venom – and concluded with, 'I need advice... AND SO DO YOU!'

Other highlights were Marr's subtly overdriven Rickenbacker 330, surely the definitive early-Smiths guitar sound, and a beautifully delicate 'This Night Has Opened My Eyes' with a few lyrical improvisations, such as 'I'm never happy and I'm never sad'.

The TV transmission stopped at the end of the stage invasion on 'You've Got Everything Now', but I'm fairly certain that they played another two songs. I remember Morrissey pleading, 'Civility, please,' as everyone was ushered off the stage. As for us four, on Derby station we pledged to sell the keyboard and become a guitar band ourselves but, to coin a phrase, the world never listened.

### NICK HOWARTH

I used to go to a record shop on Swan Street called The Record Peddler. He sold a lot of Factory Records stuff and my mate's older brother asked for a Smiths record and the bloke played it before he purchased it and I instantly knew that was the band for me. From that day on I bought everything they released and started going to gigs. Me and a mate purchased tickets for Derby Assembly Rooms, told our parents we were going skating with the youth club and off we went. It was an amazing gig, only spoilt by the fact we missed the last train back to Manchester and had to call reverse charge to my mate's parents, who weren't impressed with us because they had to drive to Derby to pick us up. The crowd at Derby was amazing. I've not been to a gig like that since.

## TRINITY COLLEGE DUBLIN XMAS BALL

### 9 DECEMBER 1983, DUBLIN IRELAND

### DECLAN HASSETT

I saw them a few times but most memorably their first gig in Dublin. They played in Trinity College and The Blades supported. They played 'Hand in Glove' and 'This Charming Man' twice as their encore and I met my wife for the first time. My three kids, all now in their twenties, are fans.

### MILL BUTLER, AGE 20

I was roadie for The Blades downstairs – I still am – and watched The Smiths' whole soundcheck. We finished just in time to catch them play.

## A FLAT

### 27 DECEMBER 1983, HULME, MANCHESTER, UK

### DAVE HASLAM

The second issue of *Debris* wasn't going to write itself, so I made plans, wrote some ideas on scraps of paper and knocked on doors. Within a couple of weeks of the launch party, I'd arranged for Morrissey to come to my flat in Hulme.

The day after Boxing Day, 1983. That was the day Morrissey came for tea, and I cooked him cauliflower cheese. Sometimes stuff happens and it's only later you realise it was one of the highlights of your life.

I was always wandering in and out of the Crazy Face offices where the Smiths' management was based, saying hello to Liz Taylor (who worked for the band's manager, Joe Moss) and nosing about. Most of the visitors were people in the rag trade; it was through Joe that I met Leo Stanley, who ran the clothes shop Identity in Affleck's Palace. You could always tell if Joe Moss was in the office as the cassette player would be belting out the likes of Chuck Berry or John Lee Hooker.

When I first started this stalking stuff, The Smiths had just released 'Hand In Glove'. By November 1983, I was popping in once or twice a week. I asked Liz if she would ask Joe to ask whether Morrissey would grant me an interview, and word came back via Liz that he was happy to oblige.

I panicked a little because I didn't know where to go to do the interview. It was scheduled for when Joe was having a day off, so we couldn't meet at the management's office. I didn't know much about Morrissey and there was no internet to go on to search and research. I'd heard two singles and their B-sides and some other stuff on the radio; I'd seen The Smiths play; I knew Morrissey was a vegetarian, and I knew he was celibate (or, at least, he said he was); from what I'd seen and heard, I concluded he was a delicate soul and I decided that maybe we'd not meet in the pub. He didn't give me the impression of a man who wanted to be out in public, sinking pints all evening.

Another major reason for avoiding the pub was that I needed

*Morrissey interview in Debris magazine (Dave Haslam)*

somewhere quiet. It was only the second interview I'd ever done. I had a tape machine that recorded on to cassettes, it was bulky, and you had to press 'play' and 'record' at the same time, plus you had to make sure that neither you nor the interviewee was too far away from the built-in and not very clever microphone.

With all these issues worrying me, I decided that the best rendezvous point for me and Morrissey was my horrible little flat in Amberidge Walk in Hulme. I'd be there on my own and we'd not be disturbed. So I asked Joe if he thought Morrissey would mind coming round to my place. Joe said it wouldn't be a problem, and Liz said, 'I'll pick him up in the car and come over.'

I was 21 and Morrissey was 24. I suspect Joe had told Morrissey I was enthusiastic and harmless, and encouraged Morrissey to accept my request for an interview.

Ian Curtis had once said, 'Fanzines are the future of the world.' Morrissey was another true believer in the importance and potential of fanzines in that era, and in the local scene.

Morrissey was a fan of *City Fun* fanzine, as was Linder Sterling, Morrissey's close friend from the band Ludus (her work for *City Fun* included the front-cover design of issue eight).

Liz Naylor and Cath Carroll, the main characters piloting the fanzine in 1982, were also in a band together, the Gay Animals, and they managed Ludus for a time. City Fun printed the first-ever Smiths review, from their gig at Manhattan Sound in January 1983. A few months later, Morrissey, using the pseudonym Burt Macho, wrote an 800-word feature for *City Fun* about Sandie Shaw. If you followed only the mainstream media, you'd never have known all this stuff was happening.

Thinking ahead to my evening with Morrissey, I wondered if I should cook him his tea, because we'd agreed he'd come round at seven o'clock and I wanted to be hospitable. Liz Taylor said, 'Yes, I think he'd like that,' and we talked about what I might cook. These were the days before Quorn or ready-meal veggie versions of meat dishes, and I didn't do dinner parties, so I had a very limited repertoire in any case, meat or non-meat. Liz told me Morrissey liked eggs, but I was much less of a fan. So I decided to make a massive bowl of cauliflower cheese.

Morrissey arrived wearing a dark grey pullover, brown shoes and what appeared to be the same jeans he wore on *Top Of The Pops* during the week of the Haçienda gig (or maybe he had a whole stock of 32-34 inch jeans that sagged off his backside). I spent some time getting the cheese sauce just right while he browsed my bookshelves and cast his eye over a pile of magazines next to the TV. I put on some music.

It turned out that Morrissey's mum had already cooked him something, so he wasn't hungry. He told me to go ahead and feed myself and Liz, though, and then sat there and watched us eat cauliflower cheese with some carrots and a slice of white bread. A New Order track started playing, and he asked who it was. I told him I thought he might

*Morrissey interview (Dave Haslam)*

WHAT SORT OF INTERVIEWS DO YOU PREFER TO DO: THE SORT WHERE YOU PHILOSOPHISE ALL THE TIME, OR THE "WHAT'S YOUR FAVOURITE COLOUR MORRISSEY?" SORT OF QUESTION?

I think "what's your favourite colour?" is a great question...

SO WHAT'S YOUR FAVOURITE COLOUR?

I'll have to think about that. It's always the really simple questions that you can never answer. If somebody asks you about foreign policy you just snap it off (click) like that and you've got the answer.

Most interviews I've been very displeased with because, obviously, you don't have any control; you can be very merry in an interview and it can come across as being very dour. Or you can say something flippantly which will be written in blood in the music press and it sounds as though you're deadly serious. You're throwing yourselves on the mercy of a journalist who can be friendly during the interview but can turn out to be something of a bohemoth in print.

*   *   *   *   *   *   *   *   *   *   *

YOU SPENT OVER £200 ON FLOWERS AT THE HACIENDA. CAN YOU EXPLAIN YOUR REASONS WHY ALL THESE FLOWERS?

Yes, I think so. In a really perverse way it was really originally linked with the whole nuclear debate. Because at the time I introduced the flowers the daffodil had become like the Greenham Women's symbol. I wanted to introduce something on that level; that could speak politically. But have known it was New Order. 'Oh,' he said and melodramatically raised his eyebrows.

After the food, I pressed 'play' and 'record' simultaneously and we talked. He told me he'd had 'a very monotonous teenage existence'. We talked about how he'd fallen in love with music. He recalled buying 'Come And Stay With Me' by Marianne Faithfull (the first record he ever bought, purchased from the Paul Marsh record shop on Alexandra Road in Moss Side). 'In the history of my life,' he said, 'the high points were always buying particular records. And hearing records and being immersed in them and really believing that these people understood how I felt about certain situations.'

I asked him about the Haçienda show from a few weeks earlier, and the fact that Joe and the Smiths had spent £200 on flowers. He linked the flowers to CND and the nuclear debate. I remember several years earlier being struck by the power of a photo of a young woman at an anti-Vietnam war demo in Washington, confronting armed soldiers by holding up a flower. It was a strong image, so I knew what Morrissey was getting at. He was very specific, though, and had a more contemporary anti-war movement on his mind. 'At the time I introduced the flowers, the daffodil had become like the Greenham women's symbol,' he said. 'I wanted to introduce something on that level that could speak politically. But people never actually saw it that way.'

We talked about some of his songs being 'genderless'. (He said,

'We're dominated by very cemented and boring ideas about what is sexual; this completely revealed sexuality.') Cath Carroll rang up for Morrissey and he said he'd call her back. The conversation spiralled off into a discussion about 'the cult of the beautiful', the François Kevorkian remix of 'This Charming Man' and Morrissey's frustration that 'you can say something flippantly which will be written in blood in the music press, and it sounds as though you're deadly serious'.

We finished the interview, and I said, 'So, shall we go to the pub?' and, contrary to my preconceptions, he was up for it.

He called Cath from my phone, and we arranged to meet at a pub near where I lived, called the Grants Arms, on Royce Road (near the PSV Club). We got into Liz's car and drove along Boundary Lane and over Princess Road.

We ordered bottles of lager and sat there cringing at whatever people put on the jukebox. Liz (Taylor) was still with us, and then Cath and the other Liz (Naylor) arrived. I still threw questions at him, and we chatted for another hour or so. We returned to talking about the François Kevorkian remix, which Rough Trade distributed even though Morrissey hated it, and he consequently told fans not to buy it. Morrissey was annoyed with Rough Trade and looking back I guess it was one of the first of several incidents that caused him and the band to fall out of love with the label. At the time, though, everyone was convinced that the only way for a band to keep

*Morrissey interview (Dave Haslam)*

```
;   HOW SERIOUS ARE YOU ABOUT YOUR SEXUAL
CHEEKINESS?
    Intolerably serious really.We're dominated by
very cemented and boring ideas about what is
sexual;this completely revealed sexuality.I feel
very strongly.'Cheekiness';in a way I like that.
But I don't want to sound like some disobedient
schoolboy talking about breasts and 'Chesty'
Morgan.
    HOW MUCH AFFINITY DO YOU FEEL TOWARDS
OTHER MANCHESTER BANDS?
    None at all,but I wish I did.
    DO YOU EVER LISTEN TO PICCADILLY RADIO?
    Never.
    WHAT'S YOUR IDEA OF A PERFECT NIGHT OUT?
    The perfect night out is...a night indoors for
me personally.
    ON YOUR OWN?
    Yes.Just stroking the cat...The perfect night
out?That's so difficult.I could give you a little
itinery,but that would be pointless.What's import-
ant is who you're with.If you're with people you
like you can swim in a canal and it can be a per-
fectly relaxing atmosphere.People feel they can't
have a good night out unless they spend £39 at the
bar;you know,if they spend £39 they come home
and feel totally wasted.
```

*What Difference Does It Make?*

their vision pure was to sign to an independent. He said he hadn't wanted to sign to a major record label because 'it just seemed like going back to school'.

I took off on some long exposition of the status of the artist in a capitalist society, saying that all relationships, including those between a band and a label and between a band and an audience, are no more and no less than one based on money.

'You're a commodity, Morrissey. Our connection is really a transaction. And don't you think the whole idea of 'artistic integrity' is a fallacy?'

He said, 'I don't know.'

## DANCETERIA

### 31 DECEMBER 1983, NEW YORK, NEW YORK

Johnny Marr: We had to play at midnight, and we went to this club, Danceteria, which was this pretty trendy hip predominantly hip-hop club, or electro as it was then. We went and played on New Year's Eve at our very first American show. It was a little bit of a weird show for us. We didn't have too great a time. We had some sound problems, and we were just trashed (from jetlag). Supporting us was the girl who worked on the coat check, and we didn't really pay too much attention to her, but it was Madonna. She played for about 20 minutes before we went on. I think she went down pretty well.

## 'WHAT DIFFERENCE DOES IT MAKE?'
### RELEASED 16 JANUARY 1984

'What Difference Does It Make?' climbed to number 12 in the UK Top 40, with Morrissey briefly on the picture sleeve until actor Terence Stamp consented to his image being used. Actor Albert Finney and footballer George Best both declined similar advances from La Moz.

### SUE LONGSTAFF

I worked at BBC Television Centre during the height of their fame so I used to watch *Top Of The Pops* from in the audience whenever I could. If you watch 'What Difference Does It Make?' on YouTube, right at the start there's a guy kicking off in the audience because his girlfriend wouldn't leave the studio. I'm the girl in white turning round and laughing to my friend at how bizarre it was. I'm thinking (I don't remember, as it's 40 years ago) that there were several takes as, within seconds, I can see the back of my head in front of Johnny Marr. I'm from Manchester, so I remember feeling quite proud that they were too!

### ROB LEVY

When I first heard 'What Difference Does It Make' it was a moment I could easily relate to it because, at this time in the eighties, we were all scared of Reagan and war, and we thought a lot of things were pointless. Despite all the gloom there's a celebration of having fondness for someone that really connected with me as I ploughed through the perils of teenage crushes. As both a mushy lover paean and a snide retort at the same time it fits the needs of both sides of a relationship: the start and the end.

### MAGS BURKE

My journey into The Smiths began in 1984 when my then boyfriend, Guy, later to become my husband, talked about the music he enjoyed. My taste in music at the time was very average and he suggested I watch them on *Top Of The Pops*. Honestly, a guy singing with a bush sticking out of the back of his pants? Nah, not for me! I bought Guy their debut LP with the instruction, 'Don't play it when I am around!'

After a long gap in attending gigs due to having children and money being tight, in 2004 Guy received a bonus from work enabling us to buy tickets for us and our now two grown up children (also Smiths fans) to see Morrissey at Lancashire Cricket Ground.

Reminding Guy that I didn't know any of the music, he said he would 'educate' me. Over journeys to and from work, I began listening to The Smiths and Morrissey, starting with *Viva Hate* on a cassette. When I listened to the songs, the lyrics jumped out at me and I thought, 'This is fucking good.'

I became the most obsessed of Smiths and Morrissey fan. Guy and I went to gigs all over the UK and Rome. We began to attend the famous Smiths Disco at Manchester's Star & Garter and have now been going regularly for 20 years. The Smiths' music has taken me to places I would never have visited, but best of all we have made some wonderful friends who share the same taste in music and the same moral compass in life…

# CITY HALL

## 31 JANUARY 1984, SHEFFIELD, UK

### ADRIAN KEELING

I was probably 15 and a fan of pop when I first saw The Smiths doing 'This Charming Man' on *Top Of The Pops*. I thought, 'This is something different. They look a bit weird; I'll try and watch this and see if I can expand my horizons.' Weird wasn't my thing so unbelievably it didn't grab me.

My parents were members of a society called the Independent Order of Foresters that put on social events and raised money for charity. I was in the Young Foresters and one of the things we did was go to a gig once a year. In 1984, we booked to see OMD at Sheffield City Hall, but they cancelled and we booked The Smiths instead. By this time 'What Difference Does It Make?' was in the charts and I did like that so I bought the album and played it to death. The gig at the City Hall though was something else. I remember a very bright light behind Morrissey at times, making it look like the sun was shining out of his behind. Pity it doesn't anymore, but I digress.

*Mags & husband Guy were regulars at the Smiths disco*

## NORTH STAFFS POLYTECHNIC

### 1 FEBRUARY 1984, STOKE-ON-TRENT, UK

### GARY DONALD

The guys had just made it into the charts and were either just about to or had just done *Top Of The Pops*. I was part of the student union team manning the door and doing security at front of stage. It was a brilliant night, with possibly 400 to 500 there. It was packed. Morrissey was chilling out in the bar in his long brown raincoat, cool as fuck. Gladioli were in full swing. Before the show, I stopped a fella at the door and asked him for his ticket. He replied, 'Nah, but I've got one of these', holding up his guitar. I had just asked Johnny Marr for his ticket!

### GLYN WADE

I saw them three times. The first time was at this gig. It was packed.

They had broken big since the gig was announced but I managed to get to the front. Big mistake! The stage was about shin-high and I spent the whole gig crushed against it, unable to move as swathes of people pushed against me. Flowers were spinning but it was hard to concentrate as I was in so much pain. My shins were bruised for days afterwards but – hey! – I saw The Smiths at one of the smallest ever venues!

## UNIVERSITY OF WARWICK

### 2 FEBRUARY 1984, COVENTRY, UK

### RICHARD DYER

The Smiths had come to the attention of my student friends at Warwick through the release of 'Hand In Glove' and 'This Charming Man'. Marr's jangling, hypnotic guitar and Morrissey's sexually ambiguous literary-referenced lyrics and monotone crooning set them apart from many of the new wave post-punk indie bands of the time.

Tickets for the Warwick concert went on sale in January and sold out almost immediately. I worked the student union bars and theatres in the evenings to supplement my postgrad grant and jumped at the chance to work the concert. I was on the small stage with the band, stage right and facing the crowd, as The Smiths unceremoniously strolled on. Marr and Rourke plugged in their guitars and Joyce sat at the small drum kit.

*North Staffs Poly ticket*

NORTH STAFFS POLYTECHNIC STUDENTS UNION

presents

**THE SMITHS**
+
**TELEPHONE BOXES**
+
**DISCO**

at COLLEGE ROAD

on WEDNESDAY, 1st FEBRUARY, 1984

☆

Ticket £3.00

Doors open at 8 pm

Morrissey followed, clutching huge red gladioli, white shirt open to the waist, bouffant hair. Warwick was an easy audience that loved to dance, so the energy was instant.

I jigged along at the side of the stage, next to Andy Rourke, hypnotised by the proximity of the band, the immediacy of all the previously unheard tunes and Morrissey's self-absorbed arrogant posturing. Once all the gladioli were tossed to the crowd, the band skipped off. We got only 30 minutes of fast melodic tunes, which was probably all they had written at that point. No encore, they were off to London. I was left with jangling ears and a red gladiolus, aware that something special had happened, but not quite knowing how special. A couple of weeks later, The Smiths' first album was released. I like to think that the fiver I earned that night at the concert was the fiver I used to buy the album. I am sure that the playlist that night was the album in its entirety, short and sweet.

### IAN GREEN

I saw The Smiths at the University of Warwick in February and, on 10th March at Lanchester Polytechnic, both in Coventry. Whoever arranged the tour may have thought one was in Warwick and one was Lancaster – a regular mistake. They had a backdrop of the 'What Difference Does It Make?' cover and Morrissey waving gladioli around and them all being trampled underfoot afterwards.

I first heard the band when John Peel played 'Hand In Glove' as a new release on his show and I bought it from HMV in Hertford Street, Coventry the next day. It sounded a 'bit sixties' with the harmonica riff and the chord sequence. I wasn't a fan of the single that elevated them, 'This Charming Man', but was excited by their first Peel session - especially the stunning 'Reel Around The Fountain'. I remember discussing it avidly with friends a day or so later. We picked up on all the 'kitchen sink' film references, in which there was a revival of interest as a mirror to the grim, bleak and desperate feeling of early eighties Britain. One was the country in its ascendancy, the other one the fag end of the engineering industry.

The Smiths were compared to a UK version of REM, who I also saw in 1984, probably due to both having enigmatic frontmen and guitarists who used Rickenbackers as much as their melodic pop music.

### NICK WATT

In sixth form at school, I was one of those kids who would turn up at gigs and always manage to squirrel my way backstage. If I wanted something, I was pretty shameless in ringing people up and asking for it. I was one of the first people ever to study media studies at 'A' level and I wanted to film a band. The only band that interested me at that time were The Human League. I didn't know how to get hold of Bob Last, who was their manager, but I knew Geoff Travis at Rough Trade probably would. So I contacted Geoff and through that I got to know Geoff a little bit. I used to write to him.

I was at Coventry Poly, which was down the road in the centre of town. I'd gone to Coventry was because of The Specials and the whole 2-Tone thing, and Coventry was a pretty good place to see a lot of bands. Within the first couple of weeks, I saw U2, Echo and The Bunnymen and The Dead Kennedys.

But I soon realised I was studying the wrong degree. I was trying to get onto a radio journalism course at London University and part of the deal was you had to interview a local politician or somebody equivalent. I thought, 'Well, I don't really want to interview a politician. I'd rather be interviewing bands.' I persuaded Geoff to get me an interview with Morrissey and Marr at Warwick University.

I was told to turn up backstage before the concert and I'd get my interview. I walked into the dressing room. Johnny – always a lively character – was dancing around. Morrissey was lying flat on his back on the dressing room floor, and he had a Parka over the top of him with the hood over his head. He looked like he had no interest in actually moving. I don't know whether he just didn't want to do an interview or whatever. Obviously I wasn't anybody. But I did write it up for the college magazine.

Johnny turned round and said to me, 'Oh, you're Geoff's friend, aren't you?' and he let me interview him. He was fantastic. He gave me a heck of a lot of time. Bruce Kent, who had been the Archbishop of Canterbury, had just resigned to become head of CND and he'd done a rally at Warwick that day.

So the first question I asked Johnny was about politics. I'd read most of the stuff that had been written about them in the music press and politics hadn't really been anything people had picked on with them. So I sat there and we talked a bit about politics, and we talked a bit about The Smiths. (I've still got the tape of the interview in the loft.). At the end I said, 'Okay, what's your favourite record of the moment? What track are you listening to the most?'

He said, 'Oh, it's a really old song. Do you know 'Walk Away Renee'?' I said, 'Well, it depends which version you're talking about.' He looked at me and went, 'Well, The Four Tops of course.' I said, 'Yes, it's a brilliant song,' and, being a bit of a clever clogs, I said, 'Do you actually know who wrote it?' He said, 'I'm assuming Holland-Dozier-Holland or one of the classic Motown writers' and I said, 'No, you're a million miles off.' And he went, 'Okay, smart arse. Who was it?' I said, 'Have you ever heard of a band called The Left Banke?' And he went, 'Left who?' I said, 'Next time I see you, I'll give you a copy of the record.'

I was doing a bit of Ents at the time at Coventry Poly and the Head of Ents was a real goth, so we had Spear of Destiny, The Mission, most of the goth bands. And I persuaded him and Mike Hinc at Rough Trade to book the The Smiths for the Poly. And when they turned up after the gig I wandered into the dressing room and handed Johnny a seven-inch reissue of 'Walk Away Renee' by The Left Banke in this lovely gatefold sleeve. He was running around the dressing room going, 'Look, look, look!'

We still didn't get a heck of a lot of response out of Morrissey.

## OXFORD ROAD SHOW

### 10 FEBRUARY 1984, MANCHESTER, UK

### KARREN ABLAZE

We were supposed to be interviewing The Smiths after their appearance on the BBC television programme *Oxford Road Show* but, although Andy Rourke said he'd make sure our names were put on the guest list, the receptionist refused to let us in. Instead we spent an hour standing outside the doors until Johnny Marr came out to sign autographs. He was very helpful and he took us inside to do the interview, but half the group had gone home so there wasn't much point. Well thanks, Andy!

## LYCEUM THEATRE

### 12 FEBRUARY 1984, LONDON, UK

### CHRIS MADDEN

Hearing 'Hand In Glove' on John Peel piqued my interest. I've still got it on a seven-inch single and it's an amazing record. But 'This Charming Man' was doubly amazing – amazing guitar music with a lyrical sensibility and really different from what I'd been listening to before. I can remember being at the school disco and going out with mates who were rude boys and punks. At 14, 15, 16 I was a headbanger – a heavy metal kid – only it was called heavy rock then. The New Wave of British Heavy Metal (NWOBHM) was starting to be a thing. But our mates were into all sorts of stuff, and it was a really brilliantly visceral shared experience. So I was going to see Thin Lizzy, Queen and Motorhead but also The Smiths, Aztec Camera, Orange Juice and Black Uhuru with Sly and Robbie. That was from the influence of mates who just wore slightly different clothes and who bought into an identity. My identity really began to evolve and change when The Smiths came along. I took signifiers from Morrissey and Marr and started to develop a style of my own. What an amazing time to be alive.

My mum and dad were very young when they had me, in their teens, so I came from a household steeped in listening to music – Motown, Stax, Zeppelin, Floyd. Thin Lizzy were the big one for my dad, and The Beatles and the Stones. The Smiths were something completely different. I was 17 or 18 and I just found them utterly entrancing, totally beguiling. I found my band in that moment.

I was very, very lucky to see them quite a few times. The first time was around the time 'What Difference Does It Make?' came out. They played at the Lyceum with The Redskins and Billy Bragg. I was doing a graphics diploma at Bradford College, and we went on a graphics course on a trip down to London. We took the train down to London on the Sunday, went straight to the hotel and me and

*Lyceum Ballroom ticket*

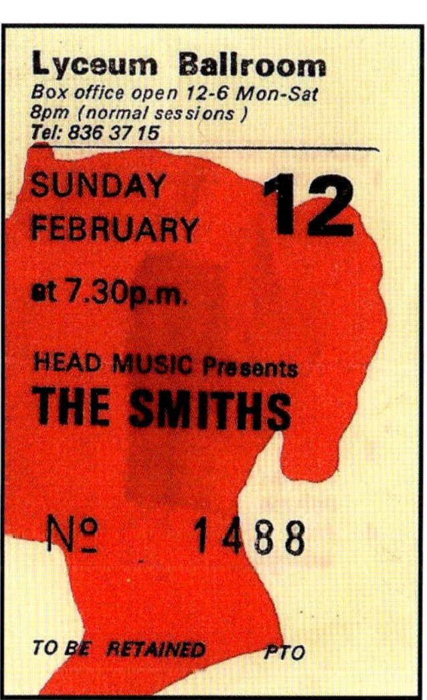

my mate Gary threw our bags in the room and bombed down to the Lyceum in the middle of the afternoon.

It was a sold-out gig, but I really wanted to see them. We were dead lucky – as we were walking down the street without tickets, on the other side of the street were Johnny Marr, Mike Joyce and Andy Rourke. So we wandered over and said, 'We've come down from Bradford to see you' – which was a slight variation on the truth – 'and there's no tickets left.' And Johnny Marr said, 'Don't worry, lads.'

We just walked in with them and watched the soundcheck. Johnny said, 'Look we haven't got any room on the guest list. But I reckon if you hide in the toilets you'll be okay.' So we went and hid in the toilets after the soundcheck and then the doors were opened and we watched the gig.

### EVE WENTWORTH

I'm American, but I was doing a year abroad and saw them live a couple times when I was a university student in London. I'd seen a short film of them singing 'This Charming Man' on some music show, maybe *The Tube* on Channel 4 or something on BBC2. I picked up the album as soon as it was out and wanted to see them live.

Back then, you got concert info on the radio or in papers like the *NME* or *Melody Maker*, or in *Time Out*. I'd heard they were touring and I was excited to see Billy Bragg was also on the bill. He was playing a lot of gigs around the time of *Life's A Riot With Spy Vs Spy* in 1983, so I'd already seen him a few times.

He was still busking on occasion with his busted old guitar and that backpack amp thing he used to do.

My first Smiths gig was at the Lyceum. The Smiths were headlining and the opening acts were The Redskins and Billy Bragg, who had had actually been playing outside the venue before the show. When he took the stage after The Redskins, he thanked those who'd tossed money in his case outside. The amount he mentioned was '27 quid' and the crowd were laughing because some clearly hadn't realised he was on the bill and not just some funny, mouthy guy with a guitar entertaining bored concert goers queuing up outside.

When The Smiths finally came on (ah, young and pretty Morrissey and cool Johnny Marr, be still my twentysomething heart) the crowd roared. There were flowers in Morrissey's back trouser pocket and eventually some got tossed into the crowd. Or maybe some originated in the crowd, who knows? There were definitely flowers flying around at some point. The sound was decent, the crowd was loving it, and it was a fun though not terribly long set. So much lovely guitar jangle.

I had some kind of lecture or school thing the next day and my ears were still ringing.

### MICHAEL FARRAGHER, AGE 19

I discovered them through hearing 'Hand In Glove' on John Peel and Kid Jensen. They were playing it fairly regularly when it came out. I thought, 'That's an interesting record.' And I remember being in my bedroom and Peel having The Smiths 'in session'. I was just dumbstruck. I was hugely into The Jam before that and then The Smiths just appeared. Even before I'd seen The Smiths live or seen a picture of The Smiths or heard Morrissey speaking, I knew from hearing their session tracks that this was a band I could really get into. The lyrics were just completely different to any other band.

I tried to get to see them towards the end of '83 when they were playing in London, but I couldn't get a ticket. I was almost the same age as The Smiths themselves, apart from Morrissey. My sister Rita, who's 18 months younger than me, had the same feeling. I got into them first and then she became obsessed with them as well. We were extremely close and we went to a lot of gigs together anyway. We first got to see them at the Lyceum. They were only on stage for about 45 minutes because Morrissey wasn't well but that sealed it for me. By this time, I was buying all the music papers – *NME, Melody Maker, Record Mirror* – and Morrissey was on everything at that point. The music press was in love with The Smiths.

### HENRY WOOD

Such was Smiths fervour at this point that tickets for this show had sold out weeks beforehand. Tickets were like gold dust, but I would not have sold mine for love nor money.

The harsh truth is that had not purchased my ticket to see The Smiths. I'd come to see Billy Bragg, who over the course of the past twelve months I had followed from tiny, partially empty venues across London to this, probably his biggest gig to date – supporting The Smiths at the Lyceum. By the end of the year, Billy would be headlining this very same venue himself.

Apart from being completely rammed, I remember the gig being a joyous celebration of jangling guitars, a great deal of audience beer-throwing and a sea of daffodils. Morrissey had some stuffed in his back pocket when he walked on stage and huge swathes of the audience had brought their own! I remember nothing of Telephone Boxes, but The Redskins were loud and aggressive with lots of left-leaning songs. Billy was on top form, delivering his set with aplomb, a clever combination of moving love songs and political tirades. Fantastic songs, but it was the way he delivered them that made them so special.

When The Smiths finally appeared, the place simply erupted. They were very, very good and I could now see for myself what all the fuss was about. But, if Billy had not been on the bill, I would never have been there, so in a weird kind of way, I bore witness to what has turned out to be a legendary Smiths gig purely by default.

## UNIVERSITY OF EAST ANGLIA
### 14 FEBRUARY 1984, NORWICH, UK

### NEIL KIMBERLEY

The first time I heard The Smiths was in the autumn of my first year at the University of East Anglia in Norwich. We were listening to old Doors albums, dancing to New Order and being inspired by U2. Then The Smiths changed everything. Whether it was the jangly guitars, the angst or the sense of humour, The Smiths spoke to me as they did to many others. I began to get obsessed and inspired.

When we came back from Christmas holidays, UEA announced that despite the closure of the Lower Common Room (LCR) for refurbishment, the university would host a gig by The Smiths. I had already been working as a stagehand, so getting a ticket to the show was not an issue. But I was attempting to become a host on UEA's Nexus TV and thought it might be a cool thing to interview The Smiths. Having no idea how to make this happen, I went to see the master of all gigs at UEA – Nick Rayns. He listened to what I wanted to do and gave me the name of Scott Piering at Rough Trade Records. But he said, 'There is no way they will do this.'

This was way before mobile phones or even phones in individual rooms, so I went to Nexus and used the office phone to call Scott Piering. Every day. For two weeks. He finally picked up the phone, and we talked for 15 minutes, and I pitched him on an interview. To my surprise he said, 'Okay' and I nearly fell over. I was to go to their dressing room at 5pm and would have Morrissey for 30 minutes. There followed two weeks of panic as I found a cameraman and thought of questions.

The big day came and at 5pm it was apparent all was not well. Morrissey was nowhere to be

found. Apparently he was 'under the weather'. But Johnny Marr stepped up. The rest is a bit of a blur. I walked him up to the Nexus studio where we chatted on camera for 20 minutes. He was energetic and funny – and made my job really easy. We talked about Manchester, Joy Division, guitar sounds, their writing process and the aspirations of The Smiths. We continued to laugh and talk on the short walk back to the dressing room. Then he said, 'Fancy a drink? We never finish our rider', and so I was ushered into the room and introduced to Mike and Andy and saw the world's largest supply of gladioli and other flora laid out on a table. Where was Morrissey? The management was flustered. The rest of the band was used to it. In later years, I would find out that renowned photographer Paul Slattery photographed the room. Back in 1984 it seemed big and glamorous. Today it all looks a bit naff.

Morrissey finally showed up and the band performed a 45-minute set. The stage was mobbed as the band were in their flower-whipping, jangly heyday. In later years I would see them multiple times in the US where the shows were amazing. But back in 1984, I was just happy to see the amazing Smiths songs live. After the show, I got the chance to have a few beers with the band and some other fans. I even got to meet and talk for five minutes with Morrissey. I fawned horribly but he was funny, thoughtful and patient. I was truly meeting a hero, and he was all I hoped he would be. The evening ended and I took a bus home, not quite sure that I had been so close to my heroes for a couple of hours. From today it is a distant dream.

## PAUL GRIGSON

My mate who worked in Backs Records in Norwich told me I would like this group. He was so right with their first album, which is still one of my favourites, especially 'Reel Around The Fountain'. I was there with my best friend, Lynn, and brother Colin. It was Morrissey at his best, with gladioli everywhere, and one girl decided to give me a horrendous love bite in reaction to 'This Charming Man'.

## ANDREW HOOK

There was a second Norwich gig, Valentine's Day 1984, almost exactly six months since the Gala, at the University of East Anglia. The venue was in the process of being refurbished and the stage was temporarily in the foyer, so the capacity might have been less than the usual 1,200. Either way it was full, no longer intimate. There was a queue. Everyone held gladioli. Everyone sang along. It seemed as though I was now part of a club and I didn't want to be a member. They played eleven songs. None of them twice. Morrissey hurled flowers into the crowd. I still have a stem.

Red Guitars supported that evening. I was blown away; I felt they were the better band. I saw Red Guitars twice more that year, but I didn't cross paths again with a Smith until a Morrissey gig in Auckland, New Zealand on 8 September 1991. He didn't play any Smiths' songs. The gig was surprisingly good, although the backing band looked to be the same age as when I'd first seen The Smiths, back on that August evening when I was only 16.

## NEIL WARD, AGE 17

After a foggy drive over from West Norfolk, I set foot on the UEA campus for the first time that night. The Smiths had broken onto the national scene in late 1983. Their first two singles – 'Hand in Glove' and 'This Charming Man' – were a breath of fresh air, with Johnny Marr's exquisite guitar bringing to life Morrissey's radical lyrics. They had taken *Top Of The Pops* by storm with an iconic performance of 'This Charming Man' on 24th November. Beginning the New Year as the hottest new band in an age, they embarked on a 32-date tour to promote their eponymously titled first album.

On 14th February they rolled into Norwich. Because the LCR was being refurbished, the gig was held in the foyer of Union House. A stage was constructed under the balcony, and the crowd packed the foyer and filled the main staircase, straining to get a good view of the spectacle to come. After the Red Guitars finished their support slot, the atmosphere of anticipation became spine-tingling. As the lights dimmed, roadies tossed several armfuls of gladioli into the crowd. Amidst a euphoric storm of flowers and leaves, The Smiths took the stage.

The set that foggy February night contained much of the first album, which was released just six days later. 'Still Ill', 'Pretty Girls Make Graves' and the new single,

'What Difference Does It Make?' were highlights, with Morrissey pirouetting around the stage, gladioli aloft. They also played 'Heaven Knows I'm Miserable Now', their next single, and a new track – 'Barbarism Begins At Home' - which appeared on their second album, *Meat Is Murder*. Morrissey kicked off the encore of 'You've Got Everything Now' by saying, 'Thank you Norwich, you're very convivial people,' and more flowers were strewn around with joyful abandon. I was wide-eyed at the front, and when Morrissey left the stage casting off his necklaces into the crowd I managed to grasp a fistful of his beads, which I still have. The crowd slowly shuffled off, gradually revealing a mass of mulched foliage all over the floor. Inspired, I set about growing a quiff straight away, which I carefully maintained for the rest of the decade.

*Dumpy's Rusty Nuts weren't enough for Cris*

# ROCK CITY

## 15 FEBRUARY 1984, NOTTINGHAM, UK

### DEAN DRAKE

'That bloke looks like you, Morrissey,' said Andy. I was and still am such a big Smiths fan. I was such a Smiths fan that I even looked like a young Morrissey with quiff and all and have on three occasions been told I looked like him. I was mistaken for him in a bar once and played along – but left quickly to keep the illusion going!

When a friend announced that she had two tickets to go and see The Smiths on their debut tour in Nottingham I jumped at the chance. We travelled from Leicester. The atmosphere was amazing and the set list – although short – was played like the album. It was fabulous. I'm not a big crowd fan, so we stood around at the back of the gig enjoying the magic and watched the fans go mad for a piece of Morrissey's shirt at the end.

After the concert, I was buzzing and suggested we go around the back of the building to see if we could see the band leave. There were only a dozen people milling around and a coach parked up close to the building. As we approached the small crowd, a door opened to my left and some bloke barged into me. I gasped, 'Hey, steady on mate!' (This was Leicester talk). It was only Mike Joyce, followed by Andy Rourke (best bass player in the world), then Johnny Marr and then the man himself — Mozzer! They ran on to the coach one by one, and the coach's engine started up. We were at the front right hand side window of the coach behind the driver's seat, and Moz sat down on the right-hand side at the front right next to me. The band were clearly fired up and already had beers in their hands. Mike was already seated on the left side and Johnny was stood in the aisle.

Andy was looking at me, and I could see him say to Moz, 'Hey, that bloke looks like you!' Moz turned and looked at me and smiled. I put my hand up to the window and he did the same – tap, tap on the window from both sides before the coach was on its way. I will never forget it!

### CRIS TYLER

A whole bunch of us got a minibus over from Lincoln where I was doing a two-year Art & Design diploma. I went with my girlfriend at the time, Claire, plus friends Hilary, Lizzy and Teresa. It was one of many trips organised by Pete Thacker and Leigh Reynolds, who worked in a record store in Lincoln called Pride Records. Pete was a guy from the official Lincoln 'alternative' pub, the Jolly Brewer, and he'd organise the trips, tickets, bus hire etc. He organised another one to see King Kurt at the Retford Porterhouse. Lincoln, despite being a city, was – and still is – pretty rural and well away from the circuit for visiting bands. Anyone who wanted to indulge in anything more diverse than Rusty's Dumpy Nuts needed to travel, although I do recall some great local bands. (Well, I thought they were great at the time!)

The first album had just come out. I don't recall even owning it at the time but we were riding on the hype of the first three singles. It was during that initial wave of lazy journalism where they were being lauded as 'the most miserable band in the world'. I liked Morrissey's flat tones under Marr's upbeat semi-acoustic jangle. It was totally unique and obviously spoke to me in some capacity. It must have worked as I still listen to it today, unlike pretty much everything else I was listening to at the time (with the possible exception of the Cocteau Twins).

The Smiths at Rock City was probably my first experience of seeing a band at a venue where more than 100 people were in attendance. It was quite magical.

## LEICESTER UNIVERSITY
### 16 FEBRUARY 1984, LEICESTER, UK

### LEE THACKER

I saw The Smiths in concert three times between 1984 and 1985. I'd heard (and taped) 'Hand In Glove' and 'Handsome Devil' from John Peel's Festive Fifty in 1983 as well as the band's first Peel session and loved what I heard. A live gig was also aired on national television around the same time, and I was equally impressed by what I saw, especially the quiff-sporting individual who swung a bouquet of flowers around on stage and sang about things that actually meant something to me about my life. The stage invasion at the end of this performance was the cherry on the cake – I couldn't wait to see them play live. I ordered the 'Hand In Glove' and 'This Charming Man' seven-inch singles from Rough Trade and still treasure them both to this day.

In early 1984, an advert in the *Leicester Mercury* newspaper announced the band's forthcoming appearance at Leicester University and I immediately bought a ticket. I also did a drawing of the band in black marker pen on a plain white t-shirt (which I copied from a photo in the *NME*) and wore it to the gig. It was a great show despite the fact nobody attempted to clamber onto the stage. I sweated so much from dancing that the freshly applied marker pen ran, and I had to redraw it!

The band's debut album was released a few days later. One of my friends bought it (I had no funds back then) and I listened to it round his house whilst he transferred it onto cassette tape for me. What a disappointment. Their live sound had been reduced to what sounded to me like watered down and under-produced versions of their songs. The piano on 'Reel Around The Fountain' (a song which sounded perfect in the Peel session version) and the flat delivery of 'Miserable Lie' (another song which sounded perfect on the Peel session version) was the last straw and I didn't actually purchase a copy of the album until the band had split up.

# UNIVERSITY OF ESSEX
## 18 FEBRUARY 1984, COLCHESTER, UK

### JO COOPER

This was my fifth Smiths gig. I had been lucky enough to meet them in January 1984 at a *Top Of The Pops* rehearsal so went to the gig hoping to meet them again. My friend Emma, who was like a big sister, managed to talk her dad into giving us a lift there from London and he waited patiently in the car until the end.

We met them – which I was very excited about – especially to meet Johnny Marr. He gave us 'This Charming Man' t-shirts and I still have mine, although it's not in great condition!

The gig was packed. I was at the front on Johnny's side. The gig became livelier and the student audience began to mosh; I started to levitate up the barrier and someone's feet ended up under mine. The foam covering the metal barrier in front of the stage came off and I eventually ended up halfway over it. Johnny noticed and asked his guitar tech, Phil, to pull me over the barrier. I watched the rest of the gig from the wings.

I really enjoyed it – a small venue, close to the band, with a very tight lively performance in their more 'punk/folk' days. Nothing beat the feeling of seeing The Smiths live, and I was totally immersed in how different they looked, sounded and presented themselves, and how they connected with those of us who were struggling to find our place in the world.

After the gig, we waited to speak to Johnny, and I managed to get a photo with him but there were a few people waiting and he was trying to avoid being smooched by a drunk female student and dashed off without saying goodbye. Emma and I walked across a muddy, grassy grounds back to her dad's car for the journey home.

I saw Johnny four days later at the Reading University gig and he said he had got into their blue tour van with Phil and tried to look for us. I was given a copy of their debut album at Reading, fully signed and with the aqua font (not that that meant anything) – so that made up for it!



On *Top Of The Pops* The Smiths looked like four people on a stage who had never met before and paid each other almost no attention but – my God – the music! They made my palms tingle with excited electricity. I had a Saturday job in a shoe shop and spent everything I earned on fags, vodka and music. I bought a lot of Smiths music. I began to wear my school jumper hanging off one shoulder and walked about sighing like it was just too much like hard work for an aesthete such as me. Rather than giving me admiring glances, people kept asking if I was okay.

I was already spiking my hair but started to favour black frayed clothes, massive tweed overcoats and pale make up. I wore black lipstick and eye makeup and so much mascara that a child on a train said, 'Mummy, that girl has spider eyes.' One day I was so surprised by something that, when my wide eyes blinked, I left one false lash stuck to my eyebrow. I was such a beautiful creature that the poor bloke in Parrot Records had no option but to give me publicity posters, some of which I still have. I've a feeling, 'If you give her stuff she goes away,' might have been muttered every time I shuffled in.

So where else was I going to spend my eighteenth birthday than with The Smiths?

I queued with four friends: three with tickets and one without. Amanda South nee Ormerod, a school friend, was there with her boyfriend and future husband Mike South. She remembers buying the 'This Charming Man' single in Boots and we never knew why they insisted on stamping the sleeves of everything they sold. We talked about the gig recently and she said, 'The 'How Soon Is Now?' riff takes me back to my local, smoke-filled pub.' All very lovely, but she also said she's 'very embarrassed' that she and Mike preferred The Red Guitars. She said Morrissey was 'to type, as in being rather remote.' Well, what's wrong with that? Cathryn Bower, also a school friend, was there to see The Smiths and definitely rated them on the night.

The non-ticket holder was Neil Gosling. I'd met him at a party, and we had a lovely friendship that involved lots of music, making mix tapes and getting high on gloss fumes while I painted a monochrome homage to Edvard Munch's 'Scream' on the back of his bedroom door. The Smiths and The Birthday Party played on a loop punctuated by his mum's head round the door asking, 'Do you eat bacon/chicken/sausage rolls? That's not meat, is it?'

I lived over 20 miles away, so Dad dropped us off unfashionably early and came back to meet us. I ran between my mate without the ticket and my mates who wanted to get in and down the front. If I didn't leave a gig with bruised ribs then it didn't count. Neil got a ticket for the extortionate price of £4.25.

We made it downstairs and began filling up on pints and vodka and orange. The union at Essex Uni was an odd shape, a long space with the stage in the furthest two thirds. The ceiling was covered in eggbox shaped panels and during the main act the sweat would condense on the ceiling and drip on the crowd.

I shoved forward until I was two people away from the stage for The Smiths. It was so hot that layers were lifted up over heads and tied around waists. Denim and plaid crushed together trying to find space to flail and express. Me lifted off my feet and feeling my boots being prised off. Elbows hitting my cheeks and my toes crushed under the crowd. I was five foot four and at risk of drowning in the tidal wave of limbs. Neil got hold of my arm and stood me back upright.

Then Morrissey took his shirt off and began to helicopter it round his head. Neil predicted what I'd do and took hold of my collar. I jumped, straining to reach Morrissey's pale blue shirt as he let it go. I felt the material graze my fingertips and with a last stretch hooked the

cotton and pulled it toward me. But a man taller than me or Neil leant over our shoulders and snatched it from my hands. 'Yoink,' I think it's pronounced.

As the crowd dispersed under the harsh lights that clearly said, 'Stop shouting, they're not coming back on stage,' we kicked our way through plastic glasses and bottles until we stood together for the obligatory debrief. I looked at Manda and Mike differently after that day 35 years ago, when she said she'd preferred the support. But we've worked through it and are still friends now.

Cathryn and I are also friends, and music is still important to us all. I lost touch with Neil after a boyfriend of mine got jealous and treated him appallingly. But if you ask my mum what she remembers about my eighteenth birthday it will be making me, Neil and Dad cocoa when we got back from the gig and Neil raising his forehead from the kitchen table to say, 'It were 'ot, weren't it?' And he was right.

### JONATHAN FORSYTH

The Smiths played the entire first album plus 'This Charming Man' and then half the album again as that was all the material they had at that point. Morrisey came onto the stage with a bunch of cut eucalyptus gunnii in his back pocket (I am an arboriculturist – I know these things). Halfway through, somebody chucked him a bunch of daffodils and he decided he preferred them, tossing a couple into the crowd before removing said eucalyptus and disposing of that in my general direction, where

I caught the stems. He then stuffed the daffs into his back pocket instead. Anybody with pics of that gig can see the difference in floral decorations!

## *THE SMITHS*

### RELEASED 20 FEBRUARY 1984

The debut album by the band was released by Rough Trade and immediately reached number two on the UK album charts.

## TOWN HALL

### 21 FEBRUARY 1984, BOURNEMOUTH, UK

### GAVIN UNDERHILL

I never saw The Smiths when they performed at the Midnight Express in Bournemouth. Unlike most of the local music scene, mainly current or ex-art students, I wasn't very impressed with their singles apart from 'This Charming Man'. I thought they were a bit of a hype and, from the second hit onwards, that Morrissey was a one-trick pony.

The following year the guys who had run the by then defunct Midnight booked them to perform for a much larger audience at the local town hall, as befitting their new status as Blighty's favourite indie band. A mutual acquaintance asked me if I was interested in working security on behalf of the promoters, but as it wasn't a paid gig I declined.

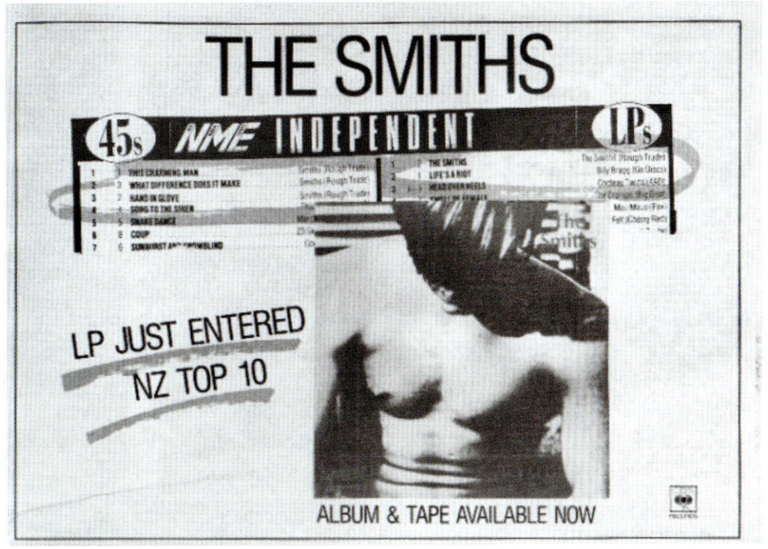


*New Zealand advert for debut album*

Later, I used to hang out in a secondhand record shop in Manchester, and the owner somehow managed to get hold of a job lot of badges that Morrissey had custom made as a 'gift' for punters when he did a gig at the MEN Arena. They were apparently placed on each seat and had various pics of him on them, each showing the date and venue, with the legend 'he stole our hearts away'. The guy tried to shift them on eBay, but I don't think he managed to sell very many. It wouldn't surprise me if he still has a few left hanging around.

### MICK TARRANT

When they started to break, Rough Trade offered them to all the people who put them on first time round and I had a good relationship with Rough Trade so I got offered them again. As a concert venue, the Town Hall wasn't bad, with a good stage and dressing rooms and a big standing area. There wasn't a permanent bar but in an ante

*The Smiths self-titled debut album*

*Mick Tarrant put The Smiths on at Bournemouth Town Hall*

room off the main auditorium they brought in a portable bar for the night. And it was pretty cheap to hire – only 60 or 70 quid. I put on loads of stuff there. But you had to employ your own staff, and you got no proceeds from the bar. If you hired the bar, you got 20 per cent off the booking fee because they'd make money from the beer they sold.

That gig was a completely different kettle of fish from the Midnight Express Club. It was sold out completely in advance. The capacity was about 800 but on the night there were so many people without tickets hoping there'd be some left and wanting to get in that the people with tickets couldn't get to the door. We had this press of people against the doors, and I could see the glass in the entrance doors bowing under their weight. I thought, 'Any minute now the glass is going to break, and people are going to come tumbling through.' I could imagine the headlines in the local paper: 'Local promoter in fracas at sold-out punk gig.'

Two guys from Bournemouth Borough Council were there to oversee it and I said, 'Look it's sold out but I've got to sell tickets and let these people in otherwise the people with tickets aren't going to get in.' And they went with it, which was the most sensible thing to do. So on the night, we probably had 900 in there. It was a huge place and by putting a few extra in there, there was no danger of people dying in the crush. It was just the most sensible thing to do on the night.

It was quite an odd atmosphere. 'This Charming Man' was out and was obviously a big seller but I forget what big waves they were making. People were initially in awe, but the audience warmed to them. I still have the contract. I also have the receipt for Morrissey's flowers. Part of the rider was 'fifty quid's worth of flowers and no thorns' which was the gladioli. That was a lot to spend on flowers and nearly as much as hiring the venue.

It was a runaway success, although as a promoter in situations like that it's a lot of stress. You've got to constantly be going round checking you've got someone on the fire doors and making sure that people don't open them and let a bunch more people in. You've got the local council on your case. You don't really have any time to enjoy it because it passes in a blur. I can't remember at any time standing there and watching a couple of numbers.

I packed up promoting soon after that. The club closed because it needed a lot of structural work doing to comply with fire regulations. It was doing okay but we weren't making a huge amount of money. We didn't have big reserves of cash where we could afford to do structural alterations.

A year or so after doing The Smiths, I was not doing much of anything and one day I was looking after a stall in Camden Market for a friend who sold old brass light fittings and stuff. Johnny passed by with his girlfriend and either Andy or Mike. Johnny spotted me. He remembered me from the gigs and said, 'Christ, you've got some strings to your bow.' They were a proper big act by this time, so it was quite nice and humble of him to stop and chat.

## UNIVERSITY OF READING

### 22 FEBRUARY 1984, READING, UK

### NICK DEAVES, AGE 21

For a music-mad 21-year-old, moving from Reading, where nothing really happened apart from the yearly festival, to London was a dream come true. I always had to come to town to see anyone. I'd come across The Smiths in the *NME* and bought 'Hand In Glove'. As I arrived in London, 'This Charming Man' was released and I bought every version I could find; the seven-inch, the twelve-inch. The song summed up my life, being a new kid on the block in the big city, as did many of the songs to come. This was my band.

The Lyceum was a regular Sunday night haunt with great four band line-ups. I can't really remember too much about the gig. I think the excitement took over. But in a matter of days, I saw them again at Reading University. Most university gigs were closed shop affairs, but this must have been open to the public. I took two friends from home who were armed with flowers, which I wasn't sure about, being a serious music fan – or snob! The gig wasn't that well attended but it gave me the chance to be right at the front. It was a fast and furious beer-soaked set.

### STANIFY NORTH

I saw them three times – Reading University in 1984, Reading Hexagon in 1985 and Brixton in 1986. In 1984, I went on my own as no mates were interested. They were interested by 1985 though!

## UNIVERSITY OF SWANSEA

### 23 FEBRUARY 1984, SWANSEA, UK

### JAYNE ALLEN, AGE 16

I met them the day after the gig and they all signed my album at the Dragon Hotel. It was the first album they had seen that had been bought (Morrissey told me it was the first one he had seen). I shared a pint of milk with Mike Joyce and still have one of his drum sticks from the gig. I can't find the other one.

## COCKCROFT HALL, POLYTECHNIC

### 25 FEBRUARY 1984, BRIGHTON, UK

### SÉAN BALDWIN, AGE 15

I discovered The Smiths through the alternative media available: namely listening to the John Peel show whilst doing my homework, reading the *NME* and rifling through record shops. I remember buying a seven-inch double A-side promo of 'Still Ill' and 'You've Got Everything Now' from Max Records in Eastbourne. I was an early adopter of the Morrissey look and dug out my old NHS specs from the days I wore them back up north. No one else dressed like that at school and no one else sounded like The Smiths. It was like they'd created their very own genre. And, of course, they spoke to me in a way that no other music of the time managed to do.

On its release I bought 'This Charming Man' on seven-inch from Virgin in Brighton and later on that day I went to a party in Burgess Hill. It was full of people from school I didn't identify with. I drank too much and someone pushed me in the swimming pool. This just made me feel like more of an outsider – having been displaced from living up north when my parents split up – and my bond with the band only strengthened.

I went to see them play at Cockcroft Hall, Moulsecoomb, Brighton with Nick Myall, a friend from school. We got to the gig early so we could get right up the front. I remember nothing about the support band, The Telephone Boxes, but the music on the PA before The Smiths arrived on stage was memorable because it was played on repeat. The band were on quite late so a Frank Chickens track they played seemed to play so many times that I can still hear it in my head.

The gig was thrilling. Wild, passionate, a crush and gladioli everywhere. The band were excellent and far more powerful than I was expecting, Morrissey waving his shirt and flowers, whipping the crowd into a greater frenzy, leaning into the monitor, chin and quiff-jutting provocatively into the melee. It was all a blur and a squash, and I don't remember many details except that Johnny Marr was playing right in front of us. At one point he stood on my hand, which didn't matter because

a) he was only wearing suede moccasins, b) he mouthed 'sorry' after he did so and c) it was Johnny fucking Marr!

I never bumped into Moz, but I often think that maybe as a kid our paths might have crossed. I used to live in Kenwood Road, Stretford in the mid-seventies, just round the corner from King's Road, where he lived. I was always cycling about Longford Park and hanging around newsagents and – who knows? Maybe we brushed past one another as he was buying a music mag, and I was getting a comic and some sweets. My family were great friends with another family called the Morrisseys (no relation) and this only compounded the feeling later on that I 'knew' him. Oh Manchester, so much to answer for!

### NICK MYALL

A dark and cold winter's night in February 1984 added to the atmosphere as I set off from home for my first ever Smiths gig. It was only my second ever gig, having seen The Jam a couple of years before, so it was a big night. I got the train down to the Poly's Cockcroft Hall, a favourite venue for indie and post-punk bands. Me and my mate from school, Sean Baldwin, had been buzzing about 'This Charming Man' and 'What Difference Does It Make?' so we had to be there. We were still too young for beers in the bar so just watched the gathering crowd of indie kids, goths, punks, etc. For several hours, as it turned out, as the band were determined to keep us waiting while they had a night out in Brighton.

At last, they took to the stage, Morrissey in his trademark tatty faded jeans, charity shop shirt, NHS specs, hearing aid and half a bush hanging out of his back pocket.

The whole of the first album was knocked out with effortless style with 'Miserable Lie', 'Reel Around The Fountain', 'You've Got Everything Now' and the singles forming some of the many high points. Sean and I were right up against the stage and the buzz coming off the band and back from the audience was massive, as it always was at a Smiths gig, with Morrissey passing round a carton of juice to the crowd.

They were rockier than I'd expected and Johnny Marr's guitar playing was superb, him not even looking at the fretboard on his Rickenbacker as he sailed through a classic early Smiths set. After a triumphant gig, it was back home to dreary Haywards Heath on the rattling BR train and off to school in the morning where we agreed it was a fantastic night. It remains one of my best gigs. How couldn't it?

### STEVE FANNING

They were delayed by about two hours. I found out years later, from their promoter Josh Dean, that he had taken them into Kemp Town for a meal, which ran over somewhat – and not a vegetarian meal, he hastened to inform me. When they finally came on stage, the excitement was at fever pitch and they went on to smash the place, much to our young and eager ears delight.

Morrissey was in full gladioli mode, and I had to chuckle with my friend who I had gone to the gig with, called Merran Wrigley. She turned to me and said, 'What is Johnny Marr doing up on the stage? I know him, he went to school with me in Manchester.' She had no idea that he was the guitarist in The Smiths. Another friend met them backstage afterwards. He was wearing a Sisters of Mercy t-shirt and regaled me with tales of Morrissey completely ripping him apart as a consequence. It was the one and only time I ever saw The Smiths, but it is indelibly imprinted on my memory.

## UNIVERSITY OF KENT AT CANTERBURY

### 27 FEBRUARY 1984, CANTERBURY, UK

### LUKA VERCAUTEREN

I was abused from the ages of four to 13 by my alcoholic father and mother. I was placed in a home for children with bad parents and at 14 placed in a foster home where I was not so well. I started the search for who I was. Like so many, punk grew in me. I remember hearing 'What Difference Does It Make?' on the radio and I immediately loved it. I began searching for Smiths t-shirts and badges. The first time I saw them was in Canterbury in 1984, and later I saw them in Belgium and the Netherlands. The Smiths saved my life – the music, the lyrics, their way of doing things. 'How Soon Is Now?' is still my favourite.

## VICTORIA HALL

### 28 FEBRUARY 1984, HANLEY, UK

#### GLYN WADE

I got near the front for this one and managed to catch a necklace and some flowers that Morrissey dropped and then threw into the audience. Being tall helped with the necklace, but then what to do with it as people clawed to try and get it? So I shoved it into my underpants. Luckily the clawing stopped, as it could have been quite painful! There were flowers everywhere so catching a few daffodil heads was easier. I still have them in a book somewhere, as I do the necklace.

## UNIVERSITY OF LEEDS

### 29 FEBRUARY 1984, LEEDS, UK

#### MARCUS AMBLER

I saw The Smiths in Leeds. They were supported by The Red Guitars. I've still got my ticket — it's number 001341.

## QUEEN MARGARET UNION

### 2 MARCH 1984, GLASGOW, UK

#### GERRY O'CONNOR, AGE 17

I saw The Smiths every time they played Glasgow and also had a ticket for the Albert Hall but sadly did not go. I went to all the gigs with friends. I bought every release on the day it came out and bought the seven and twelve-inch singles. I bought the 'What Difference Does It Make?' single again because the cover changed from Terence Stamp to Morrissey. I jumped up on the stage twice at QMU and at the first Barrowland gig.

## DUNDEE UNIVERSITY

### 3 MARCH 1984, DUNDEE, UK

#### ALAN CORMACK, AGE 16

I'd been listening to John Peel since I was about ten, in 1978, so thought I was fairly good at picking up new stuff. But for some reason I never actually heard The Smiths on Peel. I'd somehow missed the nights they were on. I heard them through the brother of my friend Craig McNeil, who came home one day with 'This Charming Man'. We put it on and listened to it over and over and over again. And also the B-side, 'Jeanne', which was brilliant but didn't sound like 'This Charming Man'. Then it was a case of going back and checking out 'Hand In Glove' and stuff like that. The only way I could find out about them was through

*Ticket for the Dundee University show exhorting fans to 'come & see how many necklaces Morrissey's got'*

*NME, Melody Maker* or *Sounds* or by what was getting played on Peel.

When the first album came out, I thought Morrissey was speaking directly to me. I always thought of myself as being a bit different to everybody else. Nobody else at school was into indie, alternative music. The closest it got to alternative for people was Simple Minds, which was pretty bad. Morrissey was talking about isolation and being different and stuff. That really spoke to me.

We saw that they were playing Dundee University. I went with Craig. Getting into Dundee University was a bit of a trial because you had to be signed in and, being still at school and underage, this was going to be doubly difficult. But somehow we managed it.

The support band was The Red Guitars. *The Tube* had done a documentary on Hull and they were on it, performing 'Good Technology', so waiting to see The Red Guitars and knowing one of their songs was a bonus. Back then Dundee had a bit of a psychobilly group that went around, quite scary-looking guys with big flat tops, who were into The Meteors, The Guana Batz, King Kurt and all that kind of stuff. You ran the risk, if you weren't a flat top, of getting a bit of a filling in from these guys. They used to go to the university discos on a Saturday night. They were all at the Smiths gig. I remember eyeing these guys and thinking, 'I need to keep out of the way of them because I don't want any hassle.'

The Smiths came on and Morrissey threw a load of gladioli into the crowd. The flat tops picked them up and were throwing them around and doing their slam dancing thing at the front of the gig. As the band started to play 'This Charming Man', somebody threw a pint glass onto the stage and it hit Morrissey. Or it might have been one of the gladioli. He walked off. The band kept playing until halfway through the song and then walked off too. So there were boos and jeers and whistling. Then a roadie came out and said something along the lines of, 'If you don't all fucking calm down then The Smiths are not fucking coming back on, you bunch of fucking idiots,' which was again met with glasses and flowers and stuff getting thrown on the stage.

Eventually they did come back out, and they started playing 'This Charming Man' again. Morrissey said something along the lines of, 'You have a funny way of showing love, Dundee,' which we thought was quite funny.

The gig was brilliant. We met a couple of girls that night, which was an added bonus. We lied about our age and told them we were 18 and studying Geography at university. I think they totally saw through us because we never saw them again.

The next time I saw The Smiths was 1985 at the Caird Hall. Del Amitri were supporting them. It's quite interesting to see how spectacularly shit Del Amitri became, because that night they were a Postcard-type jangly band and quite good. I think The Smiths came back again a year later but I had gone off them by then. When they became more successful, a lot of football casuals in Dundee started wearing Smiths t-shirts and I thought, 'What can Morrissey possibly say to these guys?' because they were all into fighting and stuff. I was starting to get into things like The Wedding Present and all that C86 stuff. The Smiths were becoming a bit old hat. By the time 'Panic' came out, I just saw them as a chart band. I thought, 'Yeah, I used to like The Smiths but now they've sold out.'

### JEREMY KIDD, RED GUITARS VOCALIST

The audience chucked beer at Morrissey, and he stormed off and refused to return for some considerable time. But when they finally did resume the whole band were clearly hyped up and played a storm. I can confirm, by the way, that it was not me who took to the stage and harangued the troublemakers on that occasion.

### ALASTAIR BRODIE, GROUCHO RECORDS

I've been in the secondhand record business for 45 years. I started on 1 April 1974 in Cockburn Street Market in Edinburgh. Then me and my assistant, who became my partner, decided to set up ourselves. Our bosses didn't want to us to set up in Edinburgh, and we had the opportunity of coming up to Dundee. I didn't know Dundee at all, but my partner came from Kirriemuir, which wasn't that far away, so we came up with a record collection and £500 and found a shop. Back then you could find an empty shop, find the landlord, get the keys to view it, say 'yes', hand over a cheque for the rent and he'd give you the keys. It would all be done in a day or two.

When we started off, it was a smaller version of Cockburn Street Market, which was a hippie market. We were young, 22-year-old hippies, and we arrived in Dundee in August 1976 and enjoyed a lovely hot summer fitting out the shop. Then the Sex Pistols brought out 'Anarchy' in November, and everything changed. By our first anniversary we were a full-blown punk shop with all the punk singles and the t-shirts. We got a badge machine and made up badges. People used to make the trek out of town and up the Perth Road just to get the latest stuff.

It went well. We had seven years there and then we got chucked out and so we moved into town, and things were even better because we got a shop at the end of the Overgate Centre, two doors along from the entrance to the Angus Hotel, which was the main city centre hotel. That was quite handy because a lot of the bands that played in Dundee stayed at the Angus and we got various well-known celebs coming in. Probably my favourite one was a hero of mine, Peter Green, and I managed to get a good chat with him.

Roll on to 1984. At that time, the punk scene was still going but the indie scene was really the thing. We never went on to dealing with the major labels. We just kept ourselves indie, doing secondhand stuff and new indie stuff and all the accessories, t-shirts and so on. Being an indie shop, we were members of The Cartel. We weren't an HMV, so we didn't get all kinds of things thrown at us because we weren't a chart return shop, but we did the chart for the *NME* and indie charts and so on. I remember the Cartel rep giving me a copy of the white label of this new band called The Smiths. I would play it quite a bit in the shop.

We had a Saturday boy who worked for DC Thomson in the *Beano* offices during the week, a chap called Alan. He did storylines for things like *The Three Bears* and *Little Plum*. But he worked for us on a Saturday and he absolutely loved it. He went from The Jam and such like to The Smiths.

Their debut album came out on 20 February 1984 and two weeks later they played at the university. I knew the Ents convenor at the university and he used to put us on the guest list for any gigs, which was very handy, particularly as I used to live on the next street to the university union. I could say to people, 'Oh, do you fancy going to a gig?' if I had people round and depending what was on, like Hawkwind, people could say, 'Yes, I fancy going to see them' or if it was Mike Oldfield, 'No, I don't think I'll bother!' We saw some really good acts there.

And on Saturday 3rd March The Smiths played there. It was an interesting gig, because the punky-type students decided to throw beer at the band and Morrissey wasn't too happy with it. I think he stomped off stage for a while. Anyway, I don't remember too much about it and I'm not even sure I saw the whole gig. But during the day on the Saturday, because the band were staying in the Angus Hotel and Johnny Marr's certainly a record fan, they popped into the shop en masse late on in the afternoon.

I wouldn't have known who they were but Alan the Saturday boy said, 'Oh, that's The Smiths in,' so he was the one that was chatting to them most. Unfortunately, he passed away some years ago. My memories are of Morrissey in a big, long coat and him buying a couple of Dusty Springfield seven-inch singles. We had a display cabinet with guitar badges in it by the front door that were one offs. They were made by chap in Fife, an ex-art college student who was making them. He was just the most magnificent miniature painter, and he would cut a badge into the shape of a guitar with a fretsaw. They were about two inches long and they sold for next to nothing at that time, five to ten pounds or something. They were exact in every detail – the wood grain, the lettering on the top, Fender or whatever, and the individual strings. I think he must have used a single hair to get some of those. Johnny Marr was having a look at them and making his choice. I think he bought a Rickenbacker one. He was absolutely delighted with it. One of the other Smiths bought a packet of Rizla king-size and some hair gel. He didn't bother looking at the records.

I remember I was standing on the shop floor and chatting away with Alan to Johnny Marr and I looked at my watch and realised that on that particular day Scotland were playing Ireland in a rugby international and Scotland were going for the triple crown. We didn't have a TV in the shop but in the Overgate a little bit further up the steps there was a TV rental shop which had various TVs in the window, so I excused myself to Johnny Marr and went out up to the TV rental shop and stood looking in the window as Scotland secured the triple crown.

I got Morrissey and Johnny to sign the white label album that I had. It was a plain white sleeve and stapled to the front was an A4 photocopy of the picture from the front of the album with the tracks listed underneath. I wasn't too sure who the other Smiths were, so I just got Morrissey and Johnny to sign it. Morrissey wrote, 'Be lucky, Morrissey' in his primary school writing with his name in capitals and underneath Johnny wrote, 'Johnny Marr digs you xxx'. I sold the album umpteen years ago.

When their stuff came out it sold in masses. 'Hand In Glove' sold okay when it came out and then it built up and up. And when 'This Charming Man' came out, that was pretty mega. Getting the twelve-inch of it was pretty good, and we managed to get copies of the twelve-inch New York Mix too. They were probably the best-selling act we had. With a lot of bands, you'd be ordering ones or twos, and with them it was more 30s and 40s.

The next time I saw them was when they played the Caird Hall in September 1985, about 18 months later. By that time, they'd exploded. I went along to that. I remember a lot of gladioli. It was one of those concerts which just put a big smile on your face. They dropped in again; certainly Morrissey and Marr came in. I've got no idea what they purchased that time, but it was good to see them in the shop. Now we could officially call them regulars! Since then, any time Johnny Marr's been around the area he's made sure he's dropped in and he was quoted as saying that Groucho's is one of his two favourite record shops in the country, the other one being a place in Manchester.



## FUSION CLUB (AKA RITZY'S)
### 4 MARCH 1984, ABERDEEN, UK

### JO BERSTAN, AGE 17
I went with a bus load of my high school chums from Buckie, where we lived, to Aberdeen, which was about just over an hour away. I remember there were gladioli flowers, which Morrissey had in his back pocket. They played songs from the LP out at that time, 'What Difference Does It Make?', 'Hand In Glove' and 'This Charming Man'. It was a fab night.

### ANDY SMITH
We were wearing NHS-type specs with the lenses poked out and we nicked daffodils from the graveyard and stuck them in our back pockets. After the gig, we were singing 'Hand In Glove' on the taxi rank in Back Wind, swirling daffies around our heads, and some guys took offence and a fight broke out. Daffies make a shite weapon.

### VIX VEX, AGE 15

I don't know if I would ever have classed myself as a fan. I was more into the goth scene – Sisters of Mercy, Bauhaus and that sort of thing. But I had few friends that were into the more independent side of things and what we would have called 'twee bands' back then, such as The Pastels.

I think it was their first big tour. The gig itself was a bit of an oddity. I don't think they expected that surge in popularity. The venue held about 700 people and on the night there were probably about 900 in there, so it was absolutely packed. The support band, Red Guitars, was of more interest to me at that particular time, although I don't think I knew who the support were beforehand.

Sometimes in those days you didn't know until you turned up.

My biggest memory of that night is just how busy it was. They would definitely have been breaking fire regulations on the night. There were quite a few people flat out on the floor, and I don't think it was anything to do with drink. It was the heat and because you were completely squashed in. That again was quite typical. It was a squishy night.

Most of that size of band would play there – bands like Spear of Destiny and Killing Joke. In those days you didn't have barriers at the front – you were right up against the stage. I must have started off there because that would have been where we were headed. But it was a squish. There was almost a sense of 'this isn't safe'. One of my friends had passed out and she was hauled unceremoniously across the stage and dumped at the side, so she watched the whole thing from the side. And a few people were coming out of the crowd a bit worse for wear. One girl was propped at the side of the bar and lying down. I asked the bar people, 'Can I have a glass of water? This girl's passed out,' and they wanted to charge me, which you're not allowed to do now. But at that time, it was like, 'Oh yeah.'

At that point I kind of went a bit nuts. For a 15-year-old, I was a bit feisty. I barged my way into the manager's office and had a real go at him, saying there were far too many people in there and it was a fire hazard. The guy was sitting there looking like a rabbit in the headlights, with this wee goth girl giving it to him!

The Smiths didn't really sound like anybody else. And of course, they had that miserable element that appealed to the goth side of things, that 'We're going to reel around the fountain and die somewhere' element. Most of my friends were on the punk side of things rather than the indie side, so there was a real mixture. There were punks, goths, the indie kids with their cardigans on. But possibly for a lot of them it was a curiosity. This was a new band that had been championed by John Peel and any club or anything you were at always had The Smiths playing. Morrissey after that became quite idolised.

He always had that swathe of arrogance. I think he always wanted to be worshipped and there was an element of that in the way the crowd reacted.

There wasn't much in the way of interaction and what there was was a bit poke-proddy. But that wasn't unusual. There was an element of bands being quite scathing towards their audience, much, much more than there is now. His interactions were quite baiting. So I don't know whether he looked out in the crowd and saw this punky element. He almost put the crowd on the back foot. There was a comment about 'playing to spotty teenagers', which didn't go down particularly well. I think Edinburgh crowds are pretty hard to please anyway.

A crowd us of walked up the road afterwards and somehow or other we'd managed to get a gladioli from the stage or his back pocket or somewhere. That was the pickings of the gig.

### KATIE LLEWELLIN, AGE 17

I had lost a bit of enthusiasm for the flower throwing. Other people I was with thought they were amazing though. I spoke to my ex-boyfriend who said, 'We saw them at Coasters and the band, and the audience were pretty annoying, so we left before the end.

### TERRY PATTERSON

This was my first concert since leaving the Army. The venue used to be for roller skating, so it was basically a dance floor. I remember being stripped to the waist and waving my shirt around.

The next time I saw them was at the Caley Palais on Lothian Road, a former cinema which is now a Wetherspoons! The girl I was with had me on her shoulders. Great gigs, great times.

### STUART RAE

I was in my first year at Napier College when I saw The Smiths on *Top Of The Pops*. Next day at college there was a lot of discussion around the performance of this new band and how 'different' the lead singer was. Then one of the guys in my class said that they were touring and who fancied going? I said 'yes' and the tickets were bought. Coasters was a strange venue because its main function was as a roller disco venue. I remember Morrissey had gladioli in his back pocket when he came on stage, that the crowd were asked to step back from the temporary stage because it had moved and just how brilliant they were live.

I saw them again in September at the Edinburgh Playhouse, a far larger venue, but they were still great live. And then I saw them playing Glasgow Barrowland in July 1986. I now know it as a great venue where the floor 'bounced', and it certainly did that night. Even since The Smiths split up, I have continued to listen to their music and have sometimes had to suffer from my friends slagging them off that they were morose. I always retort that these people are not listening to the music properly. Would I go and see them again? Absolutely. They are still one of the best bands I have seen live.

### ALAN TEMPLETON, AGE 25

I grew up a Velvets and Stooges fan and loved punk and new wave. I hated New Romantic music, and The Smiths were a breath of fresh air. I went with my flatmate Alan who got me into The Smiths by buying the 'What Difference Does It Make?' twelve-inch single. It was a brilliant night and there was a manic atmosphere. A girl was collapsed drunk in a corner at the gig, and we pointed her out to the bouncers for her own safety.

### STEVIE WALKER

I saw them twice, at Coasters in Edinburgh and then the next year at the Barrowland. They were fantastic both nights. I managed to get some beads from Morrissey's necklace.

## MAYFAIR

### 7 MARCH 1984, NEWCASTLE-UPON-TYNE, UK

### MARK SINGLETON

I went with my best friend Ste, also a Smiths fan. We were in our last year at comprehensive school. After saving up our dinner money and paper round wages to get tickets, we got the train from Darlington back in the day when you could get a train to a gig and there would still be a service to bring you home. We were both dressed in our 501s. Ste was wearing a floral design shirt and I had a paisley number on along with denim jackets (I know, double denim – shocking!). Ste was rocking the Mozza hairstyle where I was more Andy Rourke. We had bought the releases so far

– again with dinner money – so we had listened to them to death and scoured the sleeve notes so we could memorise the words. It goes without saying that we were a tad bit excited about seeing our idols for the first time. We got to the venue, our hearts pounding with excitement. We had not yet discovered beer, or how to get served underage, so Coke it was.

When The Smiths came on, the place erupted. The Mayfair had a balcony and the crowd were so loud and exuberant I thought the balcony would collapse. I don't remember the set list order – I was in a dream state – but Morrissey was gyrating away while Marr was just a guitar god who effortlessly made his guitar sing, a sound we had only heard on vinyl prior to the gig. Rourke was less animated but still rocked those renowned basslines, locking in with Joyce on drums. The best back line and songwriting team bar none in my mind. Sod The Beatles, Morrissey and Marr are the best song writing team ever.

I can't recall an encore, but what I do remember is the night went far too quickly. We left sweaty and adrenalin-fuelled, with me having had quite possibly the best night of my life so far. It may have been this Mayfair gig or the one on 17 July 1985 where, near the end, people were spitting, fall out from the punk era, which took a good few years to desist. Mozza did say, 'Stop spitting or we will stop.' People behaved but then later one numpty spat again and Mozza was true to his word and left the stage not to return. The last word was from Marr who said, 'You

*For Alan Templeton The Smiths were a breath of fresh air*

*Newcastle Mayfair ticket*

were warned. What do you expect?' The fans then gave the culprit a good slapping.

### MARK CLEMENT

They came on and I was really enjoying it and then somebody at the front started spitting at the band. The band weren't happy about it, to say the least, especially Morrissey and Johnny, and I think at one point they figured out who it was and a little bit of a scuffle broke out. But whoever it was carried on which eventually led to the band walking off the stage with Johnny saying, 'You spit, we split.' Obviously, I wasn't happy that they walked because a) the incident spoiled what was a great gig and b) they were midway through one of my favourite ever Smiths songs, 'Hand In Glove'.

## TOWN HALL

### 8 MARCH 1984, MIDDLESBROUGH, UK

### LESLEY JOHNSON, AGE 14

My first ever gig, I went with my cousin who was two years older and Smiths mad like me. I caught Morrissey's daffodil, which I still have pressed in a photo album. Red Guitars were support and it was a lovely £3.50 a ticket! I also saw the '85 gig supported by James, which was probably my favourite, and the '86 *Queen Is Dead* gig, when they were amazing, very polished and supported by Raymonde. No gigs since have ever beaten them. I could not believe they played our little town three years on the trot.

## LANCASTER UNIVERSITY

### 9 MARCH 1984, LANCASTER, UK

### PADDY SHENNAN, AGE 19

Less than ten months later, this gig was a world away from that night in Camden Town. I was now studying in Sheffield but couldn't get to their Sheffield University gig in January so waited for the concert nearest my hometown. I remember the massive queue outside the venue and the heat inside the packed hall. Some young women fainted or at least had to be helped out of the gig; it was just so hot and uncomfortable. My then girlfriend certainly felt uneasy and so we stood towards the back, within easy reach of an exit door just in case she needed to get to the fresh air. What a difference from being able to sit cross-legged on the floor at the Electric Ballroom gig!

The band's debut album had been released in the February, and, as well as 'Hand In Glove', The Smiths' growing army of devoted fans had fallen in love with floor-filling singles 'This Charming Man' and 'What Difference Does It Make?' This was a band that was already growing out of the university venue circuit. This was a band that everyone was now talking about. This was the band of the moment.

### RACHEL SOWDEN

My friend Helen was passed along the crowd and lifted off the stage after fainting. I was quite jealous as she reckoned she touched Johnny Marr's hand as she passed him. I pressed my gladioli that Morrissey threw into the crowd.



### PHILL GATENBY

October 31, a Monday. I moved out of the family home in Coventry and into a bedsit on Priory Road in Sale; a mate lived in another flat in the large Victorian house. It was a week that ultimately changed my life… The next day I bought a black-and-white portable TV from a secondhand TV shop on Washway Road, Sale. On Friday 4 November, I turned on Channel 4's *The Tube*, as I always had (apart from when in the States). The video of a band came on, not a live performance. I had no idea who the band were or where they were from. It was two minutes and 41 seconds of mouth open wide, asking, 'Who is this? Where have they come from?'

It was my introduction to a four-piece Mancunian beat combo who, over 40 years later, are still a (slight) obsession in my life… The band, The Smiths, the song, 'This Charming Man' — a title I played on nine years later when producing my own City fanzine, *This Charming Fan*.

I bought the single, yet strangely, it wasn't the A-side they played on *The Tube* that endeared me to the band, but the B-side, 'Jeane'. Having moved into a freezing cold bedsit merely four days prior, the lines:

There's ice on the sink where we bathe

So how can you call this a home
When you know it's a grave?

resonated greatly.

It summed up where I was at that exact point. It was freezing with an electric meter that swallowed 50 pence pieces like crazy if I put the two-bar fire on. It was a grave, but it was my grave...

In 1984, on my 21st birthday in February, I asked my brother to get me The Smiths' debut album on the basis of having bought 'This Charming Man' (which wasn't on the album, though it was on the cassette) and liking the follow up single 'What Difference Does It Make?'. I had a pre-prepared party tape blasting out the best punk / new wave / electro pop tunes.

I opened my present from my brother and sat there reading the lyrics on the inside sleeve and was blown away by how many songs I could have said were written for me. I wanted to stop the tape and put the album on, but at the same time I wanted the first listen to be a personal listen, which it was the next afternoon (after I had recovered from the party).

I was blown away. Punk had instilled in me an attitude and

Coventry (Lancheser) Poly (Phill Gatenby)

shaped me politically. But here was a band that was reflecting what I was feeling inside, with all the late-teen / early-twenties insecurities and questioning oneself packed into ten songs. This was a band for me.

The gig in March at the Free Trade Hall in Manchester was sold out so I had missed out on the tour – or so I thought… But Manchester City were playing away at Brighton on 10 March and on our way down on the Special, I noted in the *NME*'s gig guide that The Smiths were playing at Coventry Polytechnic that evening. And the Special was stopping at Coventry to pick up / drop off the Leicester and Rugby supporters club members.

A quick phone call from a phone box in Brighton to my mum and dad in Coventry, saying 'leave the key under the plant pot, I'll be there at 11pm', and I got off the train at Coventry and walked to the Poly. The gig was sold out but a lad was next to the door with a spare ticket. Face value and I was in. City and The Smiths all on the same day. What a day!

# HAMMERSMITH PALAIS

## 12 MARCH 1984, LONDON, UK

### MICHAEL FARRAGHER

I wanted to see them at every opportunity. I didn't have an awful lot of money. But we got to see them the next time they were playing, a month after the Lyceum, at Hammersmith Palais. They played for much longer, about an hour and a half, and Sandie Shaw came on and sang 'I Don't Owe You Anything'. Then we were looking at the music

press every week and thinking, 'When are they next playing? We've got to go and see them.'

I'd read in *NME* that Morrissey would go up to the Rough Trade offices in King's Cross fairly regularly. It was coming up to his birthday in May and I thought, 'I'm just going to spend the day up there and wait until I meet him,' because they were playing some gigs up in Scotland in June and we really wanted to go but they were sold out. I had a present to give to him for his birthday and I had a letter to give to him, and I was going to be cheeky and say, 'Is there any chance you could get us on the guest list?'

I went into the Rough Trade offices and asked, 'Is Morrissey likely to come in?' and they said, 'We don't know. He might turn up today.' Sure enough he did. There weren't any other Smiths with him, and I don't remember there being any security. I said, 'I love The Smiths and here's a present,' and, 'My sister's really into The Smiths and we'd love to come and see you in Scotland. Is there any chance you could put us on the guest list?'

He said, 'Yeah, sure. Give me your names. I'll make sure that you're on the guest lists.' I'd met Morrissey! Oh my God. It was the most exciting thing that could ever happen. And after that we started following The Smiths on a very regular basis. We started writing to them. We wrote letters to Morrissey and to Johnny through Rough Trade. My sister used to write to Morrissey every week for at least a year. And I wrote to him maybe every two or three weeks. We'd send letters and we'd send presents and we would get replies from Morrissey now and again. We've still got those letters and postcards.

We started going to radio and TV stations, wherever we knew they were going to be on and it was a live appearance. We got to know all of the band at that stage and they knew us. They would sign records for us, and they would give us records. Morrissey said we could come to any gig that we wanted to, and we would be on all guest lists, so the only gigs that we ever paid for were the Lyceum and Hammersmith Palais shows that we first saw. After that, we were always on Morrissey's guest list or Johnny's.

### AHMET DERVISH

I was just leaving school and London-based as punk kicked off, so I loved lot of the new wave stuff; The Jam (my first live gig), the Banshees, Buzzcocks, etc. Music was getting a bit stale around '82 onwards and I stopped religiously buying the *NME* every week. But I was randomly watching *Top Of The Pops* in late January 1984 when on came a band called The Smiths. I had never heard of them, but they played 'What Difference Does It Make' and it absolutely blew me away. The sound, how they looked… Everything was, 'Wow, I love this!'

The chemistry between the band members stood out. Obviously, Morrissey stood out too. In the following days I tracked down and purchased that single, and 'This Charming Man' and 'Hand In Glove'. I found out that they were playing at the Hammersmith Palais in the next month or so and booked a ticket immediately. I was hooked – I'd not heard or seen anything like them.

By that point I'm sure I already had the debut album, so all the songs were recognisable. I remember Sandie Shaw joined them on stage (for 'I Don't Owe You Anything'). The gig was something special, the crowd went mental, and the energy around the performance stood out. The gig was something else.

From then on, every record release was eagerly anticipated, and I purchased every format, studied the record sleeves, etc.

My next live gig was Brixton in 1985, and the *Meat Is Murder* tour, with James supporting. It was another crazy gig. All I remember is that leaving the gigs you were on such a high. I have never ever felt that feeling again. The closest I've got to it was seeing The Stone Roses.

The next gig was, of all places, at the London Palladium on *The Queen Is Dead* tour in 1986, and then in December of that year, Brixton again for the rescheduled Anti-Apartheid gig. Who knew that this was going to be their last live performance?

At this stage, for me they were on top point musically. I'd collected every record, collected rarities where possible, and bought every music press publication where they were on cover, plus posters, etc. When the announcement came of Marr leaving the band I was distraught.

I continued to collect early Morrissey stuff for a few years. For me, The Smiths was done. I couldn't ever see a comeback and in truth I didn't personally want it. That was the life span of the band – a start and a finish. Done.

Like Johnny Marr said in a TV

*Ahmet was at the Palais*

documentary interview: 'Between 1982 and 1987, we were the best rock band in the world!... No contest!'

## FREE TRADE HALL

### 13 MARCH 1984, MANCHESTER, UK

### STEVE BROWN

The first Smiths song I heard was 'This Charming Man' when a mate played me a video he'd recorded off *The Tube* on Channel 4. I was struck by how cool Johnny Marr was, with the sixties hair and shades. I heard the song a few more times on evening shows on Radio 1, probably the *Kid Jensen Show*, and began to adore it. It was so infectious. I was 18 in 1983; I'd had a fairly shitty childhood and life at home was still pretty unbearable. Music was vital to me, it was all I really cared about in life back then, but I didn't really like anything that was around. It was all a bit forced and I had to kind of make myself like it. 'This Charming Man' was just impossible not to love.

Kev, who showed me the video, and my other mate, Lee, were members of the Haçienda, which had been open around 18 months. You had to be, or be with, a member to get in; they used to sign me in, and we'd hang around on the balcony upstairs watching the five or ten proto-yuppies on the dance floor dancing to electro, a music which I didn't understand! The place was freezing and near empty, but we went because it was different and not full of people wanting a fight.

They went to see The Smiths there at the end of '83. I was going to go with them but by this time had watched footage of a college gig that had been shown on BBC2, which I'd recorded, and I inexplicably decided I didn't like the songs! I didn't go and to this day I regret it. They said the gig was fantastic, so I started re-watching the college gig. After about three viewings I'd decided I'd made a big mistake. I loved 'Still Ill' and 'This Night Has Opened My Eyes' especially.

I bought the twelve-inch of 'This Charming Man' and played the B-side to death. I still rate 'Accept Yourself' as one of the best songs anyone's ever written. I think the other track was 'Wonderful Woman', one of those beautiful melancholy Smiths ballads.

I bought the debut album as soon as it came out and loved it. 35 years later, it's still in my all-time Top Ten. I did the sensible thing and bought a ticket for the gig at the Free Trade Hall in early '84 with Kev. We were quite near the front and what really struck me was the near-hysteria of the crowd; I went to a lot of gigs, but I hadn't seen anything like this – people breathlessly climbing over the seats to get to the front. I sang pretty much every word along with Morrissey, except when they played 'Barbarism Begins At Home'. This must have been a full year before *Meat Is Murder* came out. It's not my favourite song by a long way but, hearing it that first time, I was really impressed that they were doing something so different from the first album. It was pretty funky and lithe. The fact that they were progressing so soon after they'd appeared made me respect them even more.

I had the album on rotation all summer, I still get goose bumps when I think of 'I Don't Owe You Anything' playing on those long summer days. Me, Kev and several other mates were on the dole and hearing Morrissey endorsing us being out of work, in those songs, was vindicating in an amusing kind of way. That year was just a succession of better and better moments – 'Heaven Knows I'm Miserable Now', and then 'William, It Was Really Nothing', which I absolutely went mad for. Taping the John Peel sessions and then *Hatful of Hollow* – brilliant.

I couldn't wait for *Meat Is Murder* to be released, but when I heard it I was a little underwhelmed. I still think it's one of those 'difficult' second albums. But I loved the humour in the lyrics, 'I'd like to drop my trousers to the Queen…' etc. Morrissey was very Marmite. Everyone I knew either loved or hated him, with no in between. I loved the fact that he was so different, outspoken and pretentious but in a likeable, funny way. He was the only person who had the nerve to slag off the Band Aid single – a very edgy thing to do; I wasn't sure whether I agreed with him, but I greatly admired his attitude. We were fascinated by his campness, the way he sang those 'la-di-da-di-dahs' in between the lyrics in the songs.

### JEREMY KIDD, RED GUITARS VOCALIST

Highlights for me include the Sandie Shaw shows, particularly the Manchester Free Trade Hall one which, if I remember correctly, was The Smiths' first hometown gig since their debut on *Top Of The Pops*. The band were on great form and all the kids in the stalls went wild, and then Sandie Shaw came on and the older folks in the balcony seats, many of whom were chaperoning sons and daughters who were considered too young to go on their own, went wild. It was brilliant, especially because Johnny Marr moved from his usual position stage left to stand next to Andy Rourke stage right. It was a simple gesture that demonstrated a grasp of rock choreography worthy of The Shadows.

### STEVE MARLAND

I was walking along Underbank in Stockport when I saw a small poster in the Crazy Face clothes shop for a new single by The Smiths, 'This Charming Man'. The shop and brand were owned by Joe Moss, who also managed the band. Days later I read a gushing review of the single in the *NME* written by local Reddish lad Paul Morley. I bought the seven-inch and later the twelve-inch remix from the Virgin shop in Merseyway. The drive of

*Steve Marland's ticket for the Free Trade Hall show*

the guitar and rhythm section along with Morrisey's unlikely yelp and yaw seemed quite remarkable. In my modest way I became a fan, buying subsequent singles in their evocative picture sleeves – chuckling at the wilfully sly and diverse cultural references.

I was eager to see them live and bought tickets for the Free Trade Hall show. I turned up and sat in the side balcony to the band's right. We all had a clear elevated view – Nia Jones, my gal, and art school pals Josephine Drazek and Steve Jordan. First up were Sheffield's Red Guitars – I still love their tune 'Steeltown'.

The Smiths took the stage to a walk on tune of 'Johnny Remember Me' (my pal). A hometown crowd were well up for a good night and The Smiths sound and presence met all expectations, I was entranced by Marr's guitar and that hi-life, McGuinn-Jansch jangle that made the night come alive. Two thirds in and they were joined by Sandie Shaw for a divine rendition of 'I Don't Owe You Anything', much to Nia's delight as she had bought a copy of Sandie's 'Hand In Glove'. The ticket cost £3.50. I later sold it on eBay for £75!

I now own none of their recordings. I sold all the records for a pound a pop during one of many cash poor life experiences. And I never listen to the tunes, although Mr Marr is a benefactor of The Manchester Modernists, for whom I work.

### KARREN ABLAZE, FANZINE EDITOR

There are many differing opinions on The Smiths gig at the Free Trade Hall. I had some very enthusiastic reviews of the event. I watched the beginning of the set, but after a while I wandered over to a distressed Smiths fan who told me, in the comparative peace of the foyer, tales of fans passing out and new chairs being destroyed in the hysteria. Apparently messages had been sent to the group after the second song, asking them to stop playing for a while so that the people who were injured, squashed or passing out could be helped.

Between us we scrawled a note to Morrissey, mentioning the possibility of an interview next time he is in Manchester ('remember Manchester?') and also suggesting that he might have been able to prevent some of the damage at the gig. He handed the letter to a girl selling t-shirts and a few days later I received a reply:

*Dear Karren,*

*I was obviously annoyed by your letter. It seems that whenever things go wrong at concerts people always blame the group. Nobody told me about your fanzine at the ORS (Oxford Road Show), so exactly what am I supposed to do?*

*Please don't give me the 'remember Manchester' nonsense; not one living soul in Manchester ever helped The Smiths in our early days – our glorious radio stations, local press, music/media people, people from local record companies. Anything we have achieved we have absolutely earned, and we quite literally do not owe anyone anything.*

*I will always speak to fanzines whenever they care to speak to me. But you are obviously entirely unaware of our true natures and ideals otherwise you would clearly realise that I would have halted any crowd unpleasantness had I been aware of it. We have sensitive people whose job it is to help people out of the crowd should they need it. Frankly, I do not care about the chairs at the Free Trade Hall. Being criminally non-sighted, I can see no further than ten inches in front of me. I do not ever recognise individuals in an audience.*

*I do not want an interview with your fanzine because you obviously don't seriously care about me or The Smiths. I don't enjoy being cross-examined; there are OTHER people to condemn, Karen… aren't there? Haven't we done any GOOD things??*

*Sadly – Morrissey*

### THOMAS JONES

The Smiths were in full swing by now. The album had been released, and this had the air of a triumphant hometown return. The flowers were mostly gone now – although four daffodil-toting boys from Crewe hadn't got that particular memo – but the Free Trade Hall was about to have the night of its life in which the seats would be literally ripped out of the wooden floor. (We stood on top of a mangled wreck of Row K at the end of the gig). The Red Guitars put in a blistering set too, one of the best support band slots I've ever seen.

Johnny had moved on from the Rickenbacker and was sporting the Cherry Red Gibson ES-355 with its squashy, fat tones, which starred on the new songs, most memorably 'Girl Afraid', which seemed to be an instrumental until Morrissey finally chimed in and – track of the night – 'Barbarism', complete with Morrissey and Johnny dancing in a duet masterclass of the 'not-quite-falling-over-dance' that was espoused and copied by a million gawky eighties teenagers.

Sandie Shaw guested on a delicious 'I Don't Owe You Anything'. The new stuff wasn't to everyone's taste though; some frustrated old fans heckled 'play something off the album' when they tried out the prototype *Meat Is Murder* songs. But yes. We ripped the seats out of the floor. I remember thinking that it should be headline news. Sod the Pistols. I was there when The Smiths played.

### KEV JONES

I saw them on *Top Of The Pops* doing 'This Charming Man' and Morrissey swinging the gladioli over his head. *Top Of The Pops* was a religious thing on a Thursday night. Sometimes it was the only chance you got to see pop stars apart from in photographs. My dad was sat there saying, 'What the bloody hell is this?' but I thought, 'These are something special. These are great.' It was when 'What Differences Does It Make?' came out that I thought, 'Crikey, these are really good,' and I went out and bought that and 'This Charming Man' and 'Hand In Glove' and anything I could get my hands on.

I found out they were playing at the Free Trade Hall, but it was sold out – I was gutted. I was living in Failsworth in Manchester at the time. I'd started working for an advertising agency and a guy at work had tickets for the gig. As an advertising agency we had one of

*Kev Jones copied a colleague's ticket to gain entry to the Free Trade Hall*

FREE TRADE HALL
Peter Street, Manchester

Tuesday 13 March 1984 – 7:30 pm

OUTLAW presents
THE SMITHS
plus Supporting Attraction

STALLS
£3.50 (inc. VAT)

No ticket exchanged nor money refunded

the very first laser photocopiers. I was so desperate to go I thought, 'I could try copying this ticket.' We went to the print production department where they had loads of different sorts of paper samples, found a paper almost identical to the paper that the ticket was printed on and copied the ticket. You could tell it was different, but it looked pretty good. I thought, 'I'm going to have to chance this.' So we cut it out and put the perfs in it.

I went with a school friend. It was all seated and we were thinking, 'What are we going to do when we get in there?' because we had my work colleague's ticket so we obviously couldn't use his seat. We thought, 'We can't do this. Let's go and see if we can buy a ticket off a tout.' So I went and asked a tout and they said, 'Oh, I can sell you two tickets for £15.' £15 was a lot of money in those days – face value was only £3.50. In the end we thought, 'We'll just chance it.'

In those days, gigs were different. There was a mass of people there just trying to get in at the door and all that was on the door were these two old boys in dinner suits and dickie bows, trying to stem the tide of people coming in and ripping tickets. I remember there being a bit scrum of people trying to get through the door. I handed my ticket over, and this old boy took the ticket, ripped it and we were straight in. And I thought, 'Oh wow, we've done it.' And then the second problem that I was thinking about was, 'Where am I going to sit?'

This was the first proper gig that I'd actually been to, if you don't count going to see Gene Pitney with my mum a couple of years earlier.

And of course it wasn't a problem at all, because once we were actually in there it was absolute chaos. Nobody sat on the seats. People were stood on the seats, and everybody ran down to the front. The ushers inside were trying to keep control but they couldn't. It was just absolutely wild.

There was something special about the connection between the band and that audience. I can vividly remember being stood on a seat and thinking, 'This is amazing.' The atmosphere was incredible. I remember Morrissey coming dancing on with the biggest bunch of gladioli in his back pocket.

## UNIVERSITY OF HULL

### 15 MARCH 1984, HULL, UK

### SEAN BRYANT

The Smiths had been scheduled to play at Dingwalls in Hull the previous August, but the gig was cancelled for some reason and a couple of weeks later Dingwalls burnt down. I first saw them performing 'This Charming Man' on *Top Of The Pops* in 1983. I didn't really like the song but was taken aback by the look of the band, in particular Morrissey who was wearing glasses and a hearing aid. I had been floundering on the tail end of the punk scene, having been a punk since 1978. But punk had become a 'fashion', something it was never supposed to be, and I must have been looking for another scene but with the same ideas. Then The Smiths were back on *Top Of The Pops* with 'What Difference Does It Make?' I was hooked.

I *had* to see them live; this song

sounded fantastic and the band looked great. I was unemployed so didn't have the money to travel to other cities to see them. However, around December '83 they announced they would be playing at Hull University – wow, fantastic! My then girlfriend said she'd buy me tickets for my birthday. My younger brother had also been impressed when he'd seen them live on *The Tube*, so off my girlfriend and I went on our bikes to Hull Uni and bought four tickets.

I can't remember how we got to the gig on the night as none of us drove and the Uni wasn't on a bus route from where we lived; we didn't want to be uncool and arrive on bikes! We had to be signed in as we weren't students and this seemed to take an age, as we didn't know anyone.

When we finally got in, I vaguely remember two guys in the Refectory performing an acoustic set. It turned out it was Paul Heaton and Stan Cullimore of The Housemartins.

The venue mainly consisted of students, of which there must have been around 400–500, and we felt a little out of place still having spiky hair. The support band, a local group called The Red Guitars, were quite good but then The Smiths came on and – wow, what a performance! I'd bought the first album a month prior to the gig so knew a lot of the songs and chanted along with the students. Morrissey was throwing out gladioli and was still wearing his hearing aid and glasses. They said everything to me; I was unemployed, didn't want a job, was Type-1 diabetic, so always ill, and oh so depressed!

It became very trendy to like The Smiths. A bit like punk, the scene was spoiled. I never bought any more Smiths albums and couldn't even watch them on *Top Of The Pops*. However, in recent times my son has become a big fan and so I have now embraced the later albums, particularly *The Queen Is Dead*, which some people think is their best album. But, for me, the first album will always be their best, for 'Reel Around the Fountain' alone. I have seen Morrissey solo a few times, and Johnny Marr, but nothing compares to the excitement of seeing The Smiths on their first tour.

### NICK SPENCE

Back in my hometown of Hull, I vaguely knew Tracey Thorn and Ben Watt, better known as Everything But The Girl, named after a local shop sign. Both studied at the University of Hull and lived nearby. One morning I bumped into Ben in the basement of Sydney Scarborough, one of the few record shops in Hull. He was raving about The Smiths, just the best thing he had heard in ages. I was sold. The Smiths came to Hull and Ben and Tracey got me tickets. They shared a very Morrissey-esque bedsit in The Avenues area of Hull, so I went round to collect them. My then girlfriend was on a school trip that day so missed out but I took her younger sister, as you do.

It's one of the few gigs from the eighties I still vividly recall, as being so close to the stage I could literally reach out and touch Morrissey. I did. It has to be said that a fair few of the 'fans' present seemed intent on causing trouble. Earlier in the night two student types were throwing beer glasses towards the stage, landing in the crowd at the front. It was scary. What I remember best though is The Smiths, mostly minus Morrissey, dancing around during an extended funky version of 'Barbarism Begins At Home.' Such a great night, such great memories.

### MALCOLM GREENLEY

I lived through punk – fantastic days – but it fizzled out. It seemed to last longer back in the day, and it meant so much. After that, I was into The Jam and all those other bands and then I was waiting around for something to get passionate about. It was the Peel Sessions – about 20 songs, a lot of them comprised of B-sides, a couple of the singles – just before the first album came out that got me hooked.

A friend brought round a cassette of the first John Peel session, which he had recorded off the radio. They did four sessions for Peel and a lot ended up on *Hatful of Hollow*. That cassette, and my friend discovering them for me, kicked it off and changed my life. The melodies were what got me first. Johnny Marr's guitar was just like a breath of fresh air, and then you got to dig around with the lyrics and thinking, 'These are pretty strange.' I was drawn in.

And then I was just dying to see them live, and I consider myself to be very lucky. The first time I saw them was at Hull University (I'm from Hull). The first album had come out about a month or so before and this was the first nationwide headlining tour, to promote the first album. They were so tight, and Johnny Marr's guitar

live was just a machine of melody. That's the cheesiest way I can think to describe it. I think it's always best to see a band just as it's about to break really big.

Hull Uni was about 500 – 600 capacity and it was one of those basement rooms so there wasn't an awful lot of air conditioning. It was absolutely boiling considering it was March. By the end of the night, all the windows were open to let some air in. It was jam packed. They were just beginning to get a real cult audience, so it was a passionate atmosphere. I've read online that there were a few hecklers there, but I don't remember that. The audience were pretty much my sort of age and in their early twenties, and mainly male. There were a lot of women there but generally all of the five Smiths gigs I went to had a predominantly male audience.

### CAT WEATHERILL

I was in my second year at Hull University. Morrissey threw daffodils into the audience. I caught one and photographed it lying on top of the poster.

## *THE TUBE*

### 16 MARCH 1984, NEWCASTLE-UPON-TYNE, UK

### DARREN MILLER

I saw The Smiths live on many occasions, and met them too. I first saw them on *The Tube*; they were on with Madness and Howard Jones. My uncle got me tickets as he worked on the show. I made the trip from Liverpool to Newcastle at the age of 17. We got to go to the rehearsals and hang out in the green room. We watched Madness do their sound check and rehearsal, and we had lunch with the crew and Madness. I was sporting a fabulous pair of leather jeans!

The Smiths didn't turn up until late. The show started and there was lots of stopping and starting, and getting groups of people together. We were on the balcony overlooking the stage.

## DE MONTFORT HALL

### 18 MARCH 1984, LEICESTER, UK

### LEE THACKER

De Montfort Hall was a much bigger venue than Leicester University. I really needed to see them live again if for no other reason than to get rid of the sour taste their debut album had left me with. It was a great gig. I was right down the front in my unique t-shirt – a few people asked where I'd bought it from – and danced and sang along to the songs, revelling in the fact that they sounded so much better live than on record. It wasn't until *Hatful Of Hollow* came out later that year (I had a paper round by that time and purchased it on the day of release) that I got over the disappointment of their debut. I played *Hatful Of Hollow* over and over again for months. It's still in my top ten favourite albums of all time.

### ALI RALPH

I went with my boyfriend, Simon, known as Christmas Simon – as we only ever see him now at Christmas! I remember the gladioli hanging out of the back pocket of Mozza's Levi's.

### DAWN OATES, AGE 20

I was with my younger brother, Ian. The Smiths were a surprisingly mutual musical interest. It was a brilliant show. Morrissey was surly, magnificent and handsome.

### SHAUN KNAPP, AGE 19

I was just the right age. The atmosphere was electric, a heady mix of excitement and anticipated violence, which always makes you pay attention. They weren't on for very long, but that didn't matter. I've been told since that they played 13 songs and I remember they did three encores. I can recall them playing 'What Difference Does It Make?' like it was yesterday. It was absolutely fantastic and it just sounded so good live – you didn't want it to finish. I've been to hundreds of gigs, but this was one that stays with you, it was so different to anything that I'd seen. Looking back, it was quite breath-taking, like being hit by a train because the audience were so up for it. The Smiths were a band favoured by The Baby Squad (Leicester City football hooligans), so there were quite a few of those in the audience that night.

### ANDY WHITE

I first heard of The Smiths via a review in the *NME* in autumn 1983. I had planned to see them at the Haçienda in November but got an offer I couldn't refuse off a girl at university so didn't go – a bad decision, by the way! I hadn't heard any of their stuff at

*Shaun Knapp was just the right age*

*Andy White's ticket for the De Montfort Hall gig*

this stage – only 'Hand In Glove' was out and I didn't get that until months later. I still don't like it much. By November 1983 there was even more of a buzz about the band, and I heard them for the first time when Peel played 'This Charming Man'. This was well before the internet and streaming, so once you'd heard it on the radio that was it – you couldn't hear it again unless you'd taped it, which I hadn't. But I knew straight away that this was very special and sounded nothing like anything else around at that time.

I got the *NME* every week and when the release date for 'This Charming Man' was announced I walked into town to try and get a copy. Alas, it was not that easy to get hold of, and I went every day for a week until I eventually got the twelve-inch. The cover was luxurious and mysterious – no picture of the band, just a random guy. I got to my flat and put it on the turntable and then played it non-stop for about five hours. I got all my mates in for a listen and almost without exception they liked it. These were non-PC times, and a few were not sure about the somewhat dubious sexuality in the lyrics, but the guitar was amazing.

You could tell before the vocals had even started that this was exceptional. I even liked both of the B-sides, which have somewhat disappeared from The Smiths' legend. My mate had got the seven-inch with 'Jeane' on the B-side, one of my favourite Smiths songs. Strangely, I never bought the seven inch version and 'Jeane' seems to have been missed off all their subsequent compilations.

I got the first album on the day it was released and was blown away by the songs. I knew I had to see them, so I started looking out for concerts. I'd moved to Hampshire, but my girlfriend was in Bradford, and I spotted that there was a concert coming up in Leicester at De Montfort Hall. It was only a small detour off my route to buy tickets at the box office, buying tickets for £3.50 on a Friday.

The set list was most of the first album. plus 'This Charming Man'. That wasn't on the album – I think it got added some years later. They also played one or two songs that I'd never heard, plus 'Heaven Knows I'm Miserable Now', which had not been released. I don't think the gig had sold out, but it was pretty full, and by this stage quite a few fans were turning up with flowers sticking out of their back pockets, which always looked a bit silly to me. Okay if you're the star on the stage, but not sat in the pub across the way. What I remember most is just what a presence Morrissey was, commanding the stage, and the great look of the rest of the guys.

### GAVIN JONES

I first heard The Smiths on John Peel and thought 'Hand In Glove' was interestingly different but I was still on a 'Jam hangover' and feeling like something would have to be really special to compete with seeing The Jam live. But a friend of mine had seen them in '83 in Birmingham and came back with photos of flowers and general carnage, saying how good it was. Then I saw the *Whistle*

*Test* gig on TV from Derby, and I think 'Charming Man' came out just before or just after – and I was hooked! I loved the sound and Johnny's guitar, so made sure when they were next around the Midlands that I would go and check them out.

So, there I was outside Leicester's De Montfort Hall on 18th March 1984, where I had seen The Jam loads. The first thing that struck me was the small truck and minibus outside with the equipment; The Jam had three artics, so this was definitely early days! There was a mixed crowd of indie kids, punks, etc. I can't remember the support band, but when The Smiths came on, they did 'Still Ill' first and I remember thinking, 'Where's Morrisey? I can hear him but not see him!' I pushed closer and there he was, rolling around the floor, loose shirt, beads and gladioli spread around. I was hooked!

Johnny looked cool as anything, standing there in Levi's jacket and with his black Riccy 330, and Rourke was pretty static as well. But the sound got me, so different and fresh, and Morrisey's lyrics, so clever and witty. Once Moz stood up, he had such a great stage presence (which was still there the next few times I saw them during '85 and '86). It was hard to take your eyes off him gyrating around.

They sped through the first album. I particularly liked 'Reel Around The Fountain', and they did two or three encores. They were so tight. It was a great gig and got me out of that Jam hangover at last!

## CITY HALL

### 19 MARCH 1984, SHEFFIELD, UK

### JONATHAN JORDAN

My group of pals were an odd mix of goths, rockers, punks and New Romantics. We watched every band that came through South Yorkshire. That week we had seen Spear of Destiny, the guitar player that had just left

Whitesnake and The Pogues. The Smiths had a good buzz, had been on *Top Of The Pops* and were playing our favourite venue, Sheffield City Hall – usual venue of choice for Thin Lizzy, AC/DC and the Halle Orchestra. We bought tickets on the door for less than £5 and found ourselves in the balcony, empty but for us. The venue was half full and totally the wrong place for The Smiths. We tried to dance and 'get into it', but it wasn't happening for us. Even the fans in our group concluded it wasn't a great night, and we ended up in the pub next door before the encores. Young people are amazed and impressed that I have seen The Smiths, but frankly it was a really forgettable gig!

## TOWER BALLROOM

### 20 MARCH 1984, EDGBASTON, BIRMINGHAM, UK

### KEVIN INMAN, AGE 25

This was not your usual venue, but it was very interesting. I went with my girlfriend Heather, now my wife.

The Smiths came on stage at 9pm. They did stuff from the first album. There were many stage invasions which I thought was irritating but most of the gig was played with people jumping on the stage. I was old for a Smiths fan at 25. We have seen Morrissey many times over the years but sadly only got to see The Smiths the once.

### SIMON WELLS

Memory is, of course, a liar. But here goes. The first time I saw The Smiths was at the Tower Ballroom in Birmingham. The first album had just been released and both me and my sixth form friend, Ian Tonks, were passionately in love with the whole group, but Morrissey especially. It was an obsession. They were our band in a way that you lose later in life but is – or was – a defining part of being a teenager. We probably outfitted ourselves in an approximation of how they dressed although I am little hazy on that point. Putting together a look was not one of our talents.

The Tower didn't host many gigs but was a pretty good venue with lots of space and big plastic palm trees, which we loved. It seemed kind of fitting, as gladioli-throwing was still a part of The Smiths live experience and I certainly took a bunch along. The band were fantastic, living in a moment of realisation where they knew they were going to be not just good and popular but important. Maybe even very important.

It's not a feeling I've had at gigs often but there was a sensation of riding a wave. Not just that this was great music but that it was sweeping away some of the horrible machismo that seemed part of becoming an adult in the early eighties. Thatcherism was in full flow, and it was easy to feel as though you were living in claustrophobic, deadening times. Here, the boundaries and the possibilities of everyone there seemed to open up. It felt like a blossoming.

### BRYAN FARLEY

When they released 'What Difference Does It Make?' the year after we'd booked them at the Fighting Cocks, they were big news. They were going on a nationwide tour which was primarily university student unions and because I'd maintained a reasonable relationship with the booking guy contact I had made at Rough Trade, he phoned me up and said, 'They're looking to do a gig in Birmingham. Would you be interested in doing it?' I said, 'Yes, of course,' because I'd liked them from the get-go and now they were becoming the band of the moment.

So we searched around for a venue and found one called the Tower Ballroom in Edgbaston, an old-fashioned dancing venue situated on the edge of this inner-city reservoir. It was used for things like tea dances and bingo, but we just saw it as a glorious place to put a band on because nobody had done it there before. It had a capacity somewhere in excess of 1,000, and we thought, 'We can do well here.'

At the time 'What Difference

*Simon Wells saw The Smiths at Birmingham's Tower Ballroom*

Does It Make?' was right up there in the charts, which helped enormously because it all fitted together timing-wise. Morrissey was doing that falsetto and it had a really good guitar riff, with Johnny Marr excelling himself. It was right up there at the top when we put them on, so we got lucky.

We did it all ourselves. We printed the posters ourselves. We advertised it ourselves. We even silkscreen printed the tickets – which I think were £4. And we sold them all. We could have sold them five times over such was the demand. And then something happened. There was an illness and they had to postpone it, so the original poster shows a date of February the something or other, but they actually played about two or three weeks later because of the postponement.

We did all right out of it financially. We'd been losing money here and there over the previous two or three years, putting on these no-hopers in the Fighting Cocks, so it had been a real labour of love. But at the Tower Ballroom we had The Red Guitars supporting them and we had a fantastic night. It was absolutely packed out. We had people trying to get in. The promoter was happy – he sold shitloads of booze – everyone was happy. We packed it in then. We both had proper jobs. Clive was a senior teacher, and I was a retail manager, and I had a young family.

After the UK tour, the band took a short break from the road before embarking on a selection of European and Irish dates.



### ANNE DE BRETAGNE, AGE 16

I saw a Smiths concert in Amsterdam. My brother lived there. I was a fan of The Cure amongst others. My brother was 22. He introduced me to The Clash. And to The Smiths!

## BREEKEND FESTIVAL

### 22 APRIL 1984, BREE, BELGIUM

### WALTER SMEETS, AGE 18

The Smiths played at the Breekend Festival in Bree, Belgium. I didn't know them very well as I was more into garage rock and punk bands. But some of my friends told me they were the next big thing. From the moment they came on stage and started the gig, I knew this was an awesome band. Good songs, a solid guitar sound from Marr and a weird guy with a bunch of flowers in his back pocket and wearing a pair of glasses but with an extremely good voice and loads of charisma. From the first minute the crowd was totally into it.

I started buying the Smiths albums, played them always in my time as a deejay and I'm sure that this unique live performance changed my way of looking at music in general. It changed my life. It probably made me a better person too.

## ULSTER HALL

### 17 MAY 1984, BELFAST, UK

### BROMLEY BOW, AGE 18

I was a bit of a die-hard so got there early and secured a stage front position. They didn't disappoint live, tight as, not a lot of interaction but just brilliant. And, yeah, he had the gladioli! I went with a friend, Anthony, who played guitar in a band I was in. I played drums. We never made it, but we had a blast and got the girls! There was a deejay on RTÉ 2, Dave Fanning, who started playing The Smiths along with all the other cool Eighties bands – James, New Order, etc. – on a Sunday night. The first love of my life bought me their first album and I still treasure it.

### DAMIEN MAGUIRE

I saw The Smiths twice in Belfast, at the Ulster Hall and then at Whitla Hall in 1986. I don't remember much about Whitla Hall but remember very clearly the Ulster Hall gig. They opened with 'Please, Please, Please…', before going into 'William, It Was Really Nothing'. My cousin got in on the soundcheck, spoke to the band and got his photograph taken with all of them. He still brags about it.

### DAMEON PRIESTLY, AGE 18

A girl I knew called Anne taped her copy of the album for me. I still have that cassette. They instantly struck a chord with me. Their angst and sound, their stories and imagery, resonated with my 17-year-old state of mind. The bleak

pictures painted of Manchester life and seaside towns, along with darkly humorous lyrics, were perfect for those teens in Belfast who were of a similar mindset. I was also a huge James Dean fan. When I found out Morrissey was too and had written a book, *James Dean Is Not Dead*, I went out and bought a copy. I still have it. It prompted me, five years later, to write my degree thesis on Dean. Growing up during the Troubles in Belfast meant that we were starved of bands playing for years. So when they came, The Smiths always received the most enthusiastic of reactions. The 'melancholy fan' label normally associated with The Smiths was not in evidence at that concert, that's for sure.

I went to the gig with a girl called Julie Mills. We met at her house first and filled up on cans of Fosters (hey, it was the eighties!) We got to the Ulster Hall early enough to see the instantly forgettable Frank Chickens, an odd Japanese pop band. Our tickets were for the balcony, but we stayed downstairs and pushed our way to the front.

I bought a bunch of white lilies from the florist at the City Hall to show my allegiance. They lasted about 30 seconds into the first song. I danced, pogoed and sang all the way through. His voice was our voice. My mates were all 23 to 25 years of age. They'd had their time in the sun with the Pistols, The Clash and the rest. I loved all of those bands, but this was our time. I remember leaving the concert and getting a lift home from Julie's mum (we'd missed the last bus). When The Smiths returned in November

*Dameon Priestley's Ulster Hall ticket*

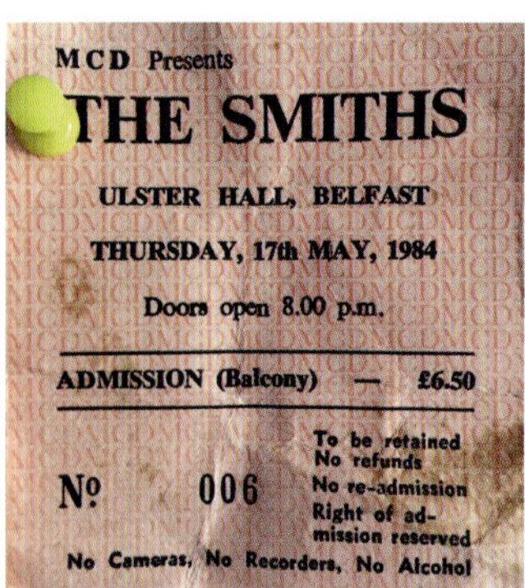

of the same year I was at the front of the queue. Reel around the fountain.

## IAN MCELHINNEY

My first concert: The Smiths at the Ulster Hall, Belfast. I had just turned 15 and had somehow discovered them via John Peel on the radio. I coerced my best friend (a rocker at heart) to tag along as my mum wouldn't let me go alone. I remember walking down the Dublin Road from the train station – black school trousers, black slip-on shoes with white socks and a shiny burgundy 'Ska jacket', trying not to break into an over excited run.

As most people say, they were like nothing before. It went by way too quickly. I had heard some of the songs but seeing them played live was a revelation. And so began my allegiance to the best band ever and I promised myself I would learn to play every song (having recently acquired a cheap guitar – I'm still learning…). The haircuts, the guitars and the flowers. I was hopelessly hooked. It was perfect. I must have glided home, high on life.

The next day I handed my ticket stub over the counter at my local record shop (to get the discount – was it ten per cent?) and bought *The Smiths*. I didn't have the wit to ask for it back. Schoolboy error… I have dined out many times on the 'what was your first gig?' discussions, and mostly people (the tasteful ones obviously) agree I was a very, very lucky boy. I still feel lucky. I still play that old record. I still adore The Smiths.

# SFX CENTRE

## 18 MAY 1984, DUBLIN, IRELAND

### NIAMH BARRETT, AGE 13

My first gig ever – whopper, right? Gladioli and dancing or, rather, writhing on the ground. Pure Morrissey magic. At 13, I was in heaven.

### PAUL LITTLE

I saw The Smiths a few times in Dublin in the eighties. They were absolutely brilliant live and Johnny Marr and Morrissey were amazing onstage. The first time, I went with my mate Giuseppe Roe. We were 14 or 15 and big into the sounds of the day – U2, Simple Minds, Big Country, etc. I have great memories of Morrissey jumping around the stage in the SFX Hall. It's the same venue and stage Bono jumped off in the 'Pride (In The Name Of Love)' video.

### JOE KELLY, AGE 16

I first heard about The Smiths in the summer of 1983 when my friend and neighbour Rob told me about a great new band his older brother had heard on the radio. It was The Smiths first session for *The John Peel Show* on BBC Radio 1 which he'd recorded on a cassette tape.

The house I grew up in in Dublin was filled with music. An English uncle brought us Beatles and Elvis records, and my three older sisters were buying classic albums from the sixties and seventies. Music radio and the weekly *Top Of The Pops* show were staples.

*SFX ticket May 1984 (Joe Kelly)*

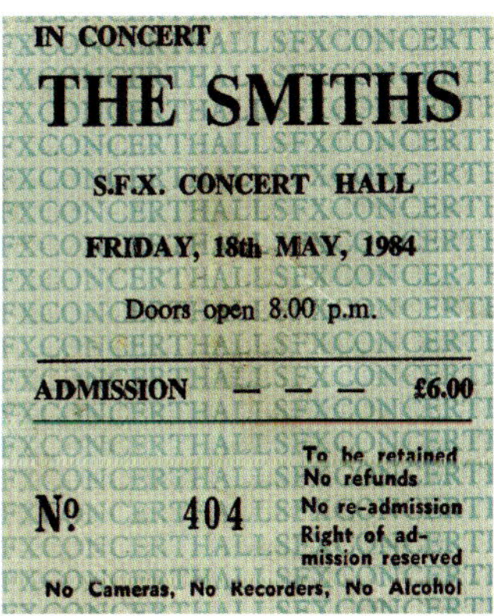

Aged 15, I was changing from a bowl-haircut chart fan into an angsty adolescent with a jar of hair-gel, and my musical tastes were changing from Top 40 pop to something with more of an edge. The Lotus Eaters' 'The First Picture Of You' single released that year was probably a kick-starter for me, and hearing The Smiths' session that same summer cemented my love for this alternative type of music. When the summer ended, another Smiths John Peel session was broadcast and recorded by Rob's brother. I worked out how to connect a ghetto blaster to our hi-fi system at home to make a tape-to-tape copy of the sessions for myself and super-indulge in listening to it.

Other bands that caught my ear soon after that were The Cure, Echo and The Bunnymen, Joy Division, New Order and Cocteau Twins. Of course, they were well-established bands with a back catalogue to explore, whereas The Smiths were new and now. An immediate bond was established. Their record releases were just starting, so there was very little material available yet.

Sometime later, one of The Smiths' concerts – from Derby – was broadcast on television by the BBC and I was enthralled watching it. When it was subsequently rebroadcast, I watched it in Rob's house because they had a black and white portable TV with a headphone socket and I was able to connect a cassette-recorder to the TV to record the sound.

My mother was originally from Southend-on-Sea in England. In February 1984 she was going there for her nephew's wedding, so I asked her to get me the just-released *The Smiths* album and the twelve-inch singles of 'This Charming Man' and 'What Difference Does It Make?' I was sufficiently unseasoned at that stage to go into Dublin city centre to look for them myself. To my endless

delight, my mother returned from Britain with all three records. However, the 'This Charming Man' one was the Francois Kevorkian remix version and the 'What Difference...' twelve-inch was the alternate one with Morrissey on the sleeve in place of Terence Stamp. I'd inadvertently stepped into the world of rarities at a tender age. I devoured all three records, and those formative months began my tendency to avidly read the covers and inner sleeves front-to-back while the record was playing and getting to know every aspect of the record – personnel, lyrics, recording studio and so on.

Those records and several subsequent Smiths records were bought in The Golden Disc record shop in Southend, which several years later would be featured in the video for Morrissey's 'Everyday Is Like Sunday' single.

In early 1984, I didn't know how or where to buy a Smiths t-shirt, so I decided to create my own. I bought a plain red t-shirt in a Dublin shop and went straight to a place in the ILAC Centre that would iron letters onto garments. I got 'THE SMITHS' pressed onto the t-shirt with a bubbly font in a curved formation. It doesn't look very rock 'n' roll now, but I knew no better back then. How proudly I wore the shirt that bore the name of my favourite band.

*Joe Kelly was at the SFX*

Around that time, it was announced that The Smiths would be playing a concert in Dublin. The venue was to be the Saint Francis Xavier Centre, a local community hall in the north inner city which was regularly used for rock concerts and known by gig promoters as the SFX Concert Hall. I was so excited and astonished that my favourite band was going to be playing in my city. I'd never been to a concert before, and my parents agreed to let me go. Rob was going too. My eldest sister must have got the tickets. She was a university student and had been to some concerts already. She was a trailblazer in my world. Being a community hall there was no bar there and no alcohol was sold, so there were no age restrictions, and therefore no issues with the 16-year-old me and my 15-year-old friend attending the concert.

The day of the concert, I was so excited, and after school was counting down the clock. My dad drove myself and Rob the four miles to the city centre and dropped us off on Gardiner Street around the corner from the venue on Sherrard Street. He was to pick us up from there afterwards. The hubbub of the people outside the hall increased my excitement. The guy on the door took our tickets and ripped off the stubs and gave us back the rest to keep, and we walked into what was the foyer. We passed through a set of double doors into the venue proper, taking off our jackets and tying them around our waists, me proudly displaying my red Smiths t-shirt. The long rectangular room was already quite full when we got in, and initially we stayed near the back. There was a small balcony above us, the middle bit was covered in and on the left and right sides of the balcony there was just enough room for a small amount of people to stand. I could see a couple of photographers up there. The room had a classic look of a community hall, with the high stage not filling the full width of the room to allow for a door either side at floor level.

Shortly after our arrival, a man with a voluminous beard walked onto the stage with an acoustic guitar and proceeded to play some songs. I don't remember his name, but the music did nothing for me: I was an indie kid now and this didn't fit the bill. I remember thinking that this was the first band I was watching at my first ever concert and it was a let-down.

After a break there was a second support: The Frank Chickens. I'd taped some of their stuff off the John Peel show, so my mood immediately perked up. They were quirky and fun and their set included the couple of songs I knew. Rob and I were still towards the back of the room, a little hesitant to move into the thickening throng in front of us.

A half an hour after The Frank Chickens finished, The Smiths walked onto the stage. The place went crazy as they started into 'Hand In Glove'. I was immediately spellbound. Nearly a year of fandom – a lifetime for a 16-year-old – was suddenly brought from written word, taped broadcasts and circular vinyl to living, breathing, heaving reality with tumultuous thunder – brought to life before my eyes and

*Morrissey & Johnny by Lee Thacker*

ears. The crowd arced into a mosh pit at the front, as if organised, yet it was a beautiful chaos that moved in waves, in and out, towards the stage.

We moved closer to the front, to the edge of the melee, to get a closer view of the band, and to attempt to dance ourselves. From the TV appearances and photos I'd seen, Morrissey often had flowers in his back pocket but here he seemed to have a whole branch of a tree coming out of his jeans, Johnny with his head flicks to arrange his fringe, Andy with his hefty bass and the high stage meaning Mike was half-hidden behind the drums. The voice, the words, and the odd dancing, the guitar riffs, the thumbing bass and the driving drum sounds forged into mesmerising music that captivated me for nearly an hour. I got a chance to catch my breath as the band left the stage after the main set, and there was that sense of wonder as to what would happen next. They came back onstage to an uproarious reception for an encore that included a reprise of 'Hand In Glove'. And then it was suddenly over.

As the band walked off the stage, the lights came on in the hall and the curtains were drawn across the stage. People started heading to the exits at the back and the room emptied quite quickly. But my dad wasn't due to pick us up for another half hour, so we waited in the hall rather than hang around outside. The few stragglers remaining started to line up at the door to the right of the stage, and when we saw the door open, we joined the queue. Within a couple of minutes, we were backstage in a small room.

The whole band were right there before our eyes. Morrissey was to the left talking to a guy in a wheelchair, while Johnny, Mike and Andy were standing around a small table in front of us. A shiver of excitement ran through me. We saw them signing people's tickets, so we approached and handed them our tickets as I tried to think of something to say. As they signed the tickets Johnny complimented me on my red t-shirt and Mike wrote 'Like the t-shirt' as he signed. There was a load of flyers around the floor for a student end-of-exam night out in a nearby hotel. I hastily reckoned that my ticket would be going into my scrapbook, so I'd need a second set of autographs to stick in there too, so I picked up one of the flyers and asked them to sign the blank back of that also. We then approached Morrissey, but he was still engrossed in conversation with the guy in the wheelchair and we didn't want to interrupt – well, not too much! We wouldn't have known what to say anyway, so we held out our autographed bits of paper, and he duly reached out and signed them for us.

We walked back into the main hall stunned by what had just happened. The merchandise stall at the back was being put away so I ran down and bought a 'This Charming Man' poster for 50p. We went outside a few minutes later and my dad was waiting there in his trusty Volkswagen Beetle. My passion for The Smiths only increased from then on and I obsessively bought every record as soon as I could, usually on the day of release, cycling into town or getting the bus and negotiating a journey home that wouldn't damage the precious cargo. That first concert experience had a profound effect on my life, cementing my love for music and live performance. I've been an avid gig-goer ever since, though alas, the hair-gel is no longer required.

### SEAMUS DUGGAN

I first saw The Smiths on *Top Of The Pops* performing 'This Charming Man' and the next morning I bought the twelve-inch. It immediately felt like one of those seismic events. The cooler (and older) kids might have had 'Hand In Glove' and even seen them play the Freshers' Ball in the JCR in Trinity the year before, but for most of us this was going to be the first chance to see The Smiths.

The crowd was one of the most mixed I had ever seen, with other dark-clad Bunnymen fans like me, ageing hippies, slightly less ageing punks and other, less defined groups of people. But many, many had flowers in their hair or pockets or hands.

Indeed, gardens on the routes to the SFX had been stripped of all sorts of plant life. A Smiths crowd were not a gardener's best friend. It was a celebration. Marr seemed like a member of a sixties band in shades and Byrds fringe, but Morrissey was Morrissey, in maternity shirt and with a bouquet in his back pocket. At one point Morrissey threw his shirt into the audience. My friend caught it but by the time he landed all that was left was a sleeve, which I had for years before it disappeared.

## SAVOY

### 20 MAY 1984, CORK, IRELAND

### COLM O'CALLAGHAN

It was shortly after midnight, early on Wednesday morning, July 29th, 1987, and it was Mark Cagney, host of *The Night Train* on RTÉ Radio 2FM who, as serenely as ever, broke the news. Home alone, and with the rest of my family off on holidays, I'd been in the habit of keeping the radio on longer and louder than usual – long enough, as it happened, to hear Cagney tell the nation's more urbane taxi drivers, shift workers and anoraks that Johnny Marr had left The Smiths. And he more-or-less left it at that, light on detail, didn't cite his sources and segued as seamlessly as he always did into his next track, which was more than likely a moderately left field, highly styled album cut, to which he was forever drawn. And, if I slept at all that night, I slept with my mouth open and my jaw hanging.

Cagney had one up on us. He'd either heard soundings of or had sight of that week's issue of the London-based music magazine, *New Musical Express*, in which one of its senior writers, Danny Kelly, citing reliable sources in Manchester, revealed that Morrissey, The Smiths' singer and Marr, the group's guitarist and co-writer, had fallen out and hadn't spoken in months. But while it was a terrific flyer, the story was vague enough on the future of the band and Kelly later admitted he may have 'augmented' his story with lines pulled from the back of his own head. The gut of the scoop was clear, though – on the cusp of the release of their fourth album, all was not well with The Smiths. And this time it was serious.

Although the influential British music weeklies – *NME, Melody Maker* and *Sounds* – all regularly hit the streets around central London by lunchtime on Tuesdays, it was usually Thursday morning or later before those titles were available on the shelves in Easons, on Patrick Street in Cork, where I routinely picked up mine. And so I had an anxious wait before I finally got my hands on *NME*'s speculative exclusive, headlined 'Smiths to split'.

History – and Johnny Rogan, the band's forensic biographer – now tells us that, although The Smiths weren't formally taken off of life-support by Morrissey until mid-September 1987, Marr confirmed directly to Kelly within days of his initial splash that yes, he'd left the group he founded in Manchester barely five years previously. And so, in its issue dated August 8th, 1987, Kelly had his second back-to-back Smiths scoop, this time flush with quotes from inside the band.

For six weeks that summer, my first as a university student, would-be music writer, part-time laundry worker and full-time dreamer, there was really only one story. One which, under sustained scrutiny, was scarcely believable in the first instance and which was always likely to end badly – few groups have, I think, fallen asunder as carelessly and as needlessly as The Smiths, undone in the end by the lack of clear decision-making and delegation that had, since the group's inception, characterised much of its off-stage activity.

The Smiths were the first band I so obsessively lived through and the first band I ever felt like I had shares in. I certainly spent enough on them and, because I'd invested so heavily in them in other respects as well, I tended to defer to Max Boyce's stock punchline when it came to analysing them – I know because I was there.

And I certainly was there, if not at the very start, then certainly close enough to it, having had my head turned as soon as I heard The Smiths on both Dave Fanning's Rock Show on RTÉ Radio 2, John Peel's BBC equivalent and, bizarrely, having caught sight of them on late night television performing 'This Charming Man' on a one-off European music initiative featuring emerging music from across the continent. Captured alongside a feeble, long-lost British outfit, The Immaculate Fools, and a number of freakish cross-continental acts trying, as can often be the case, just a tad too hard, The Smiths stood out as a distinctive star turn simply because, in the abject normality that defined every single aspect of them, they were clearly anything but normal.

I was there too in the old Savoy on Patrick Street when The Smiths played in Cork twice, on May 20th and November 18th, 1984, and when, within actual touching distance of them, they sealed the deal, almost face-to-face, as the most important and influential band of my generation.

Both of those shows took place as

I was gearing up to leave secondary school and, with half an eye and two working ears on what was around the corner, fancied myself as a veteran of the local music circuit, having already been to all of one indoor live show and a couple of random outdoor events. But although I'd been squirreling and collecting for a number of years, back-filling the gaps in my developing ELO library, acquiring and swapping new material as regularly as I could and rowing in squarely behind Sindikat, a band from our school who'd done the unthinkable and formed under our noses, The Smiths were the first group whose releases, always flagged well in advance in the music press, I regarded as genuine events and to which I counted down.

And in this respect, the radio was another vital spoke – Peel, and his long-time producer, John Walters, memorably hosted four separate Smiths radio sessions between 1983 and 1986 and, like Fanning, would play all of the group's releases well in advance of their availability in the shops. For which you'd have a second or third-hand cassette on eternal stand-by in the old three-in-one in case either of them dropped an unexpected pre-issue, without warning.

It was Fanning, of course, who alerted us to those first Smiths shows in Ireland – I still consider this sort of carry-on to define the term 'public service broadcasting' – when he announced that they were on their way to play dates in Belfast, Dublin and Cork in support of their debut album. And yet for all of the urgency that under-pinned

the band's recorded material, myself and my friend, Philip, didn't really know what to expect when we fetched up outside The Savoy on a Sunday evening in May 1984, in our long raincoats, tickets in hand and mad for road. But from early – and we were there very, very early – it was clear that The Smiths were much more than a little-known secret shared by a handful of us up on the northside.

One of the more interesting aspects of the band's history is how, throughout its career, it attracted fans from right across the social strata, much of it male-skewing and with a prominent contingent of hard shams in among the more introspective, centrally cast indie-kids. Among whom was another friend of mine, Marc Buckley, one of numerous acolytes who arrived at The Savoy clutching a bunch of freshly cut flowers and wearing a considerable quiff.

Philip and I soon found ourselves chatting to a pair of friendly girls we'd met on the tiled stairs, and, for whatever reason, we told them we were supporting The Smiths a little later. And there were, of course, numerous similarities between us and The Frank Chickens, the gobby Japanese lesbians who were *actually* due to open proceedings.

The Chickens, as with many of Peel's more random curios over the decades, sounded far better in theory that they did in practise and, with their unsteady backing tracks, loops and high-octane, skittish twin vocals, failed to convince the locals, who'd started to assemble in numbers by the time they'd finished a quite bizarre set. They left

*Morrissey & Marr by Lee Thacker*

the stage to the usual heckles and, responding to a not unreasonable suggestion from half-way back that they were, perhaps, not up to championship standard, replied – 'We think you're shit too' – before beating a hasty retreat under a hail of gob, never to be seen in Cork again. A scene we'd witness again, in the same venue and in much the same circumstances, before the year was out.

But once The Smiths took the stage to the jagged, slash-cut opening bars of 'Still Ill', and Morrissey emerged from the shadows, his outsized shirt already opened to the navel, The Frank Chickens had been consigned to the footnotes of what was to become a spectacular history. Over the course of a sharp, frenetic and powerful 16-song set, The Smiths just burned the house down. In the long and diverse history of live shows in Cork, it is easily among one of the most lethal. Because while that show has remained vivid in the memories of most of those who attended it, many of them left there that night intent on starting their own bands immediately afterwards, boldly going for it and just taking their chances. And those among the audience that were already involved in fledging groups around the city – and there were many – left with plenty of food for thought. If this was where the bar was now set, then what, really, was the point?

But although Morrissey so physically dominated that Cork show – and I couldn't believe how imposing he was, and how he so used his body for emphasis – neither could I get my head around how small and slight Johnny Marr was and how his nimble hands made one guitar sound like three. The songs were already well-known to anyone who'd bought the band's unconvincing debut album, *The Smiths*, and who was familiar with the terrific additional content on their singles. But they also introduced one new number, a protracted, funked-up, bass-prominent beauty called 'Barbarism Begins At Home', during which Morrissey baited the audience with flowers throughout the long instrumental passages and Andy Rourke stepped into the spotlight to reveal just how important his industry and frame of reference was to the band's sound. And we were just learning all of the time.

### BERNARD O'FLYNN

The Frank Chickens were two Japanese girls who were truly dreadful. The Smiths played a stormer, mostly stuff from *The Smiths* album. 'Hand in Glove' is my standout memory. Morrissey wasn't content with a bunch of flowers in his back pocket and came on stage with a large tree branch, although he did throw a bouquet to the crowd. A mate of mine caught one flower but was promptly bitten on the wrist by a girl who wanted it.

My mate suggested we go to their hotel, Jurys, after the gig. Personally I thought this was a bit suspect but went along. Morrissey had gone to bed, but Mike Joyce and Andy Rourke were chatting to fans. I wound up having a long conversation with Johnny Marr about guitars. He left me with the fact that he would be using a green

Telecaster on *Top Of The Pops* the following week. He did.

## 'HEAVEN KNOWS I'M MISERABLE NOW'
### RELEASED 21 MAY 1984

One of only two Smiths 45s to reach the UK Top 10, at number 10. 'Heaven Knows I'm Miserable Now' featured famed 1960s football pools winner Viv Nicholson on the picture sleeve. The song seared its way into the public consciousness, forever branding Smiths fans 'miserable'.

### ANA MARIA NAZARIO

I wouldn't be living in Manchester if it weren't for The Smiths. I was a 14-year-old high school kid, living in the Philippines, when I first got to hear The Smiths 'Heaven Knows I'm Miserable Now' on the radio. I can't remember exactly which radio station it was, but it's very likely WXB 102, the Station That Dares To Be Different. Filipino teenagers at the time adored that station; it wasn't always easy to get because their signal was weak, especially where I lived in Lagro (Quezon City). But whenever I could get a signal, they always played unusual music from the UK and America, ie. not the love songs and Top 40 hits you'd hear on commercial radio stations.

When I heard 'Heaven Knows I'm Miserable Now' for the first time ever, I immediately fell in love with it. There's something about that title alone, and the lyrics, 'In my life, why do I give valuable time, to people who don't care if I live or die?' that spoke loudly to my teenage self. And of course, Morrissey's voice gave it that sense of frustration and anger, and that feeling of wanting to get away, but also that feeling of helplessness.

I'd always wanted to leave the Philippines; now that I'm older, I realise I never really felt at home there and I wanted to be somewhere where I could be myself. Where, though? The second Smiths song I heard on the radio was 'Girlfriend In A Coma'. Again, I was intrigued by its lyrics:

*There were times when I could have murdered her*

*But, you know, I would hate anything to happen to her*

I thought, 'Wow, that man's hurting. That's *love.*'

Those were the two Smiths songs I fell in love with as soon as I heard them. I had to find out more about this band. In the Philippines in the eighties, we had a music magazine called *Jingle*, similar to Smash Hits, and that's where I found out that The Smiths were from this place called Manchester…

I started getting passionate about not just The Smiths but also about Manchester as a place I could aim to live in. I bought a Smiths t-shirt from an eighties shop called Top 40 and wore my passion with pride. But then, not long after that, it was all over. Sadly, The Smiths were no more.

In 1989, I finally left the Philippines and moved to the Middle East to join my mum, who was working in Abu Dhabi as a nurse. To my extreme disappointment, the move wasn't what I was hoping it would be.

*Heaven Knows I'm Miserable Now*

*Ana Maria Nazario discovered The Smiths growing up in the Philippines*

*Lana Menges read about The Smiths in Rolling Stone*

It didn't make me happy. In fact, (heaven knows) I was miserable and got very depressed. Until I discovered The Stone Roses, another Manchester band, who helped me get my focus back, gave me a renewed purpose in life, and saved me from going insane. (But that's for another book…)

Fast forward to 1996 and I am married to a Manc, I have moved to Manchester and, finally, I have found the place where I belong! This is the place I dreamt about. This is where The Smiths are from.

In 2015, I met my first Smith: Mike Joyce. I cried. I simply couldn't believe a member of the band I loved many, many years ago, and the band I was passionate about as a kid, was right in front of me! And he was so nice to me, too. People often say, never meet your heroes, because you might be disappointed, but this hero of mine, standing here before me, was simply the loveliest musician you could ever meet. This, truly, was Manchester! This is where dreams can come true.

Not long after that, I met Johnny Marr at his son's band's gig in town. And then two years later, in March 2017, I met the lovely and super funny Andy Rourke, with massive thanks to The Smiths original drummer, Simon 'Funky Si' Wolstencroft.

My teenage dream is almost complete. Almost. I'm still hoping and praying that someday, I'll get a chance to meet Morrissey too before I leave this planet. This year, I'll be celebrating my thirtieth year of life in Manchester. My home. I have been living the dream for the past 30 years.

Thank you very much, The Smiths. Rest in peace, Andy Rourke.

## ROLLING STONE MAGAZINE

### LANA MENGES

I first heard of The Smiths when I was in high school (in the Washington DC suburbs) through an article on the band in the 7 June 1984 issue of *Rolling Stone* magazine. Intrigued, I knew I needed to get their first album. As far as I knew, they weren't being played on any local radio stations. However, FM station Q107 was running a summer contest, 'The 7 O'clock Album Attack', wherein listeners had to pay close attention to everything the station played between 7pm and 7.40pm and then phone in, be the 107th caller, and answer a question correctly, such as 'what song did we play after so-and-so?' The winner each night then had to name as many artists and album titles as possible within 15 seconds, and would win all those albums from a local record store chain.

After making a list (The Smiths' debut album was at the top of mine) and practising my fast talking, I started tuning in to the station every night. On the eighth or ninth or 9th night, I won! I rattled off twelve albums to the DJ and went to the shop to pick them up at the end of June.

Listening to The Smiths' eponymous first album the next day, I was hooked. I had never heard any band like them before. I didn't realise it at the time, but that first album really spoke to me as a Gen X'er full of apathy and dread over the depressive, screwed up nature of the world of the 1980s. I knew I would be a fan forever.

## GLC JOBS FOR A CHANGE FESTIVAL, JUBILEE GARDENS

### 10 JUNE 1984, LONDON, UK

### MARTIN RODDY

The Greater London Council (GLC) Leader Ken Livingstone put on a free gig around the back of the GLC buildings. The same people I walked back with from the Essex Uni gig with in February went down to see them. Billy Bragg was the support act and unbelievably The Smiths were the support act to Mari Wilson and The Wilsations! 1984 was one of those 'Which side are you on?' years politically and living down south I was surrounded by bloody awful Tories (and still am). Ken displayed the unemployment figures (over three million) on the roof of the GLC building facing Parliament as a poke in the eye to Thatcher. Attending this gig felt important. The Smiths were an outsider's band, but when you were in the crowd it felt like a movement, or a scene that I preferred others not to understand. We left after Mari Wilson's second song. Why wouldn't you?

### LANCE GILLETT

Someone did a striptease after climbing up the side of a building, stealing Mozzer's limelight.

### PETER GALE, AGE 19

There was a naked man dancing on a ledge, and a lot of the crowd were watching him instead of the band. I also went to see Altered Images before then at Hammersmith Palais and, apparently, they supported, along with Roman Holiday, but I can't remember them.

### KAREN KELLY, AGE 19

It was a day of celebration in Jubilee Gardens, and they played in the evening on the same bill as Mari Wilson and Captain Sensible, although he played in another area in the grounds. It was a brilliant day. The Smiths were really good and the crowd loved them. I can't remember the playlist, but I knew the tracks at the time and they stole the show.

I was more of a UB40 and Style Council fan and didn't realise until many years later how much Morrissey and The Smiths would come to mean to me. After losing my husband 15 years ago, 'You're The One For Me, Fatty' and 'Bigmouth Strikes Again' made me laugh and brought me out of my grief. A few years back I saw the

*The Smiths at the GLC Jobs For A Change festival (Andy Coles)*

Stone Roses (another grief breaker) and Johnny Marr at Finsbury Park. It was like living my teenage years again, hearing The Smiths' tunes.

### CHRIS MADDEN

The Smiths were playing in a beautiful setting staged in this courtyard at County Hall. The Redskins were on there as well. I hitched down to see that. I was having a chat with my dad a few years ago and he said, 'You used to just disappear. I knew you were going off to see bands, but I didn't realise you were hitchhiking. Otherwise, we would have given you the train fare.'

It was guitar music. It was euphoric. The music was perfect for the lyrics and to this day 'The Boy With The Thorn In His Side' is still a record that I go back to. They looked so cool. They were like a mixture of The Beatles and the Stones for our generation. Who else was there who was as culturally significant at that time? They were really, really out there. They looked and sounded unique and stylistically good.

My perception of them is that they were coming from the left field, the ambiguous sexuality. They said it's all right for a young man to be fey and in touch with his feminine side, to be in touch with literature and poetry and art and looking good and using really cultural signifiers. Morrissey's gone from there to now making proclamations about organisations and people who come from those organisations which seem to be diametrically opposed to what he once was. But I'm looking at Morrissey through the prism of what I believe he used to represent. Do we have a right to change our minds? Back in those days, he was carrying a flag for the notion of a type of Britishness, which was very, very nostalgic, very parochial, and perhaps that's where he's stuck at.

### EVE WENTWORTH

The festival was free. The bill also featured Billy Bragg, The Redskins, Mari Wilson, Misty in Roots and Hank Wangford, who got beaten up by some skinheads that day, as did The Redskins – there were a couple of fairly alarming fights. The sound was surprisingly good for an outdoor gig and the crowd was insane. I remember thinking some guy dancing up on a high ledge was going to fall off and either crack his head on the pavement or get trampled by skinheads.

There were flowers everywhere – flying around, crushed underfoot, tossed overhead. I remember the band and Morrissey especially getting absolutely pelted by them at some points and wondered if they were second-guessing that whole flower gimmick. He had daffodils in his back pocket that time, but they didn't last the whole show.

I'm just five foot three so I didn't have a completely unobstructed view of everything – I've spent a lot of concert time over the years staring at the back of some taller guy's jacket – but I had a pretty good view for most of it and could hear just fine. The set list was mostly familiar. I don't know if we knew 'Nowhere Fast' yet, but the rest were the hits and album cuts.

'Girl Afraid', 'This Charming Man', 'Heaven Knows I'm Miserable Now', 'Hand in Glove' – pretty much all of 'em (at the time). The crowd was loving it.

This was the first outdoor festival-type concert I'd ever attended in the UK. It was a bit chaotic, but I chalked that up to the fact that it was free, not heavily policed and involved political stuff as well as music. A lot of us in the crowd had been to gigs and events involving the miners' strike over the previous months, and some of the bands had been doing shows in support of the miners as well, so there was a bit of overlap there and a protest vibe at the show as a result.

The Smiths did more than one encore, and Morrissey himself might have been involved in the encore chanting at some point, which surprised me. He wasn't very chatty otherwise; unlike Bragg whose stage patter was – then as now – copious and legendary.

After it was over, I remember picking my way through what seemed like a mile of mangled flowers in the gutters and on the sidewalks as I left the South Bank and headed for the Tube. I didn't have a camera with me that day but in retrospect that part might have been the most 'Instagram-worthy' part of the whole experience. I can still see flower petals scattered everywhere and I was picking bits of greenery out of my boot chains for days after. It was definitely one of the more memorable shows of my college years. I still think of it anytime I see flowers tossed around stage or into a crowd at a concert.

STEPH ROCHE

I was 16 or whatever, just before sixth form. Everyone used to go on about John Peel, but I was not a fan. But I used to hear him talking about The Smiths, The Smiths, The Smiths. And then we had a rag day. And this boy, who was a year older than me, was dressed up in an old vintage shirt and National Health glasses, and he had daffodils. I was into the sixties stuff anyway, and I was dressed as a sixties Mod, and I just fell in love with him. I basically found the daffodils and he said, 'They're my daffodils,' and I said 'hello' and that was it. And we were partners for a year. He got me into The Smiths because he was dressed as Morrissey and so we went to the gigs together.

I wrote to Morrissey early on and he wrote back – twice! I couldn't believe it. It was all teenage angst stuff. He obviously could relate to it. He sent me badges and things and one of the posters was the 'Heaven Knows I'm Miserable Now' one. It said, 'Dear Steph, Be happy, love longing Morrissey.' When you're 16 or whatever, it means a lot and I won't have a bad word said against Morrissey. I don't care what people think. I just think he's a good person and I think he's got a huge heart.

And then it was all go, really, with The Smiths. I think that must have been just before the first album came out because people had heard of him before. Then I became totally obsessed.

I only saw them twice. The first time would have been the famous free GLC concert with the naked man up on the balcony. It was a fantastic atmosphere. There

*Darren Wilkinson was there with girlfriend Bev*

*Carlisle Market Hall ticket (Peter Martin)*

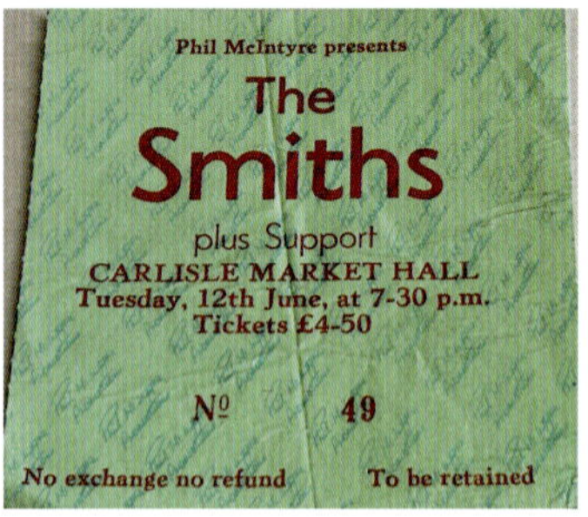

*Peter Martin's original gladioli t-shirt*

were a lot of skinheads around and I think the Redskins had a problem with them.

I live in West Byfleet in Surrey so it's only half an hour on a train to Waterloo, so we were up in London a lot. I got the train up to the South Bank Centre and walked through and I remember Ken Livingstone doing all the speeches and me loving it. It was just how things were, the battle against Thatcher and all the rest of it, but now, looking back, it just seems so radical. We can't even imagine anybody trying to organise something like that now. I mean, there's one or two things about Palestine or whatever, but it seems a lot more low-key than the fight for the GLC was at the time and the miners' strike and all that sort of thing. Also, it was to do with the UK and our politics, not that overseas stuff. We had our own problems… and still do!

I went on CND marches and all that. You could walk down Downing Street before they put the barriers up and just shout at Number 10: 'Maggie, Maggie, Maggie!' I remember doing it myself with a group of people we picked up called 'Gays Against The Bomb', who had this huge banner.

## MARKET HALL

### 12 JUNE 1984, CARLISLE, UK

### PETER MARTIN

Where to begin? The beginning, maybe? I'd heard the name, probably heard them on Peel, etc., but the first time I really took notice

was when 'This Charming Man' burst onto our screens on *The Tube* one Friday in October 1983. I went to Volume in Newcastle the very next day to purchase it on seven-inch and twelve-inch and 'Hand In Glove' on seven-inch. I was smitten.

Later that month we went to London on a sixth form trip and I bought the New York mixes on twelve-inch and the original gladioli t-shirt in yellow. From then on, I bought everything, collected everything. Although it seems like no time now, it seemed like forever then, as I waited over six months to see them live. I bought four tickets at Virgin in Eldon Square – for me, Belly, Dixon and my sister's boyfriend Paul, who agreed to drive if we paid for petrol and bought his ticket. A great deal. The Market Hall had sky lights and, as it was the height of summer, it was light when they came on. Most bands you see in the dark but seeing The Smiths in the light made perfect sense. The whole thing was a blur. I would class it as one of my favourite ever gigs, but in reality I cannot recall much about it.

### DARREN WILKINSON, AGE 18

The Smiths' two previous releases had passed me by, but I was instantly grabbed by that repeating guitar riff that runs all the way through 'What Difference Does It Make?' I loved it then and I still do. To my absolute delight the band announced a gig in my hometown of Carlisle at the iconic Market Hall, which described it exactly as it was! Glass-roofed so it never went dark if the gig was in the summer months, it had a high cast iron roof more likely to be found in a railway station, making acoustics a nightmare. The people of Carlisle loved it and reminisce about it still.

It was two days after my 18th birthday when The Smiths arrived to a rapturous welcome. I was there with my girlfriend Bev, aged 16. They opened with 'Nowhere Fast' and the crowd went nuts. I remember Morrissey leaving the stage and the band doing an acoustic version of 'William, It Was Really Nothing' before Johnny appealed to the crowd to behave or Morrissey wouldn't continue, followed by starting the song again. After three encores which included 'What Difference Does It Make?' the gig was over. Everyone spilled out of the side doors into Market Street. The Smiths headed off to Scotland. I was hooked.

<h2 style="color:green">BARROWLANDS BALLROOM</h2>

### 13 JUNE 1984, GLASGOW, UK

### ANNE MCGLASHAN, AGE 17

I was with my mate Christine. I had been to Barrowlands a few times before, but this is the first time there was a queue, all the way around the corner. We must have been early, but we stopped to have a wee roll up on the way there. There were people in the queue holding bunches of gladioli. Everyone was buzzing – the atmosphere was electric. It was so packed in the hall – really busy, tight and sweaty. We got a bit excited as we were sure we spotted Elizabeth Fraser from the Cocteau Twins a wee bit in front of us,

although this was never confirmed. During the gig we could not believe how Morrissey's jeans stayed on. There were so many hands tugging on his jeans it seemed impossible for them not to have been pulled right off!

While waiting for The Smiths, the girl next to Christine was asking her if she had any liquids in her bag as the girl's leg was soaking wet. 'Nah,' says Christine, 'No liquids.' It wasn't until later, when we managed to squeeze back to the Ladies and Christine pulled her industrial size tin of hairspray from her bag only to find it empty, did we realise the cause of the cold wetness spreading down the girl's leg.

### STEPHEN MATHISON

I was introduced to The Smiths' music by a school friend at a party. Their music was totally different to any other band around at that time. I wasn't sure if I liked them at first but there was something about the contrast between the upbeat, jingling guitars and the mournful but poetic lyrics. I missed their first gig in Glasgow but was there when they returned to play the iconic Barrowland Ballroom.

It was a warm June evening and myself and my pal joined the queue to get in, where there were mumblings about the gig starting late. Sure enough, I went up to the door and saw a notice advising that, 'The Smiths are in London recording for *Top Of The Pops*, they'll be here ASAP.'

The doors eventually opened and everyone piled in. The mood was not a happy one. Back in '84 there were still a lot of punks knocking

*Anne McGlashan was a fan from early on*

*Stephen Mathison remembers Morrissey getting a traditional Barras 'welcome' for The Smiths turning up late*

around. But the drink was flowing and the mood lifted slighted. After a delay that seemed like hours the support band, The Telephone Boxes, entered stage left. They went into their first song and the punks in the mosh pit and beyond 'welcomed' them to the Barrowlands with a hail of lager, plastic bottles and spit. It didn't get any better. They were pretty awful and I'm sure they were just as glad to finish their set as the audience were.

There was another break while the roadies got everything ready for The Smiths. When they eventually came on stage it was late and the audience were pretty drunk and extremely pissed off. The opening number didn't last long as Morrissey was soon covered in the same 'welcome' the support act got. He stormed off and it was left to one of the roadies to try and calm the crowd. He too got covered! The crowd demanded a show, they had waited hours for it and they weren't

going anywhere.

The Smiths returned and what a show it was. Morrissey was magic, he sang and danced around the stage whipping the crowd up with fabulous renditions of 'Reel Around The Fountain', 'Suffer Little Children', 'Hand In Glove' and 'What Difference Does It Make?' It was a cracking gig, despite starting hours late.

### STEVIE WALKER

My second time of seeing them and I have never experienced the like of the Barrowland gig before or since. It was more like a cult or spiritual gathering. Typical Glasgow, they sang en masse to every tune. 'William, It Was Really Nothing' was being debuted that night and went down immensely. Morrissey copped an eyeful of spit and rightly threw a wobbly. The roadie came out to warn us. It was a moment out of step to be truthful as the gig was rocking. I remember Marr looking at Rourke and his face was a picture – a bit like a kid in a sweetie shop. I don't think they had experienced such love before. Bodies were getting pulled out all over the place with exhaustion.

## CAIRD HALL

### 15 JUNE 1984, DUNDEE, UK

### JAN BURNETT

Seeing The Smiths twice, in hindsight, was rather an honour. I missed them at Dundee University – if I was going to go to that, I would have been more interested

*Flyer for the June 1984 Dundee show (with the incorrect date) (Jan Burnett)*

in The Red Guitars. 'Good Technology' was so, erm, good. My then girlfriend went to that gig with her dad.

The first and second time for me was at the Caird Hall, Dundee, my hometown and apparently one of the band's favourite venues. This is possibly confirmed by Morrissey playing a few solo shows there. The second show was good but unremarkable to my ears and they stayed at the posher Swallow Hotel just past Invergowrie. We had no chance of meeting them, unlike the first time.

The show was great, manic and hot. The band stayed at the Angus Hotel, now knocked down. That's where all the 'stars' stayed – Duran Duran, Kim Wilde, Howard Jones. We hung out after the show outside the Angus, hoping for a glimpse of the band. Way up high we could see curtains twitch and suddenly a string of various beads were launched down on us by the band, necklaces thrown to them earlier in the night. They were up to high jinks.

Friendly shouting and jaunting continued and, in the wee small hours, the band appeared to the remaining five or six of us hanging around outside. They were chatty, funny and rather aghast that we had hung about this long. All night I had held under my arm the recently-released US twelve-inch remix of 'This Charming Man'. Johnny told me they didn't want it to come out, 'But I'll sign it anyway'. In fact, all four of them signed it (I don't think Morrissey signs Smiths records anymore). We got our autographs – getting pictures wasn't really a thing then – and they headed back in, and we went home and stayed up all night chatting.

Of course, 'Everyday Is Like Sunday' is about Dundee, but then everyone says it's about their town.

### DEREK MOIR

The Smiths did a small tour of Scotland, and we went to see them in Dundee. I had been drinking a bottle of red wine, very unusual for a working-class youth but inspired by Moz's choice of tipple in Ormskirk. At the end of the gig, we hung round. Johnny Marr remembered us from Ormskirk. He invited me to join him in smoking a massive Camberwell carrot, but I declined, as I don't even smoke cigarettes. He then said we could be on the guest list for the rest of the Scottish dates. I was that excited – and pissed/stoned – that I put forward an entourage of the grooviest 25 people I knew. They weren't impressed when we turned up to Aberdeen next day. Soundman Grant Showbiz and the band stood on the steps of the gig and read the riot act to those that had misplaced guest list intentions and refused any further communication with such people – us! I was so embarrassed – it was really only the original four of us that were there on a Monday night after work. Nevertheless, we sneaked in. Next night, we travelled up to Inverness and met them to apologise as they arrived. It was sold out but they let us watch the gig from the side stage. It's a great venue and wow, how gracious.

## CAPITOL THEATRE

### 16 JUNE 1984, ABERDEEN, UK

### JEFF BRUCE, AGE 13

I had discovered them via the Derby Assembly Rooms gig which aired on the BBC. This was my first major concert. My mum bought two tickets from the box office at the venue. I remember the intro music of 'Romeo And Juliet' and then the band blasting into 'Nowhere Fast'. The gig flew by, but I remember the stage being invaded a few times.

## EDEN COURT

### 17 JUNE 1984, INVERNESS, UK

### DONNA GOODALL

As a teenager, I listened to John Peel and in 1983, I heard 'What Difference Does It Make?' and 'Reel Around The Fountain', and that was me hooked. I had never heard anything like it. They got me through my teenage years, the loss of my mum at 17 and they really have been the soundtrack to most of my life... and I am 51... very corny.

It is still very fresh. We were in the second row. The lights dimmed, the orchestral music started playing... and we ran to the front of the stage. It was amazing. Later on, Morrissey took his shirt off and threw it into the crowd. My friend Jackie caught it, but by the time we got back to our seats, all she had was a sleeve. Anyway, it was a fabulous night... we were at the front, got to hold Morrissey's arms and got pulled away by a security man... all the usual teenage stuff. Jackie split the shirt between our group of six or seven. I kept my bit stapled to my diary.

We also noticed two boys at the gig, who stood out because they were dressed really trendy. Three years later, I met a boy called Steve, who I remembered from the Smiths concert. He was one of the trendy two. We started a friendship and one day he surprised me with something... a piece of Morrissey shirt. It was the same shirt my friend had caught all those years back. He had a whole front section. We've been married 26 years now. I carry my piece of shirt with me everywhere in my purse for luck. It's been on driving tests and been taken to interviews and exams. I think it brought me a lot of luck. Steve sacrificed a piece of his for part of a handbag he had made for me. So the Smiths and Morrissey are very special. We have seen Johnny Marr and Morrissey locally and in Aberdeen and Glasgow since.

## OPERA HOUSE

### 20 JUNE 1984, BLACKPOOL, UK

### STEPHANIE HAUBER

I don't have a ticket stub, just memories I will never forget. My older sister's friend rang and asked if I wanted a ticket. She had a spare and knew I liked Morrissey. I had been to one gig before that with the same older crowd. The hardest part was getting past my dad. I was

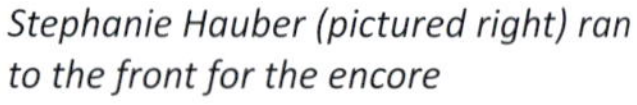

*Stephanie Hauber (pictured right) ran to the front for the encore*

dressed head to foot in my sister's clothes to look older. With girls my age it was probably more the teen crush, as Morrissey was uber-cool and I thought he looked like a modern James Dean.

The atmosphere was amazing. When I thought the gig had finished, I was about to start leaving when they did an encore. I ran screaming down to the front, or as near as I could get. My husband was a 'proper fan' who knows all the lyrics and everything about The Smiths. He is so jealous I got to see them.

### DEBBIE PARKINSON, AGE 16

I only really went because this bloke called David Smith was going on the minibus from Preston and I fancied him. I got on this minibus to go and see The Smiths and watched a bit of the gig, and it was great. Then I went off to the toilets for a wee where I bumped into Su Pollard of *Hi-de-Hi!* fame. She admired my outfit.

I had on a pair of brown paisley pyjamas in brushed cotton, like your grandad would wear, that I'd taken in and made into a skintight pair of leggings. I really can't remember if I enjoyed the gig. I do remember that it didn't happen with David Smith. He already had a girlfriend.

### STEPHEN CHRISTIAN

When Smiths tickets went on sale, a friend and I went into town to buy our tickets from the Opera House box office. It was probably my idea to take them to the local library and use their photocopying machine to make duplicates. The original tickets were poorly printed and on basic white paper, so our duplicates looked pretty much identical to the originals. We ended up with five or six sheets of A4 full of 'tickets'. We took them home and I had the genius idea of using a pin to perforate them, so the stubs were easy to pull apart from the main ticket.

We never set out to be counterfeiters, and I don't remember making lots of, if any, money from selling the tickets, but I do remember avoiding sitting in seats E23 and E24 on the night of the concert. We had given away most of the tickets, all for the same two seats, to a grateful bunch of mates and saw many of them at the concert, so the tickets were obviously good enough to fool the door staff and get them into the show. Was the concert a sell-out? It was filled beyond capacity!



*Stephen Christian's ticket for the Blackpool gig. There were several tickets for this one seat*

*Stephen Christian was at the Blackpool gig*

## CORNWALL COLISEUM

### 22 JUNE 1984, ST AUSTELL, UK

### GEORGE E HARRIS

I finished school listening to and was part of the 2-Tone tribe, very much into bands like The Beat, The Specials and The Selecter, the more political end of the music. I was a young socialist with ideals. Then I switched to being a goth and a fan of things like Echo and The Bunnymen, Teardrop Explodes and earlier Bauhaus. It was during this period that The Smiths emerged, a bright hope in a field of drudge.

I bought the first album and the singles and became obsessed with the music and imagery. I got fed up with the goth look. The indie thing had taken me. It was bright and it was speaking about us in our bedrooms, the loneliness and all that. Then I became vegetarian because of The Smiths – well, Morrissey.

Looking back on it, I think one of the reasons I got into The Smiths was the search for working class heroes and how they wrote songs about that as well as the imagery from the kitchen sink films of the past. It reflected lives in a way which could be seen as political. When Morrissey was pushing the *Meat Is Murder* thing, it appealed to my idealism. I still have that; except I do eat some meat these days on health grounds. Unfortunately, Morrissey has lost it these days, and his views make me vomit. Morrissey is now dead to me.

### NIGEL PENGELLY

I got Morrissey's shirt when he threw it into the crowd, and I met Andy Rourke after the gig at the disco around the corner.

## CND FESTIVAL

### 23 JUNE 1984, GLASTONBURY FESTIVAL, UK

### NICK FOSTER, AGE 16

I originally got into The Smiths via the John Peel show on Radio 1. I was a big Bunnymen fan, but the release of 'This Charming Man' was like nothing I had heard before. I went out and bought the single, then stayed up to watch a live gig on BBC2. I found out that they were playing Glastonbury and persuaded my parents to let me go with my best mate, Jer. We had a fantastic time, but The Smiths were the crowning point. We were of an age where we stayed at the front of the stage regardless of who was on. The Smiths came on early due to a swap with Amazulu. The set was very short – 30 minutes – but the reaction was incredible, with thousands of young fans attempting to climb up the pyramid stage to reach their heroes. Opening with 'William, It Was Really Nothing' it was a hit-packed set, which included B-side 'Jeane'. It was over far too quick, leaving us elated but also slightly deflated after all the excitement. The festival still had a day or so to go but it felt like it had already peaked.

### GREG ARCHER

I was eagerly awaiting The Smiths' performance at Glastonbury, but their performance was cut short due to a problem with Amazulu turning up late. I also saw them at Cardiff Uni in 1984. That was a fantastic gig and to be feet away from Morrissey and Marr was spine-tingling.

## PAUL HOWARD


I saw The Smiths nine times between December 1983 and November 1986. Every gig was an exuberant milestone – but the band's one and only appearance at the Glastonbury Festival is an extraordinary highlight of my life.

Earlier than advertised, The Smiths appeared suddenly on the Pyramid Stage at about 5.30pm and me and my three pals moved towards the front. Morrissey greeted the crowd with 'Hello, you wild rock 'n' rollers!' and they launched into the then new song called 'Nowhere Fast'.

When they began 'Barbarism Begins At Home', my pals, Paul Carolan and Mark Walshe, pushed me by the soles of my shoes up the greasy iron slope which, in those days, served as a security barrier. I was determined to shake Johnny's hand. I knew that his hand would soon become free to shake, due to Mike Joyce and Andy Rourke's imminent drum and bass workout at the end of this particular song. I got more than I bargained for.

Johnny came forward and shook my hand – and then, tightening his grip, hoisted me onto the stage! Two security guards ran over to eject me. Johnny told them to leave me alone. In a moment of pure, surrealistic magic, I danced around in a circle with Morrissey and Marr in front of tens of thousands of people. The crowd reaction was absolutely extraordinary!

My third pal, Jo Clack, who had moved back from the stage, saw what was happening and took a few pictures when he saw my gradual ascent.

When the song finished, I hugged Johnny, and, in a moment of inexplicable madness, I simply shook Morrisey's hand! Who does that? Everybody hugs Morrissey! I slid down the greasy slope. They played one more number, 'Hand In Glove', whereupon other people (without Johnny's assistance) clambered onto the stage. The set was then cut short.

The very next day we found a bootleg of the performance for sale on the festival site. You can hear the crowd's response to the unfolding drama… and also their response to my swift and ignoble slide down the greasy slope. You can find the same recording on *YouTube*. It's genuinely hilarious!

Years later, Angie Marr made public some photographs that she had taken from the sound desk. I mentioned in the comments that I was 'The Kid' in the photos that Johnny had often mentioned in interviews. The next day I received a beautiful message from Johnny.

Ten years after receiving that message, I queued in line to meet Johnny at Rough Trade on Brick Lane. When I told him of our previous encounter, Johnny shot back with, 'It's Paul, right?' I was absolutely staggered.

Others have laid claim to be 'The Kid' – but they are arriviste chancers. I was the lucky recipient of Johnny's invitation. Unequivocally and categorically!

In later years, Glastonbury host Michael Eavis was asked who his dream Saturday night headline act would be. Without missing a beat, he replied that it would be a reunited Smiths – as he believed

*The Smiths at Glastobury (Paul Howard)*

*'The Kid' caught up with Johnny at Rough Trade (Paul Howard)*

their original appearance had changed how the festival was perceived.

## PEEL SESSION, MAIDA VALE STUDIOS
### 1 AUGUST 1984, LONDON, UK

The band's third Peel Session saw them record 'William, It Was Really Nothing', 'Nowhere Fast', 'Rusholme Ruffians' and 'How Soon Is Now?' for broadcast on 9 August 1984.

Morrissey: Those sessions almost caught the very heart of what we did – there was something messy about them, which was very positive. People are so nervous and desperate when they do those sessions, so it seems to bring the best out of them.

*William, It Was Really Nothing*

*William Smith's wife Michaela was wearing a Meat is Murder t-shirt when they first met*

## 'WILLIAM, IT WAS REALLY NOTHING'
### RELEASED 20 AUGUST 1984

Reaching number 17 in the UK, 'William, It Was Really Nothing' had already been part of the band's live set over the preceding months.

### WILLIAM SMITH

My wife was wearing a *Meat Is Murder* t-shirt when first we met. I had no idea she'd go on to become both a Smith and a vegan. Or that she'd propose marriage with a presentation box containing a ring and a picture of Morrissey topless on *Top Of The Pops*, 'Marry Me' writ large on his puny chest. Some girls

are bigger than others. And so it was, in August 2014, 30 years after its release, that we walked 'down the aisle' at Blacksmith's Gretna Green to the opening strains of 'William, It Was Really Nothing' – and the rain falls hard on a Dumfries town. This was indeed my life.

Sure, life imitates art, and The Smiths wore their art on their sleeves. And impressions tend to last when you're an impressionable teen. I'm older now (and a clever swine) but I'm not ashamed to say we still have Smiths posters adorning our walls at home: *Meat Is Murder* in the kitchen; *The Queen Is Dead* (RIP Alain Delon, unvanquished face of French film); *Rank* (RIP Alexandra Bastedo, actress, writer, vegetarian and animal welfare activist); and the reissue of *William* (RIP Billie Whitelaw, *Charlie Bubbles, Omen*, Beckett collaborator) in the bedrooms, each representing a world beyond the world of the record. In the living room, above the turntable, a composite picture of all 23 singles' cover stars.

Halfway in between, there's a framed print of the Paul Slattery photo taken from backstage right at Glastonbury 1984: Marr left, Rourke right, facing the crowd, and Morrissey centre, turning away, arm aloft as if in goal celebration. I'm sure I can pick myself out in the crowd just by his left ear. Maybe not. But I was there. And the sense of excitement, at least towards the front, was electric. Here was the band of the moment, champions of the outre, strange and uncelebrated, vanguards of the indie movement into the mainstream – where every release was a statement of identity and intent, and none more robust, confrontational and inspirational than The Smiths. 'So?' quoth Terence Stamp (RIP, actor, writer, vegetarian and ace face of *Billy Budd, The Collector*, etc.), 'what difference does it make?'

The Smiths epitomised such 'difference' - everything from the choice of name, the exclamatory titles to Morrissey's lyrical conceits and provocations; from his awkward performances, pitch and positioning to Marr's uniquely cool and tuneful guitar arpeggios and hooks - smartly presented within iconoclastic, monochrome images that placed them at the cultural nexus of outsider art, cinema and television. A rallying point for social misfits. The music was modern, lean and punchy and a triumphant combination of Morrissey's challenging way with words and melody and Marr's elevating, energising and joyful arrangements. The tension between the two, underpinned by the muscular Rourke-Joyce combo, gave The Smiths an unmistakeable sound, as arresting now as ever it was.

It's a tribute to The Smiths' brilliance as a band – and the supremely gifted creative partnership at its heart – that, despite the sudden way in which the curtain came down (and the years of acrimony that did much to mar their memory), The Smiths' legacy is their almost perfect body of work, Morrissey (and Jo Slee's) artwork and Marr's remasters included.

It stands, beautifully, defiantly, gloriously naked and (not so) vulnerably alone, out there on its own. An unimpeachable testament to a genuinely singular voice in the wilderness of 1980s UK pop history.

Still holding the torch… can you hear them? … 'Do you love me like you used to?' Ask me, ask my wife: if it's not love, then it's The Smiths that will bring us together.



## GLOUCESTER LEISURE CENTRE
### 24 SEPTEMBER 1984, GLOUCESTER, UK

### NICK FOSTER

This was an incredible moment for us young music fans. The leisure centre was not on many bands' touring schedule, so apart from the likes of Howard Jones or Musical Youth, a trip to the Colston Hall in Bristol was generally on the cards. To top things off, not only were The Smiths playing, but Echo and The Bunnymen were appearing a few days later. It was to be the best week in our young lives! The attendance process was to get to the venue as early as possible to secure a good place in the queue and then race to the front of the stage as soon as the doors were open. This position was held for the entirety of the gig, regardless of whether you needed a toilet break or not. It was a case of 'holding it in' until the finish, and it was also a little while before I really got into the pleasure of having a few pints during a concert. This meant that I was able to witness The Woodentops set in its entirety, another Peel favourite,

*Jo Sayers made a pilgrimage to Salford Lads Club more than 30 years after seeing The Smiths in Gloucester*

who set the scene admirably ahead of the main band.

Before long, the lights dimmed, and the opening strains of Prokofiev's 'Romeo And Juliet' filled the auditorium. Where I had previously enough room to stand and watch comfortably, I now felt the air being pushed out of my lungs and my body lifted and propelled nearer to the stage as the crush ensued. The excitement was palpable and you feel the tense expectation for what could be the most important thing to happen to our young lives (up to that point).

With the entrance of the band, it all kicked off. Launching into 'William', the crowd went wild as Morrissey gyrated, teasing the front stage participants to push in further, like a musical guru bringing his clan to him. The sound was perfect and here were a band at the top of their game, Johnny's chiming guitar equally matched by the tight rhythm section of Rourke and Joyce.

The set flowed, peppered with tracks from the upcoming LP *Meat Is Murder* as well as now familiar tracks from the self-titled first LP.  But, as with all good things, it seemed to be over as quickly as it began. Starting off their first encore with a live debut of 'Please, Please, Please, Let Me Get What I Want' and finishing their second with a rousing rendition of 'Miserable Lie', I finally made my way out to the chilled September evening, with my sweat-soaked t-shirt clinging to my body. I was still warm with the feeling that I had just witnessed the best gig of my young life.

### JO SAYERS, AGE 13

My first ever gig. Me and a mate, Natalie Easton, went. They were brilliant. They were my favourite band as a teenager. People said they were depressing but I was in love and never got the whole depression thing. The guitar work is just amazing, and I suppose with Morrissey being a bit odd it appealed to the alternative youth of the day! I still listen to their music loads now. I want 'There Is A Light That Never Goes Out' played at my funeral.

### ANDY WHITE

My next chance to see the band was at Gloucester Leisure Centre. Support was from The Woodentops, who were pretty good but never really made it. The first album had been out a few months, and the band had clearly gained confidence – except maybe Morrissey who was born extremely confident. The rhythm section was tighter than I recall from Leicester and the fan base had grown. The songs were mostly well-known but included a few from the not-yet-released Meat Is Murder. I believe this was also the first live appearance for 'How Soon Is Now?' I was going through a difficult phase in my love life and

The highlight of the concert was 'Jeane', one of my favourite songs and not played in Leicester. It was a poor venue, actually, a giant sports hall with poor acoustics. You could have had a game of badminton at the back.

# UNIVERSITY OF CARDIFF

### 25 SEPTEMBER 1984, CARDIFF, UK

### SIMON DAWES

Morrissey came on swinging a fir tree in the air. He chucked it into the crowd, and I remember seeing people holding bits of twig at the end!

### ROBERT HILL

I believe it was the 'Heaven Knows' tour but I could be wrong on that. It was packed to the rafters and Morrisey appeared with a tree out of his back pocket. A slight exaggeration there, but it's my abiding memory of the concert. I can't remember much more apart from 'William' being their first number and it being a fantastic night.

### MICHAEL JONES, AGE 18

As a bored 17-year-old motor spare shop assistant, I became aware of The Smiths by hearing the singles on the radio and seeing them on *Top Of The Pops*. I was struck by the music, lyrics and image. I bought secondhand Levi's, a few paisley shirts and DM buckled shoes, my hair styled into a quiff emulating the band's look. I don't think the first album left my turntable for six months. They filled the gap that was left by The Jam.

I saw the tour announcement in the *NME*. I had Fridays off so was delegated by my friends to get the tickets from Spillers Records in Cardiff, taking the early one-hour train journey from my hometown in Merthyr. I was first in the queue buying the four pieces of gold and was then having to pinch myself that I was going to see them!

Come the day of the gig and a few swift beers and four bequiffed 18-year-old Merthyr lads are getting to the front of the stage – me, Gegsy, Treeny and Slyver. We don't pay much attention to support band The Woodentops. There is some dry ice, booming Oscar Wilde intro music and then there they are. I'm stood front of the stage to the right, looking directly at Johnny Marr. He's cool even with eyeliner. Morrissey has a tree hanging out of his arse pocket. They go right through their album. The crowd are going mental. I'm crushed at the front, soaked with sweat and beer, but I don't care. It's just sheer excitement. 'Hand In Glove' hits a nerve and is probably my best memory of the evening. Seeing a band in their prime was something to behold and I don't think I ever experienced that sort of gig again – and I've been to hundreds since. Thanks for the memories.

### ONDINA COOPER, AGED 14

I was too young to see The Smiths live. However, I do remember hearing 'How Soon Is Now?' on college radio. It was fall 1984, I was 14. I remember finding out the name of the track, requesting it be played again and sitting by the boombox to record it. I still have my mixtape with it on it. I then went and bought the single at Cutler's record shop in New Haven, Connecticut.

*Ondina Cooper remembers hearing 'How Soon Is Now?' on the radio*

### ALLAN PETRIE

I left school in 1982 having gone through punk, heavy rock and ska and also liking bands like Classic Nouveaux, Visage, Soft Cell, etc. I was always into alternative stuff. We used to drink in a small football club bar even though we were underage — Barry Town FC. One day at the football club, Chris McCarthy, my best mate since the age of six, said he loved a new single by a band called The Smiths. It was 'Hand In Glove'. I went away and listened to them and fell in love with them. I used to drive my mum and dad mad. They said Morrissey was a miserable bastard, but as a depressed type of teenager, the lyrics felt real to me. I liked the way they used to sing about real issues instead of making lines up which rhymed.

It was a sunny evening as I walked the three miles from my house to Chris's house for the gig. I was wearing my dad's shirt and my sister's beads and had flowers in the arse pocket of my jeans. I got some weird looks walking through Barry! We caught the train to Cardiff and must have looked odd. I remember Morrissey hurling gladioli around and us getting quite close to the front. There weren't loads there but there were enough to make a great atmosphere. They did two encores and I remember going mad to 'Miserable Lie' at the very end.

### ROLO MCGINTY, THE WOODENTOPS

The Smiths had come to see The Woodentops at Dingwalls, to see about inviting us to support them on the tour they were about to do.

We were a very new band, improved from doing our first tour support with Julian Cope on his comeback. We were majorly excited and off we went. The halls were big and echoey, a sports centre especially. The Smiths themselves were friendly and easy to hang around with. Morrissey was not usually visible, doing press or whatever. It was more a nod here and there and I had thanked him for putting us on the tour. Only… we were going down really well, and the flowers were all thrown away before The Smiths came on. I don't know if that's normal or not. Indeed, Johnny Marr was taunting Morrissey with our new single, 'Move Me', that was just about to go public. Johnny had an advance copy. So just maybe some bad blood was flowing. Then it happened.

It may have been Cardiff. As we drove to the venue, we spotted the car driven by our good friend Dave Harper, a vintage Mercedes. In the passenger seats were The Smiths, all asleep. We drove alongside, not too close, to give Dave a quick wave and then whizz off because we were late. Johnny woke up, raised his head and saw us and grin and waved. As did I. Morrissey was in the front passenger seat, and he turned to look at me. For a split second, as his head was turning, an undulation in the road brought the two cars a tiny bit closer to each other. In the other broken piece of second, Morrissey got a shock and thought 'crash!' just as our eyes met. He thought he was going to die and made the face.

We passed and I thought, 'First thing on arrival, apologise.' I mean I wasn't driving or anything but still. So, I did. It did not go down well. I had mentioned the bump in the road. We were waving at Dave and said the bump was 'a bad coincidence'. Morrissey repeated that back to me sarcastically.

We played a blistering set that night. I've heard from people, for example Rob from Alabama 3 (who it turns out was there), that we blew The Smiths off. Old time expression that. I don't see how we could have, 'How Soon Is Now?' was such a hit, you can't beat that.

I remember seeing a guy dancing up on a balcony with a spotlight up there making his shadow enormous as he perfectly mimicked Morrissey. You can't beat that.

In the morning, we got the news. We were off the tour. I think we had done three of the five and we were absolutely gutted. The next thing was the interview question, 'Why did you not finish the Smiths tour?' The question kept coming up. One day, I think Alice or I perhaps answered with, 'Oh, it was a silly thing, it wasn't as if we had put a cigarette bomb under the stage or anything, tried to blow them up and they found out.' This quip made its way to print as, 'We tried to blow them up'. How it goes.

I personally enjoyed seeing them every night. As a result of that Smiths tour, Everything But The Girl, Tracey and Ben, took us out on a much longer tour that was not only the damn best time, but it was also our last support tour. They came to see us at Dingwalls too, which we were now headlining. So, all three support tours we did, we were checked out firstly at Dingwalls by the artists that took us out.

# *HATFUL OF HOLLOW*

## RELEASED 2 NOVEMBER 1984

### ROB LEVY

Everyone remembers their first time. Especially when they discover a band. *Hatful Of Hollow* was one of the first albums I ever bought. I remember being wowed by the design. I loved the cover and the lettering. Once opened, I loved how thick the record sleeve was and how cool it was to have the lyrics printed on blue paper that matched the album… It very quickly became the gold standard of album packaging for me. It told me that these guys weren't screwing around.

The Smiths are one of the pivotal bands of my life. They arrived during my adolescence and nurtured me through young adulthood. Now as I drift into senility, their music speaks to me more than ever. They remain ever present. While a lot of people were drawn to Morrissey at first, I was awed by their melodies. Sure, I loved the lyrics that somehow always to spoke to me when I most needed them, but there was something about their sound. The subtle but sturdy bass of Andy Rourke, the ingeniously gorgeous guitarwork of Johnny Marr and the crisp and puissant drumming of Mike Joyce.

A standout track is the closer, 'Please, Please, Please, Let Me Get What I Want'. I often think of this song cinematically due to the fantastically sad moment in *Pretty In Pink* when Duckie is looks gutted as this song plays. He's

*Hatful of Hollow*

desperately into his friend who isn't into him. I have spent countless hours with this song on repeat after breakups. It's an anthem for those whose hearts are weary and heavy with rejection.

### CARL MANN

My sister is four years older than me. Growing up, most of the music I got into was via the sounds blasting from her bedroom. One evening I heard this phenomenal guitar riff and song coming from her room. I ran in and asked her what it was. Turns out it was 'What Difference Does it Make?' by The Smiths from the *Hatful Of Hollow* album. The next time she went out I grabbed that cassette on permanent loan. I was 13 or 14 and it was the beginning of a love affair. (I had to learn the guitar riff to that song recently; it's absolute genius -  and much faster to play than I thought it would be!)

The next cassette I purchased was *The Queen Is Dead*. It was Johnny Marr's guitar playing that made me want to play guitar and be in a band. The melodies, the sounds coming out of that guitar just blew my mind. How could it sound so melancholic yet so uplifting?

In Morrissey I was hearing a vocal style and lyrics that were totally new to me. It was like this band had come from outer space. There was nobody else like them, and there still isn't! The rhythm section was a force of its own. The intoxicating drums and bouncy melodic bass lines amplified Marr's guitars beyond the sum of their parts and gave the melodies the biggest stage to shine from.

Each element of the band was so important and made them unique. As I fell deeper into their world, I grew to love more and more about the band. The look of the artwork for the singles and albums, the clothes they wore, the haircuts and, of course, Johnny's guitars.

I can't comprehend how Johnny Marr came up with all of those amazing guitar melodies at such a young age. I treasure my Smiths albums and still listen to them regularly. They manage to stay fresh and exciting to my ears, even after all the years that have passed.

I don't know what happened to that original cassette of *Hatful Of Hollow*, but I still have my *The Queen Is Dead* cassette. I have all of the albums on CD and vinyl now too. The love affair continues...

I occasionally thank my sister, but not for the introduction to Paul Young's *No Parlez*. I still give her grief for that!

### RYAN LEWIS WALKER

There are bands that arrive at a time of your life where it felt like they were needed. This is not a random coincidence. Up until they enter what was a series of lines lacking much, if any, colour – a series of squiggles in the seat, a shadow on the street, a wire coat hanger without clothes, a paperclip without documents to hold together, an odd noise in the conversation – you're a confused shipwreck of a human being, dozing off to the vibrating drone of an air conditioner in a waiting room with no clear destination or real confidence that what you're doing is the right decision.

*Johnny Marr influenced Carl Mann's career as a musician*

In situations like this, we don't find the band. Rather, the band, and their albums, find us. And in situations like this – because of the profound impact of what has suddenly become the single-most important artifact to impress itself on our lives – it informs our outlook on everything and everyone. Folks either remember the exact specifications of the occasion it happened as though psychologically dated like sniffing a temporal popper, or it's all sort of cobbled together as an interesting whirl.

I don't remember when I found *Hatful of Hollow*. But I remember taking it, along with their 'best of' (*The Sound Of The Smiths),* on a school trip to France. It was one of those weird exchanges. I'd put up this young lad a few months prior, so now it was his turn to do the same. I remember being on the floor in a room in his house with a CD player and somehow knowing the melody (both Marr's guitar and Morrissey's vocal) before I'd ever heard a note. I remember pressing repeat when 'Barbarism Begins At Home' came on – too infectious and energetic not to keep on playing it. It felt like companionship for an hour, or day, or week, or what would turn out to be a lifetime of crisis when one set of traumas rears their ugly heads and bite your arms off. 'William, It Was Really Nothing' cast a spell on me and hasn't lost any of its special power. The Smiths are one of those bands that will never lose any of their power. Their resonance remains unchanged. Their relevance untarnished.

I'm not religious and I was born in 1995. That means no autographs or ticket stubs or anecdotes of gigs or first issues of LPs. But that doesn't mean I can't be in the pictures, waiting for The Smiths to come and save the day, or the week, or the year, or my whole fucking life.

### ROSS KENNERELL-WALTERS

I bought *Hatful Of Hollow* on cassette in November 1984, with my sixteenth birthday present money. I played it to death. For months it was all I obsessively played. Every day after school I'd retreat to my bedroom and play the album on repeat, often followed by my father bellowing up the stairs for me to turn it down. He hated The Smiths, which made me love them all the more. He'd get so frustrated he'd cut the power plug off my cassette player.

Jump forward 40 years and my mother was very ill and in the final weeks of her life. We had lots of chats and time to say goodbye. She reminded me of the times I use to 'butt heads' with my father and how she used to lie in the bath each evening, listening to me playing The Smiths. She fondly recalled these times and could even remember a few lyrics.

*Hatful of Hollow* now has an extra special place in my heart as it reminds me of my mum (a secret fan of The Smiths).

### JENNIFER RILEY

There is such joy to be found when you meet someone you connect with - it's a beautiful thing… sharing favourite songs, talking about lyrics that touch your soul,

*Ross Kennerell-Walters' mum was a secret Smiths fan*

to be hauntingly sung, when you cannot find your voice, a friend who gets you.

14-year-old me found a friend in *Hatful Of Hollow*, which has walked with me for 41 years – where I find peace, sadness, melancholy, hope and acceptance that we are loved for who we are. 'Back To The Old House' and 'Please Please Please' spoke for younger me, and holds the hand of older me…

In November 1984, The Smiths embarked on a tour of Ireland, playing seven shows in the Republic and two in the north, at the University of Coleraine and Belfast. James were the support.

# SFX

## 12 & 13 NOVEMBER 1984, DUBLIN, IRELAND

### JAMES ROBERTS

I saw them just the once, in Dublin. *Top Of The Pops* was a weekly ritual and their first performance on the show was it for me. I went to the gig on my own because no one I knew would go and so I stood at the back. The two members of Everything But The Girl were a few feet away from me as they were big fans also. Great gig!

### LISA COLLINS, AGE 16

My hipper school friend, Julie, first heard of The Smiths during one of her summers in London. Julie was really cool. She listened to Radio Luxembourg before the rest of us knew it existed. Before MTV or SKY TV reached Ireland, ourv exposure to other types of music was very limited. My other friend, Denise, was also a big fan of The Smiths. I was very new to the goth scene, having been a mod up until then. The night of the concert, Julie, Denise and myself all dressed in black, and wearing our ghostly white make-up with our hair all back combed, set off with great anticipation to see The Smiths.

I was just 16 and I knew this was one of the first gigs The Smiths had ever played in Dublin. As an angst-ridden teenager in the early eighties, Ireland felt the complete opposite to the multicultural thriving cosmopolitan nation it is today. Teenagers were desperately searching for something different from the oppressive culture that we lived in then. The Catholic Church had a chokehold on what was deemed acceptable in all aspects of Irish society. The Smiths' lyrics and music spoke to us as teenagers feeling trapped by what we felt as an oppressive society.

The SFX was a small, plain, simple, dark dusty old hall with wooden floorboards and a door at one end and a stage at the other and it was just perfect for seeing bands.

Not many people had heard of The Smiths and so the SFX was not very full that night. Because it was such an intimate concert, it felt like all of us in the audience were in on something special together. I was even right up at the front of the stage, which as a true claustrophobe I would normally never do.

At one point, someone threw flowers onto the stage and Morrissey added them to the ones he already had in his jeans back pocket. I remember a lot of flowers being tossed around that night. Morrissey seemed to glide over the stage singing our favourites such as 'This Charming Man' and 'Please, Please, Please, Let Me Get What I Want'.

Towards the end of the set, Morrissey leaned over to us girls crowded together at the front of the stage and kissed Denise on her cheek. She was in seventh heaven, and the whole bus journey home she vowed never to wash that side of her face again. It didn't matter that we pointed out the impracticality of that. She was determined. I think she waited a few days before she had to eventually wash her face!

Almost a quarter of a century later, in my thirties, I went to see Morrissey at a solo gig in the Bob Hope Theatre in Stockton, California in April 2007. I had been living in the Bay Area for a decade and had not seen Morrissey in concert since the SFX gig.

At the SFX gig he was a more mysterious brooding creature. The 2007 Morrissey seemed to exude a lot more warmth and even engaged in banter between the numbers. A number of his family members were in the audience that night and he introduced them to the fans, which was very sweet. He also shared that he had spent many summers in Stockton, when he was younger. This also cleared up, for a lot of the fans there, as to why he was performing during Stockton's Asparagus Festival as he made a lot of jokes gently poking fun at the 'metropolis' of downtown Stockton. I remember thinking how times have changed and how we all soften, as we age. There was even an array of brightly coloured merchandise for sale in the theatre, so different to the smoky dark atmosphere of the SFX gig. I bought a white tank top emblazoned with the word Morrissey in pink for my same friend, Denise, whose cheek he had kissed all those years ago, as a gift for her on my next visit home to Dublin. She wore it proudly.

### GRAHAM MONTGOMERY, AGE 13

I was about to turn 14. I was probably too young to be going to gigs in town – but if you're good enough, you're old enough! I remember the second song was 'William, It Was Really Nothing' and the place went mental. The crowd was swaying from side to side and someone stood on my shoe and I lost it for a while. I found it during 'How Soon Is Now?', which the crowd sang along to with gusto. I don't think the set lasted longer than an hour. I believe they were sick that night and that the next night was much better for the band.

### DAMIAN READE

It was my first ever gig, James supported them and they too were excellent. On the way to the gig, we met Johnny Marr outside the Gresham Hotel and chatted with him for a bit. I still have my signed ticket, and I also have the bootleg from that night.

### DES FOLEY, AGE 18

I went with my best friend from school, Brian Whelan. We were

*Damian Reade's SFX bootleg*

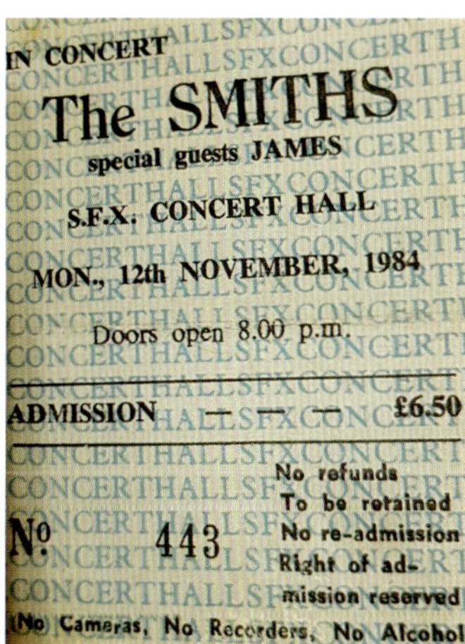

*Damian Reade's 1984 Dublin ticket*

up near the front. I remember the screams of the audience when The Smiths came on. Everyone sang along with pretty much every song. The atmosphere was great and I remember just being amazed to actually see the band in person for the first time. I was on such a high after the gig that when I got home, I blasted out 'This Charming Man' on my bedroom record player. Much to my dad's annoyance, as he was in bed at the time!

### JOHN FOYLE, AGE 19

I was a year at work, on staff for a department store. Anything but return to education. Living at home, I look back and wonder at the tolerance of my parents. I've no memory of pressure to move out, etc. I was in a comfortable, cosseted environment. I was and am a big fan of live music. I'd hear all the latest bands on 2FM and RTE Radio 2, particularly the evening shows hosted by Gerry Ryan and Dave Fanning. I wasn't and am not a viewer of much TV. It was all about the sounds. The weekly music magazine I'd mainly read was *Record Mirror*.

The Smiths were the band to see, as would REM be at the same venue a few weeks later. My memories of both shows are constantly mixed up in my head. Both shows were hysterically received. The venue, on the other end of O'Connell Street, north of O'Connell Bridge, was the north side of Dublin, significant to me as a Southsider. Basically, northsiders were poor, southsiders were rich. My dad may have dropped me at the venue. I'd seen my first show there, on an altar

boys' outing in the seventies, seeing Danny Doyle topping the bill of a charity show.

That's when the place was called St Francis Xavier Hall, very much associated with the church. It's rebranding as SFX was considered rather daring, though us teenagers would still have been very much aware of its previous associations. Seeing a rock show there was still slightly daring and a bit bold, a delight to us as we shook off the clergy's stranglehold on Irish society.

I was enthusiastic about keeping up with the new acts. All of that informed my reaction to Morrissey & Co. As the mostly male crowd swayed away under a fog of cigarette smoke and body odour, Moz appeared waving a branch of a tree, getting a roar – part delight, part mocking. His penchant for vegetation was well known – coming on with a branch seemed both appropriate and a kind of knowing irony, that he knew he was already playing up to an image.

They started with 'Please, Please, Please, Let Me Get What I Want'. It was a B-side at that point, only appearing on *Hatful Of Hollow* around the time of the show. Whatever, it was well known, with lots of radio play by 2FM. The tracks from the first album were roared along with and ones from what would be *Meat Is Murder* – 'Rusholme Ruffians', 'Barbarism Begins At Home' – less so, but seeming intriguing. The inclusion towards the end of 'Jeane' was especially welcome. It was already considered delightfully obscure, a B-side only the hardcore fans could possibly know. It was a fitting ending to a show that was going full blast all the time. People staggered out of the venue drenched in sweat, every bit of clothing damp, stinking of booze and tobacco.

My abiding memory is of a band in complete control of the stage and the audience. Reading later that Maher (Marr) was sick for most of the tour after a rough crossing on the ferry, it's hard to think how much better they could have been if they had been 100 per cent.

## COLIN KERR

I saw a lot of bands there, but my standout memory is of seeing The Smiths. The first time they played Dublin was at Trinity College, Dublin. Word spread that this was a band that had to be seen and heard. What set The Smiths apart in the SFX was Morrissey, a frontman like no frontman before him, and Johnny Marr, a guitarist who played guitar like no other guitarist of his generation. And then there were the songs – 'This Charming Man', 'Hand In Glove', 'What Difference Does It Make?', 'Still Ill' and other early classics. I didn't see The Smiths live again, but I did get to see both Morrissey and Johnny Marr play solo gigs in Dublin. Morrissey was good and Johnny Marr was great, but nothing could recreate the magic of that SFX gig.

## PAUL ROY, AGE 17

Having siblings made *Top Of The Pops* a viewing staple. There was something about The Smiths that immediately stood out. I suppose there is always the teenage musical epiphany of hearing music that resonates and perhaps speaks to you in a new way. I was 17 and went with my friend Alan and his younger sister, so we couldn't go to the pub before or after. I always remember the intensity of 'How Soon Is Now?' That tremulous guitar intro is a favourite of mine, and a track I still listen to. There was a thread of energy through the show; it all seemed more intense and atmospheric. The stage lighting was also something that transfixed me. I had just begun working in my first job and soon after I started my mother turned to me smiling in the kitchen one evening and sang, 'I was looking for a job and then I found a job, and heaven knows I'm miserable now...'.

# SAVOY

14 NOVEMBER 1984, WATERFORD, IRELAND

## MICHAEL FARRAGHER

When we went to see them in Ireland, we were hitchhiking and had places to stay. We were coming out of Dublin on what is essentially the motorway, hitchhiking to Waterford when a little minibus passed us by and I said, 'That was James!' We'd seen them the night before in Dublin. Nobody really knew James at that point, but they noticed us and they reversed back on the motorway and said, 'Are you going to see The Smiths in Waterford?' We said, 'We are!' and they said, 'Jump in and we'll give you a lift!'

During that tour, we didn't get to meet The Smiths all the time. We would always go up to the

Waterford ticket

venues for the soundchecks. We'd go up there, spend the day at the venue and wait for them for them to arrive. We'd see them going in and take some photos. We weren't pushy, we didn't ever force ourselves on them. If they were up for a chat and if they had enough time, sometimes they would hang around outside the venue before they went in, which was great and a lot more relaxed.

And as they got to know us more, they let us in to soundchecks. They would say, 'Are you coming in?' The band would be doing their drum checks and going through all the songs instrumentally, and Morrissey would be sitting there watching them and singing in the row in front. Then he would get up and sing a few songs and do a few vocal checks.

# LEISURELAND

## 17 NOVEMBER 1984, GALWAY, IRELAND

### MICHAEL FARRAGHER

When Rita and I saw them in Ireland, we got a song dedicated to us. Morrissey had written to us on one occasion and had said, 'Dear kittens, brothers and sisters must always share' and sent us a little something. And at one of the Dublin gigs he said, 'This is for the kittens,' and we were saying, 'I wonder if that's us? Do you think he means us?' It could have been anybody. But when we went to see them in Galway on that tour, we'd gone out to the venue and met Morrissey during the day.

Galway Leisureland was a sports venue. Our parents are from Galway, so we were going to go and see our cousins and our aunts and uncles and weren't going to follow the rest of the tour. The band were going on to the north of Ireland, and we didn't fancy hitchhiking around the north of Ireland because, at that time, to have an English accent around the north of Ireland wasn't completely safe. We met Morrissey and we said, 'Sadly this is our last night. Good luck for the rest of the tour.' And that night he said, 'This is for Michael and Rita. Hope you get home safe.' That was so brilliant.

I was desperate to get a recording of that gig, not as easy as it is now. Now you can go on YouTube and a lot of these recordings are there. Back then it wasn't easy. I advertised in *NME* and *Melody Maker* to ask if anybody had a recording, but no one came through. But we were living at home with our parents in Streatham in south London, and Grant Showbiz was living on the same road as us. He produced The Fall, and he did the sound at every Smiths gig. It was just a normal road but the house he lived in had a studio called Cathouse Studios where bands came to record demos. We would meet Grant walking up or down the road and he knew us from all of the gigs that we went to. We never stopped and had a chat with him. We'd never say, 'Any news? Have you got any gossip?' We'd just meet Grant and say 'hi' and 'see you next time'.

After the Galway gig I did stop him on the road and said, 'If there's any chance, Grant, that you've got

Morrissey by Lee Thacker

a recording of the Galway gig, I'd just really like to get a copy of it.' He said, 'I'll have a look. I've got a soundboard recording of practically every gig.' So I said, 'Well, if I pop a blank tape through your letterbox would you be able to give me a copy of it?' He said, 'Sure.' And he did.

### RITA FARRAGHER

I was still grieving the breakup of The Jam at the end of 1982. I completely believed I would never like any band as much as I had liked The Jam, so I had to be persuaded by my brother Michael, who was my music guru, to come and listen to The Smiths on the John Peel show. Fairly soon after that, they were playing at London's Lyceum and we went along. It was one of the most electric gigs I have ever been to, and after that gig I was well and truly over The Jam.

We then saw them at Hammersmith Palais in March 1984, where Sandie Shaw came on for the encore. Morrissey was in fine form, with plenty of one-liners. The next time I saw The Smiths was at the GLC gig in London, in June '84. Festivals weren't as big a thing then and to see a band you like playing outdoors in the daytime was amazing. Michael and I got right up the front for it and was such an exciting time. Being a festival type event, not all the audience were there to see The Smiths, but they got a really great reception, and I think that's the first time I saw Morrissey throwing glads around.

I can't remember the series of events that followed but, basically, we went to every radio appearance, TV show appearance and gig that we could. Michael went up and met them at Rough Trade offices very early on and Morrissey asked if we were coming to the next gig, but we hadn't been able to get tickets so he said he would put us on the guest list – something he very kindly did many times during our Smiths days. I started writing to Morrissey early on and he wrote back a few times, which always caused great excitement in the house. Even my mum would recognise his childlike handwriting and know to get it to me as soon as possible. Morrissey was always very kind to us – I think he liked that we were from an Irish family and that we were brother and sister – he once sent us two white-label seven-inch singles and wrote 'brothers and sisters must always share' on a postcard. He also once sent me a packet of flower seeds and said, 'Each bud must blossom and grow.'

Johnny was also very generous. When *Meat Is Murder* was due out, he was doing an interview at Broadcasting House in London. It had snowed really badly and there were no buses running along Streatham High Road so we decided to walk the three miles to Brixton – in completely unsuitable footwear because, after all, we were potentially going to meet a Smith! We got there late so didn't see him going in but waited around and met him after. Unusually, we were the only fans there – others were far too sensible to hang around in the freezing snow. He was so lovely to us, and he gave us each a copy of the album – we were buying it anyway but to get a copy from Johnny was special. I remember getting home and just playing it over and over.

The Irish tour they did in 1984 was probably the absolute best time for me. We had so little money and we were 18, 19 years old, hitchhiking around in November. We must have been mad. But Morrissey had sent a letter saying, 'You will be on all guest lists everywhere', so how could we not go?

The band were on the same ferry as us going over. They seemed like superstars to us and we assumed they would be flying over. We had a great chat with Johnny on the ferry. I think Morrissey was in his cabin unwell. It was a terrible crossing, and everyone felt ill before the night was out. In Dublin they started with 'Please, Please, Please' which seemed like a bold and brilliant move, and it was just magical. Morrissey also dedicated a song to 'the kittens' and we liked to think that was us, as he had called us that in a letter shortly before.

Our first task was to get from Dublin to Waterford in time for the next gig. We'd stayed in a hostel in Dublin and trekked out to the dual carriageway to thumb a lift. After about half an hour we spotted the support band, James, going past in their camper van and we waved. They recognised us as Smiths fans and, unbelievably, turned round and came back to get us. We had a little detour because Tim Booth wanted to find a waterfall to chant at. Michael and I were vegetarian, but they introduced us to veganism. They fed us and looked after us and got us to Waterford in time for the soundcheck – they even took us into the venue with them where we had a chat with Johnny.

That whole little tour was great. We left it after the Galway gig as they were going up north next and we weren't sure about that, with all the trouble there at the time, and we have family near Galway, so we went to visit them before heading home. I gave Morrissey a claddagh ring by way of thanks for all the guest lists. When I got home, I had a letter from him, on hotel letter headed paper, simply saying, 'I will always wear the ring' and I believe he did until it got taken off his finger by a fan at a gig – in America, I think. He dedicated 'Reel Around The Fountain' to us by name at Galway, and wished us a safe trip home, which sent us home floating on air.

## SAVOY

### 18 NOVEMBER 1984, CORK, IRELAND

### COLM O'CALLAGHAN

The Smiths returned to The Savoy six months after their first appearance there, during which time they'd been sucked slowly in from the margins. But although the group would go on to regularly feature at the business end of the album charts, they never really enjoyed the consistent successes they craved with the shorter form, which was one of Morrissey and Marr's primary ambitions for their group from the get-go.

Even so, the singer had already been rumbled by the tabloids who, picking up on the platinum-plated copy he routinely provided in interviews, had become as regular a freak feature in *The Sun* as he was on the hit parade, portrayed variously as a dangerous, anti-royal traitor, a sexual deviant and a macabre, terrorist-loving, tree-hugging weirdo. Or, if you like, the Jeremy Corbyn of his time.

The Denis Desmond/MCD-promoted, nine-date, eight-town tour of Ireland during November 1984 took place less than one month after the IRA bombing of the Grand Hotel in Brighton, where the British Conservative Party was holding its annual conference, and during a particularly dark period in modern Irish history, when loyalist and republican terrorism across the island routinely dominated the news agenda. And at a time too when many formidable contemporary bands simply wouldn't – or were advised not to – play in the north of Ireland.

With The Smiths on the road in support of their stop-gap compilation album, *Hatful Of Hollow*, Morrissey gave the London press a series of typically headline-grabbing quotes during the media campaign to promote it, one of the most notable of which referred to Margaret Thatcher, then Britain's Prime Minister, and who had survived the Brighton bombing, which killed three people and injured 30 more.

'The sorrow of the Brighton bombing', Morrissey claimed, 'is that Thatcher escaped unscathed. I think that, for once, the IRA were accurate in selecting their targets'. And it was against this backdrop, six weeks after U2 released *The Unforgettable Fire* and five months after Bob Dylan's

show at Slane Castle was marred by riots around the County Meath town, that The Smiths returned to Ireland. During which they played shows in Letterkenny, Belfast and Coleraine, as well as the usual stop-offs, fetching up in Cork for the second and last time on Sunday, 18 November 1984, one week before Midge Ure and Bob Geldof recorded the Band Aid single, 'Do They Know It's Christmas'.

The mood inside The Savoy, second time around, was just as frenzied and excitable as it had been earlier that year, and maybe overly-so. The crowd was bigger, as you'd expect, and the promoters had put an extra 50p on the price of the tickets. Once again, Philip and I were there, close enough to see the magicians work the stage but far enough away to avoid the on-going bash-ball inside the moshing zone. The support this time was provided by James, yet another fledgling and already-highly-regarded Manchester band (is there any other kind?) who'd released a fine first record, the *Jimone* EP, on the Factory label and who, during their formative years, enjoyed Morrissey's very public patronage. For better and, possibly, for worse.

The Smiths' set had changed quite drastically in the interim. Although they were ostensibly promoting *Hatful Of Hollow*, the band was also roadtesting several of the tracks that would buttress its second studio album, *Meat Is Murder*. They opened bravely with one of their more introspective cuts, 'Please, Please, Please, Let Me Get What I Want', which had featured as a quality B-side on their 'William,

*Image: (Stephen Wright)*

*Image: (Stephen Wright)*

It Was Really Nothing' single earlier that summer, and into which they quickly segued.

Foremost among the clatter of new material was a frantic take on 'What She Said' and, close to the end, a bionic, souped-up 'I Want The One I Can't Have', by which time the atmosphere inside the hall had turned sharply. Marr had become the unwitting target of a hail of spit halfway through, an unfortunate knuckle-walker's pastime that many of us suspected (wrongly) had died after the Sex Pistols signed to a major label.

And after two audible warnings – at one point he arched his callow body back and looked like he was going to lash out – he eventually walked off just shy of the hour mark, taking the rest of the band with him. The Smiths returned, reluctantly enough it seemed to me, to do a two-song encore, finishing on a high with 'What Difference Does It Make?', but Marr had the last word; he leaned into a vocal mic on the way off and told the crowd, not incongruously, how he'd 'come to play and not to be spat at', before leaving again, this time for good.

As the house lights came up around The Savoy, a section of the crowd, some checking their watches, began to vent, booing initially – more, I suspect, in the direction of those who'd caused the walk-off than at the band itself – and then, once it was obvious that the show was over and that The Smiths weren't returning, broke into a ridiculous chorus of 'We want James'.

So, while the Cork crowd was given an early flavour of some of the more sinewy cuts from *Meat Is Murder*, it also experienced the shortest Smiths set, by at least three songs, of that leg of the tour. But not before Morrissey, as the band set up for its encore, returned to the stage with a small sapling, which he wielded like a bicycle chain during 'Hand In Glove', and then deposited with gusto into the audience.

The Smiths certainly knew how to make an exit, like they knew how to make an entrance. And they never returned to Cork. As regards the spitting, several shows in Cork were disrupted during this time by the same core of eejits, and in much the same manner. Most of them have, no doubt, gone on to be pillars of Cork society. Why Marr? Quite probably because he was a) close and b) tended to stand his ground, unlike Morrissey who was a moving target.

From where I was, I'm not sure if Morrissey was as keen to abandon ship, but abandon ship they did and, although they returned for a two-song encore, that was the last Cork saw of The Smiths.

### DENIS CARROLL

I got into music in the early seventies, my favourites being T. Rex, Marc Bolan and David Bowie. I was obsessed with T. Rex and Marc Bolan, buying all their records and any magazines in which they featured. In late 1983, after seeing The Smiths on *Top Of The Pops*, I became a massive fan of the band and Morrissey in particular. The Smiths have become the band of my life. I have seen The Smiths live twelve times and Morrissey over one hundred times around the world!

I first saw The Smiths live in May 1984 at the SFX Concert Hall in Dublin and two days later at the Savoy Theatre in Cork. Later that year, I saw The Smiths again at the Savoy. This is where I had my first encounter with Morrissey. I was working in a nightclub called Cocos, which was attached to Cork's Victoria Hotel, where the band were staying. That Sunday afternoon, I went into the hotel with their first two albums – The Smiths and Hatful Of Hollow – under my arm, hoping to get them both signed.

I waited for an hour or so whilst listening to the chants of 40 or 50 Smiths fans outside the main entrance. Word got to the hotel's manager that the band did not want to enter via the main entrance and asked if there was another entrance that could be used? The manager informed them that, yes, there was a back entrance on the street behind the hotel, and he instructed them where to go. He also informed them that someone would be there to meet them to bring them through the hotel…and that someone was me!

I arrived at the back entrance to find the band and one or two other people waiting to be let in. I introduced myself to all four members of The Smiths and, en route to their rooms, chatted with them about the two albums and that night's concert. They all signed the first two albums for me.

That night's concert was one of the best shows I saw, only slightly marred by some idiot spitting at Morrissey while he was on stage. After the show finished, I went back to the hotel, where I met with all four Smiths members (Morrissey was really upset by the spitting incident) and all signed a *Hatful Of Hollow* promo poster for me. Morrissey proceeded to go to bed while the rest of the band went on to party in the nightclub of the hotel.

My next encounter with Morrissey was on the afternoon of The Smiths' final Dublin show in the National Stadium, 10 February 1986. While walking along Grafton Street, my three friends and I bumped into Morrissey and one other person. Morrissey stopped to talk to all four of us for ten or 15 minutes about that night's Dublin show and mentioned that they were eager to have a Cork show but that they could not secure a venue for that particular tour. He asked if we were going to that night's show at the National Stadium. We told him that three of us had tickets but that we were short one ticket for my friend Tony. We then said our goodbyes. When we got to the show that night, Tony went to the box office counter to be told that Morrisey had put his name on the guest list. He was escorted to a great side-of-stage seat while the rest of us proceeded back to the seated area in the main auditorium.

## ULSTER HALL

### 22 NOVEMBER 1984, BELFAST, UK

### ROYCE HARPER

They were and still are a big part of my life. I got into them like a

17-year-old would if it was their first band, even though I was in my twenties. That's the sort of effect that Morrissey and the boys had on me. I was a punk, but I was listening to music from the age of 13, 14 and I remember my father taking me into the old Smithfield Market in Belfast and buying secondhand albums because they were so cheap. And it would have been everything – a Pink Floyd album, a Simon and Garfunkel album, a Roy Harper album. There was even a Billy Connolly album! Even when I was a hardcore punk, I was still buying other stuff. I had no hang ups about what was cool and what was not.

After the punk thing, I really liked what people did when they progressed. I was a massive Magazine fan. I hate boxes but they seemed to marry punk with prog. And before The Smiths, I was listening to Echo and The Bunnymen, The Cure, Siouxsie and The Banshees – all the best of the indie stuff.

I was living in Anglesey in North Wales when I first came across The Smiths. I'd met some local musicians, and I was singing in a band. A friend of a friend was talking about the music that he was really into, and he lent me The Smiths debut album. He said, 'You've got to listen to this.'

The first time I heard it, I thought the production was a bit muddy but that there was something there. By the third listen I was hooked – hook, line and sinker! Even through the muddy production Morrissey's genius lyrics got me. I saw them when they made their debut on *Top Of The Pops*. It knocked me off my

*Moz by Lee Thacker*

seat. The band were so talented and tight. They were like The Beatles and yet this loose, Wildean figure at the front, being able to jump about with his gladioli because they were so tight behind him, was just amazing. There was nothing else on the show that week, or the week before or the week after, that could touch that performance.

There was no work in Anglesey, so I got a job back in Belfast. They played Queens University very early in '86 and I went to that gig. It was a brilliant concert. They played a lot of *Meat Is Murder*.

I saw them at G-Mex as well, for the Festival of the Tenth Summer, which was a must because everybody who was anybody played that. The best bands in the world came from Manchester and Liverpool. They played in the afternoon. I was always a festivalgoer, so I was used to seeing bands playing in the afternoon, at Glastonbury and at those Irish festivals I went to. I was happy as Larry to see so many of my favourite top bands in the one afternoon. It was tremendous.

I read Oscar Wilde in my early teens and Morrissey was coming out and saying, 'This is one of my great inspirations' at a time when Wilde was probably seen by other people as an incredibly uncool and one of yesterday's things. He reinvented Oscar. He reinvented James Dean. He reinvented a lot of people that had been left behind in that decade because he said, 'They mean so much to me.' He was so much of today but also this intelligent sharp lyrical wit in a pop song where other people are singing, 'I want to hold your hand.' His lyrics were sometimes like knives in the back – but done with a smile!

## 'HOW SOON IS NOW?'

### RELEASED 28 JANUARY 1985

'How Soon Is Now?' fared relatively badly in the charts, only reaching number 24. It had featured on *Hatful Of Hollow* and was originally the B-side of 'William, It Was Really Nothing'. The re-released single was edited down to four minutes from its original seven.

Johnny Marr: 'It's most people's favourite, I think.'

## *MEAT IS MURDER*

### RELEASED 11 FEBRUARY 1985

### LEN LIGGINS, THE UKRAINIANS

In January 1985 I was a 27-year-old, Leeds-based music obsessive. I was deeply into the northern England indie scene, I was in a band called The Sinister Cleaners and I'd already published fourteen issues of my free fanzine, *Roar*. One day I took it into my head to hop onto a National Express coach to London's Victoria Bus Station and made my way from there to Rough Trade, the indie Cartel HQ, to see if they had any new albums I could review for issue 15. I'd already been blown away by The Smiths when I'd heard them on the John Peel Show, and my bandmate Andrew Middleton had kindly gifted me a copy of the single-sided seven-inch 'This Charming Man' single, so when I got handed a pre-release promo copy of *Meat Is Murder*, I could hardly contain my excitement.

The next day, back in the living room of my little terraced house in Brudenell Mount, Leeds 6, I put on the first track, 'The Headmaster Ritual'. It was an unusually sunny and warm winter's day, so I flung open the bay windows. Johnny Marr's effortless, melodic, jangling riffs burst out into the street at full volume through my massive Celestion Ditton 44 speakers... and, I can tell you, Andy Rourke's bass on that track sounded GREAT through those twelve-inch woofers! Then, 45 seconds in, Morrissey's voice chimed with the beautifully bitter lines: 'Belligerent ghouls run Manchester schools, spineless swines with cemented minds...'. Meanwhile, across the road, a household of cool-dude anarchists soaked up the sounds wafting over them as they lay on the roof, toking on a generously-packed spliff.

There was no way I could have known then, but seven years later – to the month – I would be recording an EP of Smiths' songs and singing them in Ukrainian. Yes, in 1991 I'd co-founded a Cossack folk-punk band called, quite definitively, The Ukrainians, and we were about to release our four song *Pisni Iz The Smiths* CD featuring Slavic reinterpretations of 'Bigmouth Strikes Again', 'The Queen Is Dead', 'What Difference Does It Make?' and, of course, 'Meat Is Murder'. It was a heartfelt tribute to a band I loved.

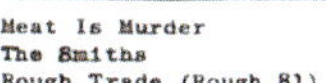

Meat Is Murder
The Smiths
Rough Trade (Rough 81)

This album is truly beautiful! It is more sophisticated than "The Smiths" in the same way "With The Beatles" was more sophisticated than "Please Please Me". Each song speaks volumes & is permeated with real-life atmospheres – continuing Morrissey's obsessions with women, his school days (the belligerent ghouls who run Manchester schools), & his own feelings ("If the day came when I felt a natural emotion/I'd get such a shock I'd probably jump in the ocean"!). Strangely, the whole is not unacceptably self-indulgent.

Compared to "The Smiths" there are more 'up-tempo rock' numbers on this record: "What She Said", "Nowhere Fast" (with mock r'n'b intro), & "Rusholme Ruffians" (with quasi-Bo Diddley beat). But, the slower-paced tracks are the real nerve-exciters: "Well I Wonder", & "That Joke Isn't Funny Anymore". Makes me feel like someone's stimulating all my brain & body cells simultaneously! Head & foot music par excellence! The band also stick their necks out with the last (title) track 'Meat Is Murder' – a straight-on-the-line pro-vegetarian statement. Yep, to my mind listening to this L.P. is almost a substitute for living itself!!!!     L.L.

*Len Liggins reviewed Meat is Murder after receiving a promo copy from Rough Trade*

*Len's band The Ukrainians covered The Smiths on their Pisni Iz The Smiths CD EP*

*Meat is Murder*

### DAMIAN MORGAN

As a classic back-bedroom rebel, struggling to find my own identity in the middle of the chaos that was adolescence, music became my refuge. I'd spend hours alone in my room, surrounded by posters of bands that felt like they understood the isolation, the frustration of being me. I'd listen to China Crisis, Lotus Eaters, and generally anything with a jingly-jangly guitar sound. When The Smiths came on the scene, it was like the universe had finally given me the soundtrack to my inner world. I knew, almost instantly, that I had found my band.

Their music was deeply introspective, laced with wit, melancholy and a sense of disillusionment that mirrored everything I was feeling. Morrissey's lyrics spoke directly to me, his biting psychosocial commentary, his romanticism of the mundane and every day, his embrace of alienation, all delivered with a voice that was both fragile and defiant. Add to that, he was from Stretford. I could barely believe it that someone from my little town had managed to claw his way on the airwaves. It gave me hope. And then there was Johnny Marr's guitar work: intricate, jangly riffs that were quite unlike anything else at the time in their complexity. It definitely wasn't punk, but it had that same spirit of defiance and nonconformity, yet with a melodic beauty that set it apart.

When The Smiths released their second studio album, *Meat Is Murder*, it was a landmark moment. It changed how I felt about music, about life, and what a mere 'band' can come to mean to a person. This record transformed how I felt about Morrissey. From The Smiths being my favourite band, my interest in them became something approaching religious. I suddenly became obsessed with him. How did he know me so well? Every word on that album felt like it spoke to my deepest, private thoughts.

*Meat Is Murder* wasn't just another collection of songs; it was a lifeline, a beacon of understanding and empathy in a world where I often felt misunderstood and alone. From the moment I first heard the opening lyrics of 'The Headmaster Ritual', I felt as though someone finally understood the intricacies of my inner world, speaking directly to the struggles and experiences I grappled with daily.

What struck me most profoundly about the album was its unapologetic authenticity, rawness and particularly in its portrayal of the challenges of growing up and navigating the complexities of feeling like society doesn't understand you, and vice versa. As a resident of Stretford, the fact that the album was written by someone from my town, about our shared experiences, lent it an even greater resonance. The raw emotion and sincerity with which Morrissey, Marr, Rourke and Joyce crafted each track made it feel as though they were speaking directly to me, articulating the feelings of alienation and isolation that had long plagued me. I felt released, and I felt seen.

The themes explored in *Meat Is Murder* resonated with me on a deeply personal level. While 'The

Headmaster Ritual' captured the oppressive atmosphere of school life, the title track spoke to my burgeoning vegetarianism and the ethical convictions that set me apart from my peers. Through their music, The Smiths provided a voice for those who felt marginalised or misunderstood, offering a sense of validation and camaraderie that I had longed for.

Perhaps most importantly, *Meat Is Murder* served as a reminder that I was not alone in my struggles. In Morrissey's lyrics, I found solace in the knowledge that others shared my experiences and understood the pain of feeling like an outsider. Listening to the album became a form of catharsis, allowing me to confront my emotions and find a sense of solidarity in the midst of my loneliness. I played it over and over.

It seems melodramatic to credit an album with 'saving your life', but I feel *Meat Is Murder* did. I was on the point of despair with life at 16 years old. I didn't feel like I had much point in existing. Then Morrissey reached out his hand, his songs, his words, and I was rescued.

The Smiths provided a sense of belonging that I had never before experienced, offering me the support, and understanding I needed to navigate the complexities of adolescence. To this day, the album remains incredibly important, its songs serving as a constant source of comfort and inspiration.

This was music that understood what it felt like to be different, to be angry but also deeply introspective. The Smiths gave a voice to the voiceless, the outcasts, and the rebels, particularly those like me, who spent hours locked in their bedrooms dreaming of a world beyond the ordinary. Their aesthetic was striking too: an odd mixture of fifties glamour and gritty, grey Britain. The cover art for their records often featured black-and-white images of actors or scenes from old films, giving their releases an art house feel that was distinct from the garishness of mainstream pop at the time.

By the time they released *Meat is Murder*, they had cemented themselves as the band for the alienated youth of Britain, and their influence only continued to grow. Marr's intricate guitar playing became iconic, with songs like 'How Soon is Now?' demonstrating a depth and complexity that few bands at the time could match. Meanwhile, Morrissey's lyrics grew bolder, tackling issues like vegetarianism and animal rights with a conviction that resonated with a growing counterculture.

The Smiths didn't just provide a soundtrack for rebellion, they embodied it. They were unapologetically themselves, refusing to conform to the music industry's expectations. While other bands were following the trends, The Smiths created their own, and for a teenager looking for authenticity, they were the perfect heroes.

The Smiths embarked on a UK tour to promote *Meat Is Murder*, playing 23 shows in 39 days. The album had gone to number 1 in the British charts. Most dates were quickly sold out.

## GOLDDIGGERS

### 27 FEBRUARY 1985, CHIPPENHAM, UK

### RICHARD SHIPMAN, AGE 18

It was the first date of the *Meat Is Murder* tour. It was my local venue and being a huge Smiths fan I could not believe they were playing on my doorstep. I managed to get onstage during a couple of the songs (it was the done thing back then) and got myself chucked out. But I knew the bouncers, so was straight back in again!

## CIVIC HALL

### 28 FEBRUARY 1985, GUILDFORD, UK

### ANDREW BLACKHURST

It was a very good concert. The only downside was that most of the numbers were from the new album, *Meat Is Murder*. We were disappointed they didn't play much from their back catalogue, and I am sure neither 'What Difference Does It Make?' nor 'This Charming Man' were in the set. But top class all the same. Good concerts were coming thick and fast at the time at the Civic. You didn't need to go to London to find the best acts. They were coming to us in Guildford!

### NICK DEAVES

I had moved to Guildford, again with work. I had a bedsit for my first year right opposite the Civic Hall. A group of us went including my girlfriend Jenny, now my wife, and some of her friends. I felt a bit protective and apprehensive of the band, as this was my first real gig with Jenny and they had a lot to live up to. But I had nothing to fear as it was a very raucous crowd and lifting one of her friends on to my shoulders broke the ice. Her friend still goes on about it now!

In what was a short-lived career, the band were a brilliant moment in time for me and just hit such a chord. I still have all my vinyl and all the reissues. As the lyrics of 'Paint a Vulgar Picture' say, 'Re-issue! Re-package! Re-package! Re-evaluate the songs, Double-pack with a photograph, Extra track (and a tacky badge).'

### DEL BOXALL, AGE 20

I might have heard them on something like the Peter Powell Radio 1 show and I thought, 'This is different.' I liked a lot of the New Romantic stuff at the time. I'd liked ska. And then in '82, I started liking Simple Minds a bit before they went a bit too big, and then The Smiths came along.

Guildford Civic Hall was a two-to-three-minute walk from where I lived, and I used to go up there when various bands were on. The staff there got to know me, and they used to give me the posters. You could buy big posters for the whole tour, but they'd have specific ones for that venue, and they'd usually get about ten of them. But I went up there to see if I could get one for The Smiths and they said, 'Well, we've only got three. We can't let you have one this time because we have to put them all outside.'

On the day of the concert, the

posters were all pasted to the boards outside and two of them got ripped to pieces where people had tried to take them down. But I managed to get the other one. I started peeling at one corner and peeled it off, complete and still wet with paste. I walked home and put it straight on my bedroom wall. That is quite possibly the only one of those posters in existence. It was easier than I thought it would be, back when I moved many years ago, to get it off again because I had some laminate running down one wall and I had managed to put it on there, so it came off. It's not in a great condition now. It's all rolled up and I'm worried to touch it in case it all crumbles to pieces.

I loved the way The Smiths came on with Prokofiev at the start. That was the only time I ever saw them. I had a ticket to see Morrissey for the first time last year, in Brighton. But we had loads of snow and we couldn't even get out of the end of my road. I finally got the ticket, and I never bloody made it. Maybe one day.

## GLENN CORPES

I was only vaguely into them. I'd bought 'This Charming Man' on twelve-inch and had a cassette copy of the first album but I was into much more obscure stuff. I went to see the support band, The Sid Presley Experience, named after three acts, that had died of drug overdoses and with songs mostly about heroin addiction. The people I was with made a point of getting pissed at the bar rather than watching the band. At some point, someone mentioned it was their last tour, so I walked into the hall and watched them from the back for about 20 minutes. I actually got much more into The Smiths several years later and again about six years ago, when my then 18-year-old son got more into them than I ever had been.

## LISA VINE, AGE 17

I discovered their music from the charts. I bought their *Hatful Of Hollow* album, which I've still got and still play, and their songs were played very regularly on the juke box in the King's Head pub in Guildford, which attracted the town's rockabilly/alternative crowd. I remember Morrissey coming out on stage and them opening with 'William, It Was Really Nothing'. The Civic just erupted. It was bloody brilliant.

## TIM NAYLOR

'How would you react if I said that I'm not from Guildford at all?'

It was fair to say that The Smiths gig at Guildford Civic Hall was approached with some trepidation. I had seen the band just over a year earlier at the notorious Reading University gig where fractious elements in the crowd had upset the singer by spitting, throwing water and generally not behaving in the approved manner.

Morrissey at Reading Uni was disengaged and bored with a crowd that was by no means hanging on his every word and, as he got more distracted, the audience sensed their quarry was weakening and taunted him further. The band performed manfully despite their singer's obvious displeasure at how

*Tim Naylor was at Guildford Civic*

the gig was unfolding, although Johnny Marr played much of the set with his back to the audience after getting a soaking early on.

Rumours that Morrissey was indeed 'still ill' following a bout of alleged man flu circulated among the onlookers prompting further heckling. The inevitable happened and he flounced during the encore of 'You've Got Everything Now'. The encore was a bad idea in the first place and, with just ten songs played in full but with little passion, many in the audience left feeling severely short-changed.

This made the Guildford Civic gig the equivalent of a make-or-break date. The night itself was notable for dense fog over the Hampshire-Surrey borders, making the journey over the A31 Hogs Back exceedingly treacherous. With visibility down to a few dozen yards, we crawled along the dual carriageway at 20 miles an hour, bringing out the inevitable quips of going 'Nowhere Fast'.

Guildford Civic was a premier circuit venue back in the day with a decent capacity of around 1,400 people and attracted some of the biggest names including Eric Clapton, King Crimson, Bowie's Ziggy tour, Dire Straits and local boys The Stranglers. Numerous punk-era acts had played the venue and notably the Civic had hosted the first night of the *White Riot* tour and The Buzzcocks' *Tension* tour, with Joy Division supporting.

Because of the poor driving conditions, we'd left for the venue quite early, so got to see James' support slot. And what a belter it was. This wasn't the chart-storming (and frankly much duller) seven-piece band of the late eighties/early nineties, but the intriguing four-piece version that dabbled in edgy indie tunes with a folky twist. Tim Booth was mesmeric at this point in his career, dancing bastardised versions of the Hucklebuck or the Mashed Potato as the band thrashed out their skinny beat tunes. James were already the stars the press said they would become; it was just that no-one else knew it at that stage.

If James were aiming for the stars, then The Smiths had already sealed their place in the firmament. This was a confident, assured band fully in control of their destiny, with a stunning sophomore album under their belts and discovering their groove in more ways than one. The crowd was rammed into the venue by this stage, with a good smattering of Mozzer look-alikes, down to NHS specs and even a few hearing aids no doubt purloined from elderly relatives just for the evening ('Nan… can I borrow your hearing aid?' 'Whaaat?').

This was effectively a coming out for the Smiths tribe of Surrey and Hampshire who had grown in number as the band's stature had similarly grown with a run of hit singles. Interestingly, the girl superfan who many of us believed to be muse for 'Sheila Take A Bow' was at this gig. I couldn't possibly tell who she was, but she was definitely named Sheila…

Thankfully, the band of a year earlier were unrecognisable. Much of the previous short set had focussed heavily on the debut LP and this had been replaced with some choice cuts from *Meat Is*

*Murder* and its attendant singles. Only four songs survived from Reading – 'Hand In Glove', 'Heaven Knows I'm Miserable Now', 'Still Ill' and 'Barbarism Begins At Home'.

A spritely 'William, It Was Really Nothing' kicked off proceedings and it was a heady rush through the early part of the set, so much so that Morrissey didn't address the audience ('Good evening trendsetters…') until the end of 'Handsome Devil', the fourth song they played. And they were loud, very loud… proper rock band loud, in fact.

The first real showstopper followed immediately, as 'How Soon Is Now?' rang out, with Johnny Marr's vibrato guitar drawing cheers from the crowd. The swooping chords and Morrissey's sonorous vocals prompted a sing-along from some parts of the crowd, now supremely familiar with the song from the flipside of 'William' or from the Peel session from earlier in the year.

The forthcoming single 'Shakespeare's Sister' was introduced as a 'kind little single' followed by a headlong rush through 'Heaven Knows I'm Miserable Now', 'That Joke Isn't Funny Anymore', 'Rusholme Ruffians' and 'Hand in Glove'.

The main set drew to a close with a double whammy of 'Still Ill' and a creepy and affecting 'Meat Is Murder', the buzzsaw ringing out even more ominously in the opening passage than on the LP version. The band exited stage left but were soon back as the fervent crowd yelled and screamed for more.

The encore of 'Miserable Lie' / 'Barbarism Begins At Home' was the icing on the cake for the by now supplicant masses, with dancing on the venue floor. It has been said many times, but the boys in the rhythm section really earned their corn on the latter track, which was simply huge in every respect. Then they were gone. The crowd filtered out towards the car parks, bus station and railway platforms, peering through the by now near freezing fog. We hung around for a bit while the crowd dispersed, hoping to see the band but gave up as the temperature dropped.

The drive home to Fleet was almost surreal as four of us crammed into my Toyota Celica, sliding through the dense murk in silence along the deserted road. We probably wouldn't have heard anyone talking anyway – the band were loud and the ears were still ringing the next day.

It was, in many ways, the near perfect gig. A fabulous and arguably surprising support slot from James, followed by an all-conquering performance from the headliners. I even got a poster for the gig, which I still own 34 years later. I would see The Smiths several times again, including the Royal Albert Hall gig, but they were never as good for me as they were on that night at Guildford Civic. But it's not quite my favourite gig at that venue… a few years later I trod the same boards myself with my band Handsome Bastards and, sorry Mozzer, nothing would ever beat that!

## MALCOLM WYATT, AGE 17

1985 was an important one for a lad not long turned 17. So many

*Malcolm Wyatt was on his first proper date when he went to see The Smiths*

personal landmarks with live music at the forefront. I was a lower sixth-former, wondering now how I fitted in my studies amid such a busy diary. Things took a major turn in the second half of the year, dating for the first time while Saturday and holiday work at my hometown branch of Boots helped pay for a growing vinyl obsession. If my diaries are right, the visit of The Smiths to Guildford Civic Hall was my nineteenth gig, just three days after the thrill of catching the Ramones up the A3 at London's Lyceum.

The Smiths also turned out to be my first proper date… of sorts. I'm not convinced my college friend Karen saw it like that mind. She was hardly hanging off my arm. Way too good for the likes of me with self-esteem low on my list of attributes. I can't recall how we ended up going along together or how this fairly shy lad asked her. I'm pretty sure she bought her own ticket, so maybe it was just a case of meeting nearby.

I wasn't obsessive about The Smiths, but I'd been a fan since first hearing John Peel and David 'Kid' Jensen play them. The *Hatful of Hollow* compilation album collecting those BBC Radio 1 sessions resonated far more than the eponymous debut.

I even cited Mozzer in a General Studies O-level exam that summer, my discourse on vegetarianism ending with the line, 'In the words of Steven Patrick Morrissey, 'Who hears when animals cry?'' I like to think the examiner raised his eyebrows, impressed, wondering how this obscure poet had eluded him.

I was learning bass guitar too, a left-hander spending far too much time copying intricate Andy Rourke lines in my bedroom, 'Barbarism Begins At Home' and 'This Charming Man' being particular favourites.

Like The Clash before them, Rourke, Mike Joyce and Johnny Marr looked the part, the latter always the genius for these ears. Ah, those melodies and that delivery. As a backing band they were similarly impressive, and who could resist Sandie Shaw out front?

I never quite knew what to make of Morrissey, but he was engaging and funny in the (mainly) *NME* interviews I read, and those lyrics were often sublime. The gladioli and hearing aid stunts left me cold, only serving to fuel non-believers' arguments in countless pub, workplace and common room arguments as to the band's merits. But there was no doubting the artistry. I guess I saw him the same way I saw many more aloof, camp great poets down the years, such as John Betjeman. A genius wordsmith, so to speak. So many great lines.

A gay workmate later questioned Mozza's tongue-in-cheek celibacy claims from his own memories of nights out in Manchester, but it didn't really matter.

I hadn't warmed to *Meat Is Murder*, but it had its highpoints, with the Guildford show impressive from the moment the searchlights swirled around the dancefloor to the accompaniment of Prokofiev's 'Romeo And Juliet', a perfect curtain-raiser. I can recall little more about that night, something that embarrassed me when interviewing James' Saul Davies and Jim Glennie in later years. Had I even seen them?

Nothing came of my date with Karen. Not so much as a stolen kiss under the iron bridge, or even outside nearby music venue. the Wooden Bridge. Nature hadn't made a man of me … yet. Youth, eh – wasted on the young. We're still in touch, both impressed at having been there.

### JULIA DODD

I had tickets for this but sold them on the door, my friend and I making the monumentally stupid decision to go and see our friends rehearse their band in Cranleigh Scout Hall. I'm still bitterly regretting the decision.

### ANDY COLES

I was at art college in Farnham in Surrey. I saw them three times. The first time was at Hammersmith Palais, when Sandie Shaw came on and sang 'I Don't Owe You Anything'. Before the gig, Johnny Marr walked past us, and I was surprised how slight he was. He was wearing a yellow roll neck sweater and black beads.

I then saw them at the GLC Jobs For A Change Festival. This was a beautiful day. I got to see Billy Bragg twice, The Redskins and Mari Wilson before The Smiths came on. There'd been quite a bit of trouble during The Redskins set and I seem to recall a punch up down the front. One of the guys who tagged along with my college friends and myself was on a photography course and

managed to get right down the front during The Smiths' set. One of his photos subsequently appeared on the back of *ZigZag* magazine. The band were amazingly tight and played a few fairly new numbers. My prominent memory of the day is getting the sleeve on my old suit jacket almost getting torn off in the melee. A puce-faced middle-aged man was trying to get to the back of the crowd after initially being trapped down the front and we were laughing at his angry face as he passed by. That'd be me these days!

Guildford Civic was probably the favourite of my Smiths' gigs. The band were on top form. James looked like folk group The Spinners, dressed in fisherman's jumpers, but went down a storm, possibly as Morrissey had raved about them and had chosen their 'What's The World?' song as one of his favourites on Janice Long's Radio 1 evening show. The Smiths went on to cover and record their own live version.

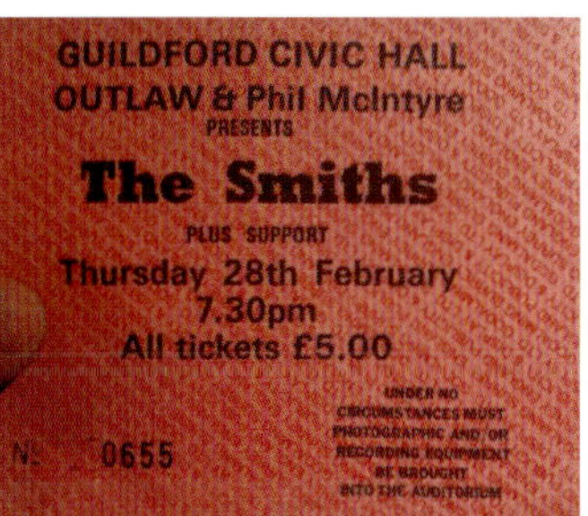
*Andy Coles with his Guildford Civic poster & his ticket*

During The Smiths' set, I managed to get right down the front and held Morrissey's thumb at some point. The journey home was memorable as we decided, possibly fuelled by excessive quantities of cider, that we would walk the eleven miles back to Farnham. The evening was dreadful, really misty and spooky, and as we walked along the Hog's Back, the headlights of passing cars silhouetted the trees, making it look like a Spielberg movie. We thought our hitchhiking attempt was successful as a car pulled up and we ran to accept his 'offer of a lift'. We reached the car and peered inside at the driver sorting out his seat belt. Three black-clothed figures stood expecting the bloke to open the door and as one of us tapped on the passenger window, he looked up in total fear and sped away as if the ghostly ship's crew from Jon Carpenter's *The Fog* had come for him. Perhaps he'd not seen us and had just stopped to adjust his seatbelt? He probably still tells the tale of how he saw three ghosts on the Hog's Back.

I bought a couple of the posters for the gig for £1 each at the merchandising stand. Amazingly, they survived the journey home. I advertised one on eBay a few years back and it went within half an hour for £300, not a bad investment. I still have one framed on my landing.

### STEPH ROCHE

The second time I saw them was at Guildford Civic. It was a Thursday night and a school night. Getting the tickets was interesting. The Army and Navy store was selling them. It was snowing and I left it quite late to get one. I don't know why, but I think we phoned up and they had eight left. And I begged my mum to go and drive and pick them up for me.

Guildford Civic was a great venue. It's not huge, and you could get straight to the front. James were amazing. And the Prokofiev music was on for the intro. My boyfriend and I, the Morrissey lookalike, started up in the balcony and I just wanted to go downstairs but he wouldn't. I think he was jealous of me wanting to go down and see Morrissey, so I just went down on my own and gazed up and got as close as I could. I was at the front, with my fingernails on the stage. You could get that close. It was mad. You used to be able to do that. And I touched Morrissey's shoes!

There wasn't a mosh pit or anything. It was just really gentle. I don't remember being squashed or anything. I remember it just being a really mixed, friendly, young crowd. Girls and boys and a lot of Oxfam shirts, obviously, and the quiffs. I just loved that look. It was just great. The style out then made you a freak. We used to dress in all the second-hand clothes and stuff anyway, before The Smiths, so we were already you know could relate to him on that level.

My boyfriend would get laughed at and spat at in the street because he was wearing Hush Puppies and he had the specs and an old shirt on. He was like, 'Well, that's what Morrissey thinks, isn't it? People laughing at you because of how you look.' And he wore the glasses because he actually did need glasses!

We felt pretty special to have him write to me and also to have seen him. Because Morrissey's got this way of just connecting.

They were on *The South Bank Show*, and I remember knowing about that and making sure I watched it and reading about it in the *NME*. On the day *Strangeways* came out I was at the record shop first thing. I just played it to death. I was really upset about the split, but I realised it couldn't go on forever. And all the albums are perfect, each one of them.

I don't know why I didn't see them again, but I've seen Morrissey multiple times since. Just seeing a lot of the clips of the recent gigs, his interactions are really kind. He seems just more human than he used to on stage.

I remember seeing Chapterhouse supporting The Sundays at Leeds Warehouse one time. Someone in the crowd shouted at (Sundays' singer) Harriet, 'Get your tits out, Morrissey!' Because she basically was a female Morrissey.

## BRIXTON ACADEMY

### 1 MARCH 1985, LONDON, UK

### KEITH BRADBURY, AGE 24

A neighbour who worked in radio had heard 'This Charming Man' on John Peel and when he put it on the turntable it just blew me away. I must have played it hundreds of thousands of times since. It's my 'go to' song to put me in a good mood or before I go out. I remember seeing them on *Top Of The Pops* and I just fell in love. The fact that Morrissey was from my home city and that he sang about places I knew, and about things that I was going through, made it even more special. I didn't get to see them until 1985 but – wow – what a concert. I had never experienced anything like it. I'd seen mass hysteria before – my first gig was T. Rex at Manchester Free Trade Hall in 1971 – but not on this scale! It began quietly enough as the crowd gathered, and with so many Morrissey clones it was wonderful.

I went with a close friend, and we stood about halfway up the sloping floor. After a while, I noticed people turning and pointing at us but then realised it was not me they were pointing at but the guy and his girlfriend standing next to us – Pete Burns, eye patch and all, of Dead or Alive. I remember swaying back and forth with the surge of the crowd and Moz asking people to invade the stage. People said there was some fighting, but I didn't see any.

I couldn't take my eyes off him so there could have been a free for all right in front of me and I doubt I would have noticed. It was the *Meat Is Murder* tour. I remember some people, who clearly didn't share Moz's sentiments, booed over the opening notes of 'Barbarism Begins At Home'. But they were soon drowned out – hey, I didn't care – I just sang along. I was spellbound and have been to this day. My wife is still convinced that if Moz knocked on my door and asked me to run away with him I would. Well, maybe!

I found out when Moz's autobiography came out that he

had worked in the same office as me when he was 15 and I was 17. So near and yet so far! I bought every single including twelve-inch ones, and every album, and still have them all. I've seen Morrissey solo many times; he is still amazing, but the electricity of that night can never really be repeated.

### KRISTIN COLLINS, AGE 17

I was in England from the US for several months on a long holiday before starting college. A few months earlier I was having drinks with a sound engineer friend – no one asked for ID back then – who knew Morrissey and Marr. So, when they walked into the pub we were in, they sat down with us for a few rounds. I knew who they were and liked the band, but they weren't huge stars in America, so to me the whole thing seemed quite casual. Various musicians frequented the pubs in the area, so them showing up was not a big deal. I remember chatting with Morrissey about different things, including music, and I specifically recall both of us saying we liked The Go-Betweens.

That same friend was able to get us into the venue early the night of the show so I could be up front. But things quickly got crazy, so I didn't stay up there long. After a few songs, I moved back where I was less likely to get bruised and could actually breathe. Honestly, the band sounded pretty rough, but Morrissey was quite happy, exuberantly dancing and interacting with the crowd. He was obviously having fun and was fascinating to watch.

The highlights were 'That Joke Isn't Funny Anymore' and 'How Soon Is Now?' while the 'Barbarism Begins At Home' encore was great. The energy of the whole night was pretty intense, and I left with the feeling that I had just seen something special.

I couldn't know that a lifelong obsession had been ignited. Three decades on I've been to well over 50 shows, including shows at this same venue, and I have tickets for more. That first Smiths show opened with 'William, It Was Really Nothing'. And when I last saw Morrissey live, he also opened with this song. What a nice way to bookend 34 years of absolute and unwavering love for The Smiths and Morrissey.

## GUILDHALL

### 3 MARCH 1985, PORTSMOUTH, UK

### DEBBIE CALLAWAY, AGE 23

I remember Morrissey walking off the stage because fans were spitting at him and him saying, 'It's not 1976!' I was so relieved when he came back on stage. I was devastated when they split up. I think I just heard it on the radio. I have three sons aged 35, 29 and 23 who all love them too as they grew up listening to them.

## HEXAGON THEATRE

### 4 MARCH 1985, READING, UK

### MARC BEATTIE, AGE 16

I remember Tim Booth's horrendous fluffy blue jumper

more than anything the main band played, apart from they said they were playing a tune for the first time. I can't remember which one. I really remember nothing about it other than being underwhelmed.

### ROBERT PARKIN, AGE 16

It was my first gig, and I lied to my parents to say a friend's dad was taking us so I could go on my own. I remember trying to emulate Morrissey's quiff with loads of Mum's hairspray, an over-sized collarless grandad shirt and a bunch of daffodils in the back pocket of my 501s. People were selling knock off t-shirts and posters outside the venue.

James supported and Tim Booth was dancing like an epileptic. All I can really remember from The Smiths is Morrissey whirling his gladioli around and Johnny Marr just looking so cool. I think the backdrop was the cover photo from the 'That Joke Isn't Funny Anymore' single.

### MICK ROWLEY, AGE 17

I became an instant fan. Morrissey's lyrics and the music touched me like nothing had before. I had just left school; Thatcher was in power and everything felt directionless and very dull. The Smiths changed everything from then on. I, and so many others, clung on to Morrissey's every word. He made me feel accepted for being an outsider and definitely less alone.

I lived just outside of Reading, so it was great to be able to see them so close to home. I took my 13-year-old sister. She wasn't a huge fan, but she wanted to see them. I still tell her how lucky she was to have seen one of the most exciting live bands of all time, especially at such a young age. I danced all night, trying my best to imitate Morrissey's every move.

The second time I saw The Smiths was on 24 October 1986 on the *Queen Is Dead* tour, at Brixton Academy. The Railway Children supported and, like James at the Hexagon in Reading, they were brilliant too.

A few months later I bought the *NME* as usual. I was more than heartbroken when I saw the news they'd split. It was the end of an era for me and something that still upsets me today. But at least I got to see them twice, which, is more than most people I know. I'm still a huge fan of Morrissey and have seen him 20 plus times, once in Rome. He'll always be a huge part of my life. I don't ever want The Smiths to reform, as I want my wonderful memories to remain intact. There's no way they'd ever get back together anyway. So many bands mean a lot to me, but The Smiths, and especially Morrissey, changed my life forever.

### ANDY WHITE

I saw The Smiths twice on the *Meat Is Murder* tour. Reading was notable due to me losing my car. I parked up on a side street near the venue. My intention was to get drunk and sleep in the car, something I did a few times in this era. Trouble was I bumped into Julie, a girl I knew from Basingstoke. She persuaded me to go back to her place with her on the last train – and she took advantage of my good nature. I

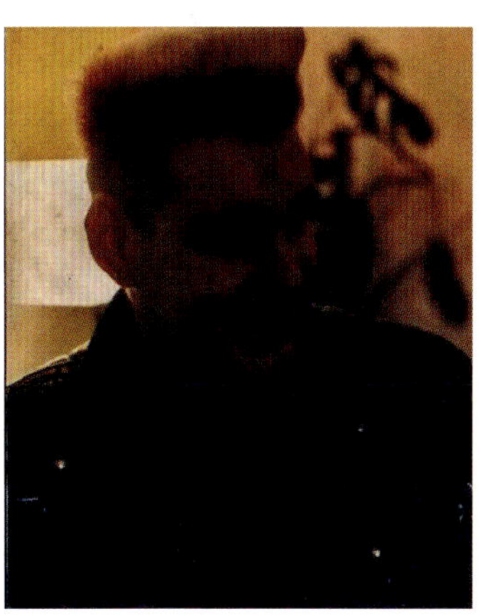

*Mick Rowley became an instant fan*

*Andy White saw the Meat is Murder tour twice*

awoke in her bed the next morning with a massive hangover and had to get to work in Overton, about ten miles in the opposite direction from Reading. I got a bus to work, spent most of the day throwing up into the River Test, which ran through the site where I worked, and then persuaded a mate to give me a lift to Reading to collect my car. But when we got to Reading, we had to drive around for about two hours before I found it.

Back to the gig. I got in the hall early to make sure I saw them and there was a sparse crowd for their short set. I hadn't seen Tim Booth doing his crazy dancing before and drummer Gavan Whelan was out of this world, the best I've ever seen by a distance.

By now The Smiths had massive support. The venue was heaving and I got to the front of the stage during the first song. I got quite a few bruises from the crush – you've not really been to a concert unless you get a few cuts and bruises. Their set was mostly from *Meat Is Murder* plus a few old favourites. I always loved it during 'Still Ill' when Morrissey used to collapse on stage during the chorus. I remember him introducing 'Shakespeare's Sister' as their new single – it was released about two weeks later.

I rate Mike Joyce and Andy Rourke as a functional rhythm section, but they are relatively weak compared to Hook and Morris in New Order, Whelan and Glennie in James, Reni and Mani in The Stone Roses. Just think – The Smiths could have been even better. They made it really on the strength of Morrissey with his ego and lyrics – he's not a

great singer – and of course Marr's guitar and tunes. Joyce and Rourke were really just filling the gaps, and not contributing that much, relatively speaking. Hence all the later anguish in the courtroom over the royalties.

# POOLE ARTS CENTRE
## 6 MARCH 1985, POOLE, UK

### STEVE CATTERALL

Down to Poole. By this time, as well as Paul and me, we'd picked up three other regular passengers – Jo, who was a big fan of Johnny's and who we'd initially met at Chippenham, and two Japanese girls, whose names I can't remember anymore. Jo had a history of following The Smiths around and had been to quite a few of the 1984 English dates, so she was a bit of a veteran. The Japanese girls used to turn up at the start of each tour and then disappear afterwards. Those three were with us pretty much right through until late 1986. We were also starting to recognise a number of regular fans that would turn up at every venue. By the Scottish tour later in the year, the band of regulars made the travelling and hanging around waiting much more bearable.

The venue at Poole was down by the sea. I remember hearing the soundcheck sitting in the car park round the back, although the combination of being outside and the wind off the sea made it hard to make out what songs they were playing. I think it was here that I first heard them playing 'Bigmouth'. Even with the muffled sound it sounded quite different to all the other songs.

Going to many of the shows, you got to hear the songs grow. Actually, our experience was probably the opposite of most people's, as we often got used to the live versions of songs before we heard the recorded version. I remember being distinctly unimpressed with the recorded version of 'Ask'. The version they were playing live was much more jangly and urgent.

### CHARLIE PINDER

1985 was one of the best years of my life. I had just started a new job and only a few days later I was about to see the best band that the world has ever seen and will ever see. However, at this stage nobody I knew was of the same opinion! Like many early Smiths fans (I assumed), I travelled to the gig alone, a half an hour bus trip from the Dorset market town of Wimborne Minster to the bright lights of Poole.

I wish I had a phone back then, to look back at a selfie of me in my flowery shirt. I'm sure I looked a lot less cool than I remember it today. The bus stop was just over the road from the Arts Centre. I had no idea what to expect from the new 'love-hate' band from Manchester. My only other gigs at the Arts Centre had been Black Sabbath with my sister, which was frightening and exciting and obviously deafening, and Madness with school mates, which was great as I actually knew the songs.

I can't remember if there had been a support, but I can remember the thrill of The Smiths walking out to Prokofiev and the loud cheer when the music stopped. The rest is a blur. I stood in awe, first staring at Morrissey and singing every single word of the songs I knew, and then glancing over to Johnny Marr and starring once again, this time in wonderment of his guitar skills and craft.

As the night went on, they did a hauntingly beautiful song that was unknown to me. Months later, I bought a bootleg cassette recording of the following night's gig in Brighton and the song was titled 'Take Me Out'. On the day of the release of *The Queen is Dead*, I picked up my pre-order copy from Square Records in Wimborne and played it to death that evening. To my absolute joy, 'Take Me Out' came on, I realised it was actually called 'There is a Light That Never Goes Out' and it confirmed that my love for The Smiths would live for eternity!

I probably remember the gig more because of my Brighton bootleg cassette, which I still have. I know I got home safely, and I know that no one at school the next day was particularly impressed that I went to the gig. But I didn't really think that I'd be playing Smiths songs as much as I do today. My pretty impressive vinyl collection on vinyl is one of my most prized possessions. For the record my favourite songs, now the dust has settled on The Smiths, are 'Still Ill' and 'Ask'.

The best feeling was taking my daughter to see Morrissey at Bournemouth a few years back. She wanted to go and bought the tickets as a birthday present to me. We stood together and Morrissey was at his brilliant best.

### RACHEL WALDEN, AGE 17

I went with my boyfriend. Morrissey (I think) had 'Meat is murder' written across his chest or back. The end of the concert was very shocking – it was the sound of the abattoir, the animals screaming and the sound of saws! The *Meat Is Murder* album was one of their best. I'm now 50 years old and my ringtone on my phone is 'There is a Light That Never Goes Out'.

### TIM BAIGENT

In 1983 / 84, I was floundering around looking to fill the hole in my overheated little 16 or 17-year-old head. Then this lot appear on *Top Of The Pops* with Sandie Shaw, a super cool guitar player with, yes, the ultimate seal of approval, playing a fat semi-solid Gibson 335! Wow, this isn't Kajagoogoo or Wham!

I started hoovering up The Smiths early singles but the sound on the debut LP was slightly underwhelming. No fear, thank the gods for the *Hatful Of Hollow* compilation with its ace fold out sleeve featuring the lads in portacabin heaven at Glastonbury. I played this to death!

Breaking it to my girlfriend Alex and best friend Stew that I really liked this lot ('yes, that twat with the flowers in his arse off *Top Of The Pops*') felt like a confession to some weird cult… but it was too late. I was gone on this lot. Stew soon joined the tribe. Alex and I started to drift and then split. I'm not sure if The Smiths confession was responsible for this, but I am sure it didn't help…

My favourite of those early singles by some distance was 'Shakespeare's Sister', a chaotic, audacious, messy two minutes and nine seconds rockabilly mash up with hamfisted piano and a cello on the outro. In January 1985, it got in the charts! This was a 'chart act' single.

I was already two years out of school but I got a call from Stew at work to say that the sixth formers at the school I had been thrown out of two years previously were running a minibus to see The Smiths play at Poole Arts Centre. Mr Porter, one of the few coolish teachers attempting to educate the hordes at Holyrood Comprehensive School in Chard, had pulled it all together. So it was that 15 lucky bods made the hour and half trip up the coast to Poole in the school minibus.

In support were James. Not your major label run of the mill band who had paid to be on the tour. They were an odd-looking four piece. I had seen their single 'Hymn From A Village' riding high in the *NME* chart but had not heard a note of their music. They looked cooler than they sounded – but with the jumble sale jumpers and prewired Manc confidence they obviously had 'it'. They finished up their entertaining 40 minutes and we were left sandwiched at the front, sweating… waiting.

I had attended the local Sunday School and large church services as a cub, but what was to come next was the closest thing I'd had to a religious experience. There was a complete black out of the hall with no sound… and then the opening, rolling thunder of Prokofiev's Romeo and Juliet's 'Dance Of The Knights'. It came in gentle but sinister, with then a sixty-piece orchestra in my chest and over the massive wall of black speakers we were squished against.

*Tim Baigent caught The Smiths in incendiary form in 1985 in Poole*

Still disorientated, we were struck by blinding white light which burnt over the crowd like a laser. I picked out Morrissey and then Marr in a denim jacket, collar pulled up with a fat Les Paul with trem arm reflecting in the white.

The deafening opening chords to 'William, It Was Really Nothing' exploded. It was like nothing else, even better than seeing The Jam in March 1982. There may have been flowers flying around but the 'lad' Smiths fans were still a rough-arsed lot and down the front it was getting tasty. But the wonderful sounds ploughed on and the discomfort of being in a moving, mutating ruck was worth it. We got everything from *Meat Is Murder* plus *Hatful Of Hollow* highlights.

It was an incendiary gig, finishing with 'Meat Is Murder' itself, complete with five-minute slaughterhouse wailing of mother bovine. Then it was over. Afterwards, dazed and soaked, we hit the cold spring night air. There we were met by loads of Manc grafters selling massive hooky tour posters, hollering, 'Two Pound The Big One'! Basically, it was the *NME* full page advert, scanned and blown up and printed to A0 size. I bought two.

# THE DOME

## 7 MARCH 1985, BRIGHTON, UK

## WAYNE LUNDQVIST FORD, AGE 16

I first remember hearing The Smiths with the release of 'Hand In Glove' when it hit the indie charts.

But it wasn't until the release of 'This Charming Man' that I started to sit up and listen. I had just turned 16 and the lyrics spoke to me. I wasn't sure I was getting the full meaning of them, but I didn't really care. It was the bright, chiming guitar of Johnny Marr that really grabbed me.

I bought a copy of the self-titled debut album on cassette so I could listen to it on my Sony Walkman. The image of Morrissey waving his gladioli about on *Top Of The Pops* stuck with me and made me giggle when I listened to the singles and album, but Marr's guitar was brilliant and that, along with the rhythm section, blew me away musically, the first time this had happened to me since The Jam.

A few months after 'This Charming Man', the *Meat Is Murder* album came out. I bought it the same day, again on cassette so I could listen to it through headphones on my motorbike. The abattoir sound at the beginning of the album was haunting, although not so much that I jumped on board with being a vegetarian. 'Rusholme Ruffians' was my favourite track, and I loved the way it sounded like '(Marie's The Name) His Latest Flame' by Elvis. I wasn't an Elvis fan, but I had liked that track as a kid and thought it was cool nod to the past, taking something and making it part of our own culture.

My mother was working for a publishing company in Haywards Heath, Sussex and said she worked closely with the promoter Phil McIntyre. So when I saw that Outlaw and Phil McIntyre were promoting the *Meat Is Murder*

*Wayne Lundqvist Ford was at Brighton Dome*

tour, I asked if she could get me a ticket for the gig at Brighton Dome. A few days before the gig, my mother came home with two tickets with 'guest ticket' stamped across the front. I felt really special and went out that night to tell my mates all about it. A friend I rode motorcycles with me then was interested in the gig so I said he could have the other ticket. I can't recall his name now and I think I probably sold it to him a bit cheaper in order to get some petrol money for my bike.

We took the train from Burgess Hill to Brighton so we could have a couple of (underage) beers on the way there, or even at the venue. Brighton Dome is a seated venue, an old-fashioned concert hall, which seemed an odd setting for The Smiths to play. Most people remained seated through James, and I was impressed at how the band swapped and played different instruments during their set.

Finally, the lights dipped and 'Dance Of The Knights' started playing, probably the first piece of classical music that caught my attention. I later spent ages hunting down who it was and what it was called. There was no internet then and going into a record shop and humming the bit you could remember to a fellow spotty youth in HMV was completely out of the question. But I found it a few years later and I still associate it with seeing The Smiths.

As soon as the band hit the stage, people were up and out of the seats. Me and my mate opted, like many others, to stand up on the back of the old wooden seats.

Many seats and people were seen collapsing through the opening number 'William, It Was Really Nothing', much to the despair of the middle-aged female stewards who were probably only a little younger than my nan at the time. As much as they pleaded, nobody was sitting back down to watch The Smiths. Morrissey and the band were also showered with gladioli, which was hilarious.

I can't remember too much about Morrissey as I was pretty much transfixed by Marr and his black Rickenbacker 330, a guitar that I decided I would one day own. (I do now own one, but it is the Sunburst version, and I still can't play like Johnny!) Apart from studying Marr, I didn't really pay much attention to the rest of the band. I thought Andy Rourke's hair was cool and I had a similar cut a few weeks later, but it didn't look as good on me and I grew it out.

They played my favourite songs – 'Rusholme Ruffians', 'Nowhere Fast' and 'That Joke Isn't Funny Anymore'. Everyone left with a smile on their face. My mate wandered around to the back door of the Dome to see if we could catch the band coming out. There weren't many people there and we were about to leave when the band exited the stage door.

Morrissey was the first one out. I said 'hi' and was about to offer up my ticket to be signed but he just rushed past. I thought he was quite aloof, but what did I know really? I turned around and Marr was there. He took my ticket and scribbled across the back of it. I told him I enjoyed the gig, I think he said 'great' and then he was gone too.

I stuck with the band and their records right until the end, although I never saw them live again. As a radio deejay, I still get a kick and a laugh out of playing 'Hang The DJ' ('Panic') and I think I always will. I still love Marr's guitar and as I got older, I started to understand Morrissey's lyrics more and got the humour in them that others missed. I was so glad I saw them live that once.

### PAUL THOMAS SCOTT FULKER, AGE 18

To this day, this is the best gig I ever saw. It was incredible. I went with three close mates and a few girls. I was in a band, and we were mad on The Smiths, The Icicle Works, The Church, Echo and The Bunnymen and Lloyd Cole. I hadn't been to many gigs, so I guess I was in awe. I remember the seats had vegetarian and antivivisection flyers on them. We were all veggies and into animal welfare.

We all ended up on the backs of the chairs on the front few rows. I was stuck behind a guy with a massive spliff. It was a crush waiting to happen. At some point, the seats snapped and everyone was on the deck on top of each other. I remember scrambling about trying to get up. Somehow, I managed to get close to the front and stayed there for the whole gig.

It went dark and the classical piece by Prokofiev played. Then the lights came on and 'William' started. They looked larger than life. Marr was smiling his head off and I remember him playing his Rickenbacker 360 Jetglo. Rourke was statuesque. He reminded me of a Thunderbird puppet. Weird, I know, but they all did – they must have had make up on or maybe the lights were over-exposing their faces as they looked exactly like popstars!

At the end, Morrissey stripped off his shirt and threw it into the crowd. It was like a pack of dogs ripping at flesh. One of my mates, a girl called Tina, had hold of the whole sleeve and was hanging on to it for dear life! She was smiling and determined not to let go of it. It was a gold base shirt with loads of coloured diamonds all over it. I had Morrissey's glass mineral water bottle off the stage. I kept it for years. I'm not sure if I've still got the shirt remnant.

### NICK LINAZASORO

There was the hearing aid, and flowers thrown from the back pockets. Nothing out of the ordinary!

### KAREN PARKER

I nearly didn't go and thank God I did. I have loved Morrissey ever since.

### NICK MYALL

The Smiths had released *Hatful Of Hollow* and *Meat Is Murder* since I had seen them in early 1984 and had amassed an amazing catalogue of classic tunes. Most people go for *The Queen Is Dead* as their favourite Smiths album, but I always thought *Meat Is Murder* was when they added some extra colour to the tunes with Johnny's intricate guitar patterns lighting up Morrissey's lyrics. I had been playing it to death since it came out, so tickets for the Dome gig were snapped up from Virgin Records in Brighton as soon as the date was announced.

When the day arrived Matt, James and I left Haywards Heath Sixth Form extra early and headed on down to Brighton for the gig. James from Manchester's Factory Records were an inspired choice as the support band on the tour. Morrissey had been banging on about them for weeks in the *NME* and *Melody Maker* (both essential weekly reading at the time) and 'Hymn From A Village' and their other early tunes went down well with the crowd, but the main event was about to happen...

'William, It Was Really Nothing', 'What Difference Does It Make?', 'This Charming Man', as well as 'Nowhere Fast', 'What She Said', 'I Want The One I Can't Have' and 'Headmaster Ritual' from the new LP all had the Dome jumping. A strobe light lit up a plain white backdrop as the eerie vibrato intro to 'How Soon Is Now?' signalled another heartfelt sing-along from the audience. Blood red lighting underlined the message of 'Meat Is Murder' while 'That Joke Isn't Funny Anymore' hit home with heart-breaking impact. Some of the first album also got a run out and 'Miserable Lie' built up to its impressive climax with as much force as ever.

We were also treated to a new song, and the rush of 'Shakespeare's Sister' was a high point, the latest single and a bonus for the fans as a standalone track. We were right up the front as usual, bashing Jonny Marr's desert boots in time to the tunes. It was fairly messy but, luckily, I managed to hang onto my watch and shoes – unlike at a Bunnymen gig in Crawley!

As the gig came to a triumphant finale, Morrissey threw his patterned psychedelic shirt into the audience. I can still picture the hilarious sight of a mob of teenage Smiths fans ripping it to shreds. I still have a piece of it somewhere.

### KAREN WALDON-SAUNDERS, AGE 16

I was really into Duran Duran to begin with, and Depeche Mode, Nik Kershaw and Kajagoogoo. I got into The Smiths as an adolescent. I loved the lyrics and Johnny's guitar playing, the jangly guitars. Their music is very funny and witty and downbeat and sarcastic. It's not depressing. It's sardonic and witty. I can remember dancing around my room to *Hatful Of Hollow*. My best friend John was also a fan. We went to secondary school together. We went to all the gigs together.

I remember the red seats and it being an all-seated venue. Tickets were £5. My memory is that James were booed off. I also remember it being really dark when The Smiths came on and them playing against a black background. There were lots of flashing strobe lights and lots of cow noises for 'Meat Is Murder' and that line, 'heifer whines could be human cries', made a real impression on me.

There was a huge bundle down at the front and I was desperate to go down the front, but we didn't. My mum and dad used to drop us off and collect us and we always had to sit. I wasn't allowed to stand at gigs. But if you were close enough you could lean on the stage with your elbows. The bouncers were just keeping people back. I feel really, really lucky that I saw The Smiths live because they didn't last very long. I felt like Morrissey was singing directly to me.

## WINTER GARDENS

8 MARCH 1985, MARGATE, UK

### DAN WELLER

Margate had received more than its fair share of battle scars during the two world wars, so I never considered it 'the seaside town that they forgot to bomb' which Morrissey would sing about so scathingly in 'Everyday Is Like Sunday'. Though in 1985 you could have been forgiven for thinking our little resort might be a candidate for dystopian fiction as we continued to struggle on in an era of cheap holidays abroad, our hotels gradually replaced by B&B accommodation for the ill-fated. So, when The Smiths added the Winter Gardens to the *Meat Is Murder* tour that year, my initial euphoria was replaced by thoughts of, 'Who the hell is going to attend?'

My fears worsened when I noticed that the ticket I'd paid a fiver for at the box office bore the number 001. Sadly, having given this blue slip of paper the reverence I might have reserved for a winning Wonka bar wrapper, it was turned to confetti at the door on the night of the concert, although I did manage to secure a promotional poster.

So what would Moz make of a Margate audience not known for its exuberance at shows? The Smiths stepped out of the wings to pockets of rapturous applause, but it was clear that some oafish louts had gone along to heckle the rising star. Wearing gladioli in his back pocket while twirling around like a drunken ballerina, they believed, mocked traditional values of masculinity. A few beers were thrown.

In Thatcher's Britain, Boy George was too obvious a target. With Morrissey, the lines were blurred. A challenge if you like. There wasn't a lot of banter. It was hot in the mosh pit and I had half a mind on keeping my tour programme free from creases. Andy Rourke's thundering bass riff rode tandem with Mike Joyce's workmanlike drums. My ribcage vibrated like a road drill as I studied Johnny Marr effecting his best Keith Richards impression, the chiming notes picked on his Les Paul Gibson ricocheting off the hall's neo-Grecian interior.

And the joy of a new song! 'Shakespeare's Sister' was premiered, which I instantly loved as it surely paid homage to the Buzzcocks. Neutrals may have gone along hoping to hear 'Heaven Knows I'm Miserable Now', but they'd have been disappointed. I personally would have loved the beautiful 'Well I Wonder'. It was a night for the devotee, so an understaffed chant for an encore at the end of the set was rewarded with a sarcastic, 'Well, if you're sure? I mean, we wouldn't want to twist your arm or anything.'

Ah, Morrissey. You may have thought you were misunderstood, but did you ever really get us?

### STEVE WILLIAMS

When I got into The Smiths, I was about 14 years old. I was quite an awkward 14-year-old and it was like they were singing directly to me. The songs spoke about how I felt and my life. I'm from East London but grew up in Kent. I was living in a small village called Borden, just near Sittingbourne. There were quite a few kids about the same age as me, and virtually all of us got into The Smiths at the same time. My brother was a couple of years younger than me, and he was really into The Smiths too.

I bought the first album on the day of release from Woolworths in Sittingbourne. I couldn't wait to get home and play it. It was never off the turntable for weeks after it came out. We only ever saw them the once. I went with my brother and my best mate at the time, an older lad called Tim Melia. He had seen them previously at the University of Kent at Canterbury. Part of the attraction was that James were supporting them.

My parents got me the tickets as a sixteenth birthday present. It was a school day. My brother and I rushed home from school, very excited to be going. It was only a few weeks before I was due to start doing my O levels and CSEs and I remember my parents saying, 'Whatever you do, don't be late.' Tim drove us to the gig. It was a 40-minute drive from Sittingbourne to Margate so to have them playing so close to home was fantastic. It was the first time I'd ever been to the Winter Gardens – I've seen loads of bands there since – and it's a very atmospheric venue.

It's a very old-fashioned venue, over 100 years old, but the way it was decorated was perfect for The Smiths. I don't believe it was sold out because it never felt packed in there. We got there as the doors opened. They played quite a strange, eclectic bunch of songs, lots of album tracks and obscure tracks. They came on and barrelled straight into 'Nowhere Fast'. There was no 'hello'. The crowd were more taken aback watching, whereas I think Morrissey wanted everyone jumping and bouncing and it wasn't like that in there at all. I don't think Morrissey was in the right frame of mind. At the end of the first song, he was moaning at the audience, telling them to get more into it and get more involved. It was quite a subdued atmosphere. I don't think he liked that.

He also had lots of problems with feedback on his microphone. Every time he crossed paths with Marr he seemed to get massive feedback, causing him to throw his microphone down mid song. I was thinking, 'Does he actually want to be here?' It was almost like he was fulfilling an appointment. But it didn't take anything away from it for us, because we were so overjoyed to be seeing The Smiths. At one stage something got thrown on the stage, which Morrissey didn't like. 'Turn the light up. Who threw that?'

To this day, my all-time favourite song is 'What Difference Does It Make?'. They didn't play it on the night so I went home disappointed. Their two biggest songs were that and 'This Charming Man', which they didn't play either. They made a big thing about their next single when they played 'Shakespeare's Sister'. The crowd got excited for that song because it was new and we hadn't heard it before, so that went down very well.

At the end of the main set, they ended one instrument at a time. Morrissey went off and then Andy Rourke and it was just Mike Joyce left on drums and Johnny Marr. And then, Mike Joyce stopped and that left Johnny front of stage, just playing the outro to whatever song for probably two minutes before just quietly fading away and playing as he walked off the stage.

### GLEN WILLIAMS

We were brought up in a rural part of Kent so me, my brother and a really good friend throughout the eighties went to gigs whenever we could because there was nothing else to do. We were very into indie and alternative music. I had a particular affinity with The Smiths because of the political messages and the outspokenness of Morrissey's lyrics. I became vegetarian almost immediately on the strength of 'Meat Is Murder' and I still am to this day, which is an example of how passionately I felt about the messages Morrissey was writing.

It was an absolutely outstanding gig and they played all of the songs I wanted to hear. I vividly remember the end of the main set as they finished on 'Meat Is Murder'. All of the band left the stage at different times. Morrissey left first and then either Joyce or Rourke, but the very last person left on stage was Johnny Marr. He played a few more bars towards the end of the song just on his own under the spotlight.

Morrissey gets an extremely negative press now. Half of me thinks, 'Oh Morrissey, what are you talking about now?' But half of me thinks it's a freedom of speech issue. 'Well, if that's your opinion, Morrissey, then good for you.' Back in the day, The Smiths seemed quite different from other people, and quite isolated intellectually. They were hopeful, courageous, different and outsiders. Those words stay with me because of Morrissey's lyrics and the political message, the anti-Thatcherism and the vegetarianism. They weren't really things that were written about and sung about in mainstream pop.

It's an emotive subject. He's always been outspoken. He's always been courageous. Perhaps back in the days of The Smiths he wasn't as controversial as he is now.

## GAUMONT THEATRE

### 11 MARCH 1985, IPSWICH, UK

### MARK COWLING

I saw them three times. Ipswich in March '85 was the first. It was an official school trip from Samuel Ward Upper in Haverhill, Suffolk. Our English teacher Mr Lund – a double first from Cambridge – told us, 'Sort the tickets out and get me 40 Marlboro and I'll get the school minibus sorted.'

### CHRIS SHARY, AGE 14

In the summer of 1984, my family moved from McGuire Air Force base in New Jersey to Bentwaters Air Force base in Suffolk, England. I was to be entering high school in the fall and my parents wisely decided to rent a home in the tiny English village of Charsfield. While our village was indeed a very small pig farming community, we did have a lot of teens in the neighbourhood. My brother and I quickly became fast friends with the village kids, and they introduced us yanks to all sorts of music we had no idea even existed.

At the time Billy Idol and Duran Duran were about all I wanted to listen to. That changed rather drastically once I discovered *Top Of The Pops*, *Sounds* and the *NME* and started borrowing records and tapes from the kids in my village. I was taking in new music at an alarming rate. When some of the older kids (who could drive) mentioned that they were planning on seeing The Smiths at the Ipswich Gaumont that following winter I was all in. I was just 14 and my parents were a bit sceptical about me being driven around by other kids. But, along with me and my brother, they had seen The Smiths on *Top Of The Pops* and I suppose they figured, 'How much trouble could that be? I mean, the singer wears a hearing aid and what appears to be his granddad's old jumpers, for crying out loud.'

If I recall correctly, The Smiths set began with siren sounds and flashing police type lights scanning the audience. It went on for what seemed like an eternity, clearly building tension, and then it all cut to Morrissey's fragile voice saying, 'Hello'. They then kicked into 'William, It Was Really Nothing'.

The place erupted with dancing, flowers being tossed and the jangliest guitars I have ever heard sweeping over the heads of a few hundred spotty-faced teens. While a lot of the set was unfamiliar to me, I immediately felt like I was in on a massive secret, one I didn't necessarily want to share with the other kids. I recall 'How Soon Is Now?' being haunting and beautiful at the same time, like it was putting us all in some kind of weird trance. That night we all belonged to The Smiths, and they could do what they wanted with us.

Things really got intense with 'Meat Is Murder'. The stage became bathed in red light, and I want to say there were films of slaughterhouses projected over the band but maybe my mind was producing those images. While I was not a vegetarian, I couldn't help but think that song was the best reason I could think of to abandon meat from my diet. I simply couldn't believe anyone was singing about such topics. It didn't seem like you could and not get in trouble – remember, I was 14 at the time. 'Meat Is Murder' was dark, cathartic and powerful, completely unlike anything I had ever heard before – or maybe since?

At the end of the evening, I had no idea how to even describe it to my parents or friends. It was musical bliss and all I knew was I wanted to keep going to shows and being exposed to music. All these years later, I am still going to shows on a very regular basis and have devoted my artist life to working with punk bands. The Smiths ignited my love of going to see live music.

### SHELLEY LINE, AGE 14

I'm a rather lumpy 48-year-old woman that lives in Norfolk. For my sins I enjoy watching *The Apprentice* on TV. However, the best part of the whole show is the opening music. 'Oh gosh, she's a prick!' you may be thinking. Can a Smiths fan really enjoy such banality? Well yea I do, but it's that piece of music, Prokofiev's 'Romeo And Juliet — Dance Of The Knights' that I love most about the show. It was the band's entrance music for the *Meat Is Murder* tour in 1985 and, no matter where I am or what I'm doing, that piece of music takes my thoughts back to one of the most exciting times of my life.

At the sweet and tender age of 14, I had booked myself a coach ticket to travel from Norwich to Ipswich to see my favourite band live. Actually live in the flesh. I was frenzied. As I was one of the very few, if not the only, Smiths fan at my school, I went alone but I figured I would be amongst friends. (Naivety will either be the end or the making of you). I am not criminally shy nor a social butterfly, but I knew I had to go. I was terrified of being alone but desperate to see them in equal measures, having missed the opportunity of seeing them in Norwich in February 1984 when, at 13, a chance of a snog at the local disco was too potent a lure. I was a titchy, tiny four-feet-eight and looked like a boy, so snogs weren't regularly on the radar. But having bought the debut album I was hooked.

I boarded the coach and sat alone with my Walkman and a cassette of *The Smiths* blaring into my ears and probably staring into my own reflection in the window. What a narcissist! I had booked a seated ticket, C4, but as a 14-year-old kid from Norwich, how was I to know about the joys of the mosh pit? Inside what I thought was the wonderous Ipswich Gaumont I found my seat and waited.

Morrissey uttered one word, 'Hullo', and the crowd erupted. The set kicked off with 'William…' but to me it was the furthest thing from nothing. It was utter glory. I was watching my God. I sang myself hoarse through each and every song, having bought and played the album relentlessly in the months preceding the gig. I was completely mesmerised by the band. Morrissey said very little throughout the set but sent the audience on a tempestuous journey. There was mayhem for 'How Soon Is Now?' and veneration and complete affinity for 'Meat Is Murder'. The set ended with 'Miserable Lie'. I made no forever friends on that night.

Except The Smiths.

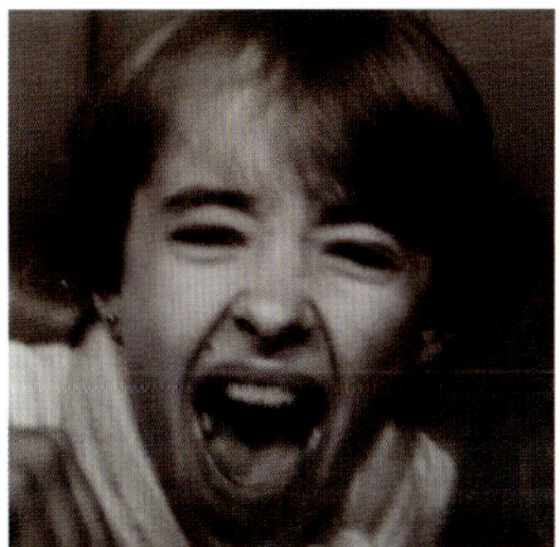

Shelley Line's Ipswich ticket

Shelley Line fell in love with The Smiths

## ROYAL CONCERT HALL

### 12 MARCH 1985, NOTTINGHAM, UK

### DAVID CRAMPTON, AGE 19

They were booked into the wrong venue as the RCH is all seated and they should really have played at Rock City. Moz said something along those lines from the stage. Great gig though. I went with my girlfriend, now my wife, and a couple of friends. The whole gig had a celebratory atmosphere. The

*David Crampton remembers a celebratory atmosphere*

Smiths were our group and seemed to speak to us on a personal level.

### LYNNE DICKENS

They were fantastic and it was a completely different atmosphere from the Assembly Rooms in Derby in 1983. They were really well known and successful by this stage. The crowd knew the songs and Morrissey knew how to play to an audience. I heard they were originally going to play at Rock City in Nottingham, but it wouldn't have been big enough.

### LIZ NETHERWAY

We were all about 17 and lived in Grantham. Not very much happened there, to be honest, so getting tickets for Nottingham Royal Centre was a dream. The *Meat Is Murder* album had only just come out and we all had it, or a tape of it, and had studiously learnt all the lyrics.

Six of us crammed into a Renault 5 which had no working tape player, so we had to sing all the way from Grantham to Nottingham, constantly repeating our favourite new line, 'He killed a policeman when he was 13 and somehow that really impressed me' which wasn't nice, as one of the blokes was the son of a local policeman.

We were there easily in time for the support group, James, who were superb, with amazing dancing from Tim Booth (who looked about twelve) plus all his crazy earwig stuff. Sadly, only about 100 people watched them; all the Smiths fans were there but hanging out in the bar or foyer. Their loss. We were in the middle of the stalls – about the tenth row – but when The Smiths came on hundreds of people clambered over the chairs and squeezed into the front rows. I don't remember any security.

What can I remember about the set? Two new songs, 'Shakespeare's Sister', which I didn't really like, and 'Stretch Out And Wait', which I loved immediately. 'That Joke Isn't Funny Anymore' was right at the heart of the set, with a spot-lit Morrissey repeating, 'I've seen this happen in other people's lives and now it's happening in mine'. The audience could hardly breathe; it was really dramatic. I remember 'Meat Is Murder' with the abattoir video screen and Morrissey off stage making horrific screaming noises. It was truly shocking; I'd never seen or heard anything like it. And it ended with 'Miserable Lie' as the last encore, one song that we'd all agreed they most definitely wouldn't play.

I'd been to see The Pretenders at the Royal Centre the previous year and after the gig the queues at the big McDonalds next to the venue were hundreds of people long. After The Smiths there was not one person queuing.

### SIOBHAN KILGANNON

I went with two friends. It was an absolutely brilliant night. Afterwards we went to a club in Nottingham called The Garage where they played The Smiths all night and where I bumped into my brother. I didn't even know he was going to the show. We never ever went out together and I remember having a great if unexpected night with him. He died suddenly last Christmas Eve. We played

The Smiths at his funeral – 'This Charming Man'.

JO RIDDEL, AGE 15

I liked The Cure, The Jesus and Mary Chain and New Model Army so I suppose I was always that little bit alternative. I went with my school friend Emma Wilson. We were both absolutely crazy about The Smiths. Her boyfriend was called Stephen, and he really looked quite like Morrissey. He had the quiff and everything. And in the eighties, if you were a little bit different like we were, you were into The Smiths.

I remember seeing them do 'Meat Is Murder'. The concert hall went really dark and then the *Meat Is Murder* backdrop came up in red. You could hear cows mooing at the slaughterhouse and then the blood dripping down the back. Morrissey came on and he started singing, and at that point it made me think, 'Oh my God, where does meat come from?' You don't put two and two together very often when you're 15. And I thought, 'Oh my God, yes meat is murder.' I was so influenced by what Morrissey said that I thought, 'Well, if he says it, it must be right.' So I've not eaten meat since that day.

I worked at Woolworths at the time, doing a Saturday job in Eastwood. I got into real trouble because I was just so obsessed with playing Smiths records. I played 'Shoplifters Of The World Unite' and my boss came up to me and said, 'This is totally inappropriate for Woolworths.' So then I put on 'Panic' – 'hang the deejay' – and he wasn't very impressed with that either!

# VICTORIA HALL

## 16 MARCH 1985, STOKE-ON-TRENT, UK

NICK BARBER

I saw them on six occasions, including twice at the Victoria Hall in Hanley, Stoke-on-Trent. On the second occasion, Morrissey walked off stage when someone threw a sausage at him.

KEV JONES

About a year after the Free Trade Hall show I saw them on the *Meat Is Murder* tour in '85. Me and the friend I worked with, and whose ticket I'd copied, used to religiously buy the *NME* every week and we saw an ad for the tour and got tickets for a few gigs – Hanley, Bradford, Sheffield, and Manchester. The ones that hold great memories for me are Hanley Victoria Hall and Bradford, both lovely old ornate Victorian town halls and fantastic venues to see bands in with fantastic acoustics. They were both completely standing on the floor, and then they had a couple of balconies around the side. Sadly, a lot of those venues have fallen off the gig circuit with the advent of arenas.

They'd started using the Prokofiev intro music. When that started, it went totally pitch black in the auditorium and they had these big searchlights flashing around the audience whilst the intro music was playing at full volume. It was pretty intense. They'd got a little bit bigger by this stage, and it was just as wild, if not wilder, with the fervour in the crowd. It was absolutely crazy.

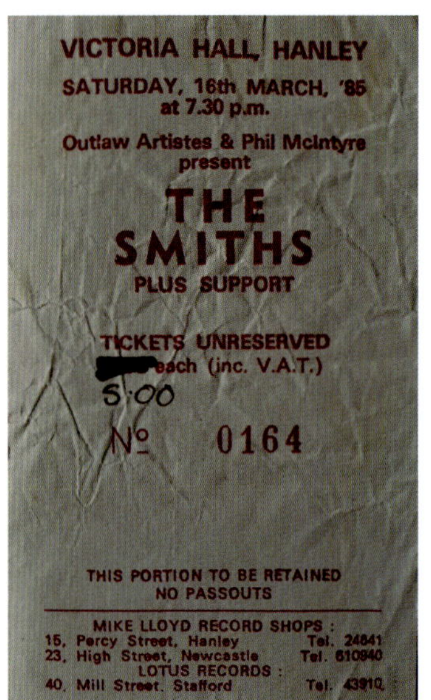

*Hanley Victoria Hall ticket (Craig Hatfield)*

### CRAIG HATFIELD

It's interesting to see that between the venue printing the tickets and putting them on sale they appear to have upped the price from £4.50 to £5! This was the *Meat Is Murder* tour; the band's only UK number 1 album. Maybe this increased popularity prompted the small price hike?

I was in my first year at North Staffs Poly. They were the archetypal student band. I couldn't not go and I made sure I got inside the venue early enough to get right down the front; about two back from front and centre of the stage, a good vantage point.

Part way through a song somebody threw something that hit Morrissey in the face, right between his nose and his eye. He flinched and then stropped off stage for a few minutes. The band carried on playing until he returned. I had no idea what it was that had been thrown until later. As I was filing out of the gig with my housemate Steve, we bumped into somebody off his course. He told us that he was stood about halfway back but was right next to the bloke who threw the object. It was a sausage! And the song that his 'pork Meteor missile' interrupted? 'Meat Is Murder'! I'm not condoning such loutish behaviour, but I must admit that I was more than a little impressed by the accuracy of the throw, hitting Morrissey square in the face from such a distance. Even as a vegetarian, I still find this story just a little bit funny.

### RUSSELL HARPER

I went with a schoolmate who always seems to remember a lot more about what we did when we were younger. Someone lobbed a flower at Morrissey, and it hit him in the eye during 'Meat Is Murder' and he walked off. The band carried on but walked off eventually. They came back after quite a break and Morrissey said something to the effect of, 'Someone always has to spoil it.'

### DARREN APPLEBY

I can't really remember when I first heard about The Smiths but the originality of the music and the connection I had with the lyrics made an instant impact. Soon after, a friend gave me a copy of a bootleg tape with the Haçienda gig on Side A and the Kid Jensen session on Side B. Those words, 'The only thing to be in 1983, is handsome, Handsome Devil!' have stuck with me ever since.

Growing up at a school with few friends due to never fitting in made me a prime target for bullying both by fellow pupils and the belligerent ghouls who ran the place. They believed that beating with cane and slipper was an effective way of teaching, and it was formative to say the least. To hear Morrissey talk about being an outsider made my day, knowing that this was someone who just knew my life.

My first gigs were tagging along with my brother to Hawkwind, Motörhead,

Scorpions, Black Sabbath, etc. but here was a band that was mine. The Smiths were my band, my passion, my life. I had limited funds as a 14-year-old but was able to buy the early singles and avidly listed to Peel and Jensen to hear more. When the chance came to see The Smiths

at Stoke Poly I had to be there. My
memory is hazy, but I remember
that the gig was quiet compared
to later tours and the set list rather
short. However, the band were as
tight as a drum and way ahead of
everything else that was around.

Other gigs with other bands
came and went, and I sunk all my
paper round money into seeing
as much live music as I could, but
my next Smiths gig was in Hanley
at the Victoria Hall. In the pit, the
crowd was amazing with passion
and singing. This was the *Meat Is
Murder* tour and the new material
showed a fantastic development of
the band as writers and performers.
They played a blinding set and
to see them develop into such a
complete gang was fantastic.

But of course, the show went
down in Smithdom history as
'The Sausage Incident'. As the
evening went on there were several
moments of sheer joy and I almost
got to the stage barrier to get up
and get close to my idols. Then,
as the show was getting close to
the end, the strains of the factory
machines played out as the first
bars of 'Meat Is Murder' quietened
down the crowd. I didn't see the
Phantom Sausage Flinger, but I saw
them hit Morrissey. I can't say for
certain that one actually went into
his mouth, but by God it was a good
shot! I think the shock was felt by
the man himself, but more so by the
audience, who couldn't believe what
we were seeing.

### GLYN WADE

I saw them three times as I was back
at the Victoria Hall for the night
of the sausage throwing incident. I
know who did the throwing... but I
won't tell. And, no, it wasn't me! My
mate got on stage and did a backflip
to which Morrissey commented,
'What a charming man.' It's such
a shame that someone so talented
turned into a fascist and it makes
it hard to listen to The Smiths now.
I know someone who sold all his
Morrissey records when he turned.
But those gigs were special, intimate
and memorable and will remain
fond memories.





## HIPPODROME

### 17 MARCH 1985, BIRMINGHAM, UK

### CLIVE ADAMS

By 1983, it almost seemed like punk
had never happened. In terms of
English guitar bands that captured
the soul of suburban youth, The
Jam, who disbanded in late '82, had
left a void in popular music. The
charts were awash with synth pop
bands with long winded names
such as A Flock of Seagulls and
Orchestral Manoeuvres In The
Dark. Don't get me wrong, as with

all genres of music, there were some gems to be found but much of it left me cold and uninspired.

As MTV took off in what had become the age of the music video, it appeared that once again style had become more important than substance. As a young college student, I would hang out at the Powerhouse, a medium-sized venue in Birmingham that played host to many of the independent, post-punk and goth bands that dominated the pages of the *NME*. I first heard The Smiths when on club nights the doom would be interspersed by 'This Charming Man' and 'What Difference Does It Make?'

The surname Smith is ubiquitous and originates from Northern England. The Smiths were a Manchester band, but their music sounded fresh, providing a welcome relief from the blandness of corporate pop. With a strong rockabilly rhythm section, poetic lyrics and uplifting jangly guitar, The Smiths were to define eighties English independent rock.

Mother's Day 1985, and the Smiths were in town playing at the Birmingham Hippodrome. It seemed a strange choice of venue at the time but looking back, playing the Hippodrome reenforced the idea that The Smiths were apart from their contemporaries. This is a seated venue, and we were held back by security from rushing the stage to see the support act, fellow Mancunians James. However, security could not hold us back once The Smiths took to the stage. From the opening bars to 'William, It Was Really Nothing', Morrissey owned the stage but at the same time held a sense of vulnerability as he gave in to repeated requests from the crowd to show us a nipple. I now appreciate how lucky I was to see The Smiths play my hometown in such an intimate venue.

### LAWRENCE BRACKSTONE

The Smiths were the only band that I fell in love with on hearing them for the very first time. The song was 'This Charming Man'. I had pretty well all their releases to date in my collection and was a massive fan of the jangle guitar style of the magical Marr.

I'd been working in London for the whole week, and I caught a National Express coach back to Birmingham on Mother's Day, where I was met by my mum. I gave her some flowers and then went home, got some tea and went out to the gig where I met my two very best friends, Gary Fox and Clive Adams. James were the support act, but we weren't interested in them and choose to have a beer in the theatre bar instead, blissfully unaware of how big they were to become.

The Smiths were growing in their popularity and getting front row tickets, as we tended to do for other acts, proved difficult. We had seats that were maybe ten rows back. Interestingly, the bouncers were preventing fans getting to their seats in the front stalls with about five minutes to go before the band came out. Suddenly the lights went out, and I took a cheeky chance to get a better seat. I literally seat hopped all the rows in the front until I got to the stage and took a place right in front of the microphone stand!

On came the band and the whole place erupted. I couldn't believe my luck at the advantage I'd got with my place. There were two occasions when I had Morrissey's microphone lead in my hand while he was singing. Later on I also had his shirt in my grip. There is a bootleg of the gig and a fan in the balcony can be heard shouting out at my actions!

My memory of the night is that it was too short. I remember the final encore of 'Barbarism Begins at Home'. As the song came to an end, one by one each member put down their instrument and departed. It left Mike Joyce as the only one left, tapping away on his drum kit for a couple of minutes. It's the best exit I've ever seen.

To this day I am still a massive Smiths fan, and my two teenage sons have independently followed the band. I love the classic sound of The Smiths. They were a massively influential part of my growing up.

### SIMON WELLS

It was less than a year after I'd seen them at the Tower Ballroom in Edgbaston. The Smiths were getting bigger and I went as part of a crowd. This may sound like some kind of prescient revisionism on my part, but Morrissey had already begun to rack up some things in the press that were disappointing. Most notably, in the *NME* that 'reggae is vile'. As someone who grew up in the city of Birmingham in the seventies, this was somewhere between laughably ill-informed and dumb.

The band were disappointing. The Hip is a fantastic place for theatre and dance but a poor space for gigs – seats only – and everyone on stage oozed a kind of tiredness and tetchiness. Perhaps being at the nexus of so many hopes and dreams was difficult to handle over time. At the end, Johnny Marr kicked down the drum kit for no reason that I could see, and I remember thinking how that was the kind of tired rock nonsense *my* Smiths were not supposed to be about. It was clear that, for me, they were already over.

As a coda, that was not actually the last time I saw Morrissey live. Some years later, Madness reformed to play in Finsbury Park, and he had the name support slot. He sang draped in a Union flag with a skinhead picture for a backdrop. To an integrated audience playing in one of the world's great multicultural cities. It looked – it almost certainly *was* – a pathetic attempt to borrow a boot boy kudos that had long been recognised as often racist. How sad that someone who initially looked like he could help us throw doors wide open was, in the end, actually a lot more interested in closing borders.

### JULIE SABINE, AGE 22

I was a punk at the time. I used to go to Romeo and Juliets, an alternative club in Birmingham and which was where I first heard The Smiths. 'How Soon Is Now?' is the song that got me hooked on them. The lyrics, the guitar riff and, of course, Morrissey's voice. It's still one of my all-time favourite songs. I bought *Hatful of Hollow* and never looked back. The lyrics all seemed to resonate with whatever I was going through emotionally at the time. Also, I found that some of the songs were far from depressing.

*Julie Sabine screamed her head off*

*Paul Miles saw The Smiths on the Meat is Murder tour*

They were funny. If only people would really listen to the songs and not judge them as depressing, surely they would see for themselves?

My then boyfriend surprised me with tickets to see them live. We managed to get to the front, right in front of Morrissey. I don't recall there being too many people there, but I do recall people staring at us as myself and my then boyfriend looked very different to everyone else, with our Mohican hairstyles. Mine was white-blonde all sticking out and we were dressed in black and generally we both stuck out like sore thumbs. But we didn't take any notice.

As soon as I saw Morrissey, I screamed my head off with excitement! I sang and danced. They were amazing and still one of the best bands I've ever seen live. The gig was ending and my boyfriend said, 'Let's go to the stage door at the back.' There weren't many people there at all – just us and a couple of others inside the door, waiting for the band to come out. Their coach was waiting for them. The band came out, but no Morrissey. Then I saw him! He had a black hat on. Some girls got his autograph, but I just stood and couldn't quite believe it was him. He looked over to me and my boyfriend. He was really staring and he waved at us. I was in a state! I was waving like an idiot, saying, 'Oh, he's waving at me – look, look!'

He then got on the coach, pulled back the curtain that was covering the window and waved again and beckoned me to the coach. I was all shy and just shook my head, 'No.' He then smiled at me, I waved one last time and then I turned and went home. Who knows what story I could've told if I'd gone on over to him and got on that coach?

### PAUL MILES, AGE 14

I was seriously gothic as a young teenager. I had three older sisters and so was going to see bands like Southern Death Cult and The Sisters of Mercy. My sisters were happy because they were going to these alternative clubs. I had long black crimped hair. I was still at school, and I remember going in on a Thursday and having to take my black nail varnish off. Then my sister decided to cut my hair. She cut it right up at the top and said, 'Right, you're a Smiths fan now.' I was absolutely livid. But within six months I went to see them at the Hippodrome. From that gig I became quite a big James fan, seeing James 26 times in total.

I got totally into The Smiths, and started buying their vinyl. That was the only thing I would save up for. It was just so different. They didn't seem that mainstream even though they were on *Top Of The Pops*. It wasn't the electro-pop thing that was going on. It was the lyrics more than anything. They were so poignant. As a teenager, you were just taking in those lyrics because there wasn't another lyricist like that around at the time. Or ever. I just used to stand in my bedroom singing along, playing their music album after album after album.

They just epitomised cool. Johnny Marr was and still is a legend while Morrissey had this really weird privacy around him as well. You never really knew much about him. He was enigmatic and I really liked that dark, secretive 'fill in the gaps' side to him.

I've never got that 'depressing'

thing out of it that people talk about. Their music makes me really happy. I saw Johnny Marr perform with The Killers at Glastonbury in 2019 and when they kicked into 'This Charming Man' it still seemed so relevant. The crowd were going mad. The music is very buoyant and joyful.



### BRIDGET DUFFY

The Smiths at the Winter Gardens in Margate was my husband's first ever gig. He enjoyed James. I saw that same tour at Birmingham Hippodrome and couldn't wait for James to finish their set as I just wanted to see The Smiths. I went with my friend Lorraine. I wore black sixties ski pants and a paisley sixties rave shirt with a boxy suede sixties jacket. Lorraine and I both thought Johnny was the bee's knees – and I had just gone veggie!

## 'SHAKESPEARE'S SISTER'
### RELEASED 18 MARCH 1985

The sleeve art featured Pat Phoenix, *Coronation Street* actress, in character as Elsie Tanner in Britain's favourite TV soap opera. The single was less of a favourite, only reaching number 26.

## CITY HALL

### 22 MARCH 1985, SHEFFIELD, UK

### JOHN GOODWIN, AGE 14

I had been into music for some time before I discovered them. I have a sister, years older than me, who forced me to listen to ska and The Specials. Where I grew up, there were lots of influences from The Human League and electronic music, so my taste was quite eclectic. But noting gripped me like The Smiths. I first heard them doing 'What Difference Does It Make?' on *Top Of The Pops* when I was 13 in early 1984. I bought two versions of the seven-inch single, one with Terence Stamp and the other with Morrissey, at the time not realising the significance. There was something immediately alluring about them that had me transfixed; the music, the lyrics and of course how Morrissey looked. I had talked to some girls I knew who were into music and they said I should get *The Smiths*, their first album. It grew from there. I followed them from then until the day they split and beyond.

I bought everything I could – records, cassettes, pictures discs, imports. I bought all my records from Hudsons Records in Chesterfield. Mr Hudson recognised my interest and would save me posters and marketing materials relating to The Smiths, which I have to this day in my loft. I clipped magazines like *Smash Hits* and the *NME* for anything Smiths-related.

I had a great family and was not lonely or locked in my bedroom. But I had been ill and I didn't do things other kids did. I stayed in a lot, and I remember many holidays where I would make my parents play *Meat Is Murder* on cassette in the car. My mum would say, 'Oh, this is dreary,' but I didn't see that

*Shakespeare's Sister*

at all. The songs were sad, but also funny and uplifting. I would mainly listen alone in the front room of our terraced house. However, I would also listen to them at my friend's house. She was not a girlfriend but a friend who was a girl. She had a letter from Morrissey that we would look at endlessly. I was so jealous – when I wrote to him all I got were some Rough Trade postcards.

The impact of The Smiths was massive. It is a cliché now, but The Smiths changed my life. I was not the best at school, but Morrissey's lyrics opened up a world of culture – books, film, TV and other music. It seems cringe-worthy now, but I started reading Oscar Wilde, Keats and Yeats. This really changed my ideas about books, words and knowledge.

The first time I saw them was at Sheffield City Hall. I had a deal with my friend that I would go with him to see Howard Jones (who was rubbish) and he would come with me to The Smiths. James supported, which was a real bonus. My dad drove us into Sheffield. My dad helped me get tickets every time. He would call up and pay with his giro bank card. Mum and Dad took us to all the gigs. They would go and eat or wait in the car. They were patient and supportive.

The gig was amazing, if not overwhelming, but some things stand out. The ticket I had said 'restricted view', but what this actually meant is that we were right at the front where the seats had been taken out. I have a distinct memory of this bloke calling me over from the seats and asking if we could swap. I did not want to

get into trouble so ignored him. I remember looking up at the ceiling of the City Hall, seeing the band's shadows silhouetted against the ceiling by the lights and thinking that I had to be there at that very moment to see that and how it would never be repeated. I also remember being so far forward one could not help but dance. My shirt was sweat-soaked. And the sound the grinding saw made for 'Meat Is Murder' was so powerful, visceral and raw.

### DAVID GRIFFITHS, AGE 17

I was 17 years old and lost. I'd been a punk from the age of 12 to 15 but fell out of love with music as there wasn't anyone around that blew me away. Then one day a friend called round and said he had a spare ticket to see The Smiths at Sheffield City Hall the following day. I accepted the ticket and went to my first ever gig. I remember the excitement of my 15-year-old friend on the day, and this rubbed off on me on our way to the gig. Outside the City Hall, the excitement and passion of all the Smiths fans made me inexplicably nervous. The sound in the City Hall was breathtaking and a band I had never heard of entered the stage. From that night James also became a favourite band. I especially relate to their early material, and I think it is all to do with them being the first band I ever saw live. Then it happened – The Smiths entered the stage to a barrage of flowers and love. I can remember being blown away by the energy and the stage invasions, the band doing an almost instrumental for one of the encores as Morrissey was mobbed and could not sing, and Morrissey having his shirt ripped from him. The main thing I remember is that I fell in love with music again.

### MIKE POWELL

I recently scanned five rolls of film I shot of The Smiths at Sheffield City Hall whilst I was at college studying photojournalism. I had heard 'Hand In Glove' and just a couple of others when I knocked on the stage door and asked their manager if I could take some pictures. I was led past the band waiting with guitars to go on, sat at a table full of drinks and flowers, and sat on their PA speakers on the City Hall stage. The crowd barely filled the stalls, and the circle and upper circle were virtually empty, all of which would change for the band in just months. A few minutes later they were all squashed at the front reaching out for Morrissey, who was flailing around the stage swinging a bunch of flowers (slowly reduced to mere stalks) and Johnny Marr played a gorgeous cherry 1959 Gibson ES355 with block inlays all night. Fair enough – if I were him, I wouldn't let it out of my sight either.

I was amazed at how tight they were. I've been a fan ever since and am now the proud owner of my own cherry 335. Funnily enough I received an email from their drummer, Mike Joyce, some years after telling Radio 1's Mark Radcliffe the story. I sent him the contact sheets, and he was really pleased to see them. I remember crawling around the stage and sitting right by his kit as he belted out some unbelievably solid drumming.

Completely brilliant. There is some amateur footage of this gig on YouTube shot by the road crew.

### JONATHAN JORDAN

My group of pals were an odd mix of goths, rockers, punks and New Romantics. We watched every band that came through South Yorkshire. That week we had seen Spear of Destiny.

The Smiths had a good buzz about them. They had been on *Top Of The Pops* and were playing our favourite venue, Sheffield City Hall, the usual venue of choice for Thin Lizzy, AC/DC and the Halle Orchestra. We bought tickets on the door that were less than £5 and found ourselves in the balcony, which was totally empty but for us. The venue was about half full and was totally the wrong place for The Smiths. We tried to dance and 'get into it' but it wasn't happening for us. Even the fans in our group concluded it wasn't a great night, and we ended up in the pub next door before the encores. Young people are amazed and impressed that I have seen The Smiths but, frankly, it was a really forgettable gig!

## CITY HALL

### 24 MARCH 1985, NEWCASTLE-UPON-TYNE, UK

### PETER MARTIN

This time we got the bus as it was our hometown gig. I remember the song 'Meat Is Murder' and realising how much I hated it. I wanted the fast ones, the early stuff that they had abandoned to play this dirge. I remember the seats and how it wasn't

*Newcastle City Hall ticket (Carl Hinde)*

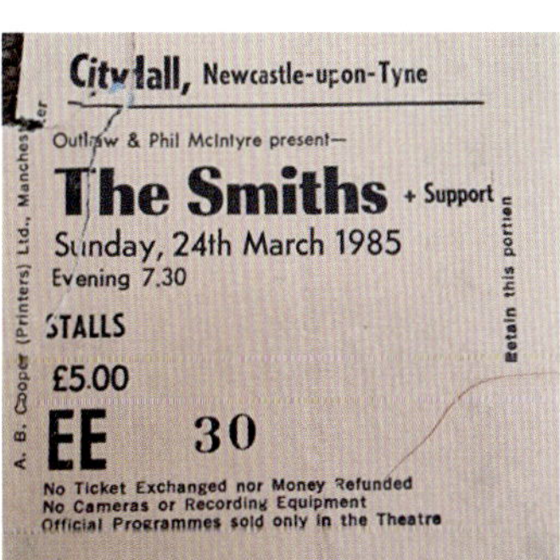

*1985 tour programme (Peter Martin)*

nearly as good as standing the night before. I also recall 'Shakespeare's Sister', still one of my favourite Smiths songs. I bought the badges of all the singles sleeves and wore Pat Phoenix for about two years solid.

### DAVID TIMLIN

The first time I saw The Smiths I went with Peter Martin. He's a year older than me, and had seen them the year before. James supported them. I was 17 and on the dole with no money but, somehow, I managed to get to see them.

I lived in Ashington. I remember sitting on the bus and my friend got on. We first met around the time that 'What Difference Does It Make' came out. I was telling him how great the song was while he was still into Wham! with a Wham! lampshade in his bedroom. Then he got into The Smiths. If you see the footage of 'Shoplifters Of The World' on *The Tube*, he's on the stage dancing.

I'd often wear a hearing aid like Morrissey did and I deliberately failing an eye test so I could get some National Health specs, as well as wearing brooches and beads and such.

The gig was riotous. I nearly got kicked out of that gig about three or four times by the bouncers for dancing and going crazy. By the time they got to 'Meat Is Murder', I was desperate for the loo. I thought it would be a good time to go as I didn't like that track. That really ignited a spark. I wanted to see them again.

### ALYSON LAWS, AGE 16

Most girls in my year liked Spandau Ballet and Wham! but I liked the sound of the guitars and Morrisey's

quirkiness. My music taste made me different from the other girls, and I really liked a lot of different music. I was gutted that I could not get tickets to see them at the Mayfair in Newcastle in 1984. It was a club and you had to be 18 to get in. I really did look 15!

When I saw them at Newcastle City Hall, I was forced by my parents to take my 14-year-old sister along, so I brainwashed her with the music before the show. I still remember the feeling as the hall was dark, the stage was lit red and booming out of the speakers was Prokofiev's 'Romeo And Juliet'. I was holding my breath. It was totally inspiring to me. Then Johnny Marr's guitar started and I was in awe of this band. I would love to say that the meaning of the lyrics to 'Meat Is Murder' inspired me to become a vegetarian but I may have thought about it for five seconds on the way home.

### SCOTT P RICHARDSON

The first time I saw them, my sister took me. We were sitting upstairs at the back, but the atmosphere was amazing. The next two occasions were part of the same tour – *Meat Is Murder* – and we had to travel to them. They were both amazing shows and I was standing right at the front and got to shake Morrissey's hand on a few occasions. The fourth and last time that I got to see them was at a small local venue where they threatened to walk off the stage as there were a few mindless morons spitting at them, but they did finish the show. I now live in Manchester and have been to Salford Lads Club and had my picture taken there. It was an amazing feeling standing there and knowing that they stood there for that iconic picture.

## CHRIS TAIT

The Smiths were the band to see on stage at that time and were my generation's shining light. I'd been a fan since their early *Top Of The Pops* appearances and some terrific Peel sessions, but I'd missed their previous visits to the city for one reason or another (studying, raising a young family, holding down two jobs, money was too tight to mention, etc.). When *Meat Is Murder* was released, missing the Newcastle City Hall gig to promote the album was not an option. Tickets were purchased, arrangements made and my friend Mark and I took up our positions in the stalls on the big night immediately behind the mixing desk, with a clear view of the engineer's set list and the delights that were to follow. Arch rivals Sunderland had lost the League Cup Final earlier in the day (with an own goal, a penalty miss and relegation to follow – beautiful, what a time to be alive!), so spirits were already high. This was despite the gig being on a Sunday evening, with the dreaded four-letter word – 'work' – in the morning. Tomorrow could stretch out and wait.

Soon-to-be stadium darlings James provided support showcasing, if memory serves, material from their forthcoming debut album, the stunningly eclectic *Stutter*, a masterpiece in itself. But nothing could have prepared you for the main event and that unique entrance which became The Smiths' trademark.

As the lights dimmed and the opening bars of Prokofiev's 'Romeo And Juliet' drifted out into the crowd, the place erupted. Then, amid strobe lighting and flying beer, The Smiths took to the stage, immediately bursting into the intro to 'William…'. Cue further mayhem, a mix of flailing arms, swirling guitar and a classic four-piece English pop group at the very top of their game, delivering songs unlike anything I'd heard before or since.

The set list was remarkable by any standards – melodic, catchy, experimental and in places, dare I say it, there were essences of what I would have described at the time as heavy rock, proof once again that, aside from being the coolest dude on the block, Johnny Marr is undoubtedly the best guitarist this nation has produced, in any genre.

All of the tracks from the new album were given an airing apart from the wistful 'Well I Wonder', alongside some of the early songs which were already gaining cult classic status – 'Hand in Glove', 'Still Ill' and 'Heaven Knows…'.

The new single, 'Shakespeare's Sister', was included and after two encores, the closing song, 'Barbarism Begins At Home', saw Morrissey leave the stage first to huge acclaim and ended with Rourke and Joyce playing that amazing bass and drum rhythm outro to close the show. It was an undoubted triumph and there was a palpable feeling that this lot were something special.

## ROYAL COURT THEATRE

### 27 MARCH 1985, LIVERPOOL, UK

### JULIE DANGERFIELD

Memories? Pete Burns in a royal box thingy. James in support. Morrissey opening with, 'We're the other funny Manchester band.' Johnny Marr removing his leather jacket before they did the title track. Me being young!

### THOMAS JONES

This was a much more sedate affair. We had only managed to get balcony tickets this time around and had missed out on Manchester tickets altogether such was the explosion in their popularity. James – in their quirky, pre-stadium-friendly incarnation – did a decent set and then our heroes showcased the newly released *Meat Is Murder* LP. The light show had improved dramatically and I remember some laser-like projections accompanying 'That Joke Isn't Funny Anymore', holding the band in a cradle of pink and green light. We also laughed on the way home about how Johnny had listed 'humping' as his main hobby in the souvenir programme.

## ST GEORGE'S HALL

### 28 MARCH 1985, BRADFORD, UK

### GRAHAM CLARK

James were the support act, and Tim Booth wore a multi-coloured jumper. I still have the (unofficial) t-shirt I bought outside the venue.

### ANDY WHITE

The fourth and final time I saw them was at St George's Hall. I met some mates who were going in a city centre pub and told them we had to go early to see James, but no-one was persuaded so I ended up going in on my own. Again, a great set from James.

I was at the front again. In those days you had your hands on stage if you were at the front, no sterile zone for the bouncers to parade in or folk giving water out. You could get on stage easily if you fancied it and plenty did, but not me at a Smiths concert. The crush was too much for some people, so these folk – usually girls – were normally hauled out onto the stage and then reappeared at the back of the hall, only to try to get back to the front. I remember Morrissey having a moan about the poor chart position for 'Shakespeare's Sister', which had now been released. Truth be told it was a poor choice for a single – they had plenty of better songs. There was a bit of trouble from some yobbos in the crowd who were spitting at Morrissey. He left the stage at one point, and I thought he wasn't coming back, but after about five minutes he did. The band jammed while he was gone.

### ANDY WALSH, AGE 17

I'll never forget it. I was a young 17-year-old watching my football team home and away when one of lads I knocked about with said he'd got two tickets to see a band in Bradford, and did I fancy it? I never expected to be almost bloody hypnotised by this young odd-looking band, but they just blew me away and gave me one of the biggest pleasures in life. They are the only band that makes my heart pump like mad when one of their songs comes on.

I think the reason The Smiths really impacted on me was that I went through many music phases such as reggae, Mod/ska, punk, etc. like any normal young lad but never really stuck with any in particular. When I saw The Smiths, I stood there in such awe at four Northern lads like me who just looked normal but had something that grabbed me instantly. The music was brilliant but the look of the band, and I suppose Morrissey in particular, made me want to be different. I loved the fact that they weren't really mainstream and weren't on TV or radio every two minutes. They felt like they were mine. People would mock and take the piss about The Smiths being miserable and morbid, but I'd just think, 'You don't get it, poor you.' And I still do!

I still probably can't explain it, and it can be embarrassing trying to tell people I thought these four lads were gods. I got the whole Morrissey thing where lads would try to get to him as if he were some Messiah. You just had that feeling in your gut. If I tried to explain this to mates, they'd just take the piss and call me a homosexual or whatever. No other band have ever touched me like The Smiths.

### PETER HOPTON

I saw The Smiths in Bradford at St George's Hall. That was a brilliant night because the support band were James and they were just as good. It's my claim to fame, along with seeing Madness just as they formed at the S Club in Leeds. That was an eye-opener in itself. It was a rough place and I was 14. You had to be 18 to get into this place, but my mates sneaked me in. It was full of skinheads fighting all the time and I'll never forget it. It was a brilliant night!

## DERNGATE THEATRE

### 29 MARCH 1985, NORTHAMPTON, UK

### JAMIE CRAMP

The gig had that buzz about it that bands have when they're at the top of their game and the height of their popularity.

### ANDREW FARMER

I married my wife Carol in 1984. Money was tight but we had got tickets. The only problem was that it was all seating. How can you sit for The Smiths? Tickets cost the princely sum of £5 each and we were about seven rows from the front. The day of the gig arrived, and hair was teased into the best quiff possible.

The venue was very busy, with animal rights activists handing out flyers. These had a dramatic effect on both of us, so much so we both gave up meat. The gig opened with the band James, Tim Booth doing his best to get the crowd going, but mostly everyone stayed seated. They went off.

There was a brief interlude, the lights dimmed and then pandemonium as the band took the

*Andrew Farmer saw The Smiths at Northampton's Derngate Theatre*

Morrissey — musical Messiah

The Smiths at Derngate.

A MESSIAH arrived in Northampton at the weekend and the result was ecstatic bedlam.

Since they exploded on to the music scene two years ago, thought provoking lyrics combined with a guitar based sound have made The Smiths one of the most electric bands to tour the country for years.

Much of their adulation is undoubtedly due to the power of lead singer Morrissey, whose captivating voice and distinctive delivery gives him an almost Messiah-like presence on stage.

At Derngate on Friday night, long starved town trendies and rock fans were amply rewarded for their patience by 80 minutes of near perfection as the four piece incredible band romped their way through most of the tracks on their recent Meat is Murder album.

But the biggest cheers were most definitely saved for earlier singles Heaven Knows I'm Miserable Now and This Charming Man, the highlight of two encores.

Morrissey has said that his ambition in life is to achieve immortality. He can rest assured that his Derngate performance has made him a legend — something that will not be forgotten for a very long time.

Suzanne Smith

*Moz was hailed as a musical messiah by the Chron*

*Paul Greenwood was in heaven with The Smiths and a new date*

stage. Even if you wanted to remain in your chair you weren't going to be allowed to. The atmosphere was electric as everyone rushed towards the stage. The music kicked in and everyone was dancing and singing, with the band whipping the crowd into a frenzy. My personal favourite songs were 'Hand In Glove' and 'How Soon Is Now?' I think they played 16 or 17 songs including two encores and then they were gone. If they had played for six hours it would have been over too soon. Our bills money was spent on tour programmes, t-shirts and a massive tour poster, which still hangs in our hall.

I kept the review from our local paper, the *Chronicle and Echo*. It opened with the words, 'A messiah arrived in Northampton at the weekend, and the result was ecstatic bedlam.' The reviewer went on to say, 'Morrissey has said that his ambition in life is to achieve immortality. He can rest assured that his Derngate performance has made him a legend – something that will not be forgotten for a very long time.'

The Smiths were, and still are, our Beatles, and we still follow Morrissey and Johnny Marr whenever they tour. Theirs is a light that never goes out.

## PALACE THEATRE

### 31 MARCH 1985, MANCHESTER, UK

### GILLIAN ANDRIA, AGE 23

Me and my friend Julie went together. It was the first time we'd seen Morrissey and also Tim Booth. We related to the music, with us coming from Manchester, and identified with the same life experiences. The most vivid memory I have of that night is the way both of them danced! You couldn't really hear the music that much. I was 23, Julie was 20. We are still best friends and still go together to watch Morrissey and James. Our kids loved both bands, having grown up with the music. My daughter has a Morrissey tattoo and coincidentally my grandson, her son, shares a birthday with Morrissey.

### PAUL GREENWOOD

I had just started in a new relationship and I was besotted. It was our first proper date. The Smiths played 'The Headmaster Ritual' and I swear the hairs on the back of my neck stood on end. It was musical euphoria with gladioli all over the stage. I think they did three encores – it was a great set. My girl loved the show, so it was a great date. For one night I was in heaven. Sadly, the girl didn't last but I still love The Smiths.

## JOHANNA ROBERTS, AGE 17

I can't remember when I first heard 'This Charming Man' by The Smiths. It was when Radio 1 played good music and deejays didn't sound like guys who run fairground rides. All I know is that I heard it and it changed my life. After punk and new wave in the late seventies, there had been a move to synthesisers, with bands like OMD, Visage, Duran Duran and Spandau Ballet topping the charts. Suddenly, here were four lads – drums, two guitars and a vocalist – and it spoke to me. I was 15.

I was already an avid record buyer. I would go the Play Inn in Eccles on a Saturday and come home with a variety of singles or albums. This was no different. Off I went to purchase the single, in a picture sleeve, with 'Jeane' on the B-side. This was new and this was mine. My first week's wages from my Saturday job went on The Smiths' eponymous album and a pair of jeans. The album was never off the turntable, and as singles and albums were released, they got bought.

I had to be at the Palace. I was too young to go to clubs, but this venue was accessible. I rang up the morning they went on sale. Aged 17, I didn't have a credit card. I appealed to the guy on the phone that I needed – needed! – twwo tickets. He told me he would hold two. I jumped on the bus on a wintry morning and went to the Palace to get them. I had never been so grateful.

Cut to Sunday 31 March, I had on a paisley pyjama top and some sixties beige chinos of my dad's. Outside the Palace were kids with daffodils (FFS, he had gladioli). I bought a programme and ten button badges, which I still have. I was on the second row, aisle seats. I was so close to the stage. James were on first and, boy, did they wow me. I got into them from that moment too – the freaky dancer and the unusual songs – and for a while ended up in a pen pal situation with Jenny, one of the then line-up's girlfriends.

When The Smiths came out, I was mesmerised. I only had eyes for Morrissey and Johnny, who was stood on my side of the stage. I'd been to other gigs, but this band was mine. Every song meant something to me, and I was seeing them live. It blew all the other gigs away.

The stage was bathed in red for 'Meat Is Murder' and the 'heifer whines' rang out across the theatre. It was at that point I became a veggie. Reading back on the set list they did 13 songs and three encores. All I know is that it was fantastic.

## JULIAN DYSON, AGE 14

I saw The Smiths three times in Manchester – at the Palace, at G-Mex and the second Free Trade Hall gig. I grew up in Baguley in Wythenshawe, a few hundred yards from Johnny Marr. I've met him loads of times. I went to school with Ian Maher, Johnny's brother.

## ALAN NEAL, AGE 17

I was living at home in Baguley and only later became aware that both Andy Rourke and Mike Joyce were from literally just up the road. Being from Manchester and yet too young for the likes of Slaughter and the Dogs, the Buzzcocks, The Nosebleeds and Joy Division, I listened to the 2-Tone bands of the early 1980s. Nothing really changed for me as a young teenager until 1983. Seeing 'Hand In Glove' for the first time on the telly really changed things for me and others I knew, particularly my best mate Deano.

Deano and I had tickets for what would be my favourite gig to this day – The Smiths at the Palace. That night ended in overwhelming enjoyment and disappointment. The Palace Theatre is just that, an old theatre building in the heart of the city. It was the first time that I had been there since watching panto as a kid. I remember the atmosphere, the subdued but expectant anticipation of the audience, the constraints of the seats and the dark empty stage. Suddenly we were blinded by bright flashing lights and deafened by booming instrumental music.

Here we were, standing in the aisles of plush velour seats, surrounded by Victoriana and 1,500 other kids with quiffs, NHS glasses and the odd hearing aid. Despite this obvious physical similarity, I felt disconnected from everyone else there and I suspect most other people around me felt the same. Then the band appeared out of the gloom, and I felt nothing but pure joy. This was my band playing my songs. It is hard to put into words how I felt for the next hour and a half but wonderment – the wonderment at pure utter genius. The rest of the gig comprised of Deano and me trying to invade the stage to snatch a few seconds with Morrissey, a mission in which Deano was the victor and I very much the loser, still tethered in the mass of heaving youngsters. It was one of the strangest gigs I had ever been to – this unconventional band in this traditional rarefied theatre setting.

Deano and I had spotted the tour bus behind the venue earlier and decided to follow the bus after the gig. We lay in wait in Deano's inconspicuous bright yellow Mark 1 Escort, with its only one working headlight. Our hope was that, as this was the band's hometown gig, the bus would take us to one of their homes. We tried to keep our distance from the bus but very quickly the driver became aware of a single beam of light following them down the Parkway headed out of Manchester. We overtook the bus and, anticipating that they were going to Hale Barns, stopped a few miles up the road and pulled out behind the bus to follow it again. At this point the bus then pulled over, waited for us to drive past and then pulled out behind us. This cat and mouse happened a few more times and then we decided to lie in wait just outside Hale Barns. The bus passed us yet again and, to avoid detection this time, we waited two minutes before following it.

We never saw the bus again, so I can't tell the story of having a cup of Twinings and a choccie digestive at Morrissey's house.

### KEV JONES

When they played the Palace, me and my mate went down during the afternoon on the off chance of getting their autographs. We took all our records down with us. There were loads of people crowded around the front of the theatre, but we stood on the corner of Oxford Road and Whitworth Street. We thought that if they were going to turn up they'd come in a coach and that they'd come in somewhere around the back. This coach started coming down the road and pulled in behind the Palace and we thought, 'Crikey, that looks like that could be it!' There were me and my mate and these two girls who were hanging around there. The four of us just legged it and followed this coach as it pulled into the loading bay at the back. These big, corrugated doors opened and this huge coach vanished. We were just behind it and we thought, 'Oh, they've gone in. They're not going to come out.' One of the girls peeped through the crack in the doors and she said, 'They're coming out. They're coming back!' They must have seen us legging after them. The doors opened and, lo and behold, there's Morrissey, Johnny, Andy and Mike just stood there with us. I was absolutely lost for words. We got our records out and said, 'Please could you sign these?' And then we got pictures with them. That was pretty special.

## DE MONTFORT HALL



### 1 APRIL 1985, LEICESTER, UK

### VAL LOVE

My school friend Kerry and I rushed to get our tickets after working all day at Richard Roberts hosiery factory. I didn't really know many other Smiths fans but I do remember other people not getting what all the excitement was about. The big day arrived and I couldn't wait to get home from work. We arrived early, as I wanted to get near the front. There were rumours that some skinheads were

*Kev Jones met The Smiths outside Manchester's Palace Theatre*

out to get Morrissey. It was so hot in there, standing right at the front, jammed against the stage. Kerry couldn't hack it and moved further back, but I wasn't going anywhere!

The place was heaving and I was getting lifted with the crowd to the sounds of 'This Charming Man' and 'How Soon Is Now?' – my favourite tracks. They were so much better live than I expected. Morrissey was resplendent, complete with his trademark hearing aid. I actually touched his legs so many times.

I was getting so hot now. A great lanky skinhead's arm was jammed across my chest, and everything was becoming unfocused. I vaguely remember some girl stopping me from sinking to the ground and then the bouncers lifting me out of there and placing me down towards the back near my friend. I can recall it as if it was yesterday. It was one of the highlights of my teenage life.

### LEE THACKER

*Meat Is Murder* had been released earlier that year. It was the album that finally made me decide to become a vegetarian (33 years and counting). I'd been heavily into the anarcho-punk band Crass and read their vegetarian manifestos, but it was hearing the track 'Meat Is Murder' that hammered the point home to me. This gig was also the first and last time I ever tried to emulate the look of a band. I was at heart a punk, wearing mostly black clothing and button badges and spiking my hair. For this one and only time, I made a misguided sartorial decision to attend the gig 'as Morrissey'. I only owned straight leg black denim trousers and a number of home-made t-shirts (no way could I afford to buy 'proper' t-shirts at gigs: I continued to make my own well into the late eighties), so I'd have to improvise.

I procured a pair of blue jeans, the first and only time I've ever worn such apparel, and a white button up shirt from my father. I finished the look with a string of beads from my mother's jewellery box. I gelled my hair into the best quiff I could muster, and I must have looked a complete fool. (I only just realised the gig was actually on April Fools' Day!) At least I avoided the temptation to pull up some flowers

from my back garden and stick them in my back pocket. I got to the gig later than planned as I'd arranged to meet up with a few friends at a bar in town beforehand, so I ended up missing the first half of James' set. However, I pushed my way to the front again and danced my ass off, my mum's beads swinging with every Morrissey-inspired move I made!

## HIPPODROME

### 4 APRIL 1985, BRISTOL, UK

### GREG ARCHER

They were so tight as a band it was unbelievable. I count myself so lucky to have been around at this time to witness one of the finest bands this country has produced.

### JON SMITH

We travelled by coach from Exeter. The next year, for the *Queen Is Dead* tour and still at school, a friend and I organised our own coach and ticket travel to St Austell. So it was that I organised the largest school bunk off in history as 54 students got the coach!

### ANDY KING

The Smiths played the Bristol Hippodrome in 1985 on the *Meat Is Murder* tour and all my friends were big fans, so we had an entire row to ourselves. Back then I used to sneak in a recording Sony Walkman so that I could tape the bands I saw, although not for bootlegging/selling purposes! (I also have a few Billy Bragg ones, The Clash, SLF, Ramones, etc. from around that period.) The Smiths came on stage to the overture to

*Lee Thacker's ticket for the De Montfort Hall show that he attended dressed 'as Morrissey'*

Prokofiev's 'Romeo And Juliet', so I set my Walkman going as it started and one of my mates piped up, 'I wasn't expecting Torvill and Dean!' All on tape for posterity.

When my son was born on 27 May 1989, I wrote to Morrissey at HMV, his label at the time, saying that I had given my son Morrissey as his middle name in homage, and how it would be a great honour if Morrissey would be his godfather – not expecting anything to come of it!

A week or so later, I got a reply with a Smiths postcard and on the back in Moz's own hand was, 'The honour is mine, Daddy,' but strangely with a date of 23 July, well in advance of when it was posted. I wrote back saying that if that was the date he could be available for a christening, I would book it in (it was a Sunday) but that I obviously didn't expect him to turn up. I said I could name him as a godfather by proxy, and if he was okay with it, could he send me something I could give to Lewis when he was older?

A week or so later, a second reply came, this time with a Morrissey publicity pic and a dedication in green crayon to Lewis – so he was christened with Morrissey as his named godfather, all on official record, which I think is pretty cool!

# ROYAL ALBERT HALL

## 6 APRIL 1985, LONDON, UK

### ALAN HAMMETT

'This Charming Man' on the radio was a breath of fresh air. There was nothing else like The Smiths around at the time. I only got to see them three times. The first time was at the Royal Albert Hall. I went with three friends who'd seen them before. The big surprise of the night was Dead or Alive's Pete Burns coming on to sing a song which went down well. All too soon it was over.

### MICHAEL EVANS, AGE 17

I've probably been to over 1,000 gigs since my first one in 1981 but this is still what I'd call my best ever live gig. I saw them do 'This Charming Man' on *Top of the Pops* and that was it for me. Rickenbacker guitars always make my eyes pop out and there was this strange man smashing flowers on the floor, so after that moment they were the band for me. Previous to that, I'd been into Big Country, Simple Minds, Echo and The Bunnymen. I chucked all those. I'd been to gigs to see Adam and the Ants and Japan, so I was slowly going away from guitar and indie. Then The Smiths came along.

It was a miserable rainy day, which was perfect. I'd been there before for Echo and The Bunnymen. I used to go on my own because I was the only one who liked indie music. Everyone else was into soul music. I still remember it as if it was yesterday. Not that it was a particularly memorable gig. Morrissey said on the night that they'd chosen the wrong venue. Pete Burns and Morrissey were quite good friends, so he came out to do the encore of 'Barbarism Begins At Home' with them.

I was at the very front. I got absolutely crushed. Violence is the wrong word but there was an atmosphere there that was more than worship. It was more than passion. It was beyond anything I've ever witnessed. Even to this day I've never witnessed anything like I witnessed at that one Smiths gig. They are my Beatles. I deliberately didn't go to the *Queen Is Dead* tour. And after that they only did the one gig, in Brixton. My parents wouldn't let me go. I thought The Smiths would be around forever. Half of me is disappointed that they weren't and half of me is glad.

### NICK MYALL

To go to two dates on one tour was a bit extravagant in the cash-strapped eighties of my youth. I did it for The Fall and now for The Smiths. (The Brighton Dome gig remains one of the best I've ever been to.) Matt, James and I headed up to London in the week for our first ever gig in the capital after another dull day at Haywards Heath Sixth Form College. I remember talking to Brett Anderson and Matt Osman from Suede, who both went to Haywards Heath Sixth Form, about the gig that morning. They were both massive Smiths fans and were envious of our trip. The Royal Albert Hall was a brilliant, classically English setting for The Smiths. I don't remember many bands playing there, although I'd seen old film of Cream there in the late sixties.

The Smiths entered the stage through a cloud of dry ice, smoke and swirling white lights to the sound of 'Dance Of The Knights' by Prokofiev. They started with 'How Soon Is Now?' a massive favourite with the fans at the time. Then they turned their attention

to the brilliant new album, *Meat Is Murder*. 'Nowhere Fast', 'What She Said' and 'I Want The One I Can't Have' were perfect live rockers and got the fans jumping. They didn't forget the early stuff either, with 'Hand In Glove', 'Still Ill' and 'Handsome Devil' all getting a look in. Two new tracks off the 'Shakespeare's Sister' twelve-inch added to the mix and the slow build of 'Miserable Lie' worked perfectly as the finale. Another brilliant gig from a band at their peak.

### MICHAEL LIKELY

My enduring memories of the gig are that someone threw a string of sausages at Morrissey and that they really screwed up 'How Soon Is Now?'

### STEPHEN REID

The finale of the *Meat Is Murder* tour. I had seen the band at Gloucester and Chippenham before this. It was the 'big' gig but not my favourite one. I had seen Echo and the Bunnymen here the year before, and it's a wonderful venue with difficult acoustics. The sound was still poor (my father played there a few times in the trad jazz days and I don't think much had changed). My friends all rushed to the main floor but I stayed in the stalls, which was feeble of me and I regret it still! James supported that night and were the highlight, although Pete Burns came on for 'Barbarism Begins At Home', which was fun but felt a bit stilted, rather like the whole night. I bought a huge *Meat Is Murder* tour poster after the show. I still have it, framed on my office wall.

*Royal Albert Hall ticket (Stephen Reid)*

# ARAGON BALLROOM

## 7 JUNE 1985, CHICAGO, ILLINOIS

### JOHN FEATHERSTONE

I worked the tour where Billy Bragg came in as support. He's just a truly lovely, kind human being and having Billy as part of the camp, with his encyclopaedic knowledge of blues and R&B music, he fitted right in. I just remember show after show, him and Johnny being huddled together, talking and kind of nerding out on music. And Billy was the one that awakened the band to the notion of their ability to use music to influence the way people think, politically as well as emotionally. He was obviously involved with getting the band aligned with Red Wedge and involved in some other political activities.

I stumbled upon a clip of Morrissey being interviewed when the band did Glastonbury and him talking about his desire to use The Smiths being at this kind of hippie festival to focus people that were more aligned with a sort of indie rock modality to get engaged with politics. I think Billy was the motivator for a lot of that. 'With great power comes great responsibility', to use a cliche from Spider-Man. 'You've got all these kids that are all listening to you.

You've got a pulpit here. What about using it?' And I've often wondered whether Billy had more influence over some of the subject material of *The Queen Is Dead* than perhaps he's sometimes given credit for. Billy's influence invited the band to think about using their popularity in ways other than just to sell records.

### GARRETT JENNINGS, AGE 19

They had placed folding chairs out for people to sit in so everyone folded the chairs and threw them in a huge pile in the back of venue, and everyone danced/moshed as close as we all could get to the stage. I went with my friends Mike and John. We were all 19 and it was a great show!

### JIM JOLL

I saw them twice in Chicago. The first time I was with one of my college mates. I had discovered The Smiths by word of mouth at the University of Wisconsin in Madison as a 19-year-old freshman. I was fortunate to have some very hip dorm mates, and they turned me onto many of the singles. I was immediately struck by Moz's voice and Marr's rhythm guitar and hooked from there on in. I combed through the 'zines I could buy at the record stores on campus and was never disappointed by the coverage I found in *Melody Maker* and *NME*. They started playing their videos, or what I always called anti-videos, on MTV's *120 Minutes*. What I recall most about the show is Moz dancing and spinning in place with his unbuttoned, white Oxford dress shirt over his head. An image that's still seared in my mind.

### THOMAS LENZ, AGE 21

I grew up in Illinois. Not Chicago. About three hours away, nearly Iowa. During my time at university, I spent a year abroad, in Spain. On a spring break in April 1984 I travelled to various countries including the UK. While in London I visited HMV on Oxford Street and saw lots of posters and promotions for the first Smiths album. I had not heard them, but I asked a salesperson about them. On a whim I purchased the cassette. In the remaining months of my year abroad, I listened to the cassette many times on a Sony Walkman and shared this new discovery with my classmates in Spain. Before too long I heard 'This Charming Man' playing around Madrid, in the edgy Rock-Ola club, hang out of La Movida in post-Franco Spain, and in the Rastro flea market, where bootleg cassettes abounded.

By the fall of 1984, I was back in the US and some of the students I knew on campus had heard of The Smiths. I found out *Hatful Of Hollow* was released during my winter break from university. I walked a mile in the snow to my hometown record store to buy a copy.

Spring arrived and I graduated from university. My sister, a few years younger than me, and two of her friends had also taken an interest in The Smiths. The *Meat Is Murder* LP was out. I do not recall how I found out The Smiths were playing in Chicago. There was no internet. Perhaps hard copy tickets were sold at a local record store. We bought four and on the day of the concert I drove us in my VW Beetle the three hours to Chicago's Aragon Ballroom.

It seemed all the songs I wanted to hear were played. Morrissey crooned and moved about the stage. Johnny Marr played brilliantly. The band was in top form. When it was over I knew they were a band I'd like to see again if the opportunity presented itself. We had a great time and drove the three hours home.

As the records came out, I bought them all. I recorded them all to cassette tapes, memorised the lyrics and probably sang along at far too loud a volume.

In the fall of 1985, I moved to Louisiana for law school. The Smiths were a regular part of the long drive back and forth on Interstate 55, through St Louis, Missouri, and Memphis, Tennessee and the north to south length of Mississippi over three years. As law school ended, my hope of seeing The Smiths another time also ended. The band broke up. I bought the cassette of Morrissey's solo debut, *Viva Hate*, at a record store in Baton Rouge around the time I graduated from law school. I listened to it on my last voyage north on Interstate 55, returning to Illinois.

Not long after my return to Illinois, I moved again. I was looking for a job and then I found a job. In Los Angeles, California. More than 30 years later, my sister and friends who attended the concert in Chicago are spread across the US. We still talk about the show we saw in Chicago.

My oldest child is a daughter, 18 years old as I write this. She asked me if I had heard of an English band from the eighties. She said she likes them a lot and their music speaks to her more than other bands. She asked, 'Are you familiar with The Smiths?' 'Yes,' I said. And I told her this story.

### THOMAS AUGUSTINE

The opening act was three drag queens lip synching. It was confusing at first, then amusing. I enjoyed both the concerts I saw but the second one was overshadowed by going to see Del Amitri for the first time afterwards. Justin put out so much more energy than Morrissey did on stage. It wasn't that The Smiths put on a bad show. I just stopped being impressed by them or, more specifically, Morrissey.

# KINGSWOOD THEATRE

## 9 JUNE 1985, TORONTO, CANADA

### CHRISTIAN PATRICK, AGE 12

My parents made my older brother bring me to the show, at a theme park outside of Toronto called Kingswood Theatre. It was a very strange setting for a band like The Smiths. It's stranger still to think that my brother was into The Smiths, considering that he was a massive metalhead and into bands like Metallica, Judas Priest, Iron Maiden, etc. But over the years I've realised that metalheads love Johnny Marr's guitar playing. When people talk about great guitarists in music history, Johnny Marr's name rarely comes up. But metalheads know what's up. Seeing him really stoked the fire in me to want to play guitar.

Morrissey was at his peak in 1985, really embracing himself as an icon and front man. It was ego and arrogance, but was easily forgiven because of his flippancy and sense of humour. That's the thing about The Smiths; they've always been this band that's super dark on the surface, but when you really dive into them you realise that Morrissey – for all his morose and dark undertones – is one of the funniest, most clever lyricists of all time.

I remember them playing 'How Soon Is Now?' and it really changed my life. It seemed like a familiar song, even though I'd only heard it for the first time that night. It is such a haunting, complex ear worm that in reality is a simple, repetitive song, as I realised years later. I found a tape of that show that someone was trading a couple years back. So, in a weird way, listening to it brings all those memories back even though I should have been too young to remember.

### PHIL GUERRERO, AGE 14

It was such a long time ago that I don't remember much. It was at Canada's Wonderland at the Kingswood and one of the very few times they played in Canada. I was

*Billy Bragg & Morrissey backstage at Kingswood Theatre (Billy Bragg)*

big into new wave/New Romantic music at the time. I was with my best friend Russ. We were two new wave peas in a pod. I had *Meat Is Murder* on vinyl as well as the 'Barbarism Begins At Home' EP.

### KEVIN HOLMBERG

The weather that day was great and anticipation for seeing the show was in the air. The Kingswood did a great job of having great UK 'artist of the day' concerts. CFNY was a strong promoter of post-punk and new wave acts. My two favourite Kingswood shows were The Smiths and Siouxsie and The Banshees. My first recollection of them was hearing 'Hand In Glove'. At that time they were *NME* and *Melody Maker* darlings. I remember buying 'This Charming Man', the second single I purchased by them, and playing the grooves off the EP. There was such a great, happy feel to that record. I purchased the debut LP as a UK import. It was on Rough Trade and missing 'This Charming Man'. The Sire US release would soon remedy this, as 'This Charming Man' was garnering lots of airplay.

The Smiths replicated this when *Meat Is Murder* was released as an import without 'How Soon Is Now?' The concert crowd consisted of fans that knew all of the songs. Morrissey was a rock star frontman that had the crowd's complete attention. Marr quietly displayed mastery of his craft, but it was Morrissey's stage. The show was a little over one and a half hours and had two encores. They left an amazing legacy. This music was so fresh and timely. I have The Smiths poster with my ticket stub mounted in my music room.

### DAVE KAPLE

The show took place as part of the *Meat Is Murder* tour in Toronto, or more specifically Vaughan, in Ontario, Canada at the Kingswood Music Theatre, an open-air theatre with a covered bandshell and exposed lawn seats for the audience. I only had a handful of concerts under my belt at this time.

Truthfully, I didn't know what to expect. Billy Bragg opened the gig. We as a crowd were shy but we got louder and then Morrissey encouraged the crowd to come closer. By the end, fans were on the stage hugging and kissing him and he soaked it all in. Fans even threw the newly laid turf up on stage, throwing the sod like frisbees. It was bizarre.

### LORRAINE RENNER

I was in high school when I first started listening to them. 'How Soon Is Now?' was soon pretty much was on every mix tape I made, as was 'The Queen Is Dead', 'Panic' and 'This Charming Man'. I would crank my stereo, Walkman or whatever I was listening to music on at the time whenever I heard any Smiths song come on. I first saw them at the now defunct Kingswood Music Theatre just north of Toronto in 1985, and then again in 1986. They were amazing! Every song they played, every lyric that Morrissey sang in that oh-so-distinctive Morrissey voice, Johnny Marr's riffs on guitar and of course Mike and Andy... it was awesome. The crowd started cheering and banging on the seat backs in front of them hoping for an encore. It was such a racket, but Morrissey loved it. He said, 'I am not sure how you are making that sound but keep on doing it.'

We bought the tickets for the concert and the amusement park. A few hours before the concert was to begin, we heard the famous guitar riff for 'How Soon Is Now?' echo through the park and my anticipation grew into a frenzy. At that time in my life, The Smiths meant everything to me during a high school unrequited love period. Funnily enough his name was William (Bill)... (It was really nothing, ha!)

Morrissey was gorgeous and our seats were close enough to the stage that I went from noticing only him and then acknowledging the power artists have to instantly connect with millions of people, making them physically feel connected. I adored the seemingly whimsical delivery of poignant political and authority hypocrisies in the lyrics.

# WARNER THEATRE

## 11 JUNE 1985, WASHINGTON DC

### LANA MENGES

By autumn 1984, I was a student at the University of Colorado in Boulder, Colorado. Unable to find any forthcoming US tour information, I wrote a letter to Rough Trade Records in London. Months later they actually wrote back!

They listed the tour dates for the summer of 1985, including for my hometown of Washington DC on 11 June. Yay! Knowing I would be back in DC for summer break 1985, I went to the local library and combed through the DC newspapers for the concert ads. Aaarrgghh, the show was already sold out! But I was *not* going to miss The Smiths first ever tour of the States!

I stood in line outside the ticket office at the Warner Theatre for hours on show day and got one of the few returned tickets ($15) for the show – Row J centre. As a bonus, Billy Bragg was in the opening slot. Billy was the best opening act ever.

And The Smiths blew me away; they were so good! 'How Soon Is Now' is the definitive seminal anthem for my generation. I vividly remember how haunting and tortuous the song 'Meat Is Murder' sounded. I was already a vegetarian,

*Lana Menges' ticket stub for the Warner Theatre gig*

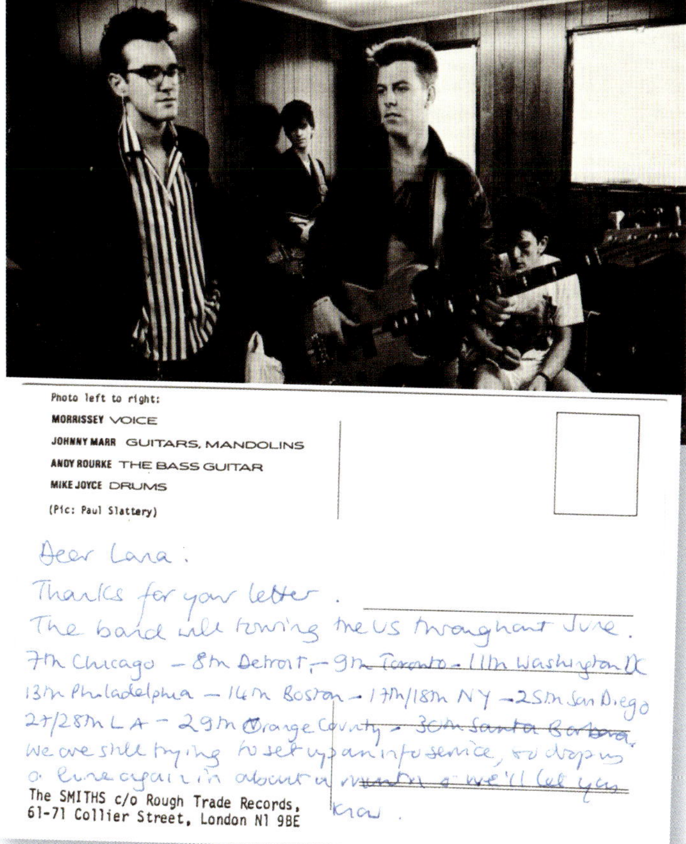



*Lana Menges' postcard from Rough Trade*

but the song really cemented it for me. The crowd was so wild; we kept screaming and applauding when the band left the stage, even after the house lights came up – they did three encores to finally appease us!

### CHRISTOPHER QUINN

I discovered The Smiths in the spring of 1984 and became obsessed over that summer. I frequented a local independent record store called Yesterday and Today. Owner Skip Goff employed local musicians like Archie Moore of Velocity Girl and Ted Nicely, bassist for Tommy Keene and producer for groups like Tripping Daisy, Jawbox, Shudder To Think and Fugazi. It wasn't unusual to see Tommy or Henry Rollins perusing the bins any day of the week. I became friends with Tony Cohen who worked in the store, as we shared the Smiths obsession. One day in early '85 a signed copy of *Meat Is Murder* turned up in The Smiths' section. The price was $50 and I asked Tony why he hadn't short stopped it. He said, 'I'm not buying it and neither should you. We'll get our own!'

I got tickets through a broker for the DC and Philly shows. I had second row seats for Warner and a different friend of mine (also named Tony) came with me. The show was amazing and, to this day, remains my greatest all-time favourite concert. Billy Bragg opened the show (we had never heard of him) but I fell in love with him that night. He played 'Jeane' and asked us to be more careful next time we elect a president as we elect one for England too. I was surprised at the negative response he got. (Reagan was a pretty popular president and had just won re-election in a landslide, but in that room?)

Record store Tony came climbing over the seats during the encore, headed for the stage and handed me his jacket as he passed. He said, 'Don't let *anything* happen to this. I'll see you at Poseurs.' Poseurs was a dark wave / new wave nightclub in Georgetown where a bunch of us were going to an after party. On the way there, I discovered a tape recorder in Tony's jacket and we listened to the concert all over again in Tony II's car.

The next morning, one of Tony's friends had arranged for a group of us to have breakfast with The Smiths at the Shoreham Hotel in DC before heading up the road to Philadelphia. I didn't really know the other friends that came with Tony.

I think the young lady who had put together the breakfast was the owner of the bootleg tape… I know she was there. Any road, this group of people came from different places and by the time we were all in the lobby, we found out there would be no breakfast. The Smiths were running late so Tony and I decided we had to go find them.

We got a look at the registration (such things were printed back then) and that saw Andy and Mike were sharing a room and that there was a 'Kevin' Morrissey down the hall. We got to the sixth floor and saw the door to the shared room was ajar. We didn't disturb. We headed for 'Kevin's' room and found Mike walking down the hall eating a bowl of cereal. We told him how great the show was and that we were headed to Philly too.

I pointed to the door and asked if it was, in fact, 'you know who'. He said yes but that it would be wise to follow the instruction on the sign dangling from the door and not to disturb him, so we didn't. There was a housekeeping cart nearby so I switched out the signs and used it in the lobby for autographs.

Later, in the lobby, Mike and Andy sat on a sofa barely disturbed while Morrissey was surrounded. He seemed a bit overwhelmed. One guy handed him a card that was clearly bulging with handwritten pages and he commented he would read it in bed. Tony's friend (and now mine), Nalinee Darmrong, had brought a set of coloured markers and asked Moz to draw her a picture. It looked very like something Linder would have drawn. Very Picasso and angular.

I asked him if was aware that there was a meat packing firm in the MidWest called Morrissey Meats. He was not and was duly appalled. Johnny slipped out to the bus somehow and while I didn't get him to sign my new treasure, I contented myself with the fact I'd shaken his hand through the window of the tour bus the night before.

## TOWER THEATER

### 12 JUNE 1985, PHILADELPHIA, PENNSYLVANIA

### CHRISTOPHER QUINN

Tony, Nalinee and I rode up to Philly with my good friend Jay and my sister's best friend, Marcella. We had four decent seats and two up front. We'd agreed to switch in intervals but Tony and Nalinee stayed down front for pretty much the whole show. Tony was stood next to a guy who kept demanding 'What Difference Does It Make'. Moz came over, looked the guy dead in the eye and said, 'We don't do THAT song anymore!' Tony and Nalinee got on stage for the encore, and Nalinee got Andy in a lip lock. Great show!

Nalinee got talking to Johnny at some point over those two days and got herself on the guest list for the Beacon Theater, New York. She continued on the rest of the tour. She and Tony also did the Scottish *Meat Is Murder* tour. (Tony got on stage at Barrowlands and hugged Moz – it's on YouTube.)

They had extraordinarily access to the band and Nalinee did the *Queen Is Dead* tour as well. She became the house photographer at DC's 9:30 Club and later released a Smiths photobook. Her beautiful live shot of Andy was used for the recently installed mural / memorial of Andy in Manchester.

I saw The Smiths again on the *Queen Is Dead* tour in DC. It was a great show but a shadow of the year before and something wasn't quite as it was. Had I known, of course, I would have attend a couple more shows at the very least but a year later, it was all over.

### JEANNE CARDAMONE

I still love them like I did when I first heard them, in my hometown of Rochester, New York. We didn't have cable at home so I would go to my friends' houses who had MTV and watch TV all night instead of sleeping. It must have been 1984 when The Smiths came on the TV playing 'How Soon Is Now?' and I was hooked. We have a record store in Rochester called House of Guitars and I went there to find *The Smiths*. I

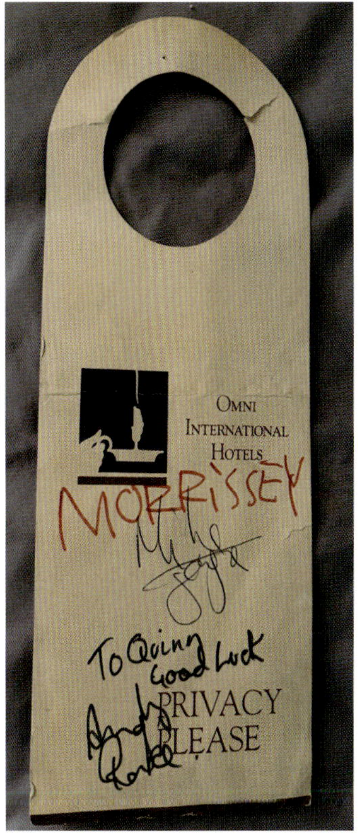

Christopher Quinn's autographed *Do Not Disturb* sign liberated from Morrissey's hotel room door

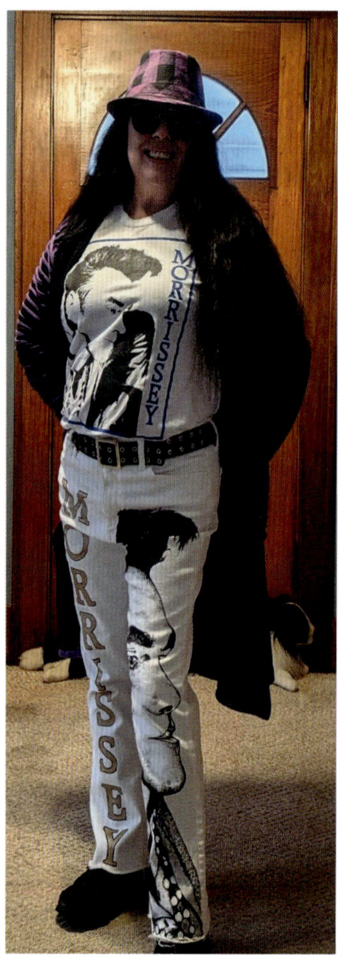

Jeanne saw The Smiths at the Tower Theater

got the album and played it to death.

In 1985 I went to New Jersey for a couple of months to help my aunt. While I was there, I read in the paper that The Smiths were coming to Philadelphia, not too far from my aunt's house. I asked her if I could go and see them (I was only 18) and she said yes, but only if I could find someone to go with me. This was a problem because I didn't know anybody there. My aunt said, 'Why don't you ask John and Cindy?' They lived in the same apartment complex, and I had met them just a few weeks earlier. So I asked them and they said yes and I paid for them to go and they got me a date too! How weird was that? Not one of them had ever heard of The Smiths (and I can't remember my date's name) but what a show!

My ticket cost $12.50. The concert was at the Tower Theater, an old, run down theatre in a bad part of Philadelphia and I was so glad I didn't go alone. We had to wait for the doors to open, and the crowd was so cool. There was a very tall, slender young man who was in all leather and sporting an awesome five-inch-high Mohawk with black roots to blond tips. In the shaved side it was bleached out blond with leopard spots in black.

The doors opened and we got to our seats on in the middle right side of the theatre. I could see The Smiths very clearly. They let so many people go up on stage to dance with them. It was so cool. The concert was awesome and the people I brought with me loved them too, even though they had never heard of them before. It's one of the greatest concerts I have ever been to.

# DULLES INTERNATIONAL AIRPORT

## 13 JUNE 1985, WASHINGTON DC

### LANA MENGES

Two days after the DC show, I met the band at Dulles International Airport while waiting at an airline counter. I spied some people way down the concourse, one of which I swore was Morrissey. (After all, Morrissey does have a distinctive flail to his dancing and movement.) I asked my companion to keep our place in line while I walked down there just to make sure it was *not* Morrissey. As I got closer, I realized it *was* the whole band, hanging out before going to their gate. I effused about their show, hugged and kissed them all (perfectly acceptable in the 1980s) and asked for autographs (no photos though, as people didn't really carry their cameras around back then). Morrissey dug through his book bag and found a piece of paper with instructions for contact lenses on one side and which was blank on the other side. They graciously talked with me and signed autographs on the floor in the airport. I got the feeling they wanted to chat longer and find out more about how the DC show went, but I had to return to the airline counter. It was the best experience ever!

# OPERA HOUSE

## 14 JUNE 1985 BOSTON, MASSACHUSETTS

### JAY P MORGENSTERN

This was their debut gig in Boston. It included three encores and a stage invasion for the final track, 'Barbarism Begins At Home'. Shortly thereafter in 1985 I started graduate school at UCL. There I saw The Smiths multiple times, the highlight being their gig at the Palladium in London in 1986 to support *The Queen Is Dead* where, after the show, I met Morrissey's mum. (I kid you not!) I also caught their last gig ever at the Brixton Academy later that year.

# BEACON THEATRE

## 17 JUNE 1985, NEW YORK, NEW YORK

### JOSEPH HUGHES, AGE 16

It was the night before the French Regent's Exam in NYC (a comprehensive subject exam for third year of high school). I went with my girlfriend at the time. Her parents drove us home. It was life-changing. Every song was magic. When they opened with 'Meat Is Murder' the stage backdrop turned blood red. I can still see it. They closed with 'Barbarism Begins At Home' and left the stage one at a time. It was unforgettable. I'm pretty sure I was gape-mouthed the whole time, and I can honestly say that gig still looms large in my memory as a milestone event. My whole concept of bands and live music and art all started forming that night. I went to Tower Records in the next day or two and bought whatever imports or compilations I could find.

### CHRISTINE LICAUSI, AGE 20

My first concert ever. They opened with 'William, It Was Really Nothing', my favourite Smiths song to this day. I went with my new 17-year-old punk rocker boyfriend Larry, who had turned me onto their music soon after we met that month. We were both from Long Island but spent a lot of time in the city that summer. I immediately fell in love. With the music – and the guy.

That show holds a special place in my heart because it was my first but also because of the music and their showmanship. It was about love, and death, and angst and loss. All emotions I could relate to at the time, and now... I loved that band for speaking to me that way.

Morrissey was in top form and put on an amazing show. He really whipped us all into a fan frenzy with his stage persona. Larry and I had an amazing time and hated to see it end. They did three encores.

After the show, Larry and I got up to leave and started walking out of the theatre. We noticed a group of people ahead of us who really stood out. As we got closer, we realised it was Andy Warhol and his entourage. They had been sitting just a few rows back from us the entire show. I will never forget saying hello to them in the lobby as we left. How could I ever forget that night?

# BEACON THEATRE

## 18 JUNE 1985, NEW YORK, NEW YORK

### JOHN BAXTER, AGE 16

My older brother was in the Ron Delsener ticket club and procured tickets for me. Delsener was a concert promoter, and club members were guaranteed seats at sold out shows. My brother was mostly attending large stadium shows, but I was interested in all the new music shows that were playing the smaller venues.

I took the train into the city from our home in the suburbs of Long Island, about an hour away. The Beacon is a former movie theatre opened in 1929 with three tiers and just under 3,000 seats. And to my surprise our seats were twelfth row centre! I brought three school friends who also loved The Smiths. In 1985, the suburbs could be pretty conservative in terms of style and music taste. If it wasn't Top 40, most teens weren't interested. I was happy to find my tribe in school, and we were easy to spot, with Mohawks, thrift shop clothing, combat boots and cardigans. Our classmates dressed like their parents, and we wanted none of that!

After Billy Bragg, The Smiths took to the stage and opened with 'Meat Is Murder'. With only two albums at this time, every song was well known and much loved. I remember they closed with 'How Soon Is Now?' before several encores. We had read and seen pictures in the music magazines about how Morrissey let fans storm the stage and sure enough my friend Edna made her attempt. One security person decided there was enough teens on stage, but she wriggled past him and bounced around onstage, victorious. If only I hadn't run out of film in my camera and could have captured that moment for her. There was no digital in those days and I could barely afford the 24 exposures I had!

The concert ended and I bought a *Meat Is Murder* t-shirt and a tour programme and lingered outside the theatre afterwards. Then Billy Bragg strolled out alone and unnoticed, his guitar slung over one shoulder. I asked him to sign my Smiths programme and he kindly obliged. I rode the train home on that special concert high, where your ears are still ringing but you hope it lasts.

### RACHEL FELDER, AGE 16

I grew up listening to British and American punk rock, and I subsequently became close to the Ramones. I was always obsessed with British indie music from early on. For me, British punk rock had a straight line to British indie music. My trajectory ended up with a lot of professional and personal musical connections.

I'm American, but I did sixth form in England at a very traditional school. I had a little radio. I'd listen to Radio Caroline, and John Peel and Radio 1 in the evenings were where I heard many artists for the first time, and where I first heard The Smiths. I don't remember which song but I do remember it sounding earth shattering. The sound of The Smiths that evening was arresting and distracting and so assertive that there was no way you couldn't pay attention. I used to listen to the radio as background music but that was not background music. That pulled you in.

Billy Bragg opened up for them, who I was also super-duper into at the time. Still to this day it's one of the most compelling concerts I've ever seen. I remember how Morrissey moved on stage. Today we live in a world where gender-bending and sexual ambiguity is embraced and it's a good thing and it's widely accepted. But that wasn't the world then. The artists that played with gender roles and their sexuality were more in the Bowie direction, much more overt. So it wasn't just what Morrissey would say in interviews. It was the way he moved on stage and even his choice of clothing, these blousy shirts that were clearly feminine although there wasn't make up or long hair or any of that. I found that fascinating. That made him and his band feel unique and relevant and cool and music your parents would hate, which is exactly what you wanted when you were 16.

It was assertive music, jangly but not spiky, sharp but not overly angry. A lot of the English bands I had been into beforehand were bands like The Jam, whose last American show at the old Palladium I remember vividly. The Jam had a certain anger about them. That wasn't what The Smiths were about. The lyrics had a darkness, but the music was so upbeat, and it just grabbed you.

I saw that show and then I saw all the other New York shows, because they would always play New York on their tours. I was always compelled and I loved them to the end. Although I found the direction they went in progressively a little less interesting as they got more mainstream, their records were always good. The concerts were always that way too.

I'm lucky enough to have seen many influential bands. I started going to gigs very young and saw a lot of seminal English bands play reasonably small places in New York. There's not that many gigs that you remember so vividly so many years later. I still think of The Smiths as the standard that other bands have to meet.

There was a passion and a potency about The Smiths that was, and is still, huge. It felt like there was a purity to what that band was doing that today is a little bit harder to achieve, in the age of Instagram and hype. We live in a world that is much faster to get 'buzz' happening. In Britain and the world at the time, that wasn't the case. So you could almost sense that excitement of them playing in New York for the first time. I became a journalist that wrote mostly about music for years. I ended up working at a record label doing A&R. I ended up reviewing a Morrissey album for *Rolling Stone*.

It wasn't a small evening, that night at the Beacon, in the big picture of evenings for me. It had a great impact on what I ended up doing professionally and with my life.

I'm not very into seeing reunion shows. I've seen Morrissey solo once. He played a big run of shows here on Broadway in May 2019. I didn't get tickets on purpose. Seeing The Smiths are precious memories to me of young, passionate, naïve – in the most beautiful way – men. I'm not eager to see middle-aged men try to repeat that magic. It doesn't usually happen that way.

*Bekki Newton saw The Smiths at the Hollywood Palladium & the London Palladium*

## HOLLYWOOD PALLADIUM

### 27 JUNE 1985, LOS ANGELES, CALIFORNIA

### BEKKI NEWTON

I saw them night one at the Palladium (when they had to stop the gig for a few mins as someone in the crowd pulled Johnny Marr's battery pack off him) and a few days later at Irvine Meadows.

I then saw them at the Kilburn National, one of the *Rank* gigs, after moving to Britain in October 1986, and again at the London Palladium. The Palladium show was sold out, and my friend and I tried to buy tickets from touts but there were barely any available and super expensive. Then a guy at the side door motioned to us, said he'd get us in for £5 each, and let us into the show. He also gave us stubs so we could find a seat!

### GREG GABRY, AGE 21

I was only really familiar with the songs that I had heard on KROQ (106.7FM radio in LA) like 'This Charming Man' and 'Heaven Knows I'm Miserable Now', but I had heard everything else at my friends' houses or in their cars and was quickly becoming a fan.

When we got to the Palladium, I felt like I may not be the only one who didn't quite get it yet, as there were almost equal size contingents of punks, surfers, Hollywood glam types and even some hair band-looking dudes – it was quite a mix. I will admit we 'partied' rather heavily before getting into Hollywood, so recollections of the evening are quite hazy, but the opening act was very bizarre, as it featured an incredibly robust drag queen on stage who serenaded the crowd with operatic selections. The crowd wasn't all that appreciative.

The crowd became a bit unruly with lots of yelling, some booing and minor skirmishes amongst us standing on the floor. Perhaps this was out of boredom or nervousness, and of course drugs and alcohol, but the unruliness continued throughout the show, so much so that it was mentioned from on stage a few times. I recall feeling a bit scolded. If I could go back and give my 21-year-old self some advice it would be that when he spends money on tickets to see potentially iconic bands, he should scale back on the alcohol and hallucinogens so he can remember things more clearly in the future!

When the band finally took the stage and a long, slow melodic introduction started, the tension and excitement in the crowd shot up tremendously. It was the second song I remember vividly, for when I heard the introduction to 'Hand in Glove' and wished for harmonica, which was absent, I and the people I was with went a bit nuts. That's when it sunk in that I was actually seeing The Smiths and it felt like a really big deal; you got the sense that this band was capable of big things. Morrissey up on stage held your attention like no other lead singers we were seeing at that time, and the guitar work was mesmerising.

Seeing The Smiths felt like our generation's 'Beatles at Shea Stadium' experience; something that could never be duplicated and which we would remember forever.

### PHILLIP LÓPEZ JIMÉNEZ, AGE 16

In '85, I was getting more into music and started reading *NME* and *Melody Maker* to find out what was happening in England and *Flipside* and *MMR* for the States. I first heard The Smiths in '84 on KROQ, a radio station out of Los Angeles. The song was 'What Difference Does It Make?' I loved it but I figured it was a new song from The Polecats! When the deejay said it was a band called The Smiths, I made a mental note. The first album I got was *Hatful Of Hollow*.

The Smiths were getting a big buzz in the UK and US, and they were right up my alley. My tastes leaned toward more guitar-oriented stuff than techno. I liked Depeche Mode but so did twelve-year-old girls! When I read in *NME* that Morrissey was the president of The Cramps fan club and that he preferred American bands like X, I became more interested, as The Cramps were (and still are) my favourite band.

I went to the show with some people I knew but they were a bit square and hung out on the balcony. I was on the floor at the stage. Because there was a buzz about the band and this was their first LA show, the crowd was a mix of punks and bubblegummers. The opening act was a bunch of drag queens. That's when it started raining spit.

I had hooked up with this chick there earlier and I threw my leather jacket over her and said, 'Shit this is like a fuckin' Fear show!' Loogies were flying everywhere. The final drag queen was dressed like a baby with diaper and bottle and singing 'Shortnin' Bread'. (I am not making this shit up). The crowd started getting a bit violent. Then some guy started groping the girl I was with, and I popped him in the face. I remember thinking, 'This is the fuckin' Smiths, not some local HC show!' The drag queens left and the lights came on and we waited.

After a while the lights shut off, and it was total darkness. Then – boom – a bright spotlight popped on from the back of the stage, pointing up and forming columns of light. Then pre-recorded music turned on and I recognised the tune. A few other people in the crowd recognised it too. This went on for a minute or two and then the band came out and jumped right into 'Meat Is Murder'. I was like, 'Okay, now I get it.' That sure was an attention grabber!

People were jumping on stage and halfway through their set someone grabbed Johnny Marr's leg, and he fell and someone took his wireless and Morrissey stormed off. Marr said that if he didn't get his wireless they were going to leave. Then someone in the crowd screamed that he was gonna kick the shit out of whoever had it. Finally, it flew out of the audience and into Marr's hands. Then Marr had to persuade Morrissey to come back out. He came back out and said that we were the most unruly crowd he'd ever seen and lectured us some more. Then they finally started playing again.

I wish I could remember the girl's name I hooked with. I'm not a big Morrissey fan and never got his solo stuff, though I like some of the songs. I love The Smiths but don't really listen to them often. Being Latino and liking them has become a bizarre stereotype, to say the least. That show was predominantly Anglo. Now, I'm sure, it would be different.

### DONNA KLAUSER

I first heard them on KROQ. I remember scrounging for change to get tickets for me and my boyfriend (now my husband) for $15. $15? Those tickets are priceless now! I remember Morrissey swinging his flowers. 'Meat Is Murder' was their first song and I remember hearing a cow mooing and the sound of a butcher's saw in the background. I thought I saw an image of a cow. Many young gay men were crying and hugging themselves. This was the height of the AIDS crisis, and I now understand the relevance of having The Smiths performance with a gay lead singer. My little sister kept trying to squirm her way up the front and we kept pulling her back. There was no mosh pit. I just felt that this was an intense musical experience.

### LARRY WEATHERFORD, AGE 17

The Smiths were a great band for four 17-year-old dudes to see. We walked up to the Palladium as a limo pulled in the back and the guys got out. All four of them! Johnny Marr bummed a cigarette from me. I had to hand it to them through a chain-link fence.

They were pretty cordial. Morrissey didn't say anything, but Mike Joyce was friendly. They were on their way in as we were all saying, 'We really like you!' They humbly thanked us and went inside. When the show started it was very aggressive, more like the punk shows I went to and what I envisioned The Smiths show would be like. We were pretty big guys, so we rushed to the front. Had we not been big we would've been crushed against the wooden barrier between us and the stage. We were front and centre – Morrissey's wingtips were in our face. The band sounded amazing and we had a fantastic time.

### JUANITA MANTZ

I grew up in Ontario, California, which is about 60 miles from Los Angeles. It was a pretty poor neighbourhood. My dad was a truck driver and Mom a waitress, so I had a lot of time on my own. I was what they would call a latchkey kid back then, where you literally had a key on your neck to get in at home.

I used to smoke behind a section of the apartments across from our house and one day these guys walked by in black trenchcoats and had the words 'The Smiths' in white tape or maybe white paint on their backs. I thought, 'Who are The Smiths?'

I must have been 14 years old because I was really into them by high school. Me and my best friend would take the bus to Hollywood and go to Tower Records to look through the imports. That's how I found The Smiths' first record, the self-titled debut. I remember listening to 'Hand In Glove' and 'This Charming Man' and, oh my gosh, I just lost myself. I'd take my Walkman to school and just listen to the album on repeat.

My favourite album is *The Queen Is Dead*. I'd never heard someone talk about literature the way Morrissey did until that album came out. Those were my two loves, music and literature. I loved the songs 'Frankly, Mr Shankly' and 'Cemetry Gates'. And 'Half A Person' from the compilation *Louder Than Bombs* touched me in a very deep place. I got what that meant; I grew up in a very abusive and alcoholic household, and I just wanted to get out...

I saw The Smiths with my best friend, Melinda, who I've known since I was four or five. Her mom used to watch us as kids and we're both Latina. How did we get to the Hollywood Palladium? I don't even know. I think Melinda was driving by then, as back then you could get a learner's permit. She had this old 1964 Corvair, and we'd take a boombox with us and play the cassette of whatever band we were going to see. I'm sure she drove, or maybe it was her boyfriend Todd, who was a couple of years older than us. He was a big punk, and he was in a band.

The Hollywood Palladium was, and still kind of is, grungy. It's not a huge space. It's a general admission space where it's standing room only. I'm sure we drank in the car. I don't drink anymore, but I was a big drinker then and we were buzzed. I remember hearing Morrissey as he took the stage and I lost it. I went to the front of the stage and was just standing there with my arms outstretched, singing along to every word. I will never stop loving Morrissey. I will never stop loving him. He gives everything in a show.



### TONY JASICA

It probably started around the time I graduated from high school in 1983. What intrigued me about The Smiths was the intelligence in their lyrics. A perfect example is in the lyrics to 'Cemetry Gates', when they talk about Keats and Yeats. I ended up going to our local library and reading up about John Keats and WB Yeats to decide which one I liked best.

I was going to college in Southern California and Los Angeles when my college girlfriend and I went to see The Smiths. It was a wonderful show, and at the very end of the concert, after their encore, Morrissey stopped the concert and said to the audience, 'So everybody's here having a good time tonight?' 'Yeah, yeah, we're having a great time.' 'But you aren't having a great time because the security is doing their job. And they're not letting you come on stage – is that right?'

And everybody screamed, 'Yeah, right.' And so Morrissey said, 'Well, I'll tell you what. Fuck the security and get up on stage right now.' And then something happened that I'd never seen at a concert before: everybody stormed to the stage, and we all ran on stage.

I forget what song it was the band was playing. But you could hear the full band and then, as more people got on stage, you know, one of the guitars dropped out because people were, you know, grabbing the guitar, and then the drummer stopped, and then Morrissey stopped singing. Until eventually, there was nothing on stage, but the audience was on stage. And we were just making noise, you know, just to be on stage. I stayed on my feet, but the security ended the show right there. And that was it. We all went home happy.

*The Boy With The Thorn In His Side*

## 'THE BOY WITH THE THORN IN HIS SIDE'
### RELEASED 16 SEPTEMBER 1985

'The Boy With The Thorn In His Side' was accompanied by a video that featured The Smiths in the studio, helping it to reach number 23. Truman Capote was the cover star on the picture sleeve, although not all the band were familiar with him.

Morrissey: When I put him on the cover of 'The Boy With the Thorn In His Side', a certain member of the Smiths (who unfortunately is still alive) said, 'Is that Ernie Wise?'

After a two-month break from touring, The Smiths were back out on the road in September, undertaking a seven date Scottish tour taking in Edinburgh, Glasgow, Dundee and Aberdeen but also less familiar stop-offs for Rock bands – Irvine, Lerwick and Inverness.

## MAGNUM LEISURE CENTRE
### 22 SEPTEMBER 1985, IRVINE, UK

### MICHAEL FARRAGHER

All our money went on travelling around to see The Smiths and sometimes on places to stay. A lot of the times when we were travelling to see them in England, we would stay in a coach station or a train station or even a public toilet, because we couldn't afford a hotel. The great occasions were when they went further away. That was too far to come back and forth to London from the gig, and we stayed in youth hostels. Those were really good.

There was a planned tour of Italy, I think in '85, and we were all set to go and Morrissey sent us the dates and said, 'We are playing in Italy,' and then they cancelled it at the last minute. There had been a death threat and Morrissey decided that the tour was off. In all, when I counted up how many times we saw them, it was around 50.

### YVONNE BENNIE

My sister Liz and I were from Kilmarnock and my sister always says I was the first girl in our town to walk around wearing my shirt outside my jeans like Morrissey. I also once ran into our local butcher's shop on our main street and shouted, 'Meat is murder!'

We saw them at the Magnum Leisure Centre. It's since been demolished. It's the only gig we went to in the eighties where they retained our tickets, and my sis and I were not happy. We begged to be able to keep them but to no avail. The Smiths were my favourite band then. I dressed in all black as I was indie then, but for the gig I wore one white glove as homage to the song, 'Hand In Glove'. A few years later, I was talking to a work colleague who had been at the gig and who said, 'There was a girl there wearing one white glove, we thought that was strange?' I replied, 'That was me!'

### FRANCIS LOPEZ, AGE 21

I was unemployed, skint and playing in my own band, Catch 22. Music was my life. I was always first into Speed Records in Ayr the morning of a Smiths release and the guy that ran the shop always gave me a poster to go along with the records I bought. I still have a couple, my most cherished being the 'Shakespeare's Sister' poster featuring Pat Phoenix as Elsie Tanner.

The only time I'd seen The Smiths live was on BBC – it might have been *The Oxford Road Show* or *Rock Goes To College* or one of those shows. But it was awful and they were awful so when I saw the advert for their gig at Irvine Magnum, I thought, 'On record they are great but live, I might give it a miss.'

No one I knew wanted to go and see them so when the Sunday arrived, I eventually encouraged myself to go. I set off at three o'clock in the afternoon and hitchhiked the 28 miles from New Cumnock to Irvine. It was a dark and dreich night, so everything that was keeping me in the house was being thrown at me: they were shit live; no money for the bus; the cold, damp evening; the thought of hitchhiking it back at nighttime; and not knowing what time in the morning I'd get back home. They all combined to keep me nudging towards just staying in my warm room. But I got there. I can't remember how many lifts it took!

When I got into the hall at the Magnum it was already pretty busy. I decided to position myself roughly in the middle of the crowd. Even though I was hooked on The Smiths, I still recall feeling sort of ambivalent and more amused to be seeing them than excited.

Down went the lights, on went 'Dance Of The Knights' by Prokofiev and on they came. 'Guess who?' roared Morrissey. How stupid I'd been. Right from the off, a tsunami of being was blasted at me. It felt like getting the biggest punch in the stomach. At the time I compared it to Motörhead starting the set off with 'Ace Of Spades'. The sheer power just amazed me. It was the complete opposite to the limp and unenthusiastic performance on BBC2 that I'd watched that Saturday afternoon.

It was awesome – and I never use that word to describe anything. What made it even more special was that they were using us, us in tiny insignificant Ayrshire – a place that had been devastated by Thatcher's cruel pit closures after the miners were defeated, battered and bruised by her bitter and twisted cruelty on a population she knew nothing about and didn't want to know – to debut three songs. We were the first to hear them live. They could've chosen anywhere to play them live first, but they chose us. That meant so much to us because we had so little to cheer us up at that time.

After three encores, the gig finished, and I was completely knackered. It felt great. I hitchhiked it home alone (see what I did there?) but I can't recall a single thing about the journey or what time I got back. All I remember is that I was in no hurry – I'd just been to the best gig I'd ever go to.

## PLAYHOUSE

### 24 SEPTEMBER 1985, EDINBURGH, UK

### PETER MARTIN

I remember mooching about Edinburgh all day, throwing stones at Steve Joyce, as we met him for the first time, and kissing Morrissey on the cheek as he came out of the soundcheck. We missed the train home as we refused to leave before the band had finished. We had to

*Playhouse ticket (Peter Martin)*

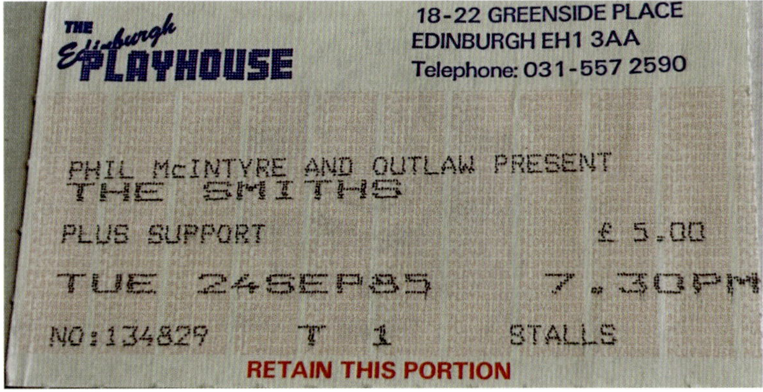


get the next one, which didn't stop at Cramlington, meaning a taxi back from the town.

## BARROWLAND BALLROOM

### 25 SEPTEMBER 1985, GLASGOW, UK

### PETER DORIS

I still have a bit of Morrissey's shirt from that night. The audience tore it to bits.

### ANNETTE FLYNN

You can hear Morrissey, on a bootleg of this show, saying, 'This song is dedicated to someone who gave me something this afternoon.' Well, that would be me. But I didn't know at that time. I had delivered a parcel to the Barrowland containing a card with a huge black false moustache, a very random gift which I thought would appeal to his sense of humour. The following week, I received a letter to my home address on Rough Trade letterhead, containing album postcards and on the letter was, 'Were you out there? I waited at the Fountain, and you didn't come. Do you still care?' I was at work when I got it. My mother called to say, 'That freaky fucker has sent you another letter – what's all this about?'

### GILLIAN DOUGLAS, AGE 17

I went to both gigs with a school friend who I later found out was also going out with my boyfriend, so we had a serious falling out and haven't spoken since! The 1985 gig was on a school night but just before the Scottish September holiday weekend. I was allowed to go on the proviso that my grandfather dropped me off and picked me up. Thankfully he agreed to do so round the corner in East Campbell Street – we were trying to be cool. In 1986, I was going home on the bus at lunchtime after a morning's shopping in Glasgow city centre when I noticed a queue for the gig forming outside the Barras. I jumped off the bus, called my mum from a payphone and begged her to pick my friend up and bring her and our gig tickets down to the Barras as I was joining the queue.

### JAMES MACNEIL

I was lucky enough to see The Smiths three times at the Glasgow Barrowlands. I attended the concert on the *Meat Is Murder* tour with my late brother John. The build up was made even more special because *The Tube* was filming it. You could feel the crowd were at fever pitch before the group came on. They didn't disappoint from the first note of 'Shakespeare's Sister' to the last song, 'Miserable Lie'. I was holding on for dear life with the crowd swaying. The atmosphere was electric, with the group and crowd playing off each other. We walked home that night knowing that we had witnessed something truly special.

### ALAN MCADAM

A friend from school and college was a big Smiths fan, and so I went along to see them for the first time. I had liked the first few singles but hadn't really got into the debut album. *Meat Is Murder* was very

different and I loved it from the off. The experience of hearing this live was incredible. They came out to demented, wild applause and launched into a great set, with Andy Rourke stock-still and Mike Joyce appearing to enjoy the experience, but not really giving much away. Johnny Marr looked cool and floral, with some beads and looking at the crowd going wild. Morrissey was spinning around and encouraging the crowd into delirium. The songs were fantastic live, particularly 'Meat Is Murder', which sounded creepy and haunting in the vast space of Barrowlands.

### SEÁN Ó DONNGHAILE

I saw them twice at Barrowlands. I've seen hundreds of bands since, but nothing has ever matched the first time I saw The Smiths. A girl fainted on me, I took her over to First Aid. When the band came off, Andy Rourke saw her and came over to see if she was okay. Nice touch. There was only nine months between the gigs but by the second gig it was almost out of control. Lots of people who I felt never really got The Smiths had jumped on the bandwagon.

### STUART DOUGLAS

The Smiths had played Glasgow back in 1983 as a virtually unknown band, and again in 1984 to support the release of the eponymous first album, later broadcast on Radio Clyde as a full show. But this would be different. This was The Smiths at their absolute peak.

I had been into the band since the early days through John Peel and the fabulous *Whistle Test* live performance from the Derby

*Barrowlands ticket (James MacNeil)*

Assembly Rooms broadcast in 1983. I had bought the first album on cassette, I had bought *Hatful Of Hollow*, I had bought *Meat Is Murder* and, as the band's trajectory soared, I was loving the ride.

This show was to support the release of *Meat Is Murder* and, after spending many warm summer days indoors listening to it, I found myself in Virgin Records a few weeks before the gig, parting with my £4.50 fee for a ticket.

The venue was the iconic Glasgow Barrowland, now the favourite venue of many a band, deep in the East End of Glasgow. It was first opened in the 1930s by Maggie McIver, The Queen of the Barras, as a dance hall for the use of the barrow owners in the market below. It had then become a dancehall and pleasure dome for Glasgow's working class. Now it was better known for being the hunting ground of Bible John, the world-famous serial killer who murdered three customers in the late '60s. Simple Minds had resurrected the venue in 1983 when they recorded the video for 'Waterfront'. The venue never looked back.

The best venue in the world and the best band in the world. The venue was a sweat-soaked cauldron of heat with the audience being doused with water from the fire hose as the gig was delayed well past the expected start as The Smiths had recorded *Top Of The Pops* that night in London and flown to Glasgow in a helicopter.

On their arrival, the atmosphere in the venue was feral in anticipation. Suddenly Prokofiev blasted from the speakers as the atmosphere reached fever pitch. Morrissey, resplendent in red cardigan, announced their arrival with a passionate 'hello Glasgow' and stood on his monitor as the band broke into 'Shakespeare's Sister'.

What followed was a stramash of joyful celebration and adoration as the band marched through an incredible set: 'What She Said', 'Bigmouth', 'This Charming Man' and 'William', as well as the only time they played a cover of fellow Mancunian band James' song, 'What's The World'.

This was the night Glasgow and Scotland took The Smiths to their hearts as the full show was interrupted by multiple breathless, sweaty fans being dragged from the pit to save them from almost-certain injury had they hit the ground. The famous Barrowland blue and red star which adorned the ceiling dripped sweat back onto the audience below due to the venue's microclimate as the glitter ball revolved furiously and the bright white and yellow stage lights frantically strobed.

And then it was over. In the encore, Morrissey returned with a small tree and announced, 'Anyone missing a tree, come to my hotel room and they can get it back,' as they burst into a furious 'Hand In Glove'. It's on YouTube and it's the best piece of live Smiths footage anywhere on the internet.

Leaving the venue and as life would have it – and due to the late arrival of the band – public transport was finished and I faced the prospect of a ten-mile walk home in the rain.

My faith in love was still devout, and I sang all the way home.

### DEREK MOIR

The last time we saw them was the *Meat Is Murder* tour. They had become a screaming teenage pop band, kinda 'phoney Beatlemania, bitten and tossed...'. I had never experienced that, and it was weird as they were still great, but some essence had been taken away.

They were beautiful and warm and welcoming and clever and working class and phenomenal. I had been raised on Radio 1 and The Beatles, *Pet Sounds* and Motown as a kid and got punk rock at the age of eleven. I spent all my paper round money on back cataloguing The Adverts and Desperate Bicycles. Now the DIY post-punk Indie Rough Trade scene was ours and we made sure to use it. I started a band, did a Peel session, released two singles, got single of the week in *Melody Maker* and worked in a cooperative that brought bands like McCarthy, GFL, My Bloody Valentine, The Wedding Present and 1000 Violins to Perth and to Scotland. Truly inspirational.

Johnny Marr disallowed David Cameron to like The Smiths (What did Cameron not get about 'The Eton Rifles'?) and I have so much more sympathy and empathy for Johnny Marr. Morrissey has abandoned what we felt was the political, sexual, leftist intellectual revolution of the eighties.

## CAPITAL THEATRE



### STEPHEN RAFFERTY, AGE 16

I went with a couple of mates. The Capital Theatre was an all-seated venue with the front four rows taken out. You weren't allowed to stand but as soon as the band came on there was a huge surge that the bouncers couldn't control and the front was full, most of them pretty rowdy Aberdeen soccer casuals. I stayed back in the sixth row where I could see everything. I remember seeing them that day on some morning programme and they played 'The Boy With the Thorn in His Side'. That's probably the song that sticks with me the most. They kicked off with 'Shakespeare's Sister' so it would have been pretty mental.

On the bus back to Peterhead, a lad who was a couple of years older than me had a piece of Morrissey's shirt. It must have been all of two inches by two inches square. He was chuffed to fuck.

### RITA FARRAGHER

The Scottish tour in 1985 was an amazing little tour. I loved it that The Smiths played in out of the way places. Starting in Irvine, somewhere we had never heard of before, that tour took us to Inverness and the Eden Court Theatre. We had to kill a couple of days in Inverness and we loved it there. I actually moved there about 15 years later. The gig was also the only time they performed 'Asleep'. We couldn't afford the ferry from

*Morrissey & Johnny photographed by Michael Farragher.*
*Top: Postcard from Morrissey to 'the kittens' - Rita & Michael Farragher*

Aberdeen to Lerwick, so we missed the Shetland show, which we heard was amazing. We just hung around in Aberdeen for a few days feeling miserable and I have hated Aberdeen ever since.

On maybe a half dozen occasions, Morrissey invited us into the venue to watch the soundcheck. That was always great, they sometimes did songs that weren't part of the set. We saw them do 'Unloveable' at a soundcheck and I don't think they ever did that live.

### ROY SHARPLES

I first came across The Smiths aged eleven when they performed 'Heaven Knows I'm Miserable Now' on *Top of the Pops* in 1984. My grandma bought it for me from Woolworths on Union Street. The whole package was an art statement and quintessentially northern British. The 'two up, two down – it's grim up north'. It was about seeing the beauty in the ugliness, the poetry in red brick industrial architecture, smoking chimneys and factories. The Smiths were the outsider's outsiders. They influenced people's perceptions, values and how they looked, dressed and sounded whilst fuelling movements such as the 'real' independent music scene, vegetarianism and animal rights. Many of their songs are like a time capsule in that they capture a moment in time in my life. My Uncle Stewart took me to see them. An unforgettable experience, they kicked in with 'Shakespeare's Sister', with the highlights being How Soon Is Now?, 'Heaven Knows I'm Miserable Now', 'This Charming Man' and 'William, It Was Really Nothing'.

### IAIN WELLER

I won the tickets from the local radio station, Northsound, probably from the Bryan Burnett slot. He played all the post-punk stuff on a Saturday night. The tickets were for the balcony, so I spent the first couple of songs trying to get downstairs past the bouncers. I managed that and went down the front as far as I could go. I remember people asking for 'Barbarism Begins At Home' and Morrissey saying, 'We don't play that anymore.'

## EDEN COURT

### 1 OCTOBER 1985, INVERNESS, UK

### MICHAEL MORRISON

I didn't know much about them at the time. I just went along with my mate Graham Maclennan, who was a big fan.

### GRAHAM MACLENNAN, AGE 18

I was a student at Inverness College. It was a great venue. I was seated and it was my first experience of live music. I also remember buying a yellow *Meat Is Murder* t-shirt with the iconic cover on it and no mention of The Smiths. The support band, Easterhouse, really impressed me but The Smiths blew me away, particularly 'William, It Was Really Nothing'.

In December 1985, the band assembled in Salford for a photo session that was to yield an iconic image.

## SALFORD LADS CLUB

### 13 DECEMBER 1985, SALFORD, UK

### STEPHEN WRIGHT

I took the photograph of The Smiths outside Salford Lads Club that was used for the sleeve of *The Queen Is Dead*. The shoot really should have gone to a big-name photographer – an Anton Corbijn or a Pennie Smith – but it went to me, a fan using my first Nikon with the 'wrong' lens. I'd sent Rough Trade pictures of the band playing, and Morrissey liked them. The first Smiths live show I shot was in 1984 at the Free Trade Hall. I was so skint I could only afford one reel of film and had to walk a long way home. From this show, I caught the shot of dead flowers hanging from Morrissey's jeans. My favourite live shot is of Morrissey waving flowers above his head. I took it from the side of the stage hidden in the lighting rig.

More live shows followed and then Rough Trade asked me to shoot the Salford Lads session. Morrissey wanted an iconic Manchester location. We also tried Victoria Station, but it was too dark, so we ended up at Salford Lads Club. It was shot on a cold, dark, winter day – yet somehow it has a darkness that sets the right mood. You can see Johnny Marr shivering in some shots. I like the casual, staggered way they are standing, and they're nicely framed by the arches. But I always say it's the band, not the photo, that is classic. Morrissey has a Mona Lisa expression: it's neither a smile nor a smirk, but he's very much in command. If you look at the body

*Iain Weller remembers an amazing gig by The Smiths*

Image: (Stephen Wright)

*Image: (Stephen Wright)*

*Whitla Hall ticket (Ian McElhinney)*

language, you can tell he was king of the pack.

My darkroom was also my bedroom. I kept my processing chemicals in old lemonade bottles. I think the cheap equipment, and the fact there was so little light, gave the photo a grittiness, like a 1950s picture.

Morrissey ultimately chose the picture for the sleeve. He sent me a postcard afterwards to say thank you. It was written in his famous spidery handwriting: 'A sweeter set of pictures were never taken. I smiled for a full minute (phone Roy Castle – that's a record).'

Apparently, it's the most famous photo of The Smiths and that makes me smile. Fans come from all over the world to recreate the shot. The round trip from the centre of Manchester is probably £25 by cab, so I've done my bit for taxi drivers over the years. Years later I've got to go into the Salford Lads Club and meet the people there, which has been a real honour. I gave an image to the Salford Lads Club to raise funds, and they managed to raise over £60,000 from t-shirt sales using it.

I love it that people enjoy the image years later and that I caught them at their magnificent peak. I count myself as very lucky, as a huge fan, to have got the opportunity to see and shoot them live and then to get to meet them and produce the Salford Lads image. Of all the bands I shot it was The Smiths I loved seeing most and none of the albums really beat the atmosphere of their live shows. You can see some of my images of The Smiths and other artists at www.smithsphotos.com.

## APOLLO THEATRE

### 25 JANUARY 1986, MANCHESTER, UK

### MARK ATHERTON

I was a big Smiths fan. I had seen The Smiths many times but, to my disappointment, they had never played 'Back To The Old House'. This was a favourite of mine as, prior to the gig, I stole some of the lyrics to put onto a card that was hand delivered by me, mid-bike ride, to a girl I was madly in love with. 'When you cycled by, here began all my dreams,' etc. Imagine my delight, on seeing the Red Wedge tour at Manchester Apollo, when Billy Bragg came out with both Marr and Rourke and they nailed that number. I saw The Smiths quite a few times after that gig, but that performance with Billy was the only time I ever heard it live by anyone. Thanks Billy!

## CITY HALL

### 31 JANUARY 1986, NEWCASTLE-UPON-TYNE, UK

### ALYSON LAWS, AGE 16

I thought my ticket to Live Aid at Wembley could not be beaten. But in 1986 I was a member of the youth arm of the Labour Party and spent £5 on the best ticket of my life – Red Wedge at Newcastle City Hall. I loved Billy Bragg and his politics and how we were all going to fight against Thatcher together. I thought £5 to see Paul Weller and The Style Council, The Communards, Prefab Sprout and

Billy Bragg amongst others – and all in my hometown – was an opportunity not to be missed. My sister again came along together with my good friend.

We had tickets in the stalls, fourth row from the front, and we thought we had made it that night. The gig was inspiring and I can't remember who was on stage when they announced the next artist, 'Smith….' We stopped and thought, 'No, it can't be…'. It wasn't. Wendy Smith from Prefab Sprout came on stage. She was fantastic and we enjoyed it, but we had been taken to the edge and although we did not expect what was coming, we got a hint and thought, 'They are winding us up!'

Then the announcement, 'The Smiths!' and in front of me were – The Smiths! The excitement of the crowd was immense, just a sense of overwhelming amazement that this band were in front of us. In front of me! Four songs later it was over, but to this day I still remember that as one of the best gigs of my life. I have not felt that feeling since.

## PETER MARTIN

Only Johnny Marr was billed to perform. This was also the only night of the tour that The Smiths turned up to. How lucky was that? Four songs of absolute brilliance. I went with lads who were more interested in The Style Council than The Smiths, but all agreed that The Smiths stole the show.

## PETER SMITH

One of the most memorable gigs I have been to. Red Wedge was a collective of musicians, fronted by Billy Bragg, who set out to engage young people with politics, and the Labour Party in particular, during the period leading up to the 1987 general election, in the hope of ousting the Conservative government of Margaret Thatcher. All of the bands performed short sets; a few songs each. The Communards were impressive, Jimmy Somerville's soaring vocals were amazing, and The Style Council were also good. DC Lee guested with them and sang 'See the Day'. Local heroes Prefab Sprout also went down well.

But The Smiths stole the show. There were whispers around the hall that something special was going to happen. Without any real warning, they were announced and stormed straight into 'Shakespeare's Sister', followed by 'I Want the One I Can't Have', 'The Boy With the Thorn in His Side' and 'Bigmouth Strikes Again' – 'our new single'. There is something about a short set; it allows a band to focus and to maintain a high level of energy and passion throughout.

The Smiths were simply phenomenal that night; there was a buzz about them at the time, and everyone was delighted to see them perform. But it was more than that. It was as if they had decided to put everything into those four songs; the power, the intensity, and Morrissey and Marr's performance were a step above anything I had seen them deliver before (or since) that night. It was as if they knew that they were simply the best band on the planet at the time, and they came out with the confidence and ability to deliver a word class, stunning performance.

Newcastle running order
(Peter Martin)

Red Wedge Newcastle ticket
(Peter Martin)

We sat there, feeling that we were witnessing something special. It was that good. It was the best time I saw The Smiths, and a performance that will stay with me for ever. Perfect rock 'n' roll in four songs and 20 or so short minutes.

Johnny Marr: The Red Wedge gig at Newcastle City Hall was one of the best things we ever did. Andy and I had done a couple of gigs already with Billy Bragg in Manchester and Birmingham the week before… I was telling Morrissey about it, and he was fairly up for just doing an impromptu show. So, we drove up to Newcastle, without telling anyone. I walked into the soundcheck…the other bands were a little bit perplexed as to what we were doing there. We had no instruments, so we borrowed The Style Council's equipment and just tore the roof off the place. In the middle of the set, we just walked on to this announcement and the place went bananas.

Morrissey: When we took to the stage the audience reeled back in horror. They took their Walkmans off and threw down their cardigans. Suddenly the place was alight, aflame with passion!

*Liverpool Council benefit gig (Carl Hinde)*



# ROYAL COURT

## 8 FEBRUARY 1986, LIVERPOOL, UK

### STUART EDWARDS

I was in my second term at Liverpool Polytechnic, and the city was in a mess. The Militant Tendency factions in the city's council were in a stand-off with Margaret Thatcher. The deputy leader of the Council, Derek Hatton, had led the setting of an illegal budget with the Council spending £30m more than they had available. Hatton was an ex-fireman but frankly he looked and dressed like an ex-footballer. He claimed that the £30m excess had effectively been 'stolen' by Conservative central Government. All manner of civic services were grinding to a halt. I remember not being able to attend various lectures because the buildings weren't being opened. This was the least of the impact of the Liverpool actions – bins weren't being emptied, the city was shutting down, and council employees were being given their redundancy notices.

The issue had gone all the way to the top of the Labour Party, which was tearing itself apart to establish its own identity and values. Matters had come to a head at the party conference in October of 1985. The leader, Neil Kinnock, had given one of the most impassioned and potentially divisive speeches in living memory. Senior Labour party members walked out in disgust and Kinnock was heckled by Hatton in particular.

Things descended even more deeply as the winter drew in. Whilst the majority of the council were traditional Labour, the Trotskyite 'Loony Left' (as the British press had dubbed them) element had a stranglehold on the city. Sympathy also existed due to the collective governmental neglect that had existed since Liverpool's grand days as one of the world's foremost ports which precipitated terminal decline.

So in February 1986, one flamboyant North West socialist, Tony Wilson, reached out to another in Hatton. Wilson booked the Royal Court Theatre in Liverpool and under the catalogue reference of FAC 152 organised *With Love From Manchester* with corresponding t-shirt.

The bands played for expenses and tickets were £6 each. The object of the exercise was to support the 58 Liverpool councillors who by that point had been sacked and faced significant legal bills. Wilson started as a reporter in Liverpool in the early seventies before ending up as the mainstay of Granada TV's early evening news coverage. He had previously worked closely with Roger Eagle, who ran the legendary Eric's club in Liverpool. They shared bands between the Liverpool club and Wilson's Factory night in Manchester before the eventual opening of the Haçienda.

Wilson and Eagle eventually had a falling out over the roster for Factory which was initially intended as a North West music label rather than solely Mancunian. The straw which broke the camel's back was Orchestral Manoeuvres In The Dark, who Wilson wanted and Eagle and his colleague Pete Fulwell didn't. The pair split but Wilson still felt a residual fondness and responsibility for Liverpool, hence the concert.

I queued up for my ticket and arrived early to enjoy an evening of stellar Manchester music, featuring three bands that were all in their prime – New Order, The Fall and The Smiths. New Order opened proceedings on the basis that they had the most gear and it would be easier to clear the stage after they had finished rather than set up. Each band were allocated a 45-minute set, so the roadies went to work, and The Fall entered the arena. The feeling in the Royal Court at the time was that The Fall were the lesser of the three bands, but their set was possibly the highlight of the evening.

The Smiths followed. This was just as *The Queen Is Dead* was being finished and the set drew mostly from the forthcoming album and *Meat Is Murder*. 'Vicar In A Tutu', 'Cemetry Gates' and 'Frankly, Mr Shankly' were all debuted that evening.

After walking on to 'Montagues And Capulets' (before we were sick of it due to *The Apprentice*!), they opened with 'Shakespeare's Sister'. The set ignored the early material with Johnny teasing with the intros to 'This Charming Man' and 'What Difference Does It Make?'. Highlights for me were 'Rusholme Ruffians', which had the full '(Marie's The Name) His Latest Flame' intro, and the earliest track, 'William, It Was Really Nothing'.

After encores of 'Meat Is Murder' and 'Stretch Out and Wait', members of the bands joined John Cooper Clarke, The Farm and The Redskins on stage for a ramshackle version of 'Maggie's Farm'. I seem to remember a few Newcastle Brown bottles being chucked but can't recall what prompted it. The evening ended and I headed back to Garston reflecting on seeing these three bands at pivotal stages in their careers.

The councillors lost their court

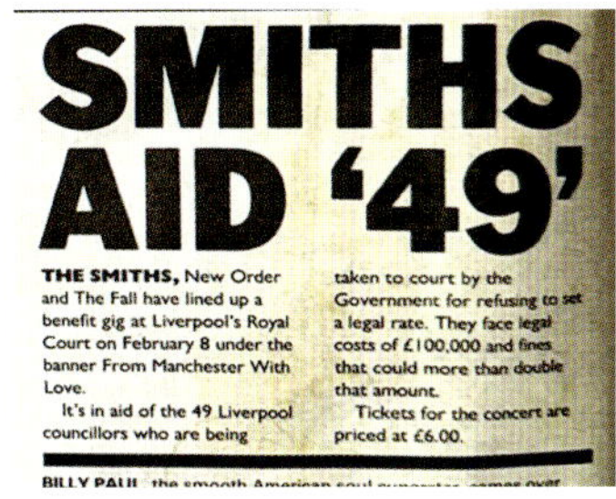

THE SMITHS, New Order and The Fall have lined up a benefit gig at Liverpool's Royal Court on February 8 under the banner From Manchester With Love.

It's in aid of the 49 Liverpool councillors who are being taken to court by the Government for refusing to set a legal rate. They face legal costs of £100,000 and fines that could more than double that amount.

Tickets for the concert are priced at £6.00.

BILLY PAUL the smooth American soul

*Sounds reported on Smiths Aid for the '49', riffing on Live Aid* battle, and the Militant Tendency contingent were expelled from the Labour Party. Derek Hatton enjoyed a chequered career in media before heading to Cyprus as a property developer at the start of the century. I doubt any of those council workers who received their redundancy notices enjoyed such a fortunate conclusion to their careers.

### NICK BARBER

The Smiths played a chunk of *The Queen Is Dead*, which had been featuring in their live set for a while. A number of the audience were familiar with the songs as there was a strong trade in bootleg cassettes – I used to get mine from an underground market stall near Manchester's Arndale Centre. The guy who ran the stall had a series of contacts, who would use the Sony Professional Walkman to get good quality recordings of Manchester gigs. You could often pick them up from the stall the day after the shows. On the bootleg of the Liverpool gig, you can hear me shouting, 'Do your Elvis impression!' (such wit) before the 'Marie's The Name' / 'Rusholme Ruffians' mini medley. I remember the gig ended in a somewhat shambolic fashion after The Smiths' set when, instead of an encore, Derek Hatton and Margi Clarke appeared, much to the audience's disgruntlement as we wanted more from The Smiths.

### STEPHEN REID

Everything about this was a cracking night: Southern public schoolboys on the train to Liverpool, my friend Pete and I sleeping on the floor in an old primary school friend's student bedsit and, of course, The Smiths, The Fall and the wonderful New Order. The gig was in aid of Liverpool Council, about which we cared little. We were 18 and thought it was kind of cool to be so right on, CND members that we already were. Derek Hatton was there. The actress Margi Clarke did Bob Dylan's 'Maggie's Farm', which was pretty awful, and I recall John Cooper Clarke and also bands I later got into, The Redskins and The Farm. All this for £6!

We drank brown ale in the Royal Court bar and then managed to get right in the centre of the room for New Order and The Fall. I loved Mark E Smith that night, pulling pieces of paper from his pocket and reading lyrics or shopping lists or whatever he was doing. The Fall were at their peak in '86 and Brix was in the band – we thought she was sooo cool. I liked New Order but after this gig they became a new obsession; they played 'Love Will Tear Us Apart' and really got things going with their new (to me anyway) mix of electronica and guitars. Oh, and some bloke on bass guitar making one hell of a sound.

The Smiths played new stuff off what we later knew to be their *The Queen Is Dead* album. The set was mainly *Meat Is Murder* tracks and B-sides, with Elvis' 'His Latest Flame' leading into 'Rusholme Ruffians'. I have seen a photo of Moz from this gig and I was wearing pretty much exactly what he was – cardigan, shirt, Levi's and black brogues. This was a memorable night with the Fall surprising me as the stand out band. To top it off we even went out afterwards, to some underground speakeasy club where the gatekeeper slid a panel back to see who you were and whether you were worth letting in.

### JULIE CALLAGHAN, AGE 27

I witnessed some amazing gigs in the late seventies in a little punk club called Eric's in Liverpool. The Clash, Siouxsie, Talking Heads, Ramones, The Slits, X-Ray Spex, Joy Division, Buzzcocks… the list goes on. I was a fervent Smiths fan, had just discovered them and was enthralled. I just can't remember much about the gig. But I have kept my souvenir t-shirt after all these years!

### MARK WILLIAMS

I recall Morrissey introducing 'Frankly, Mr Shankly' by saying something along the lines of, 'This song isn't about who you may think it's about.' Of course, he was referring to the legendary Liverpool FC manager Bill Shankly. A Liverpudlian to the side of me shouted, 'Is he taking the piss?' as the band struck up the song's debut live performance. All in all, the short 45-minute set went well, with Morrissey customarily throwing his purple-striped shirt into the audience and me being close enough to grab it in mid-air. Within a second, there must have been half a dozen of us pulling at the tough nylon garb without ripping it until an enterprising youth in the crowd pulled out his flick knife and started to cut strips off it for us all. My portion has been sadly lost. I used to have it on my bedroom

wall with a review of the concert that included a photo of Morrissey wearing the shirt it came from.

### KEV JONES

I was at the front. Nowadays there's a barrier and you've got the security in front of the stage. But back then you were right up against the stage, and you could just reach over. Morrissey was always making contact with the audience, shaking hands. He was right in front of me and I remember holding onto his shoelace and undoing it, thinking it would be a good memento to have, but I didn't actually manage it. I did get Andy Rourke's set list. I just shouted at one of the roadies.

### DAVID TIMLIN

The second time I saw The Smiths was the benefit concert for Derek Hatton, a member of Liverpool City Council. What a line-up that was: The Smiths, The Fall, New Order and John Cooper Clarke. The gig was amazing, but we'd travelled on the train from the North East and had nowhere to stay. Our plan was just to sleep rough that night.

The Smiths were brilliant. They did 'Frankly, Mr Shankly' and Morrissey said, 'This is not about anyone you might know,' making a reference to Bill Shankly, the former Liverpool manager.

As we were walking out of the gig, I got stopped by this woman who wanted to take my photograph because she thought I looked like Morrissey. She said she worked for *No1* magazine. When they went to take my photograph, all the lads I was with jumped into the photograph!

When the magazine came out

*Kev Jones managed to bag Andy Rouke's setlist from the Royal Court show*

there were pictures and quotes from other people who were there for the cause, with sentiments like, 'Derek Hatton's trying to do something for the people of Liverpool,' even though the council was going bankrupt. And then at the bottom of the page there was me saying, 'I'm Johnny Marr's sister.' They actually printed that!

We tried to find somewhere to sleep and ended up at this monument with concrete benches around it. I got to sleep but the lads I was with couldn't, so we went to the train station. It was shut but a kindly British Rail employee took pity on us and allowed us to sleep on one of the trains. It's the coldest I've ever been in my life.

### KERRY MCCARTHY, MEMBER OF PARLIAMENT FOR BRISTOL EAST

I saw The Smiths a few times back in the day, including a gig they did at Liverpool Royal Court Theatre with New Order, to support Liverpool councillors. I remember Derek Hatton came on stage in a brown bomber jacket and tried to be down with the kids; he didn't get a great response! I was also at the G-MEX Festival of the Tenth Summer in 1986; just £13 a ticket for a great line-up!

I suppose my most obvious 'moment' relating to the band would be asking David Cameron at PMQs about pretending to like The Smiths, which ended up being mentioned in Johnny Marr's autobiography. I cannot quite bring myself to look at the coverage…

On a visit to LA in 2017, I got to know Councilwoman Monica Rodriguez, and we've kept in touch. She's a massive Smiths/Morrissey fan and took me backstage at a Royal Albert Hall gig a few years ago. She was in a private room with Morrissey, and when she told him she was with a vegan MP, he said, 'Well, bring her to me then!' But by the time we did get into a group with him, there was a guy from *Newsnight* (I think the producer) with us too… and he did all the talking!

## NATIONAL STADIUM

### 10 FEBRUARY 1986, DUBLIN, IRELAND

### DES FOLEY

I went with my girlfriend Sinead. We had seats up in the stalls to the left of the stage, but facing in towards the audience rather than the stage; the upside of this was that we were directly above the entrance to the stage used by the band. Morrissey came on wearing a green jumper. The stadium was packed and I remember people going crazy. Fans always seemed to be right at the front of the stage too; I don't remember there being any barriers or gaps between stage and audience like you'd have now. The band played a blistering set. I distinctly remember them starting with '(Marie's The Name) His Latest Flame)' and then going into 'Rusholme Ruffians' and the roar when the audience recognition kicked in.

Smiths' gigs were always very exciting, high-energy gigs and audiences were always highly vocal.

Me and Sinead took advantage of our position to shout down to Mike Joyce when they came off stage at the end, asking him for the vest t-shirt he was wearing and he took it off and threw it up to us. We did the same again after they'd finished the encores and, again, he duly obliged, so we got two t-shirts worn by him on stage during that gig. We were beside ourselves as they were fantastic souvenirs to have. Sinead and I eventually split up. She kept the t-shirts!

### GRAHAM MONTGOMERY

My friend's uncle used to get us free and reserved seats in the press box at the Stadium. I think Craig Gannon was playing with them. A lot of what they played was off *Meat Is Murder*, an album I liked less than *Hatful of Hollow*.

### PAUL PAGE

I don't think I have ever witnessed such hysterical adoration for a band. There was this kind of lovely chaos about it. Fans desperate to get close to Morrissey were constantly invading the stage and constantly being intercepted by security and tossed back into the melee. Those that evaded security would throw their arms around their messiah before being forcibly prised away.

The front of the stage was a heaving mass of Morrissey lookalikes, arms outstretched, singing along to every single word. It was really something else. I was in my late teens but had only started going to gigs the previous year, seeing bands like Echo and The Bunnymen and New Order. This was a completely different experience, like an indie version of Beatlemania.

Morrissey was the main focus of attention but I had just started playing guitar and was mesmerised by Johnny Marr. He made it look so effortless, the epitome of cool. They finished the set with 'Meat Is Murder' and left with the stage bathed in blood red. They returned for a rapturously received encore and then they were gone. They never played Dublin again.

I went on to play with a Dublin band called Whipping Boy. Those formative live shows I witnessed with bands like The Bunnymen, The Cocteau Twins and The Smiths lit the fuse and inspired not just me but a whole generation of musicians in Dublin from that era.

### TOM LOFTUS, AGE 19

It was an incredible atmosphere before they came on, with a real sense of expectation. The Smiths were considered the best British band at the time and so much was going on in the background that us fans were unaware of – Andy's heroin addiction, the delayed release of *The Queen Is Dead* – but The Smiths pulled off one of the greatest gigs I have ever been to.

## 'BIGMOUTH STRIKES AGAIN'
### RELEASED 22 MAY 1986

The lead single from *The Queen Is Dead*, 'Bigmouth Strikes Again' reached number 26. James Dean, one of Morrissey's heroes, rode a motorbike on the picture sleeve.

*Moz in action at Dublin's National Stadium (Tom Loftus)*

*Bigmouth Strikes Again*

### JULIE HESMONDHALGH

'Bigmouth Strikes Again' has a very special place in my heart. It's the first Smiths single that I ever bought. I took my hard-earned cash from my Saturday job to the brilliant independent record shop in Accrington. The song has the most recognisable and brilliant opening bars of any Smith song. Also, controversially, it's possibly the best Smiths song to dance to and it is a definite contender for the most 'Morrissey' a lyric can get with, 'Sweetness, I was only joking when I said, by rights you should be bludgeoned in your bed.' When people don't understand how funny and wry his lyrics are, this is a good one to throw in the faces. If they don't get it, then they're thick.

## THE QUEEN IS DEAD

### RELEASED 16 JUNE 1986

The Smiths' third official album was released and reached number 2 on the UK album charts. The *NME* was to rank it as the greatest album of all time in 2013.

### ANDY JOHNSON

I was a little late in getting properly into The Smiths. I can remember seeing them on *Top Of The Pops* and liking the early singles. 'What Difference Does It Make?' sticks in my mind and made it one of the first *Now That's What I Call Music* compilations. And I had the lyrics to 'William, It Was Really Nothing' stuck to my woodchipped bedroom wall, next to pictures of Madonna. But it wasn't until a friend made me a tape of *Hatful Of Hollow* and then *The Queen Is Dead* that I fell really hard. I was 14 or 15 – prime 'moping' age – when The Queen Is Dead came out. I was also teaching myself to play guitar and started writing songs soon after. Trying to figure out Johnny Marr's chords was challenging when I only knew three major chords and A minor.

The first songbooks I bought were for *The Queen Is Dead* and The Clash's debut album, and my songwriting has sat somewhere in-between the two ever since. The Smiths also led me to bands like The Housemartins and The Wedding Present, who seemed to be cut from a similar Northern cloth. The towering genius of the Morrissey / Marr partnership is undeniable. All those amazing records in such a short space of time is still mind-blowing.

### LEAH CALLAHAN

In the US, if you wanted to hear new, interesting music you either tried to find a station towards the beginning of the FM dial – which were the college radio stations; or if you were lucky enough to be in the range of a bigger city on the East or West coast, you had the 'modern rock' stations. While they may have been on *Top Of The Pops* in the UK, in the US The Smiths were definitely considered an 'underground' band. Living near Boston, I first heard about The Smiths in high school on WFNX. After hearing the title track, I bought *The Queen Is Dead* when it came out on vinyl.

The music of The Smiths was wonderful; catchy, sometimes cacophonous, sad, flowery and eloquent. It was just what I needed to rebel against the current top 40 tunes.

*The Queen Is Dead*

But beyond the music and the band, what really made an impression on me back then was Morrissey.

I went to an all-girls Catholic school in a conservative, lower middle class Massachusetts town bordering New Hampshire. There were no punks, there were no art school kids, there was only the radio and MTV playing the music of REO Speedwagon and Van Halen, and then a little later Bon Jovi, Poison, Mötley Crüe. Much of this music typically promoted women as dim-witted sex objects in videos, usually wearing thongs, fake tans and big frizzy hair. Come to think of it, the men were fairly dim-witted too! The lyrics weren't exactly going to win any Nobel literature prizes. Aesthetically, I just didn't relate to the culture which was being spoon fed to us on a daily basis.

Even the lyrics of the post-punk or new wave acts were mostly by men and their relationships with women. How they want them, can't get them, or can get them, etc. It's weird to think about how much time young women like me spent listening to David Lee Roth sing about how he's 'Hot For Teacher' or Adam Ant singing about 'Deutscher Girls' when many of us girls probably didn't really feel like the girls they were talking about at all.

Into this atmosphere enter Morrissey. Aesthetically he was very cool, with his seemingly effortless looks. He is unlike any boy I had ever known, he reads books, he name drops poets! No one I had heard on the radio in the US was doing that. He was a vegetarian, and in my sheltered life I didn't know any vegetarians. He was the furthest

you could get from a strutting macho American male rock star.

And he was, of all things, a proclaimed 'asexual'. In the mid-1980s, in Catholic school, we weren't even supposed to say the word sex, never mind have it or have it 'differently' from what mainstream culture demanded of us, which was in marriage and for the procreation of children.

We didn't have the internet, and I didn't really have any access to any magazine articles about Morrissey, but I remember one of my more sophisticated friends would feed me info, and of course we would match the stories we'd heard about Morrissey with the songs, which had strong statements against eating meat, and very vague proclamations about love and desire. To me, his importance was that he came across as an outsider, and that he opened up the idea of options, that one didn't have to accept society's stifling dictates, or one's boring reality, but that there was another world out there. In 'Asleep' he sings, 'There is another world, there is a better world.'

I am aware that he has more recently stated that he is a fan of some far-right politicians in the UK, which is sad. I don't know what has made him so angry. Hopefully he will rethink this and realise the value he has as being a beacon of light for people. I put the words, 'There is a light that never goes out' next to my name in my high school yearbook. No one knew WTF it was, so it was my way of rebelling, and putting out a sort of secret code that only I knew about. I thought about suicide a lot in my teens and twenties, and this song, and other

*Leah Callahan wears black
on the outside*

songs by The Smiths (along with other artists like David Bowie, Siouxsie and the Banshees, Echo and The Bunnymen, and The Cure to name just a few) got me through some very tough times.

### DEBORAH ROPER

It was the spring of 1986, I was 14. My high school best friend had an older brother who was very much into his music and in an aspiring punk / rock band. He made us a mixtape as he was sick of hearing our 'irreverent pop music' when we were at their family's house. On that tape, amongst tracks from bands such The Clash and Siouxsie and the Banshees, was The Smiths' debut single, 'Hand In Glove'. I had been gifted a record player the Christmas the previous year and it wasn't long before I'd bought *Meat Is Murder* followed by *The Queen Is Dead* (still my favourite Smiths album.) The following year I snuck off to the Oxford Circus HMV to buy *Strangeways, Here We Come* whilst on a school art trip to London.

I sadly never got the chance to see them live... Rank was as close as I could get. But a couple of Smiths songs at a recent Morrissey gig gave me a glimpse of what it could have been like.

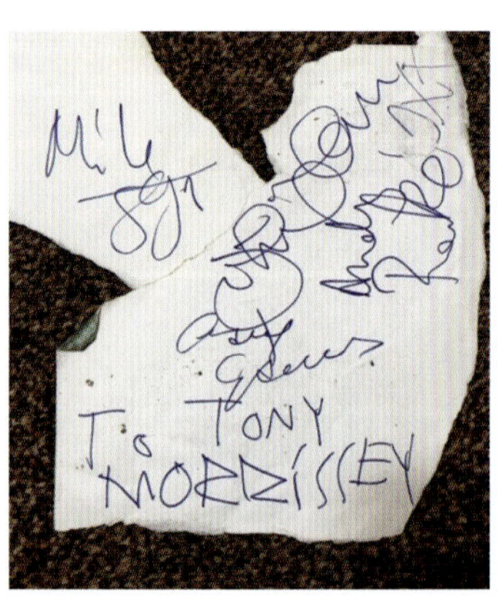

Band autographs (Peter Martin)

## *EUROTUBE,* TYNE TEES STUDIO

### 5 JULY 1986, NEWCASTLE-UPON-TYNE, UK

### PETER MARTIN

They only played two tracks, but this was one of my favourite ever gigs. We had just managed to get tickets for this Euro-Tube special. After a few too many ales in The Barley Mow, we arrived well-oiled and met Craig Gannon in the loos. If you watch the videos of this on YouTube you'll see a group dancing on each other's shoulders. Well, that is us. When we went back to the Barley Mow, people came up and shook our hands as they'd all just watched us on the TV. Fame, fame, fatal fame...

### DAVID TIMLIN

*Eurotube* was great. I'm pretty sure it was one of the first times they played 'There Is A Light' and 'Panic'. I don't know how the hell we got tickets because they were like gold dust. We were right at the front, waiting for The Smiths to come on. For some reason Carl, the reformed Wham! fan, thought the recently recruited Craig Gannon was called Darren. He wouldn't have it otherwise and when they came on but before they started playing, we were shouting 'Darren!' Both Craig and Mike Joyce were having a good old laugh at it.

You can see it on *YouTube*. I'm the one with the horrible yellow and green t-shirt, with a big black quiff, sat on one my mates' shoulders and dancing around. We caught Morrissey's eye. It was four o'clock in the afternoon and we were just going crazy. I think we looked a bit like football fans, but we were just sensitive young men who loved the songs. After the set, we ran outside to try and catch them. We found their minibus. Morrissey was sat in the back, just staring ahead. The rest of the band came out, and I got talking to Johnny Marr. He said, 'Thanks very much for dancing, lads.' Johnny gave me his yellow plectrum. I've still got it somewhere.

### JOHN FEATHERSTONE

When we started planning for *The Queen Is Dead*, Johnny was like, 'Is there any way we could have big, rich velour green curtains?' Because we'd sort of anchored back into this very, very curated colour palette of greens and whites and blues, with the exception of *Meat Is Murder*.

But Johnny got a VHS tape of the Stones playing on some TV show in the States with this really dramatic, almost overpowering bright white light, and he said, 'This looks really great, let's find a way to weave this into a song,' so we used it on the middle eight break of 'Big Mouth Strikes Again'.

There was this great energy and excitement of back and forth, lots of ideas flying around, mostly Johnny and Morrissey – they did the draft of the set list – but if the drum tech was like, 'Hey, have you thought about flipping these?' they'd go, 'Oh yeah, maybe we'll give that a go.' This was back in the day, but bands now fairly rapidly, with the scale of productions, gravitate to a fixed set list with a couple of alterations here and there.

The Smith set list was very fluid and very dynamic, as most bands were at the time. You'd get a set list sometimes 40 minutes before the show. But that's another part of the excitement. They were never super-long sets, but I think The Smiths could have done three songs and afterwards people would have been like, 'Holy shit, I feel like I need to have a lie down and a cigarette.'

I don't think their sets were ever much more than an hour. But an hour of The Smiths live? Holy crap, an hour of The Smiths life is an onslaught. The music was just so powerful. I honestly don't know if the band could really have done much more than that. I've got a

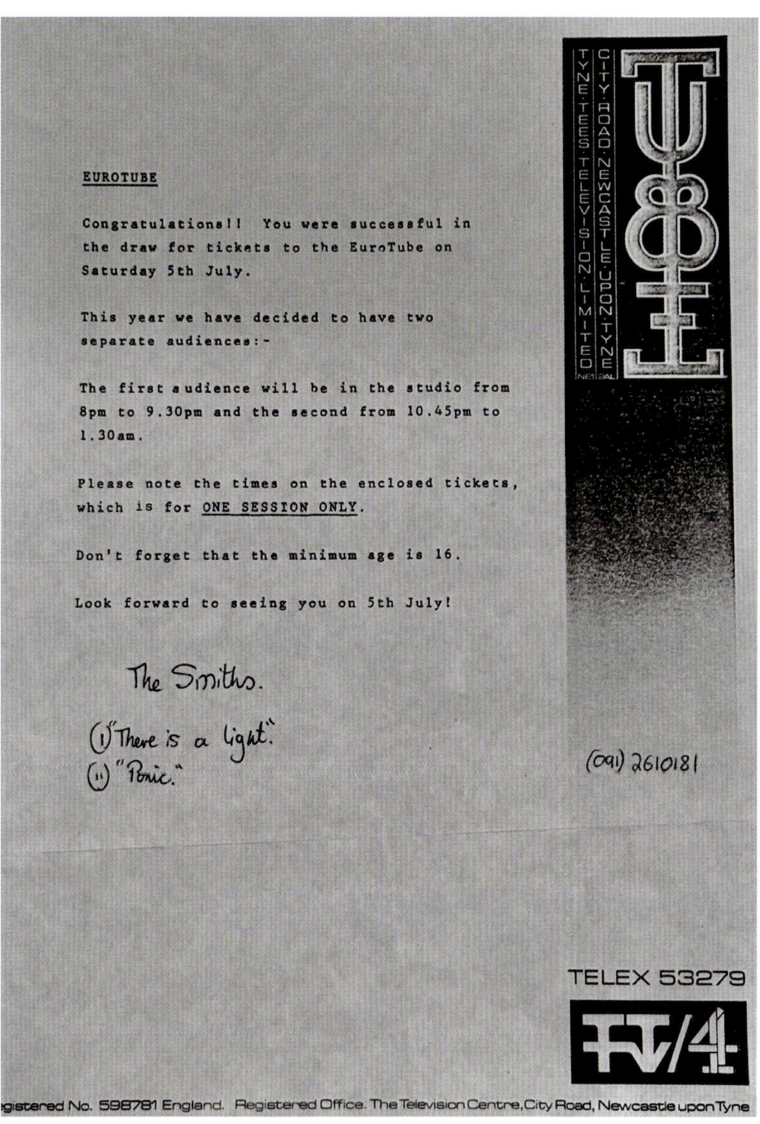



*Tube invite (Peter Martin)*

high-res video of the Derby show. It was 38 minutes. But I remember being there for the show and it felt like two hours.

There was a focus. And this is something that Johnny has always been, and still is, really good at, which is filtering and only doing or putting in or playing or performing exactly what needs to be in there. Johnny's wife, Angie, has a great expression which is kind of like 'Johnny Marr's orbit cannon' – there's just no need. Don't play the song because it's the B-side of the Latvian version of the release of 'How Soon Is Now'. Do the songs that you know the audience are going to want to hear and the songs that you want the audience to hear.

I don't remember there ever being any pushback, even in the US when we got into bigger gigs and bigger promoters, of anybody going, 'Oh, you guys should really be doing 90 minutes.' They would do the set and everybody knew they were seeing something special. A lot of that was Johnny going, 'No, let's just do the one, let's just keep hitting them, let's just do the songs which are really going to move the needle and have everything be in service to the music rather than clock watch.

Nobody's looking at their watches at a gig if the band's doing their jobs right. It's a free-for-all and you have an amazing experience and at the end of it you go, 'Wow, that was incredible.' I saw the Ramones in New York. If they played for 20 minutes, I'd be surprised. But, holy crap, what a 20 minutes.

## BARROWLAND BALLROOM

### 16 JULY 1986, GLASGOW, UK

### JOHN CANNING, AGE 15

I lived in Livingston, around 30 miles east of Glasgow, and took the bus into Glasgow with my friends Peter 'Doris' Doris and David 'Ramo' Ramsay. The bus got us into Glasgow around 3pm with the gig not scheduled to start till around 8pm.

We went straight to the iconic Barrowlands venue and hung around outside with a few other fans. After an hour or two, we thought we saw the tour bus pull up outside the front of the venue. Doris, not known for his athletic prowess, took off to reach the front door of the bus before everyone else. The bus moved off again with him and the other fans in hot pursuit. The bus then went around the whole block before arriving back at the front door of the venue after a minute or two with Doris leading the chasing pack.

The door opened and Morrissey alone got off the bus. Doris reached him first, putting his hand on his shoulder, shaking his hand and no doubt telling him how great he thought Morrissey was. Throughout all of this, Ramo and I were far too reserved to move from our spot and just observed the whole thing. Doris touching Morrissey kept us going for the next hour or two until the doors opened and we entered the venue.

We were about tenth in the queue and ran straight upstairs to ensure we got into the first row of the all-standing venue. We never moved for fear of losing our place, not for the toilet nor to try and get served at the bar as three spotty 15-year-olds.

The support band was The Railway Children. Many of the fans started spitting towards the lead singer, which was a commonplace and warped show of affection at that time in Glasgow. After about ten minutes the lead singer said, 'There's a lot of wankers in here tonight,' which did not go down too well. The spitting increased and after a few minutes more, the band walked off. For the record, I'd just like to add that Morrissey seemed to take the spitting in the spirit that it was intended!

Eventually The Smiths came on, and the place went berserk. They started with 'Bigmouth Strikes Again' followed by 'Panic'. I have absolutely no recollection of what songs followed, as the front of the gig just exploded with such an outpouring of mainly, young, male hero-worship and adulation. It was almost a religious experience, and I have never experienced anything like it since. I remember feeling like I might cry.

At one point, Morrissey reached into the crowd and was pulled in, inadvertently crowd surfing whilst having his shirt torn off. Ramo and another guy managed to grab an end each and they tore the shirt in two. Ramo later cut his part into three and gave Doris and I a bit of the great man's shirt.

The middle of the gig is a bit of a blur, as we got split up in the melée and had to drop back a few rows to catch our breath. We could not keep up that early pace, with the venue's famous spring-loaded floor being put through its paces. It might be a myth about the floor, but it was certainly bouncing that night! It was frantic, with people falling and being helped back up again by total strangers. Bedlam.

During one of the encores, I remember 'I Know It's Over' and 'Rusholme Ruffians' which merged into '(Marie's The Name) His Latest Flame' being played. All of the band members came out, and each threw a bunch of flowers into the crowd. I leapt like the proverbial salmon and caught a decent amount of Andy Rourke's bunch, which I also shared out with Ramo and Doris. I put my share of the flowers into my 1979 *Shoot* annual. They're still in a box somewhere in my mum and dad's loft, along with a section of Morrissey's shirt and Billy Bragg's used plectrum and autograph from a gig the following month.

Only when I walked outside did I realise just how soaked with sweat I was. My t-shirt, jeans, socks and pants were as wet as if I had jumped into a swimming pool and nearly everyone was exactly the same.

I still refer to this gig as my all-time favourite. I remember seeing so many lone, young, male fans keeping themselves to themselves prior to the band coming on and then exploding with passion, love and total adoration for the band, and especially Morrissey. For years afterwards, I'd argue with people who referred to The Smiths as boring, saying, 'I've seen them live, there is nothing boring about The Smiths.'

On Facebook so many of my former schoolmates now claim to love the band. But when I was at school, I distinctly remember no more than eight to ten people in my year and the two years above loving them. I'm just glad I was able to see what was so special about them when I was 14. I wasn't there at the very beginning, but I was there whilst they were still together and lucky enough to see them live.

### ANNETTE FLYNN

I started my first 'real' relationship with a rockabilly and collector of all things

fifties. He was not a fan of indie music or any music outwith this genre. I bought him a ticket for this gig. He reluctantly accepted as the new relationship meant (in hindsight, sadly) that we didn't go anywhere apart. Just before they played 'I Know It's Over', Morrissey said, 'Annette, Annette, we'll get you yet…'. The rockabilly turned to me and said, 'WTF, is that you?' Some girls behind me shouted, 'Fuck her – who the hell's Annette?' In shock, I just kept me eyes glued to Morrissey and my mouth shut. The rockabilly was staring at me to look at him, but I kept my eyes front not wanting to draw attention to myself.

The dedication was surreal. The next day, as many of us did, we visited the Barrowland's market. A stall there produced cassette tapes of the previous night's gigs so I bought it and legged it home to listen to it. I must have worn out that dedication, listening to it daily. The rockabilly quizzed me about it for days in a slightly controlling and possessive style.

The relationship didn't last. After 28 years, I saw the light. The rockabilly would not return all the letters, decorated envelopes and personal memorabilia like tickets, the Barrowland cassettes, record factory postcards to me when I left him. In the weeks leading up to the end of our 24-year marriage, all these items inexplicably disappeared.

### DOMINIC JOHN

I had missed the *Meat Is Murder* tour as I lost my sight and was in and out of hospital for about a year undergoing numerous eye operations. Consequently, I had to give my ticket to a pal, who managed to bring me a section of a huge bush that Morrissey threw into the audience. I still have it inside the cover of my *Queen Is Dead* album. The following year, even though I was still quite ill, I went to see them. My brother pulled a few strings, and I was smuggled in through a back stair in a pub downstairs and watched the show from the wings. I was almost on the stage the whole time. I had also been promised that the band would come and say 'hello' at the end, but they went off the other side and my chance was gone. I found out later that the guy who arranged it all was Arthur Thomson Jr, the notorious East End gangster. Good times.

### STEPHEN MATHISON

I moved from Glasgow to East Lothian with my work – which I absolutely hated – in July '86. I was desperate for a decent night out in Glasgow. It just so happened that the boys were playing at the Barrowlands again. The rumours of a split in the band were rife, so I had to go and see them before it was too late. I gave my pal a shout, tickets were bought and I was heading back through to the land of the living for what would be their final hurrah at the Barrowlands. The concert was going to be a classic.

We headed to the Barras and went into the bar next door for a pre-concert pint or two. This place, sadly now shut, was sight to behold, a Celtic fan's mecca and also a go-go bar. I'm not sure what the dancers thought when The Smiths were playing over the jukebox though!

The Barras was packed that night, and it was brilliant. Channel 4 were there filming. The cameramen were getting in the way of the stage divers, so the bouncers had their hands full trying to eject them and pull the fainters out of the front. At the encore, Morrissey came on stage with a massive 'The Queen Is Dead' placard just to whip the crowd up – as if they needed it. I can remember watching the show on Channel 4 and spotting myself in the crowd.

I still love The Smiths' music. I play it all the time in my shop – I'm a barber.

## ALAN MCADAM

They came onto a darkened Barrowlands to 'Dance of the Knights' by Prokofiev, the most dramatic entrance I had seen, with the tension building and building until they launched into their set. Craig Gannon was also on guitar and subsequently the sound was huge and the crowd went crazy. I'm sure stage invaders kept grabbing at Morrissey, but I can't remember. I just know that it was incredibly hot and crazy in that venue that night. My ticket was too damp to keep and it subsequently disintegrated. This band and this relatively recently reopened venue were made for one another.

## STEPHEN RAFFERTY

I arrived at 2.30pm to try and get a place down the front. The queue was already the length of the Barrowlands. I stood in the queue with one of my friends for a couple of hours but then nipped across the road to the corner shop to get a drink. I had a spare ticket due to one of my friends letting me down. In those days, touting was illegal, so I didn't shout out that I had a spare. When I came out of the shop a lad that had been following The Smiths on most of the tour asked me if I had a spare ticket, so I sold it to him. I was chuffed that I was able to off-load it.

When I got back in the queue, I told my friend I had sold the ticket. The lad in front of us turned round and said, 'Did you have spare tickets?' to which I replied, 'Yes.' He then told me that the queue we were in was for tickets that were handed back and that were going on general sale. I could have made a fortune selling mine to the highest bidder. But I was happier that the lad following The Smiths around got in to see them.

The gig was absolutely mental. If you've ever been in the Barras you'll know what I'm talking about. I managed to get down right in front of the centre stage and then afterwards went to the backstage door to wait for them leaving. I got my reward, shaking both Morrissey and Johnny Marr's hands as they left to board the tour bus.

*Mayfair setlist (Peter Martin)*

# MAYFAIR

## 17 JULY 1986, NEWCASTLE-UPON-TYNE, UK

### PETER MARTIN

Afterwards we went to Cramlington train station and painted 'The Queen Is Dead' on the newly whitewashed walls. This was in 'honour' of an appearance from Her Majesty at the station the next day. Sadly, someone painted over it before she arrived. I'm sure she would have appreciated our gesture.

### COLIN BOOTH

Halfway through the set some idiots started throwing empty bottles at them on stage. The band asked them to stop but another bottle was thrown and the band walked off. It was the only time I got to see them. They split up not long after.

### LESLEY FEARON, AGE 16

The Mayfair is sadly no longer in existence. My lasting memory, apart from the strong smell of cannabis, was the lights going out and the band's entrance music blasting out before the band came on. The feeling I had has never been replicated and I'm now aged 50! Morrissey ended up walking off-stage as some idiots at the front had been spitting at the stage.

I had seen them at Newcastle City Hall during the Red Wedge concert. There were rumours milling around that night that The Smiths were due to play but we didn't believe it. How wrong we were! They only did a short stint of about four or five songs, but they made an already brilliant night even better. That was another superb time seeing the best band in the world. In my opinion they still are.

### CHRIS TAIT

I would see The Smiths live again just once more, when they returned to the city to promote their seminal third album (or their fourth, if you count *Hatful of Hollow*). By then however, problems with their relationship with Rough Trade and the money issues which would come to define the band's aftermath were already simmering in the background. But this show, and the venue in particular, had added significance as The Smiths were booked to play The Mayfair in Newcastle, home of 'raaark'. This was the indie kids storming the citadel of the city's long-haired, leather-trousered rockers, the metal-heads we'd spent years verbally battling at school, although 'storming' may be something of an exaggeration. We were literate, sensitive soft indie kids after all.

As it turned out, the evening was something of a disaster. I recall standing half-crushed on one of the Mayfair's famous spiral staircases as the band, now a five-piece with the addition of Craig Gannon (once of Aztec Camera, so of course I approved), were subject to a torrent of abuse from sections of the audience. An element of what one assumes were Mayfair regulars in the crowd taunted the band throughout, hurling bodily fluids and verbal insults in Morrissey's direction, forcing him to eventually leave the stage during the closer, 'Hand In Glove'. Johnny then famously delivered the line, '…If the

people spit, then the people spit…'
and, after a couple of false dawns
when we thought our hero might
return, that was pretty much that.
A sad end to a wonderful period in
our musical history.

### DARREN WILKINSON

It was a further year before I saw The
Smiths for the third time, this time
on the *Queen Is Dead* tour. I still
think this is the finest album the band
produced. Every track is a banger, and
the title track possibly my favourite
Smiths song. It was the same old
rigmarole to get tickets and off we
went again across the Pennines to the
North East. We arrived in good time.

The Mayfair was an old ballroom,
and we staked our place on the low
balcony overlooking the stage and
waited. When The Smiths took to
the stage the floor went mad – too
mad – and I was pleased to be on
that balcony. Pints were thrown
and general chaos ensued. There
were scuffles and spitting and these
things were becoming the norm
and Morrissey didn't like it. My
fading memory tells me he walked
off mid-gig not to return. I have
since read reviews of the gig that
say it was during the encore. I just
remember being gutted. I bought
the tour t-shirt and headed home.
I wore that t-shirt to death until
one day many years later I couldn't
find it. My wife admitted that she
had thrown it out as it was looking
tatty, along with several others – a
heinous crime. I have only recently
forgiven her.

### PAUL JEFFREY

I discovered them in January
1984 when they were on *Top Of*

*The Pops* doing 'What Differences
Does It Make?' I thought, 'This is
a bit different, is this.' I was ten or
eleven. They stood out a mile and
of course there was a total lack of
interest from the *Top Of The Pops*
crowd.

Then I saw them on *The Tube*
doing 'Hand in Glove' and 'Still Ill'.
I'd go and buy seven-inch singles
for 50p with my pocket money
from Woolworths. I was too young
to see them on the *Meat Is Murder*
tour, but they came back to the
Mayfair in July 1986. I didn't have
any clue about it being an over-18s
venue. I managed to convince a
friend of mine to come with me.
We told our parents we were going
to the cinema and so there I was
with my quiff, my button-down
shirt, my burgundy tie, my DMs
and my suit jacket.

I went up to the venue with a
group of Smiths fans who were
milling around central Newcastle
when I got off the Metro. I got to
the door of the venue, and it was
very apparent I wasn't 18. And
the security guy looked at me and
looked at my friend and went,
'You're not coming in.' There was
no way I could say, 'I'm 18.' I wasn't
an old-looking 13-year-old. And,
to quote Morrissey, I went home
and cried and wanted to die.

Organised by Factory Records
to 'celebrate Manchester' and
specifically the first performance
by The Sex Pistols at the Lesser
Free Trade Hall in Manchester on
4 June 1976, the Festival of the
Tenth Summer culminated in an
all-day music festival at the Greater
Manchester Exhibition Centre (or
G-Mex).

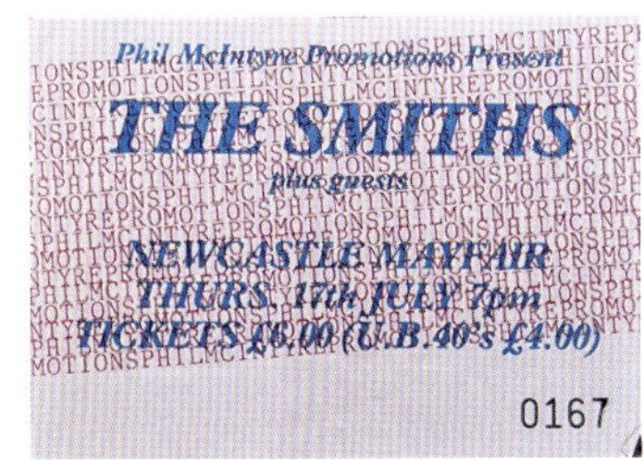

*Newcastle Mayfair ticket (Carl Hinde)*

## FESTIVAL OF THE TENTH SUMMER, G-MEX

### 19 JULY 1986, MANCHESTER, UK

### CLIVE ADAMS

I took a sickie from work and accompanied a mate up in his Ford Escort as we had tickets for the Festival of the Tenth Summer, a whole day featuring several of Manchester's most iconic artists and bands. For many of the 12,000 or so in the crowd, The Smiths were the band to bring the house down. From the opening 'Bigmouth Strikes Again', I quickly realised that, just like the Pistols gig at the Manchester Lesser Free Trade Hall ten years previously, this gig would be one for the history books of the future.

At times, Morrissey's voice was drowned out as the crowd sang along in joyous celebration. To this day, I never understood why so many dismissed The Smiths as doom merchants. I remember John Peel stating that lyrics by The Smiths made him 'laugh out loud', which very little else did for him back in the eighties. That's the point. The Smiths were – and still are – unique in their ability to make you laugh, cry, hope, and wonder. Three decades on, they are still as relevant as they have ever been.

### MARK WILLIAMS

I arrived at the Piccadilly bus terminal in Manchester with no ticket for the event and no viable way to get back home to North Shropshire at the end of the evening. But I strolled down to the event and luckily bagged myself the last ticket at face value off a tout outside the newly opened G-Mex Centre. I was in!

The huge venue was nowhere near full, and it was quite easy to mill around whilst the lower order bands played. It was around this point in the afternoon that I met some other folk from my hometown of Oswestry and happily secured a lift home with them.

Eventually The Smiths appeared on the stage after performances from Pete Shelley of the Buzzcocks, The Fall, John Cooper Clarke and the Virgin Prunes. I remember the evening sunlight shone through the pane glass roof of the hall as Prokofiev's 'Romeo And Juliet' intro music heralded their arrival and they burst into a resounding rendition of 'Bigmouth Strikes Again'. From then on it was sheer pandemonium in the front rows, with Morrissey egging us on while holding a placard with 'The Queen Is Dead' on it. I also recall him introducing their forthcoming single 'Ask'.

Morrissey changed his shirt for the last song, a white cotton polka dot one, which he subsequently threw into the crowd. I was once again fortunate enough to be able to grasp at it; thankfully, it ripped apart easily this time. You can see the photographic evidence in the middle of the gatefold slleve for the live album *Rank*, where I can be seen at the centre of the image pulling the shirt apart. I still have the piece of shirt in my sock drawer to this day.

On the way home, the minivan we were travelling in broke down near Warrington which is where we spent the remainder of the night, but not before the bizarre occurrence of a 1950s-style American Cadillac-type car that drove slowly past us with two women sitting on its wide flat bonnet waving to us as the car's stereo blasted out music. I still scratch my head about this incident to this day. In the early morning, we finally got the van started and I got to my bed for a few more hours sleep before preparing myself for my second Smiths gig of the weekend at Salford University. This time I was on a scheduled bus trip from Wrexham and, after a game of footy with my mates, I embarked on the bus that was going to take me to what Johnny Marr described as his favourite Smiths gig of all time.

### DAVID ALLEN

The first of the two times I saw them was at the opening of G-Mex with a great line-up. But me and my mates were there for The Smiths. I had the feeling that Morrissey couldn't cut it live, but I was so wrong. His vocals were brilliant, the band was brilliant and the crowd was the most enthusiastic I've ever seen at a gig. It was one of those gigs that would make the generations who got into them later envious. Even now, if I happen to mention I've seen The Smiths live, it's met with respect and envy in equal measure.

### JAMES DONNELLY, AGE 19

I went to college with a lad whose brother worked in the recording studio for the first album. He brought the demo in. It was amazing and I was hooked. That was about October 1983. I saw them at G-Mex celebrating ten years of punk. It was an all-day event with other artists performing. The crowd were only interested in The Smiths and that's all I was there for – nothing else but The Smiths! They did *The Queen Is Dead* set.

I'm from Rusholme in Manchester and I knew exactly what they were singing about in the first line of 'Rusholme Ruffians' and the last night of the fair. It was a yearly event, and I was there on the night, in Platt Fields in Rusholme. Morrissey's songs just said it all. I always thought he was singing about my school in 'The Headmaster Ritual'.

### JOHN GOODWIN

The image in the centrefold of *Rank* shows fans tearing at the shirt Morrissey threw into the crowd at the end of the set. My blond curly hair can be seen in the centre of that photo. I grabbed a huge chunk of cuff and sleeve of the spotty shirt. Despite the sweat, it smelt amazing and I had the shirt pinned to my bedroom wall until I went to uni two years later.

### MALCOLM GREENLEY

They were on about six o'clock. It was around ten years since The Sex Pistols played that famous gig at the Lesser Free Trade Hall where about 40 people turned up, Morrissey being one along with members of what would become Joy Division and also Mark E Smith. So it was a really important gig that spawned

*Malcolm Greenley got several postcards
from Morrissey*

Hello Malcolm,
"This Night Has Opened My Eyes" will be on an LP comprised of radio sessions to be released in September.
A new single is ~~fea~~ released on August 24th
I'm glad you mentioned "Girl Afraid", it seemed to have been overlooked by most people.
Not happy/not sad,
MORRISSEY.

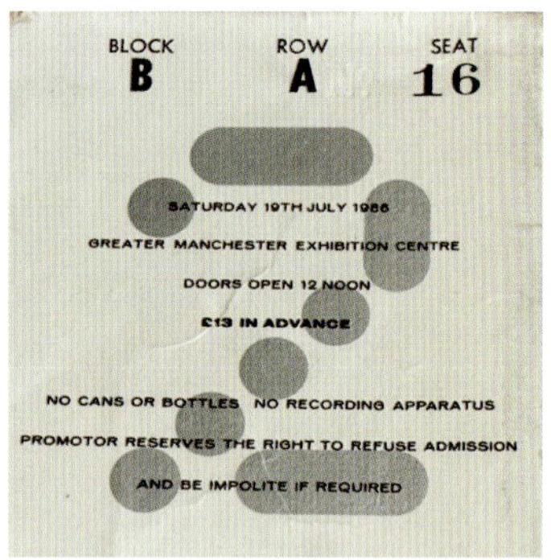


*Festival of the Tenth Summer ticket (Peter Martin)*

the Manchester music scene. As an old railway station, it was hard to get a good sound in G-Mex.

I wrote to Morrissey and he wrote back to me. I was just amazed when I got a response. I wrote because of my obsession with the band. When I get into certain bands it's full on. I tried the lucky option and just stuck a letter in the post c/o Rough Trade Records. I was lucky enough that they got to him. He was relatively famous then. I doubt you would get through to him now. The correspondence lasted for a couple of months. He got too famous, too busy I presume, but it was nice while it lasted. I sent all my Smiths covers there to get signed and he was the only one available to sign them. I'm hoping to one day meet the rest of the band and get them to sign them as well. I've still got the postcards and the letter back. And I've still got the envelopes in green crayon. I remember my mum saying, 'Who the hell is writing to you in green crayon?'

He was seriously into James Dean – I think he still is – and I sent him a cassette of this radio documentary about James Dean. He mentions that in one of the letters he sent. It was great when I met him. It was really, really, really weird meeting him. He spoke so quietly. You could hardly hear him. You had to lean in and get right next to him. I said, 'I'm Malcolm, I wrote to you a couple of years ago.' He paused for a second and said, 'James Dean,' and I thought, 'I can't believe he's remembered me'. I was amazed at that. He's a strange person; there's no doubt about it. He's an odd guy, but all the better for it.

### PETER MARTIN

We got a coach on a pre-paid package trip from Newcastle. We didn't come back on the bus but stayed over for the next night in Salford. We tracked Johnny Marr down to a big hotel in the city centre as he'd promised us tickets. To our surprise, he was as good as his word, and we duly left with spare tickets for the next two gigs. The gig itself was great. Loads of bands celebrating the ten years since punk broke in Manchester. The Smiths were on early; New Order were headliners. I really don't think we realised how great these gigs were at the time.

### STEPHEN WRIGLEY

I'm from Saddleworth originally. The annoying thing is, being from Manchester, I could have seen them a million times over. But it was that time when you start going out and not going to as many gigs, and then I went to college in mid-Wales and of course they never came anywhere near. And it was impossible then to get back; it was hours to get back to see them anywhere.

The G-Mex gig just tied in with one of the summer holidays and me and a few of my mates from school all got tickets and went down for that day. At the end of '82, all my favourite bands seemed to be splitting up. The Jam had finished, the real Clash had finished, Stiff Little Fingers. Those punky new wavy bands that people my age were all into, and there was suddenly this void. It was so funny. I was only 16 and I remember thinking, 'Oh no, this is the end of proper music.' And then of course The Smiths suddenly arrived, which was kind of perfect. I became aware of them through John Peel. He was playing them right from the get-go.

My brother was into them, and we'd hear them when we went out, but it was a slow one with me. I didn't immediately go, 'Oh, these are suddenly the best band ever.' I thought the first album was great, but the production was so bad. 'This Charming Man' was obviously brilliant, but I was already getting a bit too cynical and I was thinking, 'Ah well, this could be a one hit wonder.' In real time then, it was 'What Difference Does It Make?' We were going out in Oldham and Manchester and that was huge. It was everywhere. And we thought, 'Oh, this is going to be good.' But then *Hatful Of Hollow* came out and I was going, 'Yeah well, load of Peel sessions.' They weren't brilliant. I'd rather have something well done in the studio than new takes on other tunes.

It took me until about *Meat Is Murder*, to be honest. Me and my mates were already vegetarian, so it was great to hear that and hear what they were saying. It was such a good day. We were buzzing and looking forward to The Smiths. By then, they and New Order were by far my favourite bands. We were drinking. The Fall were on and they were brilliant. The Smiths were coming on about six o'clock and it wasn't like they were the big headliners because Tony Wilson organised it so that New Order were going to be the headliners. It seemed weird because it was still light in this massive arena. You never really went to big arena gigs in those days.

They didn't really exist unless you wanted to see the Rolling Stones or whatever.

It was just a brilliant time. *The Queen Is Dead* had been released and I was thinking, 'This is the best album ever.' I remember 'Ask' was just about to be released as their new single, which I'd never heard, and they did that live. And of course, never having seen Morrissey before, he was just brilliant. He had his 'Queen Is Dead' sign, waving that around, and his 'Two Light Ales' placard.

I remember Paul Morley being there. I remember him being funny, whatever he said.

We had all these people coming on and off. I did have a cassette of the concert. I think it was broadcast. Sandie Shaw was on directly before The Smiths, and she did 'Hand In Glove' and 'Jeanne'. It was this build-up of anticipation and going, 'Ooh, Sandie Shaw,' and not really knowing who she was other than that she was the 'Puppet On A String' woman Morrissey was obsessed with.

The Smiths were just unbelievable. They knocked everybody out of the water, including New Order, who were pretty average that night to be honest. They were still in that 'we're not very good live' kind of phase. The Smiths were head and shoulders above the rest. That made me think, 'The Smiths are just the best band ever,' which I still now believe.

### ALAN BUTTERWORTH, AGE 19
I had already seen two amazing gigs by The Smiths, at the Palace

Theatre and the following year at the Free Trade Hall. But the two that still resonate happened over the same weekend in July 1986. The Smiths were set to play a Factory Records-organised event called the Festival of the Tenth Summer and then a much smaller gig at Salford University the next day.

I remember going into G-Mex early in the day and A Certain Ratio already being on stage. Myself and my gig-going pal Mike made our way down to the front – after a quick trip to the bar to get a beer in – to watch the rest of ACR's set. The next couple of hours went by in a blur. I can remember enjoying The Fall, people throwing plastic pint pots at Derek Hatton, who was compering, and a particular highlight was someone managing to get on stage and trying to hit Andy McCluskey of OMD with a plastic tray from the bar! Andy soldiered on doing his geography teacher dance whilst simultaneously ducking out of the way of the beer tray until the bouncers were able to drag the guy off stage!

As early evening approached, I can recall getting right to the front and a buzz of excitement in the venue as we waited for The Smiths to come on. The area where we were became more and more full as people rushed to the front. Moz strolled on stage holding his 'Queen Is Dead' placard and looked immaculate in white Levi's and a white shirt, opened halfway down. 'The Queen Is Dead' kicked in and all hell broke loose down the front. In the crush, I lost a shoe but I was having such a good time I didn't care. Later in the set, I saw someone

throw it on the stage. When it was all over, 40 or so sweaty fantastic minutes later, the roadies were clearing the stage and I shouted for one of them to throw my shoe back. Thankfully he did!

Lots of drinks of water were needed and once Mike and I had recovered we both thought, 'Bloody hell, that was fantastic. And we still have New Order to come on yet!' We later took the short walk to DeVille's nightclub to carry on partying. We couldn't believe we would be seeing The Smiths again at a much smaller venue the next night.

### ANDY MCCLUSKEY, OMD

I suffer from stage fright. I'm much calmer than I was, because it finally dawned on me that if people have bought a ticket to see us, they probably already like the music so we're onto a winner. I think the most terrified I've ever been was playing the Festival of the Tenth Summer. We thought we'd do it as a 'thank you' to Factory, and because we wanted to remember that we'd started ten years previously, just me and Paul Humphreys and a tape recorder. What we hadn't factored in was that we'd be playing in front of 8,000 Smiths fans. I was more and more frightened as the day went on. I was so nervous I threw up before I went on. Matters were made worse by Paul Morley introducing us on stage as, 'And now, two rich bastards from Los Angeles.'

### CAROLINE ALLEN, AGE 16

I got to know who The Smiths were when I was about 13. 'This Charming Man' came out and my older sister bought the single. We shared a bedroom, so I used to have to listen to it all the time and got quite fond of it. From then on, I just carried on listening to whatever they brought out. My two best friends at the time, Nicky and Jenny, liked them as well so we listened to them together.

G-Mex was the first time I saw them live, with Nicky and Jenny. We got up at three o'clock in the morning, took the first bus into Manchester from Macclesfield and got there really, really early – about 7am. We wanted to be on the front row.

Outside, we got chatting to other Smiths fans. We got on the front row. I can't really remember much about anyone else who was on. All I was bothered about was seeing The Smiths because seeing them for the first time was so exciting. It started at about midday. They were on at about six. We stood at the front for hours and hours, not eating anything and not going to the toilet – nothing.

Kevin Cummins' book, *Manchester: Looking For The Light Through The Pouring Rain* has a picture of the whole front row, with me and Nicky stood looking really miserable. We weren't miserable. We were just like, 'Come on, when are The Smiths going to come on, for crying out loud?' The Smiths were just brilliant and when they'd gone off, we had to get out because we were just desperate for the toilet. But all my memories of that show are overtaken by the next day, because we went to Salford University the next day for the gig there at Maxwell Hall.



### CAROLINE ALLEN

The best gig I've ever been to in my life. (And Johnny Marr says it was the best gig The Smiths ever played.) Everything about it was just insane. We were on the front row again, because we'd queued up at the crack of dawn again.

What made it such a special gig was the whole atmosphere. It was loud, it was hot, it was sweaty. The crowd was just bouncing. It was intense but a little bit intimidating as well. A lot of lads – Smiths fans – were quite rowdy. You'd see the same lads as you'd seen the day before, rowdy and shouting. The banter between Morrissey and the crowd was really good as well. I had a bootleg tape of the concert. I listened to it so much I could mouth all the things that Morrissey said between every song. He was really, really on form.

Loads of people were stage invading. I think it was 'Still Ill', the second-to-last song, when people started getting on stage. I thought I was going to die if I didn't get pulled on the stage because it was that squashed and horrible and really quite scary. But we got pulled onto the stage and we were there when the stage collapsed a little bit.

I was covered in bruises the next day. But everybody was really lovely as well. Everybody was helping you get on stage. Nobody was pushing you out of the way or anything. Everybody was in it together and they all wanted everybody to get on stage. If the whole crowd could have got on stage, it would just have been perfect.

The bouncers just gave up trying in the end because there were loads of people on stage. You can see the whole gig on YouTube. You can see how intense it was. I love watching it back now and thinking, 'My God, I can't believe I was there.'

### KHALID AHMED

It was the day after G-Mex and a small venue, less than 1,000 people. I just remember the intensity of the gig – it was hot and sweaty. This was the tour when Morrissey paraded 'The Queen Is Dead' placard during that song. Watching The Smiths was an event, a chance to share the love we all had for them. They were a funny conundrum; Morrissey's lyrics were sensitive and intelligent but the music when played live brought out manic responses from the crowd, who were mainly manly blokes. They were just a great combination with Morrissey the poet and Marr in effect a would-be rock guitarist. Ordinarily that combination wouldn't work, but it certainly did!

### ANDY DAWSON

I was listening to Piccadilly Radio in my bedroom in 1984 when this song came on, 'How Soon Is Now?'. I was blown away and hooked on Morrissey and The Smiths from then on. I bought every twelve-inch vinyl single. This was my life. The songs said everything about my life in the North West. I scanned the *Manchester Evening News* every Friday night for Smiths

concerts. I bought my ticket for Salford University at Piccadilly Records: £4 standing. I can recall a Smiths poster on the stairs being torn down. The box office was on the side of the Free Trade Hall in Manchester. I got centre circle £6.50 and took my girlfriend at the time. All I can remember is Morrissey holding up a 'The Queen Is Dead' placard. The concert was packed. They finished with 'Still Ill'.

Afterwards I bought a 'Queen Is Dead' t-shirt from a street seller along with six by four-foot tour posters of *Meat Is Murder* and *The Queen Is Dead* tour. These were on my bedroom wall for years. I also bought postcards from the underground market in Manchester and with my saved newspaper cuttings and tickets did a framed picture, which again was put up in my bedroom. I still have it.

I lived near Altrincham in Cheshire. Mike Joyce was often seen pushing a pram down George Street. One day Morrissey came into Altrincham Post Office with a dog, and said to a girl working on the counter, 'You look sad,' and went out, returning with a big bunch of flowers for her. Kevin Cummins did a photo shoot at Dunham Massey. There used to be a car park on Charcoal Lane, on the right near the stile to Dunham Park. My friend went for a mid-week walk and saw Morrissey, parked up on his own. The car was crammed full of flowers.

### DARREN APPLEBY

Girls had started to feature in my life, and I got tickets for both me and my girlfriend to go to Salford

*Andy Dawson was at the Maxwell Hall show*

University on a coach organised by our local record shop. Knowing what the gigs were like, I was asked if we could sit in the balcony and, frankly, I was going to do everything the girl wanted in return for a cheeky snog on the bus home. So, whilst the gig was mental, we had a good vantage point to see the sheer joy of my fellow fans. Apart from 'Money Changes Everything', which I still think is one of their weakest songs, it couldn't have been a better gig musically.

But the fact that it was almost a homecoming gig meant that the cries of 'Salford, Salford!' rang around the venue. It was the most pleasurably violent gig I have ever been to. It was quite literally like a war zone. The stage invaders, the noise of the crowd, Morrissey swinging his placards around, Johnny Marr's cymbal ride leading into 'The Queen Is Dead', Craig Gannon being a shy new boy, and the fact that the band were on such good form, meant that this is still my number one gig ever.

I've seen loads of bands since – big boys like the Stones, Stone Roses and Iron Maiden in stadiums as well as tiny unsigned bands in tiny venues – and nothing has ever come close. Reading that Johnny Marr also said it was the best gig he had played in The Smiths makes me feel honoured that I was there to witness it.

Seeing Morrissey solo at Hanley a final time in 2011 was like reliving my youth once more. I bunked off work to queue for tickets. Now with my wife, we witnessed more than one 40-something grown man moved to tears. It was almost like a Holy Communion.

Morrissey might have fallen out of favour with the mainstream media recently due to his opinions, and Johnny Marr has gone on to be the 'Johnny Fucking Marr' of legend, but along with Andy Rourke's sublime bass lines and Mike Joyce's pounding beat, The Smiths are and were the best band ever and made me the man I am today. And even though Johnny inspired me to pick up the guitar at 15, I still can't play 'This Charming Man'.

### NICK BARBER

I saw the back-to-back shows at G-Mex and Salford University. The atmosphere at G-Mex was a bit subdued apart from at the front of the crowd, as the size of the venue and the Neanderthal security kept a lid on things. But Salford was one of the wildest gigs I've been to in 40-odd years of gig-going in several countries. I have photos from the Salford gig and a couple from the Liverpool Royal Court show I took on a Kodak Instamatic. The Salford ones were featured in a *Mojo* article a few years back and uncredited, which I wasn't too happy about.

### STEVE BROWN

I saw The Smiths twice in 1986 and had two very brief encounters with Morrissey. I was getting into other stuff, jangly sixties bands like The Byrds – probably a Smiths influence there – and listening to a lot of reggae. I didn't share Morrissey's views on it! And I discovered hip-hop, a big moment for me. I left home in April 1986 – the best thing I ever did – and was now sharing a house with my friend Kev, who bought a copy of *The Queen Is Dead*.

To be honest I was barely interested in hearing it. I had moved on, but my ears pricked up at the first notes of the title track. Some of the songs were beautiful, the obvious ones like 'There Is a Light…' but also 'Some Girls Are Bigger Than Others'. I had a disagreement with my son recently about that song; he thought it was meaningless and naff, but to me it was perfect Smiths: funny, quirky lyrics that no-one else could have written, with a sort of fatalism about them even though they didn't seem to be about anything, and so catchy – a lovely melody and that genius guitar playing. Morrissey's lyrics were better and funnier than ever, kind of self-referential and world-weary and soaked in black humour. The music was quite varied; it had moved on a long way from the simplicity of the first album.

One of the best things about The Smiths were the B-sides; way back from 'Accept Yourself' to later stuff like 'Half A Person' and 'You Just Haven't Earned It Yet Baby', all hidden gold; and the Peel Sessions! I recorded a Peel Session that included 'London' which sounded amazing, better than the released version. I think it was in '86 that 'Rubber Ring' and 'Asleep' appeared on the B-side of one of the singles. 'Asleep' was stunning. The darker side of Morrissey's lyrics seemed to be getting even darker, yet more beautiful. I was a Smiths fan again!

When they played Salford University, loads of us went. It was a relatively small venue for a band as big as they now were and it was heaving. The atmosphere was buzzing and quite laddish; whether it was just a Manchester thing I don't know, but the band now seemed to have a lot of everyday teenage jack-the-lads amongst its fans, lads you would normally expect to see on the football terraces. To me it showed how the realness of The Smiths' songs could reach parts that other music couldn't. I thought this was great; the fans were boisterous but good natured and there was no hint of aggro. This was how Manchester came to be throughout the late eighties; the kids who you would have previously crossed the road to avoid were now mixing with students and young professionals and everyone got on great. Gigs and clubs were amazing at that time.

Although the type of people in the crowd had changed, it was still a typical Smiths gig in that it was made up evenly of girls and lads, as it had been at previous gigs in '84 and '85.

I was determined to get on the stage. Smiths' gigs had traditionally ended with the crowd dancing on the stage with the band, although I had never got up there myself. We were stood near the back and towards the end of the gig I started to work my way to the front, which wasn't easy as it was so rammed. By the time they came back on for the encore I was right at the front and felt like I had no choice now but to get on the stage; I was being squashed by the crowd and the heat was intense.

It wasn't easy to climb onstage, but eventually I made it! I was the only fan up there. There was Morrissey, stood right there. I put my arm on his shoulder, the stage lights in my eyes, and was immediately grabbed by a security guy or roadie. I'd been onstage for about a second and now I was being shoved backwards very quickly towards the back of the stage and out through a door.

I went down the stairs and out of a fire door, walked round to the front and back in – it was near the end of the night so there was no one on the door – up the stairs and back into the hall where The Smiths were still playing. My mates were still stood where I'd left them. I said, 'All right lads?' They were laughing, 'Where did you come from?' 'Was that you on the stage?' I was a bit dismayed to see the stage was now full of people; no-one had kicked them off! I guess I was unfortunate because I was the first one up there.

### MARK WILLIAMS

It was yet another hot sticky night as we climbed off the bus, but this time into the darkened hall of the university. I wouldn't say it was the favourite of my five Smiths gigs, but it was most certainly the most manic. The security fence collapsed halfway through the concert. I also helped pull a few girls out of the crowd who were being seriously crushed. You can see me quite clearly at the start of 'His Latest Flame'/'Rusholme Ruffians' in the footage on YouTube.

### AL BUTTERWORTH

We got the bus into Manchester City Centre and then walked the mile and a half out to the university.

I recall it was a lovely summer's evening and, as we approached the venue, I recognised a few faces from the previous day's gig at G-Mex. We could not get tickets for downstairs standing so had to make do with the balcony. Mike and I made our way upstairs and tried to get as close to the front as possible. It was heaving upstairs, but the standing area downstairs it looked scarily overcrowded. It was only years later I found out how lax the security was and that lots of people were able to get in without tickets. The place felt hot and sweaty and everybody seemed to be tingling with anticipation.

The lights went down, Prokofiev came on and once again the place erupted! The set was very similar to the previous day, but we didn't care. We just danced and sang along to every word with sweat dripping from the ceiling. After each song a cry of, 'Salford, Salford' was chanted by a lot of the audience. After five or six times this got a bit annoying. Even Morrissey got fed up with it and mock growled, 'Stretford, Stretford' back at the crowd a few times.

The balcony was bouncing up and down with the weight of people dancing and I could see roadies struggling to hold the speakers to try and stop them bouncing into the crowd. The concert ended and we made our way outside. Mike and I crashed down with exhaustion onto a grass verge outside the venue along with quite a few others. And that was it, all over.

I was only 19 years old. My passion for music has stayed with me. I still get out to gigs a couple of times a month, but nothing has come close to that wonderful weekend in July 1986. The best gigging weekend of my life.

### DAMIAN MORGAN

Through the years, my love for The Smiths has only deepened. Every song, every lyric became a piece of my own personal journey. It was the sound of defiance, of individuality, and of a deep, emotional connection to a world that often felt indifferent. They didn't just speak to me, they spoke for me, and for countless others who found solace in their music. If you were lucky enough to have witnessed them live, this connection was taken to a whole new level in a sweaty concert hall.

When The Smiths played at Salford University it felt like the universe itself had aligned. A few weeks earlier, I'd queued for what seemed like a lifetime to secure two tickets at Piccadilly Records, back when it was still actually in Piccadilly, near the old bus station. The excitement as I clutched those two flimsy pieces of paper was intense; there were no apps, QR codes or any digital reassurance back then. If you lost your tickets, that was it, game over. And I wasn't taking any chances. I practically strangled them in my grip as I descended the stairs from the box office, my heart racing with the thought of seeing The Smiths live for the third time.

My obsession with the band had now reached near-religious levels. Morrissey was my poet laureate, and Johnny Marr my guitar god. Seeing them in the intimate confines of the relatively small Maxwell Hall felt like a dream come true. I was giddy at the thought. But what made this weekend truly monumental was that the night before, Manchester was hosting 'The Festival Of The Tenth Summer' at the G-Mex Centre to celebrate the tenth anniversary of the Sex Pistols' legendary Free Trade Hall gig, a night that had sparked a musical revolution in Manchester.

The line-up was iconic – New Order, The Fall and The Smiths – and it was organised by Factory Records and the Haçienda, encapsulating Manchester's rebellious, post-punk spirit. The event promised to be an unforgettable celebration of the city's vibrant creative landscape, with art exhibitions, film screenings, and performances all blending into one grand homage to a decade of Punk-inspired music and culture. But if I'm honest, the reality was a bit underwhelming. The G-Mex, a former train station-turned-venue, was cavernous and cold. The sound wasn't great, and though The Smiths were magnificent, the crowd was there for a mixed bill of artists. It lacked the electric atmosphere I craved, but it was a warm up for what was to come.

We arrived at Salford University early – Colin Foden, my then girlfriend Jenny Murray, myself and a few others. As we waited outside, we could hear the muffled thump of the soundcheck behind the doors, teasing us with the promise of what was to come. A black Mercedes Benz sped past at one point, and we half-joked, half-hoped it was the band inside, off to some mysterious rock-star errand before the show.

Then the moment came – we were in. We scrambled to the front, pressing ourselves right up against the stage. I could almost touch the mic stand. The excitement was palpable, the air thick with anticipation. We heckled the support act, Raymonde, with all the wit and impatience that comes from youthful arrogance. I remember thinking, 'Why is this guy trying to sound like Morrissey?' I had no idea that Raymonde's frontman, James Maker, had a history with Morrissey, even appearing on stage with The Smiths in their early gigs. Maker and Morrissey had their own adventures together – Morrissey once recounted a terrifying night where the two of them narrowly escaped a gang of thugs near a car park by Chorlton Street Bus Station. Maker had been kicked nearly to death, only to miraculously stand up and run. Knowing that story now, I feel a bit guilty for the 'get on with it' jeers we threw his way.

By the time The Smiths took the stage, Maxwell Hall had become a pressure cooker. The summer heat, the bodies crammed together like sardines, the sticky, humid air – it was like the whole room was holding its breath. The opening strains of Prokofiev's 'Romeo And Juliet' filled the hall, booming out at an ear-splitting volume, strobe lights flashing across the crowd. My heart was pounding. I could barely breathe. And then Morrissey appeared. The moment he stepped into the spotlight; time stopped. Mike Joyce's drums thundered into the intro for 'Panic' and suddenly I was lifted off my feet caught in the surge of the crowd.

We were a sea of arms, heads and bodies, pressed together, sweaty and ecstatic. Morrissey leaned into the crowd, his hands grazing the outstretched arms, and I screamed his name until my throat burned. The energy was electric. The speaker stacks wobbled dangerously as the band roared through 'Bigmouth Strikes Again' and 'How Soon Is Now?' Craig Gannon, the unofficial 'fifth' Smith, added extra firepower on guitar, giving the band a heavier, more muscular sound than they'd ever had before. Gone were the delicate, chiming riffs of earlier tours – this was The Smiths at their most powerful.

At some point during 'There Is A Light That Never Goes Out,' a bra sailed through the air. I recognised it immediately – it belonged to Jenny. I didn't know whether to laugh or cringe, but I had no time to process it because the next moment Morrissey was back at the mic, delivering his lines with a mix of theatrical flourish and raw emotion. His voice, haunting and deeply resonant, cut through the sweat-soaked haze of the room.

Morrissey barked into the mic before 'Frankly, Mr. Shankly' with his usual sarcastic wit: 'Who needs G-Mex?' The crowd roared back in agreement: 'Nobody!' It was a sly jab at the festival from the night before, but it perfectly captured the feeling in the room. Maxwell Hall wasn't just a venue – it was a sanctuary for us, a room full of disciples hanging on every word, every note. We weren't just fans; we were followers of something bigger, something that transcended the music.

The encore came, and as the band returned to the stage, Morrissey laughed, 'You've missed the last bus, haha!' He was right, of course. It didn't matter. I would have walked all the way home barefoot if I had to. That night was worth every second.

The Maxwell Hall gig marked the end of what Morrissey later called the 'heavy petal' phase of The Smiths' live performances. It was a shift from their earlier, more delicate sound to something more forceful, more intense. It remains the best gig I've ever been to. All these years later, I can still feel the heat, the crush of the crowd and the raw energy of The Smiths at their peak. For a few hours, they took us to another world – a world where the air crackled with possibility, where the music felt like salvation, and where Morrissey's voice, cutting through the noise, was the only thing that mattered.

### CHRIS GREEN, AGE 18

I lived in Lower Broughton. Where Peel Park is, there's a little bridge that crosses over to an estate called Spike Island. I lived just across the bridge, 200 yards on the right-hand side, half a mile from Salford Uni.

The Jam had split up, and we needed a focus and The Smiths were it for us. I found Morrissey amazing to look at. He was so different to what we'd been used to. Because I'd been into The Jam, who were clean cut and I was a Mod. And there was this political stuff going on. There was nothing for us.

We were all into music. My mate Jimmy McManus was into The Human League. My mate Stuart was a year older, and he got me into The Jam and when they folded, he got me into The Smiths and Echo and The Bunnymen. Stuart's a Mod. Stuart had a paper round and wore a two-tone suit on his paper round. With his money he could afford to buy decent stuff. I wasn't as blessed financially. When my mates all had proper Mod parkas, I had one with a red lining like little kids have.

I distinctly remember where Stuart lived on Earl Street, facing The Croft where they dropped the houses. We were stood round the fire one night and Stuart started talking about The Smiths' 'Hand In Glove' single that he'd just bought. He said, 'Come round and listen to it.' So we walked the 50 yards to his house and as soon as I heard 'Hand In Glove' I was absolutely smitten and went out and bought it. From that point on, every single that came out, we were there on the day – at HMV or wherever – buying it.

Apart from Stuart, we were all into football around the age of 15, 16. My dad died suddenly of a heart attack when I was 15 so my head was all over the pace. For a little while I lost my way. I wouldn't say I was a football thug, but we went to football and got into trouble. About 15 or 16 of us used to have a Mitchells self-drive hire van and we'd go all over the country. When City were in the old First Division, we used to have a fight with anyone we could bump into, but nothing vicious.

The gig meant so much because it was on our doorstep. I'd been listening to The Smiths for two or three years by then. If my memory serves me right, everyone knocked

on for me on the way. None of
us had tickets. We all had bottles
of cider. We walked through the
park, sat on the steps leading up to
Maxwell Hall, finished our drinks
and then we all went round and sat
on the grass. There was a group of
girls from our estate there. They
all dressed the same. They all used
to wear black Doc Marten shoes,
socks up to the knees and little frilly
skirts. They were younger even than
me. A group of 20 of us walked
up the stairs looking like Salford
scallies, not a ticket between us.

There were a lot of flat tops there,
Morrissettes, but we just looked
like we were going to a match. I
remember it being really warm,
beers, sat outside, just chatting.
Someone discovered that the
window to the girls' toilets was open
a little bit, so we forced it a little bit
more and we all got through and
managed to sneak into the gig.

So we all bowled in there and
straight away, and because we were
all drunk, we were chanting 'Salford,
Salford' all the time. It must have
been fucking totally annoying for
everyone else, this mob of drunken
youths. And when the gig started, we
realised that downstairs was where
the action was. When Prokofiev's
'Romeo And Juliet' started the hairs
went up on the back of my neck.
Morrissey came dancing onto the
stage and everyone was screaming.
The first thing he said was, 'Who
needs G-Mex?' and of course it all
went off.

Every time a song finished the
crowd cheered. And we were just
annoying. We were singing 'Salford. Sal-ford.' But it went on and
on while they were changing guitars

and tuning up. And at one point
Morrissey started singing, 'Stretford, Stret-ford', and that wound
everyone up.

I've since found on YouTube
some clips. My mate Denis Hughes,
bless him, had a big head and you
can clearly see him perched half
on the stage. Morrissey's there and
Denis is looking round for everyone
else, and you can see heads bobbing
about. That would have been us, but
it's really blurred. Our mate Steve
Bradshaw, who was a City fan and
a postman, just comes dancing on
from the side of the stage, grabs
Morrissey around the neck and
everyone goes mental and then he
gets ejected.

We pushed onto the stage and,
as we pitched forward, the stage
collapsed. I vividly remember going
head first towards Mike Joyce's
drums. There were dozens on
the stage. Morrissey came on for
the encore, laughing, and saying
something about, 'If you don't leave
now, you'll miss the last bus.'

Johnny Marr has said somewhere
that it's one of his favourite gigs
and to say you were at Salford. It
was a little gig, and I get a little bit
of a buzz about it because I can say
I was there.

I bumped into Mike Joyce going
down to London on the train seven
or eight years ago. We were both in
first class. Mike was sat in his seat
with his wife and he looked up. I
had a proper Weller haircut at the
time – before my hair started going,
I had the full-on sideboards. He
looked at me and I looked at him
and I went, 'Hiya Mike.' He went,
'Where do I know you from?' And
I said, 'The last time you saw me I

was going arse over tit over your drum kit at

Maxwell Hall in 1986.' And he said, 'Ah, that's where I recognise you from!'

### DEREK HAZELL

The Smiths had been an important part of my teenage years after listening and dancing to them on the dancefloor of the State nightclub in Liverpool. As an 18-year-old living in Liverpool and being an avid Liverpool supporter, going to Manchester with a Scouse accent was like running the gauntlet.

I remember seeing an advert in the *Liverpool Echo*. Tickets for The Smiths were going on sale on Friday for Salford Uni. This was the warmup gig for the *Queen Is Dead* tour. In the run up to the gig I was taken very ill with the flu and was bedridden. On the morning of the gig I could hardly stand, never mind go to a concert. But there was no way I was going to miss this. Somehow, I got out of bed, phoned my friend Haze and we were going!

We had arranged for a friend to drive us there, so we got picked up. We went down the East Lancs to Manchester but on the way the car broke down. Luckily, it was just the fan belt which was soon fixed and so we were on our way again. Next stop – Salford Uni. First port of call? The bar and a few double whiskies, washed down with a pint of lager. From the uni bar, we could hear cheers from inside the hall and in a rush to get there I kicked about four full pints all over the floor – but who cared? The most important band of my life were going on stage.

They opened with in my opinion their finest moment, 'The Queen Is Dead', and then flew through the whole album. The whole crowd was one in movement, with people diving on stage. This was a true rock 'n' roll event, and it will never be forgotten. The gig was over in a second, but I will remember it for a lifetime.

### JOHANNA ROBERTS

I had posters and t-shirts (oh, where did they go?) and their name scrawled on my army bag that I used for college. I tuned in to Radio 1 when they played them live at Kilburn National Ballroom (later the recording for *Rank*) introduced by Andy Peebles. I taped a Morrissey interview on Piccadilly Radio with Mike Sweeney, which I still have. I watched Moz with Margi Clarke on *The Tube*. I loved *The Old Grey Whistle Test* that followed them in the studio as they recorded *The Queen Is Dead*. (RIP *Whistle Test*, it was bloody marvellous.)

I had done my A-levels and was getting ready for university. I was looking in the window of Piccadilly Records and there it was, the last item on the gig list – The Smiths to play Salford University. I mustered all the change in my purse and went down to the box office to get two tickets. I couldn't wait.

It was a balmy summer's evening outside Maxwell Hall. I saw The Smiths come out from their soundcheck to get in a limo; unlike now, when I would have bowled over, I stood back and just looked at them. As the doors opening time got close, the crowds were vast. There were eight glass doors but they only opened two. I am little and literally got carried in by a wave of people.

We stood close to the stage. James Maker's band Raymond was on first and I remember them smashing a guitar and fucking the stage up. That had to be sorted before the gig could go on. The place erupted when The Smiths came on. I was getting crushed at the front and escaped upstairs. We found seats, which isn't very rock 'n' roll, but I could see and I wasn't dying.

The bouncers were holding on to the speakers for fear they would topple over as the over-filled room bounced. It turns out there was extra stage set out for the speakers which was rather weak, hence Raymonde's ability to wreck it.

Everyone fell out of that gig sweating. Chapel Street was swarming with Smiths fans. The wonderful thing about the internet is that videos from that evening surfaced, so to be able to watch back some of that night, regardless of how grainy, is so special.

By 1987, *Strangeways* was released and the band announced their split. I was devastated. When the (very few) other fans at Uni claimed adoration for The Smiths, I 'knew' they could never feel like I did about them. And then Morrissey emerged as a solo artist, and I have followed him religiously ever since. At 51, my love for that band has never waned. I was known – am known – as a Smiths fan. I have a Morrissey tattoo, my house is a shrine to the Smiths and Morrissey, and we married in the Smiths room at Salford Lads Club.

I have met all five of them, including Craig. Johnny is a humble, wonderful individual. To hear him do Smiths tracks is so special, given his guitar skills. I am honoured to have been alive when they were at their height and to have seen them perform. So many people, including my husband, tell me they wish they had, so I feel blessed that I did. I know every word to every song, and I still play The Smiths daily. Their music got me through the trickiest years of adolescence, and it has never aged.

### JOHN MARSHALL, AGE 19

I was a young up-and-coming drummer and a keen fan of the local music scene. I was born in Hyde, Greater Manchester and became aware of The Smiths in late 1984. The music was just so different to anything that was around and appealed to me almost right away. Johnny Marr had to be the coolest-dressed man on the planet.

I'd been into Piccadilly Records to buy a ticket for G-Mex, and they had none left but said, 'We have some for Salford.' I was unaware of this gig and bought three tickets there and then. I think I paid £6 each for them. I took my older sister, who was a keen fan, and my mate's girlfriend as he was on military service in Germany and asked me to look after her (We were just friends, may I add).

The venue was absolutely packed out. I heard later that the door staff were not taking tickets on the door and so people were just going to the loos and passing the tickets through the windows so all their mates could come in. The gig started and you couldn't breathe. It was summer and red hot. I remember going out afterwards looking like I'd just swam across the local boating lake.

As they went through the set list

the crowd seemed to get bigger and bigger, with people jumping on stage. The venue staff had to lash ropes around the speakers to stop them falling into the crowd as the floor bounced with the fans.

I've seen hundreds of live bands over the years. I was a drummer for many years and played countless gigs and became a sound engineer and managed bands until retiring from music in my thirties. I can honestly say this was the most manic gig I ever went to.

### BILLIE MCGRAIL

I was at the Salford Uni and Free Trade Hall gigs in 1986. I fell madly in love with the band and Morrissey when I saw and heard 'This Charming Man'. It was unlike anything I'd heard before and I felt I'd found my lyrical soul mate. There were cameras at the Salford Uni gig for *The South Bank Show,* and I summoned up the courage and strength to be part of the stage invasion. It was almost the end of the gig and emotions and adoration were running high. I was helped over the barrier where I clambered onto the stage and knelt on the left-hand side of Morrissey – and was awe struck. I even worshipped him like a god and was applauded by the crowd! I stayed until the end of the gig where the bouncers removed us gently off stage.

### JOHN PARKES

I managed to get in and get to the side of the stage. They were doing the soundcheck – 'Ask'. I wanted to speak to Morrissey. I don't know what I was going to say to him. But I was apprehended by, I believe, the manager and two other people who very roughly threw me out.

Salford University was a fantastic gig. It was just mental, it really was. I could see water running down the walls. The stage didn't look very secure either. I came out of there and because there were no trains back to Warrington, where I lived and worked, I was going to hitch. The very first people I asked, 'Is anybody going to Warrington or thereabouts?' this guy said to me, 'Yeah, we're going to Warrington.' I said, 'Great. Can I have a lift if there's space?' And he said, 'Yeah. But we're waiting for our mate.' It was ages. The crowd had all disappeared when this lad turned up. 'Sorry, but we're not going to Warrington. We're going to Wallington,' which is a place in Surrey.

I'm there in the middle of Salford, a young lad with no money. It was very late at night and I tried thumbing a lift but nobody was stopping so I ended up walking twelve miles down the hard shoulder of the M62. It took me all night. Fortunately, I worked at Winwick Hospital and lived in the nurses' residence there, just off the junction of the M62. It's a wonder the police didn't pick me up. It might have been a blessing if they had.

### RITA FARRAGHER

A standout gig was Salford. So many great moments and songs they hadn't done for ages. I would not want to have missed that one. They played for longer than usual and we had to run like mad to catch our coach home or face sleeping in the bus station again. I got a postcard from Morrissey afterwards saying, 'We saw you running away from Salford.'

The previous day I'd been at GMEX for the Festival of The Tenth Summer thanks to Johnny Marr, who'd left access-all-area tickets for us at their hotel in the city centre. Carl and I got in on those. It was like *Wayne's World*: 'We're not worthy!' We were backstage with Barney from New Order and his wife and Peter Hook and all these people. I remember OMD played, loads of pop stars. It was just an amazing, amazing gig, and it was great to be able to walk up to the bouncers and flash the VIP passes.

We stayed in a B&B but didn't sleep that well. We went down to Salford University and saw them as they arrived for the soundcheck. We thanked them for leaving the tickets.

Out of all the gigs I went to, this was just the best. It was The Smiths at their absolute peak for their homecoming gig. The final encore was 'Hand In Glove' and the stage was invaded by hordes and hordes of fans. It started to give way with all the people jumping up and down. People ask, 'What's the best gig you've been to?' and I still love this one by far. They were just amazing that night.



It was an unforgettable night in an unforgettable town.



My favourite Smiths gig. I drove up from Swindon with my friend Pete in my banger of a Renault 12. We were 19 and we had been travelling around the USA (watching the 1986 World Cup and having a great time) for four months. We had missed out on the launch of *The Queen Is Dead* so were keen to catch up. I remember a lovely summer's evening, everyone dressed in Fred Perrys and Levi's (I was, for sure), flowers everywhere and beads around our necks. This gig really felt like a meeting of friends.

We drank the traditional (and cheap) Newcastle Brown in the bar and were in the middle, just behind the front, for the whole show, although I remember being taken off my feet many times, just like being in the Town End at Swindon (well, probably more like the Stretford End). During 'Panic', Moz had a picture of DJ Steve Wright on a sign but maybe I am imagining that. He did have 'The Queen Is Dead' written on a sign later on and made several witty remarks about how long life was and so on. 'Ask' was introduced with a long drawn out flat 'A' and a barbed comment about the 'southerners' (like us, I guess). There was lots of dry ice, Prokofiev as usual and an extra guitarist in Craig Gannon, who had played with Aztec Camera. Johnny Marr played several instrumental B-sides that night – 'Draize Train' and so on.

On the way back, somewhere near Birmingham, the police stopped me for speeding but let me off when we

*Salford University ticket (Stephen Reid)*

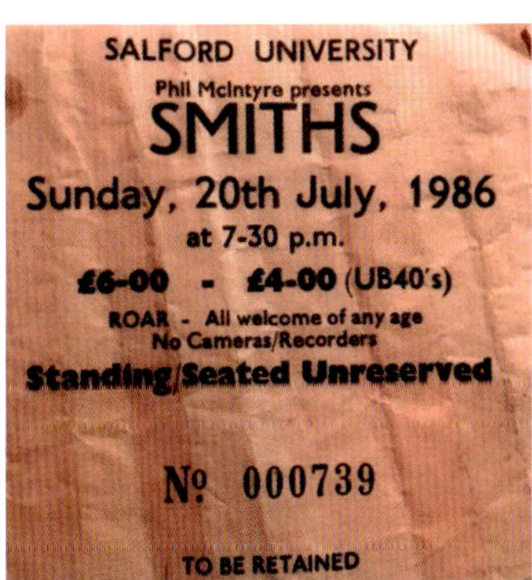

*Panic*

said we had been to see The Smiths. I don't think that would happen now!

My friend Pete worked with Craig Gannon 30 years later and he said that Craig thought this was the best gig he ever played…

In June 1988, I got a letter from Morrissey. I had it for about a year before I showed it to anyone. It came in the post and I thought my friends were playing a cruel joke on me but I kept it just in case and only showed it when someone mentioned that it was a shame that Morrissey never wrote to me when he had promised that he would.

My friend Angus, who was working at Knight Frank in Hanover Square in central London, saw Morrissey walking in the street and ran over to him. Moz was wearing a trilby hat and listened intently to my Hooray Henry estate agent friend (who was also a Smiths fan). I had had some bother recently and Morrissey said he would write to me to cheer me up. And he did!

*Morrissey wrote to Stephen to cheer him up*

## 'PANIC'

### RELEASED 21 JULY 1986

During the band's lifetime, only two singles ('Heaven Knows I'm Miserable Now' and 'Sheila Take A Bow') did better than the number 11 position that 'Panic' achieved in the UK charts. It managed national radio airplay despite the chorus of 'hang the deejay' as Morrissey reflected that 'the music that they constantly play… says nothing to me about my life.'

From Salford, The Smiths travelled to North America for their second and what would prove to be their final tour there.

## KINGSWOOD MUSIC THEATRE

### 31 JULY 1986, VAUGHAN, CANADA

### JEANNE CARDAMONE

The second time I saw The Smiths was in Canada. Living in upstate New York, Canada wasn't that far away. My best friend, Tom, and I were unemployed and decided to go to as many concerts as we could before getting new jobs. A Smiths concert was first on my list. As when I went to Philly, Tom had never heard of The Smiths before but this time I was able to loan him my albums.

The Kingswood Music Theatre was an outdoor theatre located in Canada's Wonderland. As we were getting close it started to rain. We went in and got rain ponchos from Wonderland and got right on the edge of the amphitheatre, so that only our backs were getting rained on. There were so many cool-looking people in the audience. One girl had a black wedding gown on. The Smiths let people up on stage to dance with them again. Morrissey is a gifted dancer, and it almost looked like he didn't have any bones as he flowed with the music and sang beautifully.

It was a great concert, and I have not forgotten it even after all these years. Afterwards, we began the three-hour drive home in the rain. We were in my friend's Buick Skylark, and I fell asleep in the back seat. I woke up, just in time to stop Tom from taking a wrong turn.

## STEWART ALI

The first time I ever heard them was at a dance in Hamilton, Ontario, very near Toronto. I was 15. The deejay was a bit older than all the patrons and introduced the crowd to some of the more obscure eighties music. 'Love Like Blood' by Killing Joke had just finished playing so I was already up on the dance floor. As that song finished, this beautiful distorted-sounding guitar filled my ears and struck me like no other music I've ever known: 'How Soon Is Now?' I moved closer to the speakers and just listened in awe. It was the most amazing song I had heard so far in my life. I asked the deejay who it was.

The next day, Saturday, I bussed downtown Hamilton to a fantastic record store called Cheapies. There was always a line-up of people for tickets and twelve-inch releases. I'd forgotten the name of the song but remembered The Smiths. I asked for the new Smiths song. They told

me they only carried the full album. 'How Soon Is Now?' had been released on *Hatful Of Hollow*. From that moment on I have never loved a material thing more than this record. I played it over and over again. I listened to 'How Soon Is Now?' ten times before being patient enough to listen to the whole album all the way through. Song by song they all became my favourites. Everyone has that one staple album in their lives from an impressionable age. This was clearly mine.

I have since bought it again, lost it and my son, 24, bought it me on vinyl for my 45th birthday. It's still my very favourite ever album of all time and I know it better than my own face in the mirror.

Soon after buying the vinyl from Cheapies, I acquired a Walkman so bought it on tape as well. When *The Queen Is Dead* came out, I purchased it on cassette.

The kids in my high school were exposed to an array of very eclectic, recent and obscure eighties music because of our local radio station, Toronto's CFNY, with Alan Cross. We heard 'How Soon Is Now?' often within days of hearing it at the dance. Then CFNY announced a tour was to follow the release of *The Queen Is Dead*. The Smiths were coming to Toronto. I called my friend in hysterics right away: 'We have to wait in line all night.' We were young and not allowed to do it, but knew a few boys who wanted to go and they were willing to camp out and buy us tickets.

My very best friend, Michelle, also liked The Smiths. We prepared for the concert by listening to the albums over and over. The boys that got us the tickets ended up driving (thanks, guys!) to the concert. We went early and split with the boys in order that Michelle and I could go our own way on the rides. We rode the most daring and had a blast all day.

The Smiths were due on stage at 7pm. This day was one of the best of my life, the rush from the rides and the rush from seeing your ultimate favourite band.

### DEREK RUBINOFF, AGE 15

I went with Susan Horton. We were both working at the theme park. At the back it was open-air and there was a lawn. Morrissey seemed plastered and was spinning around on stage wearing a cardigan; he was twirling a protest sign that said, 'The Queen Is Dead'. He had to leave the stage once or twice because he seemed to be so drunk. The band would play an instrumental during his breaks. The crowd got nuts; people were banging on the plastic seats. Rows of attached seats started to fail and got knocked over. People started to rush the stage. Susan grabbed me and we started to rush down the aisle to the stage; security guards were grabbing us and stopped us, but others broke through. People jumped on stage and the band fled. I remember some Mods dancing on stage after the band left. At some point security got the kids off the stage and the band came out and played more. It was the craziest show I ever saw. It was exhilarating. It felt a little like *Quadrophenia*.

### SUSAN THORNTON

At one point Morrissey wasn't looking too well. He left the stage while the band played an instrumental for quite some time. Then he came back in a different outfit and looked much refreshed!

### STEVE SINGH

The only thing I remember is Morrissey letting everyone on stage at the end. He had a daisy in his pocket. It was just another show at the time. No one knew that record and band would become such classics!

## UNIVERSITÉ DE MONTRÉAL CEPSUM
### 3 AUGUST 1986, MONTREAL, CANADA

### MARC PELLETIER

Back in 1985 I heard the song 'What Difference Does It Make?' by The Smiths and thought it was great. Then I took a chance with *Meat Is Murder*. Suddenly I was hooked, both by the lyrics and the music. I bought *The Queen Is Dead*, one of the best LPs of all time, so when I heard that they would be playing live at the CEPSUM at Montreal University I rushed to get a ticket.

A small place with a few hundred people, maybe less, and no seat reserve, the stage was low and we even could go on stage at any time and shake hands with Morrissey. I took a picture with my old Kodak when I was about 20 feet from him. It was a very friendly ambience. The set list was great, with all the hits and more, and it was the first time I'd heard the song 'Panic'.

They never came back. And Morrissey never came back to Montreal solo – until 2019!

# CAPITAL CONGRESS CENTER



### GEORGE ROBERTSON

During the course of a few songs, Morrissey gradually took off his shirt: undoing a few buttons per song, untucking it, etc., until finally he whipped it off and tossed it into the crowd. It was a relatively small venue, so lots of us were able to get up close to the stage, and I was near where the shirt landed. Immediately, several people grabbed on to it and started pulling to get a piece of it (I was reminded of a vaguely remembered biblical story about Roman soldiers arguing over Jesus' clothes at the crucifixion). One guy next to me grabbed a sleeve, pulled a lighter out of his pocket and burned the end of the sleeve off! I remember thinking at the time that he could have started a fire with a stunt like that. The show carried on with just a whiff of burnt fabric in the air.

# GREAT WOODS PERFORMING ARTS CENTER

5 AUGUST 1986, MANSFIELD, MASSACHUSETTS

### MARK NEEDHAM

I became an avid Smiths fan in 1984, as did my sister and my girlfriend of six months. I remember the loud roar and excitement from the crowd when the lights went off, and the intro music came on. The band opened with 'How Soon Is Now?' and when I looked to my left, I saw a classmate climbing up on the stage. He made it to Morrissey and hugged him and was then taken off the stage. Four songs in, and after drinking several beers, I had to use the restroom, but I said to myself, 'I've waited so long to see The Smiths and I'm not missing a second', so I grabbed a cup and discreetly peed in it so I wouldn't miss a second of the show! It was close to a two-hour concert, but it literally felt like 20 minutes.

The favourite song of my girlfriend was 'Asleep', from the first moment she heard it. Flash forward nine months and she shockingly passed away in her sleep from an undiagnosed heart condition.

### PETER APPEL

I was living in London in the fall of 1983 and stayed for about six months in Paddington, doing a semester abroad with my school and majoring in Theatre Arts. We saw 108 shows in a three-month period. It was insane and brilliant. I

*Great Woods Performing Arts Centre ticket (Lisa Plosker)*

loved Camden Palace and Camden, the Kings Road, Speaker's Corner and everything. I was out and about one day and a bloke selling cassette tapes told me to listen to this new band – 'They're pretty good.' Well I wish I had listened to that tape while I was still in London. But whoever gave me that tape launched me into a lifelong obsession with a band named The Smiths.

I got to see them at Great Woods Amphitheater – Morrissey holding 'The Queen Is Dead' sign and then the brilliant show taking off. They recently released that show with the deluxe reissue of *The Queen Is Dead*. I have seen and met both Morrissey and Marr in their post-Smiths careers and was given a pick from Johnny that I've carried in my wallet since. I have followed Morrissey forever and seen him in Manchester, Blackburn, Glasgow and London in the UK. This band has saved me over and over and over. There is a light that never goes out.

## PIER 84

### 6 AUGUST 1986, NEW YORK, NEW YORK

### FREDERICK GUBITOSI

The Pier was on the water and a lot of big bands played there. I didn't know much about them. A friend had played some tracks for me, and I thought their sound was different from everything else. I scalped a ticket because it was sold out but got it at face value. They did songs from *The Queen Is Dead* and *Meat Is Murder*. A few people rushed the stage.

### ANDY SCHWARTZ

I saw The Smiths live in NYC at an open-air show on a Hudson River pier on the west side of Manhattan. The American folk singer/songwriter Phranc supported and was not well received, which I guess Morrissey was miffed about and explains the Smiths' entrance being delayed for 30 to 45 minutes. I don't recall much about their set – I mean it was good, maybe very good, I just can't remember the tunes, the high points, etc. I do remember running into a couple of friends and innocently asking what this new drug was called 'crack'!

### JOSEPH HUGHES, AGE 17

This was a concert venue just south of the Intrepid aircraft carrier museum, jutting out into the Hudson River. I was about to start college. I went with my best friend Steve and my girlfriend. It was general admission and we waited outside all night to get in. We ended up getting about 20 people back. I remember talking to some 'old' couple (probably aged 25 or so), who had seen their infamous New Year's Eve gig at Danceteria. Even in 1986, that was the stuff of legend. They were amazing. Craig Gannon played, and they sounded great. I remember some overheads for the backdrop, including tombstones for 'Cemetry Gates' It was an exhausting, sweaty, dramatic, unforgettable time.

### PIOTR ORLOV, AGE 17

Being a Smiths fan going in – I liked 'How Soon Is Now?' but had also just started listening to the then-new *The Queen Is Dead* – it's fair to say I was a little disappointed. They were very straightforward. The *New York Times* reviewed the show and said, 'The sell-out audience… sang along on most verses and choruses' and that, 'Onstage, Morrissey moved in a kind of ecstatic slow-motion – wind-milling his arms, wrestling with his shirt, twirling as if entranced. In songs that could teeter into self-pity, he maintained an intelligent, if troubled, dignity.'

### QUINN JOHNSON, AGE 17

I'm Afro American and originally from Philadelphia. As a teenager I went away to a boarding school in Connecticut from 1980 to 1983 and was exposed to a lot of seventies music – The Doors, Jimi Hendrix, Led Zeppelin, The Beatles. Around 1981, a friend came back from England and brought back UB40, The Specials and The Clash and I started going in that direction. That music just resonated with me, so when I graduated and went back home to a town outside of New Haven, there was a radio station that played quote, unquote the new wave music. But the only thing New Haven is known for is Yale University and the first hamburger. Other than that, there's really nothing there.

Going into high school in 1984 to 1986, I went to a lot of shows. It wasn't difficult to get to New York to see shows. I went to Live Aid as well. (When I saw the groups that were billed to play, I thought that some of the groups that were in London were actually going to be in Philadelphia!)

By '85, '86, I was in a clique, some of whom really liked David Bowie and The Clash and The Violent Femmes. The off shoot, the year behind me, were into Depeche Mode, The Smiths, The Cure and New Order. When *The Queen Is Dead* came out, we listened to it. 'Some Girls Are Bigger Than Others' and the way it starts out and then fades down and then comes back in is pure genius.

When I found out they were playing Pier 84 I got the tickets and two or three of us went. From the opening moment to the last, the fans knew every verse and they sang. I'd never seen any performer get as many things from the audience – flowers, books, anything – than Morrissey. He got so much love and so much gratitude. I was just totally floored by that. It was a total singalong from the first song to the end. I'm so glad I went, because they broke up after that.



### ANONYMOUS

It was a hot summer's day in Washington DC. The general admission audience had to wait outside for a couple more hours than usual, apparently because Moz didn't like the fence being so far from the stage.

I was at the very front when 'Bigmouth Strikes Again' started to play. Moz came right to where I was standing and suddenly reached out to me. I wasted no time and grasped his hand with no intention of letting go. People started to push and climb on me as I pulled Moz towards me. I pulled him off the stage and he went head in right in front of me. At this point, it was a frenzy. I managed to give him a kiss. Nothing crazy, just a friendly peck on the cheek. The guards came to pull him out and he scrambled to the back of the stage. The band finished the song and after a bit walked off the stage.

The crowd around me immediately erupted into chaos. I remember someone saying to me, 'It's your fault they'll never come back to DC, asshole!' But to my surprise, others were defending me. A brawl erupted and I ducked under the fight and ran to the back where my friends were. One of them said, 'Some asshole pulled Morrissey off the stage!' 'That was me!' I replied. My other friend immediately interjected, 'I fucking love you!' He said he was going to get me a t-shirt that read, 'I Stopped The Smiths'. I'm still waiting.

### LANA MENGES

In 1986 my concert buddy, Evan, and I got general admission tickets ($15 each) for *The Queen Is Dead* tour at the George Washington University's Smith Center. (Yes, it's called The Smith Center!) Since it was standing only, we arrived at the venue at about 10am and were around twentieth in line. It was miserable weather: sunny, 90 degrees Fahrenheit and humid, until the late afternoon thunderstorms drenched everyone and flattened our hair.

Andy Rourke, Mike Joyce and Craig Gannon were walking around outside chatting with fans after the rain stopped. Andy gave me a guitar pick, which I still have in a ziplock bag. By the time the doors opened (an hour late), we ran for the barrier at the front of the stage. Yes! Front row centre!

I didn't manage to stay there though. I finally felt too faint from the heat of the day and the crushing crowd and security pulled me (and others) out. I watched the show pretty far back from the stage, but it was still incredible. I wouldn't have

*Lana Menges' license plates*

expected it for The Smiths, but there was a slam pit (mosh pit in today's vernacular) filled with frenzied dancers during all the fast-paced songs like 'The Queen Is Dead' and 'Cemetry Gates'. My friend Evan managed to stay in the front row and had the show of his life.

## MUSIC HALL

### 11 AUGUST 1986, CLEVELAND, OHIO

### ROB LOGSDON

I remember spilling a pitcher of Guinness on my buddy at the pub before the show. I also correctly predicted the opening song, 'There Is A Light That Never Goes Out'. We had listened to The Smiths while in college so much during the previous two years that we were in tune with everything they were performing. Morrissey had a Jim Morrison-like presence over the crowd. He sometimes didn't look at the crowd and sang whilst lying on his back. Johnny Marr seemed to be in a zone. I don't recall ever seeing a guitarist that was so smooth. His style, with his incredible breaks and timing, mesmerised us. His sound is unmistakable and unduplicated.

## FULTON THEATER

### 12 AUGUST 1986, PITTSBURGH, PENNSYLVANIA

### LISA ANN BONOMO, AGE 18

I went with my best friend Beth and we had a blast. I knew about The

Smiths from alternative/ college radio and from reading *Smash Hits* and other UK magazines. We had an independent record shop called Eide's that carried a lot of UK imports, and I bought all of my imported vinyl there.

I have seen Morrissey twice solo and Johnny Marr once – I actually met him after the gig and he was lovely! I was in the first row in a small venue for the 2009 Morrissey show – he touched my hand and my friend Janice, who I didn't know was there just two rows behind me, got a piece of his shirt which she had framed. That was a great gig.

For the Johnny Marr gig we got there super early and it was all just standing room only, so we were right up against the stage. He is just so talented, it was just incredible to see him and then meet him. His son played with him, which is so cool.

### JOHN QUALLEY

I remember Morrissey being all over the stage. It was a very good performance. 'How Soon Is Now?' was incredible. I felt lucky to have seen it as they kind of collapsed after the tour. I definitely saw them at their pinnacle.

## ARAGON BALLROOM

### 15 AUGUST 1986, CHICAGO, ILLINOIS

### KERA BOLONIK

I was a rising high school junior when David, one of my oldest friends, called and told me he'd bought us tickets to see The Smiths for their *Queen Is Dead* tour. The

*Morrissey was happy to pose for fans pre gig (Lana Menges)*

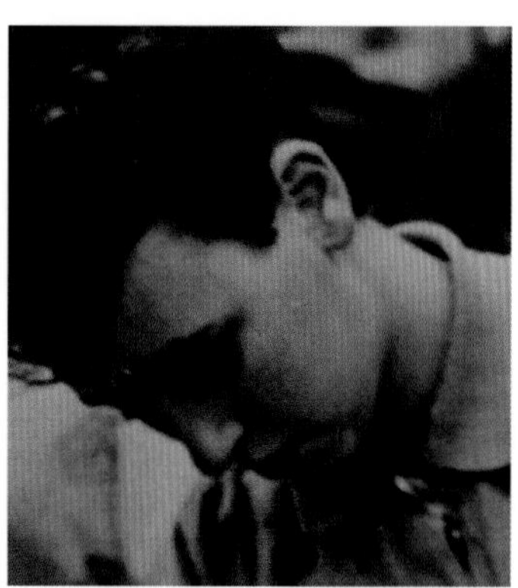

*Kera Bolonik was at the Aragon Ballroom*

Smiths were, for me, like the Prozac that didn't yet exist; I'd been in the grips of a powerful depression – heaven knows I was miserable then – and the misery of which the Moz sang, and with such candour, provided an ideal antidote.

There was only one issue: my parents. They forbade me from seeing concerts. They were overprotective and convinced that music venues were places where bad things happened. Sex and drugs and rock 'n' roll. In part this was because they had rarely been to concerts, and when they had they'd seen people pass joints, and they'd never smoked pot.

But they'd known David since he was three and they were friendly with his mother. He anticipated all my parents' issues, so he gamed it out. He bought my ticket so saying no would have been rude. He arranged for our ride to and from the venue. So my parents put me on probation for the three weeks leading up to the concert, scrutinising my every move and waiting for an opportunity to take away the privilege of my attending the concert. I'd never been so prudent and so well behaved in my life. That's how eager I was to see The Smiths.

David and I arrived early so we could stand as close to the stage as possible. A butch-lesbian folk singer named Phranc opened, singing songs about such things as physical education teachers she harboured crushes on. I'd never seen a performer sing or even speak so openly about same-sex desire. I was red in the face. Even though I didn't physically resemble her at all

– a femme clad in an Oxford shirt buttoned all the way up, clasped at the top by a vintage brooch, harem pants and Chinese slippers, my hair highlighted in bleach – and couldn't imagine pining for a PE teacher, I definitely identified with same-sex love, and was in awe of her courage in articulating it. I was not ready. My eyes were fixed on the floor.

The Smiths emerged about 45 minutes later. It felt like an eternity to us but was so welcome as the sounds of Johnny Marr's opening riff to 'How Soon Is Now?' enveloped the Ballroom. A doe-eyed young man rushed the stage with a bouquet of roses to welcome Morrissey as he came to the mic, segueing to 'The Queen Is Dead'. The Moz gave him a brief sly smile, took the flowers and proceeded to smash them against the left amp, then the right. The kid looked around with a mixture of horror and awe, not quite knowing how to react. Nor did David or me. I remember saying something to the effect of, 'Um, nice guy?'

The Moz was predictably surly, but then again that was his persona, it felt performative. They delivered an incredible performance, covering songs from the then-new album and many tracks from *Meat Is Murder*, *Hatful of Hollow* and the debut (we call it *Rough Trade* here in the States). They ended with an even more haunting version of 'Meat Is Murder', which resonated deeply with me at the time because I was a vegetarian for about five minutes.

I wish I could still fit into my *Queen Is Dead* t-shirt, then contraband in my parents' household and a reminder of that perfect night – an evening of communal sardonic sulking for me and an evening of anxiety for my parents, convinced it was the end of innocence. That would come years later.

### VIRGINIA DEVLIN, AGE 18

Seeing The Smiths live is something I brag about from time to time and a true highlight of my punk days. While the band started playing larger venues on that tour, the Aragon is a more intimate space. The concert promoters must not have been big Smiths fans, because the main floor was set up with rows and rows of folding chairs. As soon as the band started playing, and in a rather orderly fashion given the circumstances of a packed, sweaty room, we all started folding up the chairs and passing them to the back over our heads. I don't recall security intervening at all. It was inevitable – we needed to clear the floor to dance and sing our hearts out with Morrissey! At the end of the night, there was a huge pile of chairs in the back of the room.

### JIM JOLL

The '85 show wasn't 100 per cent sold out, but just one year later, The Smiths were much more widely known here in the States and Chicago, being a very progressive town musically, was ready for them. I procured tickets for myself and friends for the show and it was a complete sell-out. The band was equally amazing the second go around and I wish I'd had more opportunities to see them. I suppose that is a popular lament among The Smiths faithful. My favourite songs?

'Unhappy Birthday' and 'Vicar In A Tutu'.

### KEVIN WILLIAMS

The Smiths caught my ear at Metro, a Chicago venue with a smart bar downstairs. They were playing 'How Soon Is Now?'. I went out and bought the cassette. 'Reel Around The Fountain' took some getting used to.

### MARK MICHICICH, AGE 21

To this day, Morrissey and Marr inspire a hand-on-my-heart loyalty that I will take with me to the grave, impacting my life in a way only rivalled by the likes of Lennon or Bowie. They are amongst the greatest bands of all time, equals to The Beatles, The Clash… you get the idea!

I have old memories of hearing 'Hand In Glove', 'This Charming Man', 'What Difference Does It Make?' and 'How Soon Is Now?' on different mix tapes from friends. The first Smiths record I ever bought was *Hatful of Hollow*. I worked backwards from there, picking up the first album, the first two 1983 seven-inch singles and then all of the 1984 twelve-inch singles, including the different mixes of 'This Charming Man' and them backing Sandie Shaw.

I searched and bought up as much Smiths material as I could find – videos, magazines, books, you name it. I even sought out live recordings and Morrissey's book on James Dean. From *Hatful Of Hollow* on, I bought every Smiths record as it came out.

In 1984, I was a 19-year-old college student at the University

*Virginia Devlin took part in a mass movement - of chairs!*

of Illinois at Urbana-Champaign. I spent a lot of time in a student run concert organisation, Star Course, that promoted concerts on the college campus. The Star Course staff were all music fanatics, routinely hitting the local independent record shops like Record Swap to see if Charlie (AKA The Quaker) had put a Smiths single up on the new releases wall. We drove to other cities, especially Chicago (where I was from), to see shows we weren't able to bring to the college campus.

My first opportunity to see The Smiths live was in June 1985 at Chicago's Aragon Ballroom. I was 20 and with my girlfriend (now wife), Margie, and college friends from Star Course. I was intimately familiar with the set list but was surprised to hear Elvis' '(Marie's The Name) His Latest Flame' being mashed up with 'Rusholme Ruffians'.

The show was not sold out. I'm not sure the crowd even went much further back than the soundboard. It seemed like a gross miscarriage of justice. How could Chicago not fill this ballroom to see the most important band in the world at this moment in time? But those who were there were absolutely mad for them. My friend, Gwen, turned to me after 'How Soon Is Now?' and said, 'That was the pinnacle of human existence.'

My second (and last) opportunity to see The Smiths was back at the Aragon Ballroom in 1986. I had to miss work to see them and so told my boss that my whole family was going to my dad's college graduation ceremony after studying at night school for years. But I went to see The Smiths again, again with Margie and with friends from Star Course.

This time the Aragon was completely sold out. Chicago had made me proud and recognised *The Queen Is Dead* for the masterpiece that it was. I was intimately familiar with the set list, but they played 'Panic', which I heard for the first time that night. I also remember them playing 'What She Said' differently from the previous tour. This time it was mashed up with 'Rubber Ring'.

I was surprised that there was a fifth member of the band, Craig Gannon, on rhythm guitar. At first, I thought, 'One does not simply add a member to The Smiths. John, Paul, George and Ringo never walked out on stage with Larry.' But then I heard Gannon and had to admit that he did do a nice job filling out their sound live. Mostly I remember Morrissey just being Morrissey as only Morrissey can, frantically waving a giant 'Queen Is Dead' sign and beautifully singing songs like 'I Know It's Over' and 'There Is A Light That Never Goes Out'.

Leading up to the re-release of the deluxe version of *The Queen Is Dead*, each week iTunes released a live version of each track in order from a different night of the 1986 tour. 'There is a Light That Never Goes Out' was taken from my Aragon show. I was at that gig. Yes, I was there.

### RICH SCHUMANN

It started at 8pm and the ticket price was $13.50. (Boy, that's cheap now!) I went with my buddy, Tony

Schaffer, and we pushed our way up to the front. It got so hot in the place that stage security was dumping gallon jugs of water on people. I got soaked. A girl passed out and I remember seeing the bouncers carrying her in that area between the stage and the crowd. A bundle of roses was thrown on the stage, and when they played 'I Want the One I Can't Have', Morrissey beat those flowers over the front speakers, annihilating them.

Taking the bus home, we were freezing because of how wet we were from all the water that was poured on us due to the intense heat inside the building. My ticket is in such bad shape, with the ink almost all washed off it as a result of the water dumped on me that I had to use a pen and write all the information back on it.

STEPHANIE SNYDER, AGE 16

I was back from spending ten months in Ireland, where I had seen The Smiths in February. The Aragon is general admission and the custom for shows back then was to line up early to ensure the best spot at the gig. So, I got there at 3am. The next people to show up got there at noon on the day of the show!

My friends and I had been out there about twelve hours when we saw that there was activity around the back doors to the stage. People were lined up along the alley that separated the north side of the building from the public parking garage opposite. We could see people unloading and carrying things in at the point where the band would also access the building.

The stage was on the second floor of the building. My friend Sara and I, both 16, had successfully met musicians such as U2 over the previous couple of years. We decided we wanted to sneak in and try and meet The Smiths, and Morrissey in particular. We went up the back stairs where the roadies were moving in and out. The light was very dim.

The Aragon had ten feet high windows with heavy red drapes over them. No one really paid attention to us as they were busy setting up for the show. We ducked behind a curtain. Johnny Marr was on the stage doing a soundcheck. Sara and I whispered to each other, trying to figure out what to do.

Suddenly there seemed to be security everywhere. Then Morrissey passed near where we were and we bolted from behind the curtains to talk to him. As we got near him, a guy stopped us and was already saying we had to go but Morrissey said, 'Let them go,' and the guy did. We hugged Morrissey and he graciously hugged us back. He smelled really good. I feel bad for him because we had been hanging out in an alley for twelve hours and probably didn't smell so good! I gave him some horrible poetry I had written. He was lovely and then security had us go out the front doors.

The show was wonderful. I was up front on the barricade, and the crowd had me pinned against it, it was so full. Security gave us water during the show. When people passed out from the heat, we'd pass them over our heads to the front and help lower them to security so First Aid could help them.

*Paul Weiss' The Smiths Queen is Dead poster*

## PAUL WEISS

I was in high school. My older sister, who turned me on to The Smiths, took me to the show. I didn't have a camera with me, a mistake I would not make again. There was the longest line of fans waiting to get in; indeed, of the untold dozens of show I have seen there, I don't recall a line stretching around the building and block until years later, when Nirvana played there in 1993.

I remember standing in the crowd up close to the stage, with all these chairs on the floor that were later hauled off the dance floor and passed overhead one by one after The Smiths took the stage. I watched intently as a mysterious figure – Johnny Marr – played guitar in the back corner of the stage. He was almost hiding; he was so inconspicuous. It was incredibly tough to see him, and next to impossible to see his guitar fretwork, yet the sounds emanating from his guitar sounded like several guitars playing all at once.

I remember watching intently as Morrissey, who at that point was an almost-iconic figure – even before the internet and cell phones, when we had to get our information from fanzines and rock magazines – was flitting around the stage, gladioli sticking out of his back pocket. The strangest part of the show was Morrissey spending most of his time singing while lying flat on his back on stage; he sang many songs in that prone position.

From the cavalcade of guitar to Morrissey's *sui generis* stage presence, the first of dozens of Morrissey concerts I have attended, I have never seen anything like The Smiths, before or after.



## MIKE HEAD

The shows I saw in '85 at the Hollywood Palladium were just scorchers. They were on fire and these were some of the best concerts I've ever seen in my life. They were still a four piece then. In 1986 I saw them at both the Universal Amphitheater in Universal City, California and at Irvine Meadows down in Irvine, California. Those shows were good, but the audiences were on controlled substances like you would not believe. At Universal Amphitheater they were serving liquor to minors and one of them threw up right behind us. He was probably all of 14. At the Irvine show, there was angel dust going around. I do not partake in that stuff but there were a lot of people who did. And they were trying to climb up on the stage. Morrissey was really pissed off.

## TONY JASICA

What intrigued me about The Smiths was the intelligence in their lyrics. A perfect example is 'Cemetry Gates' when they talk about Keats and Yeats. I ended up going to our local library and reading up about John Keats and WB Yeats to decide which one I liked best.

I was going to college in Southern California and Los Angeles when my college girlfriend and I went to go see The Smiths. At the very end of the concert, Morrissey said to the audience, 'So everybody's here having a good time tonight?' 'Yeah, yeah, we're having a great time.' 'But you aren't having a great time because the security is doing their job. And they're not letting you come on stage – is that right?'

And everybody screamed, 'Yeah, right,' and so Morrissey, said, 'Well, I'll tell you what. Fuck the security and get up on stage right now.' And everybody stormed forward stage and we all ran on stage. I forget what song it was the band was playing. But you could hear the full band, and then, as more people got on stage, one of the guitars dropped out because people were grabbing the guitar, and then the drummer stopped, and then Morrissey stopped singing. Until eventually, there was nothing.

## MAGGY LIND, AGE 30

In 1985 I went on my dream vacation to Europe. I had wanted to go since I was a kid, and especially to England as I was a massive Beatles fan. My first stop was London, and I went to a Virgin record store, looking at albums. I thought they were a bit bulky to carry around Europe for three weeks, so asked the guy at the register for some 45 single suggestions. He handed me The Smiths' 'The Boy With The Thorn In His Side' and Depeche Mode's 'Shake The Disease'. I bought them both. I wasn't that familiar with The Smiths name but as soon as I played the single, I recognised the vocalist's voice and became a total fan!

In 1986 I got tickets for the Universal Amphitheater show from a ticket agency located in a department store. My seats were about halfway up the theatre so I could see the stage pretty well. I took my 28-year-old brother. He had not fully embraced the new wave/punk rock sound, as I had back in 1978, but he knew I was always looking to hear new bands, so he decided to go to the concert with me.

The concert was unlike any I had ever been to. This venue had excellent sight lines and there really wasn't a bad seat in the whole place, but everybody was on their feet through the entire show. I've seen a lot of concerts there, but usually people stand up during the encore, not for the entire show!

Morrissey was very dramatic, faux fainting and draping himself over the monitors and eventually on the floor of the stage. People were going nuts and I was blown away by his voice, which was so incredible, so original and one of a kind. He was just so unbelievably unique a performer. He was in his prime and he was magic. He had a vulnerability that was very appealing. I remember being very impressed by the band. They were right there with him and Johnny Marr's guitar playing was so memorable, he made his guitar sing! He's just a sonic guitar player. My younger brother was totally impressed and could not believe he witnessed this concert. We used to talk about it often. I personally will never forget it. The crowd was with him, and the band were with the crowd. It was a beautiful experience.

## IRVINE MEADOWS AMPHITHEATRE

### 28 AUGUST 1986, LAGUNA, CALIFORNIA

### KATHERINE RIOS, AGE 13

I went with my two older sisters. The Smiths went on at 8pm. The venue was an open-air amphitheatre and had a hard concert stop at 11pm. But they kept playing. The venue shut off the sound. They kept playing. It was incredible. Towards the end of the concert, before the sound was shut off, fans ran to the stage. I can't remember what song they were playing but the stage was full of fans. Morrissey was singing and a large breasted blonde was dancing and decided to pull her top down, exposing her breasts. Morrissey gave her a look of disgust and turned away from her. Johnny Marr just shook his head and kept playing.

### TYLER W STRINGER

Morrissey actually showed up then at gigs. To be honest, I don't remember if Johnny Marr was there or not by then. I was never really concerned with him. Once the guitar is established, any great player can mimic it, except for maybe The Edge. I was never the biggest Smiths fan. I like them, sure, but it was more for the girlfriend back then. I used to see Morrissey once in a while in Beverly Hills over the years. I always ran into him at Barneys. He shopped a lot.

## STATE UNIVERSITY OPEN AIR THEATER

### 29 AUGUST 1986, SAN DIEGO, CALIFORNIA

### MIKE MCGARY, AGE 22

The Smiths got airplay on our local radio station, 91x, from the beginning. I kind of lumped them into the bigger 'new wave' acts of the time. Once I actually heard *Louder Than Bombs*, I realised they were much better than their poppy counterparts.

I was 22 and with my then girlfriend. She introduced me to them when *Meat Is Murder* came out and I was an instant convert. She ran on stage, grabbed Morrissey and got a piece of his shirt. In those days it was primarily girls who rushed the stage. It was a great show on a beautiful San Diego summer evening. They are still my favourite band.

### TRENA BELK

I was front row centre. Morrissey gave me a long-stemmed red rose and held my hand for about 30 seconds. It was amazing! He was amazing! I can tell you he is a gentleman. You can see it in his eyes.

## COLORADO EVENTS CENTER

### 3 SEPTEMBER 1986, BOULDER, COLORADO

### SAM O'DANIEL, AGE 16

1985 was a watershed year for me. There was a lot going on for me emotionally and physically, and perhaps that's why the music from that year is so strongly embedded in my psyche. I think 1985 might be the best year for music, ever. I didn't discover *Meat Is Murder* until autumn of the year I started high school. There was a girl in one of my classes. She had teased-up dyed black hair and wore goth-style clothes and makeup, for which I'll admit to always having a weakness. I had a complete crush on her; she seemed so confident and cool. Some days she would take my spiral notebooks and write in them. Through some investigation, I eventually found that what she was writing were lyrics from *Meat Is Murder*. I was already a Smiths fan, having discovered *Hatful Of Hollow* while on a spring break trip with my friend earlier that year. Something in Morrissey's forlorn, pleading, aching lyrics connected directly to my adolescent brain. *Meat Is Murder*, with its clear anti-meat and anti-school / bullying / authority stance, both challenged me and drew me in further.

I knew the lyrics to a couple of songs before I knew the actual songs themselves, which helped me get more out of this album lyrically than I normally would have. When Morrissey starts a song with 'I'd like to drop my trousers to the world', you listen.

I don't recall that much of the show. We were pretty far back. They toured with a second guitarist and I just remember seeing them on stage and not being able to make out which was Johnny for a while. I've read that the band weren't very into it and that matches my recollection.

*Colorado ticket stub (Lana Menges)*

## LANA MENGES

I was so lucky to see The Smiths twice on *The Queen Is Dead* tour. The second show was in Boulder, Colorado at the University of Colorado's Events Center. We had seated tickets ($11 each) for this show, so there was no need to queue up. Three of us went a couple of hours before doors opened and hung around behind the venue, in a grassy area with a good sightline to the back door. Sure enough, eventually the back door opened, and Morrissey came outside by himself. We slowly headed over (so as not to scare him), had a chat and took pictures with him. He was incredibly nice and gracious.

The show that night was fabulous, and it felt like a totally different show from the one I had seen in DC a few weeks before. I wish I'd known at the time that it would be the last Smiths show I would ever see.

## MCALISTER AUDITORIUM

### 8 SEPTEMBER 1986, NEW ORLEANS, LOUISIANA

### ROY ANDERSON

In the winter of 1985, I had just started attending Birmingham-Southern College, a small, liberal arts school in Birmingham, Alabama. I had failed out of another small, liberal arts college, Millsaps. I was new on campus and looking for people to connect with other than some very button-down types I already knew. It's easy to identify the cool kids – the ones who were a little off the beaten path and into better music. I was introduced to a group of girls on campus who were obviously into that sort of thing, the Siouxsie eye liner being a dead giveaway. And it was through them I first heard 'Reel Around The Fountain'.

I had also been into a few English bands in high school like Aztec Camera and The Style Council. For people not so focused on the guitar, there may not be much crossover between those bands and The Smiths. But Johnny Marr was definitely channelling some Roddy Frame on that one. It's all about the major sevenths. And it easily drew me in.

This was just prior to *Meat Is Murder* being released Stateside. When that album finally dropped, a buddy and I went to the local record shop to pick up the vinyl. It was over for me at that point. I had become a die-hard Smiths devotee even though I was singing 'sun and air' rather than 'son and heir'.

In 1986, I had dropped out after a year at Birmingham-Southern to join a band and keep up my ill-conceived pursuit of musical greatness. *The Queen Is Dead* dropped and, pun intended, so did I. My drug of choice back then was LSD and some friends of mine and I spent a good twelve hours tripping our faces off and listening to that album on repeat.

The big news came. The Smiths were touring the US and would be doing a show in New Orleans, just a couple of hours away. I ended up getting tickets with my best friend's little sister, picked up some acid and made the trip. They played at McAllister Auditorium on the Tulane University campus, where I had also recently seen Siouxsie do an epic show on her *Cities in Dust* tour.

You couldn't get near the stage for the throngs of young gay men in their cardigans and fake horn-rimmed glasses. I was transfixed by Johnny Marr's guitar rig. He used Fender amps in the studio in the eighties, but live he was running through Roland Jazz Chorus 120s, monstrously loud solid-state amps. He had two of those, side by side, on stage and was running through a smaller unit as a preamp that I could never identify. And he was playing Rickenbacker 360s, the weapon of choice for Peter Buck of REM.

I remember being amazed by the backing tracks employed during 'How Soon Is Now?' and the beautiful backdrop projected behind the band during 'Cemetry Gates'. Being a meat eater, I remembered stepping out of the auditorium when the lights all went red and the moaning cow sounds announced 'Meat Is Murder' about to be played. It's not good to feel that guilty while you're tripping.

I remember standing there, jaw dropped, watching Johnny Marr's hands and being amazed at how simple it all looked as he played whilst knowing how difficult it is to actually do.

The coolest note about that whole Smiths experience back then was that one of the girls who introduced me to the band is in the 'How Soon Is Now?' video. Birmingham-Southern was on a trimester system where most students studied abroad for the month of January. She was in London for hers and was spotted on the street by a guy with a camera who asked her to dance for him, she in her way-too-big eighties sweater and Czech army field hat. She never met the band, and I don't think she ever even visited Manchester. It was just a random encounter that ended up being what it is.

That period in life, driving around on rainy days listening to 'William, It Was Really Nothing' and trying to make myself be depressed like any good Smiths fan would? Those were the best of times. Mopey yet sweet. And that concert memory, fuzzy at it is, is still a small peak in my 52 years.

Although the band had played to bigger and more enthusiastic crowds, the remaining four dates of the 1986 US tour – in Miami, Atlanta, Nashville and New York – were cancelled.

# CHURCH OF THE HOLY NAME
## 23 SEPTEMBER 1986, MANCHESTER, UK

### STEVEN WRIGLEY

'Shakespeare's Sister' had just been released, and we were out in this naff local restaurant in Saddleworth, where I grew up. Pat Phoenix, the cover star from the picture sleeve of the single, was at the next table with her actor partner, Tony Booth. I thought, 'I'm just going to nip home, get the single and she can sign it.' And then I thought, 'That's a bit naff. I can't do that,' so I didn't. She must have been fairly ill, because she died not long after, and then I was thinking, 'I really wish I'd got her to sign it.'

I was at university but it was the holidays. My dad was working at a hospital, doing a painting job on Oxford Road in Manchester, and I must have said I was bored because he said, 'Right, you can come and help me do this painting job.' The hospital was next door to the Holy Name Church on Oxford Road, and it was Pat Phoenix's funeral that day. So of course I'm going, 'Fucking hell, this is brilliant. My two favourite things – Morrissey and *Corrie*!' (UK TV soap opera *Coronation Street*).

That was one of the reasons I loved The Smiths and Morrissey, because those were the things that he was into – the sixties and the kitchen sink dramas and Albert Finney and all the rest of it. I was going out for ciggie breaks and I said to my dad, 'Everybody's arriving, so I'll be back in half an hour. I'm just going to watch to see if Morrissey's here, and the *Corrie* people.' We were stood at these barriers at the entrance to the church and Morrissey arrived. Next minute, all these other guests had arrived, and it was just about to start when they suddenly opened up the barriers and said, 'Right all you lot – inside the back of the church.' And I thought, 'Well, I'm not missing much. I'm only missing a bit of painting.' So I went in with my overalls covered in paint.

They had jazz bands and it was a real celebration of her life. I could see that Morrissey was quite a few rows ahead of me and I thought, 'How can I get up there? I know, I'll go and take communion. So, then I can walk around and if there's any spare seats where he is, I can go and plonk myself down next to him.' That was my plan. By the time I'd got round and done communion, coming back there wasn't anywhere. But I made sure I walked past him, right next to Morrissey.

Coming out afterwards I thought, 'I'll see where he goes.' So, we're coming out of the church and there were loads of Smiths fans outside by that time. They were filming people leaving the church and Julie Goodyear, who played Bet Lynch on *Coronation Street*, was being interviewed outside and I just walked past her straight across camera. On *Look North West* that night, you could see me going past. I wasn't thinking about the television cameras. I was just thinking, 'Morrissey, Morrissey, Morrissey.' He was outside and he wandered up the road, and he

signed a few autographs and stuff like that, but I didn't have anything with me.

I moved to London in 1988. The first thing I did was get a job application off to Rough Trade. After a few months I actually got a job in their distribution factory at King's Cross. Being a Smiths obsessive, I thought, 'Oh, Morrissey's still bound to pop in now and again.' I thought that even though The Smiths had finished and of course he did pop in a couple of times. By then everybody was a bit too cool for school at Rough Trade. But word got round that I was a big fan so every time he was in the building people would come and find me and go, 'Morrissey's in. He's upstairs. Go and hang round the doorway. He's going to be out in whatever time.' But I'd heard the stories of how he could be a bit dismissive and I thought, 'I don't want to spoil it.'

Jo Slee was still working at Rough Trade. It was her birthday. We'd been invited to her party, which was just a little pub in King's Cross. I was thinking, 'Morrissey will be coming to this which'll be great. This is my big chance to meet him.' One of the guys I knew at Rough Trade played in Luxuria, Howard Devoto's band, and they'd toured the states with Morrissey. He said, 'I know Morrissey. I can introduce you' and I thought, 'This is it!'

For some reason, we decided to go out at lunchtime and we got pretty drunk. All sorts went on at Rough Trade – drugs and all sorts, all day every day – so we were drunk at lunchtime. I don't think we did much work. And then at five o'clock we all piled down the pub and then about eight o'clock Karl, who played bass with Howard Devoto, said, 'Right, we'll all go to this party.'

By this time, I was literally paralytic. I think the excitement of it all was part of the problem. We were in this little club where this party was and Morrissey arrived. We were actually in the same little room. He had a Stetson on, and he was chewing gum and he looked really tall. He looked like a real pop star, whereas when I'd seen him in Manchester a couple of years before he was in his jacket and jeans and looking like he always looked. So we get a drink and we get another drink and then Karl says, 'Come on then, I'll introduce you.' By this stage I could hardly walk. So we went up to him and Karl said, 'This guy Stephen just wants to say hello…' and I took a step forward and was just about to shake his hand and say something when I almost tripped.

I staggered over to one wall about two metres away to hold myself up and then I pushed myself off that wall and went flying across the room to the other side and managed to just about stray upright. Then I staggered back to the back wall and just about made it back to Morrissey and fell on my knees at his feet.

All I remember is looking up and Morrissey was looking down at me with a look of utter disgust. I've never seen anything like it. He must have thought, 'Who is this absolute drunken person?' I said, 'hi' and he just walked off. It was the biggest anticlimax of my life. I was just mortified. Karl said, 'You're unbelievable.'

# THE QUEEN IS DEAD TOUR

*The Queen Is Dead* was promoted on the October 1986 UK tour, which comprised twelve dates. A thirteenth show (at Llandudno, on 28 October 1986) was cancelled after the Preston Guildhall show was cut short. Rather than gladioli, Morrissey's stage props now included a placard not unlike The Ramones' infamous 'Gabba Gabba Hey' banner, one announcing 'The Queen Is Dead' and another stating 'Two Light Ales Please'. He also waved a noose when performing 'Panic'. The Kilburn National Ballroom show was to be recorded by the BBC and later released, in truncated form, as the *Rank* album a year after the band had split.

## SANDS CENTRE

### 13 OCTOBER 1986, CARLISLE, UK

### DAVE NICHOLSON

I remember watching Johnny Marr. I loved his style and his Brian Jones haircut. I met Johnny in 2019 and told him I saw The Smiths in Carlisle – he couldn't remember playing there. I'll let him off with that one as it was 40 years ago. We were talking for over 15 minutes. I was with a friend and he said, 'How did you two meet?' She said it was years ago when we knocked about on scooters. Johnny asked if I still had mine and what model it was. He said, 'Oh yeah, Mani was into scooters,' and in my head I'm thinking, 'Mani, Stone Roses…'.

### LEONARDO MANFREDI, AGE 16

Carlisle does not feature greatly in the wider history of rock and pop. When bands announced their tour dates there wasn't usually much point rushing to see if Cumbria was anywhere on the itinerary. Quite simply, until the Sands Centre opened in 1985 there wasn't really anywhere with a meaningful capacity for them to play. In the spring of '86, I'd stood on the Sands stage as part of my school choir's performance of *Carmina Burana* – not exactly a precursor to dizzying hedonism and rock 'n' roll excess.

The Smiths coming to town generated a palpable buzz among my peers. These days, tickets would probably sell out in seconds online but back then it required the more analogue solution of going to the box office and handing over the cash. I was able to get a ticket with minimal fuss.

My first gig was Prince at Wembley Arena in August 1986, an awe-inspiring show. However, my ticket placed me half a mile away from the stage and it was hard not to feel a bit detached. It really didn't prepare me for the sound and the fury of a band at its peak and almost within touching distance.

There were many more devoted fans among the 1,800 in the room than me at the start of that night, but I felt determined to fight my way to the front, in contrast to my trip to Wembley. 'The Queen Is Dead', 'Panic' and 'I Want The One I Can't Have' offered a thunderous opening, although I was as overwhelmed by the crush behind me as much as the music in front. I lasted three songs, the bruises on my chest a testament to the ferocity of the passion in the room, before retreating to a safer distance halfway back. If there'd ever been panic on the streets of Carlisle it had moved indoors for a couple of hours, fuelled by Morrissey's 'Hang The DJ' placard, Mike Joyce's fierce drumming and Johnny Marr's bewitching, bewildering guitar. The obligatory stage invasions ensued, and I watched friends of mine attempt their own incursions, too breathless to join them.

A review of that night written by Dave Sexton in *Record Mirror,* pronouncing The Smiths 'probably the best band in Britain', included the prophetic lines, 'It remains the juxtaposition of Morrissey and Marr that makes the band (and undoubtedly will break them too) but now is their moment.'

Around nine months later the moment was over.

### GARY ROBINSON, AGE 16

This was my first ever proper live music gig! My mate who was 15 was doing the lights and gave me his AAA pass. Johnny Marr gave him his strings. Like the little fan boy I was, I brought a gift for Morrissey, a specially made mug that I had asked to be inscribed with 'Hang the Queen' with a silhouette picture of the Queen's head on it. Bit harsh I know! The shop refused but said, 'What if we put 'The Queen – Friend of the People' but cross out the 'r' so it reads 'fiend'?' My mate passed the mug and a note to Morrissey. I hope he appreciated it!

A few days later I went to Preston Guild Hall and was at the gig where the band were forced to cancel the gig part way into 'The Queen Is Dead' opener as Morrissey was hit by a coin and cut and taken to hospital. It ended up in a near riot!

### CAROLINGTON BROAD, AGE 16

It was the first proper gig I had been to. I remember seeing people climbing on stage and thinking I could get up there, so I made my way to the front. Carlisle Sands Centre is like a sports hall, so the stage wasn't very high. I got up and managed to get to Morrissey's side. It was all a blur. Years later, I found an article about the gig and through that was able to find actual footage of the gig and me dancing with Morrissey.

### DARREN WILKINSON

I didn't have too long to wait before The Smiths arrived in my hometown of Carlisle for the second time, in October 1986. Now 20, little did I know that this would be the last time I would see the band live and that less than a year later they would have split up. I remember they did 'Panic' and everyone just waited for the nod it makes to Carlisle, Morrissey whirling a noose around above his head.

Carlisle is not known for exuberant crowds. When I saw The Cult a few years later, Ian Astbury announced at the end of the gig, 'Thank you Carlisle, you have been shit. We won't be back', but The Smiths were in town, and this was different. The stage invasion during the encore was huge and thankfully didn't result in Morrissey taking the huff and walking off. And that was it: I never saw The Smiths again.

I have seen Morrissey a few times

THE SANDS CENTRE          290886
THE SMITHS      +    SUPPORT
MON 13 OCT 1986          EVENING
                          07:00
MAIN HALL
W  301  STANDING
MARTIN P CRAM/TON 716942
£6.50        INCL. VAT

*Carlisle Sands Centre (Peter Martin)*

since but it's just not the same; maybe I'm just older. I still get my fix by going to see The Smyths, a tremendous tribute to the real thing, several times a year. Each time is like a time machine where my mind is younger than my body. During a recent gig at The Ritz in Manchester I made the rash decision to enter the mosh at the front. It didn't end too well. One lyric sprang to mind, 'Does the mind rule the body, or does the body rule the mind, I dunno?' I have never tired of listening to The Smiths, probably never will.

## TOWN HALL

### 14 OCTOBER 1986, MIDDLESBROUGH, UK

### ANGELA LAMBERT

We queued around the old town hall ready for the crypt gig. I remember a lot of aggro at first in the mosh pit, although it settled down. Moz was as flamboyant as ever and whipped us all into a frenzy. I think he enjoyed taunting us. That night opened my eyes… to live indie music. Morrissey is a modern-day poet, and his lyrical genius transcends generations since.

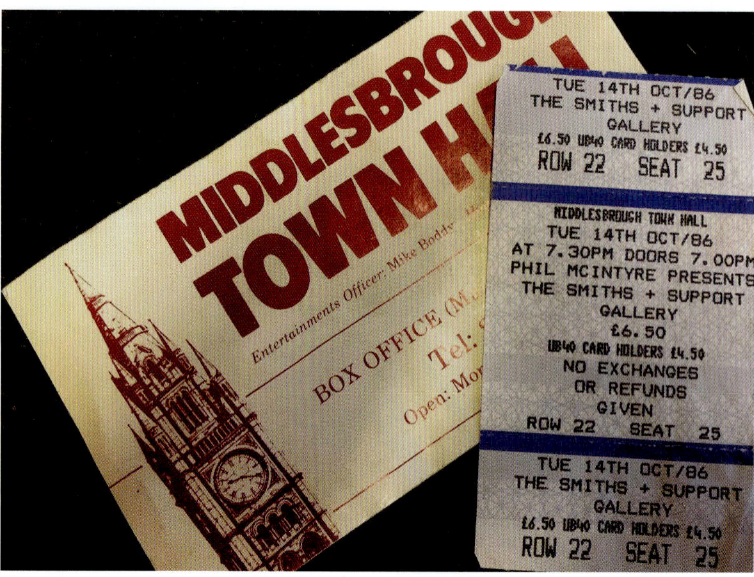

*Derek ended up at the front of the stage*

*Middlesbrough Town Hall ticket (Carl Hinde)*

### DEREK FARRELL, AGE 14

I ended up at the front of the stage despite having a ticket for the stalls. I did my paper round the next day in my tour t-shirt.

### MALCOLM GREENLEY

The Middlesbrough gig was the best I ever saw them. They were at their absolute peak live. They really were a strong unit with Craig Gannon. By then the notoriety and the controversy were well established. It was a few weeks after *The Queen Is Dead* went straight in the charts at number two so it was a charged atmosphere. It was a wild night, a really electrifying atmosphere.

### JENNY GAUNT

I fell under the spell of The Smiths from the beginning. I heard 'Hand In Glove' played on the radio and I was mesmerised. I fell in love with Morrissey's voice straight away. His lyrics took the mundane and made it glamorous. I would pore over all the music weeklies for releases, news and tour dates. I dutifully recorded all their TV appearances, which I still have on VHS.

I saw them on three occasions, all at Middlesbrough Town Hall. There was an unspoken bond between the fans, which is just as well because I was 16, clumsy and shy – too shy speak to anyone! Everyone came together on many levels and the other chart acts were irrelevant to me. Morrissey was also a fellow vegetarian, which gave me a meaningful connection.

At the last gig I attended, I remember a fan clambering down the velvet curtains from one of the boxes, pulling the curtain down with him. Devotional chaos reigned! Then, whilst ascending the stairs, Johnny Marr and Angie were coming down but I didn't actually meet him. I just grinned and he grinned back.

I am still going to Morrissey, Johnny Marr and Mike Joyce gigs. I have a large collection of vinyl, ephemera, t-shirts, posters and collectibles from over the years. Each piece tells a tale and 'it's time the tale were told'!

## CIVIC HALL

### 15 OCTOBER 1986, WOLVERHAMPTON, UK

### HELEN HULSTON, AGE 21

I went with my brother, his two mates and my sister, all of whom would have been 18 at the time, and my partner at the time and his friend from school, who were 21. I bought us all tickets and remember going to the telephone box to find out who wanted me to get them. I still have my ticket. It cost £6.50!

### NICK BARBER

I spent most of that gig near to the sound desk – I later picked up a video bootleg of the show, which seemed to have been recorded from the balcony. I was back at the Civic Hall for Morrissey's first solo gig but failed to get in – the venue was deemed full when I was about 30 people away from getting in. But I did see Morrissey arrive and he appeared at a side window to wave to those outside.

### CHRIS BUCKLEY

I was a diehard fan of Paul Weller and The Jam. However, after they split up in 1982 he disappeared up himself – I soon became disenchanted with The Style Council. Gone were the guitars and great lyrics to be replaced by keyboards and lyrics about long hot summers and being the best thing.

I first heard of The Smiths from the John Peel radio show in about 1983. When I saw them on *Top Of The Pops* with 'This Charming Man' I was hooked. I subsequently bought their LPs and played them to death. The media claimed Morrissey to be miserable and gloomy, but I found his lyrics laugh out loud funny and intelligent.

I managed to get tickets to the gig at Wolves Civic Hall and positioned myself on the upper balcony, awaiting the start of the gig. Suddenly the lights went out, and opera music played loudly for what seemed an eternity. Now this was different. The atmosphere was

*Tickets for Wolverhampton Civic
(Helen Hulston)*

now electric and there they were on stage launching into 'The Queen Is Dead', complete with Mozzer swirling a noose around on stage and doing his disjointed awkward dance. Song after song was played and I knew every song and lyric, and the crowd did too. Eventually the lights came on, and it was time to go home with my ears ringing and my body dripping in sweat. I've seen many bands since this gig, and none have ever come close – not even Morrissey solo.

### MICHAEL BUSHELL

My wife and I saw them twice, on both the *Meat Is Murder* and *Queen Is Dead* tours. We saw the latter at Wolverhampton Civic Hall. We sat in the balcony and watched the writhing mass standing below us. It reminded me of the snake pit in *Raiders of the Lost Ark*! Simply put, this was the greatest night of my life. If I'd been told this was the Second Coming, I'd have believed them.

We both remember the walls steaming as we came out (it was a cold night). They played for just over an hour and it was so intense I'm not sure we could stand any more. I've seen hundreds of gigs and some very great artists at the top of their powers but absolutely nothing came anywhere close to this. By the time they got to 'I Know It's Over' I thought I'd actually died and gone to heaven.

What amazes me is that when I talk to young music fans about what I've heard and who I've seen the number one thing I can tell them is what it was like to see The Smiths. As time moves on, they seem to rise and rise in the firmament of greatness and legend. That night in Wolverhampton is etched in my soul. The Smiths were way beyond just being a band, they were a reason to live. Seeing The Smiths live has never been surpassed as the highlight of my life. My wife would say the same.

### DAVE JONES

My then girlfriend and I were massive Smiths fans. We'd go to psychobilly gigs to see bands like The Meteors and The Guana Batz where the wreckin' (moshing) was violent and fierce, so we were prepared for a lively gig. The Smiths crowd was boisterous with fans climbing on to the stage to hug Morrissey. As the gig progressed, I launched Helen into a moshin' melee. We sang along to all the hits, danced, moshed, jumped around and finally, as we left, purchased a massive Salford boys club poster from a street vendor. It remains easily the best gig I have attended.

### JUSTIN WALSALL

They did two encores. I remember the 'Draize Train' being one of the songs.

### NICOLA WESTWOOD

The Smiths featured heavily in my teens, from that Friday night episode of *The Tube*, with the simpering introduction from the late Paula Yates, through to my doing extra shifts in my job as a cinema usherette to buy the first album. I felt I'd really found something, musically and aesthetically, that I completely got, and soon men's cardigans, shoes, old 501s and an insane quiff-and-plait combo, locked down with Elnette, was my daily garb, with the music of Morrissey and Marr being all I would listen too. I became 'that Smiths fan'.

I spent the summer of 1986 working in a bar in Sorrento in Italy, returned late August to Anita Dobson take on the *Eastenders* theme as number one, the sinking feeling I was back to school for last year of A levels soon and amazingly, to the news that The Smiths – my Smiths – were going to be playing at Wolverhampton Civic Hall, not 14 miles from my house.

Now this was a time where buying tickets meant queuing in real time and getting in line early, with no presales or suchlike, and I remember the bus journey, the box office, the four tickets I had. The four tickets that I effortlessly resold to friends – one simply invited because he had a car to get us there and back.

On the night of the gig, I wore a dress from Miss Selfridges, shoes from a shop in Liverpool, big black clumpy brothel creepers, a faded tan and a gold bracelet I'd spent my summer wages on. The venue was packed, heaving with teenagers. I remember passing comment on how cramped and chaotic it was and someone said, 'Wait 'til they come on.'

I'd like to say I remember the gig minute to minute but I don't. Luckily, my faded memories regarding atmosphere are filled with a YouTube video of the whole wonderful thing, from the infamous Prokofiev walk on music, to Morrissey's 'Heeeeelllo' to… the end. Hot, sweaty, a lost gold bracelet but an 'I was there' storyline that, even over three decades later (and despite everything, Morrissey!) still results in a 'lucky you' from those that know or knew what The Smiths meant at that time.

## MARK WILLIAMS

This was my favourite of the five concerts that I attended by The Smiths. Maybe it was also Morrissey's favoured venue as well, as he made his live solo debut here a couple of years later. The support act of the evening was a band called Raymonde who I was also a fan of. The singer caught me singing along with a couple of their songs and gave me a nod in the audience. When they went off, I necked a few pints as the bar ran along side of the concert hall.

I never usually drink at any gigs as a rule, so I got caught out slightly when the Prokofiev intro began and the band struck up 'The Queen Is Dead' and I still had a pint in my hand. The lager was quickly drunk,

and I was soon in the thick of it at the front of the stage.

The set list trundled along nicely with fans clambering on stage just for the slightest grasp of their heroes before they were led away. I was one of these folk. My first attempt at accessing the stage saw me unceremoniously pushed back into the audience, only for me to get straight back up and successfully hug Morrissey before security put a hand on my shoulder to lead me off stage. I walked off friendly enough with him, exchanging brief pleasantries until we got to the side of the stage, whereupon he gave me a push in the back as I ascended the narrow staircase down.

I landed at the bottom with no lasting injuries. But with my temper now riled, I was determined he wasn't going to have the last laugh. So I got to the front of the crowd and urged them to push me up for a third time, just as the introduction to 'Bigmouth Strikes Again' rang out around the venue.

The security man moved towards me again, but being a lad of quite a muscular stature, I told him in no uncertain terms what I would do to him if he laid his hand on me again. We came to an amicable agreement, and he let me stay on stage throughout the final song of the evening as long as I didn't interfere with their performance. Has any other fan singularly stayed on stage with them for so long apart from me?

Thankfully this concert was recorded for posterity by someone in the crowd, so you can witness me stage left and see me asking for Andy Rourke's plectrum at the end, which he graciously gave me. I also got hold of a set list, which I still have in my possession along with the Salford University one, which I acquired a few months earlier.

Poster for the Cornwall Coliseum gig in St Austell 1986 (Lee Trewelha)

## CORNWALL COLISEUM

### 17 OCTOBER 1986, ST AUSTELL, UK

### LEE TREWHELA, AGE 16

In some ways being a teenage Smiths fan in Cornwall was the epitome of what Morrissey was singing about – trapped and lovelorn at the arse end of nowhere. Cornwall in the 21st century – all hipster restaurants and TV fame – is far from the county of the eighties where there really was nothing to do. So thank heavens for the Cornwall Coliseum, a legendary venue, long since scat down (as we say in these parts) which boasted every artist of the time from Adam and the Ants to X-Mal Deutschland. You can imagine the joy of this flat-topped Smiths fanatic when the band played the cavernous venue at Carlyon Bay beach two weeks shy of my seventeenth birthday.

This was actually their second Coliseum appearance, having previously played there in June 1984. No I didn't, and I don't know why now, but I wish I had. Anyway, the 1986 gig is still ingrained on my psyche with added Craig Gannon on guitar and James Maker on stupid dancing. Morrissey strode on with his 'The Queen Is Dead' flag and there

followed one of the most sublime concerts I've ever seen.

Highlights were many, from the double opening whammy of 'The Queen Is Dead' and 'Panic' to the thrill of hearing 'His Latest Flame' meshed with 'Rusholme Ruffians'. Surely any Smiths concert which featured 'There Is A Light That Never Goes Out' – tossed away too early as the fifth song – 'The Boy With The Thorn In His Side', 'Meat Is Murder', 'Bigmouth Strikes Again', 'I Know It's Over', 'How Soon Is Now?' and 'Still Ill' has to go down in history? They even played my favourite, the steaming and storming 'London'.

I had to wait another 20 years before anything remotely Smiths-related returned to Kernow, when Morrissey played a solo show at the Hall for Cornwall in 2006. By this time, I was a reporter so how gleeful was I when he refused to play unless the daytime farmers' market in the venue removed all its meat. In fact, he bought it all and had it sent to a local homeless shelter. It's easy to forget now, but he could be loveable. It gave me a national story, and a memorable birthday stay in Cornwall for Moz, who still seemed on a high from his celebrations the night before.

### PAUL ASPLIN

I caught them twice on the *Queen Is Dead* tour. I was due to go backstage afterwards at St Austell but due to some issue with Raymonde and their dressing room the chance of a lifetime was cancelled. I remember James Maker appearing on stage. It was a chaotic evening. It was my first Smiths gig, and I spent it down the front. From what I remember there was a bit of a dressing room 'rearrangement' by Raymonde and the management were trying to sort it out, so my visit was called off.

Very annoying. Although not quite as annoying as getting an invite to appear in the 'Stop Me If You Think...' video and for a number of reasons not being able to.

### NICK BYRNE, AGE 17

Me and my mate Hag were big Smiths fans, and we saw them at Cornwall Coliseum in 1986. We were down the front, and it was amazing. There was a fantastic atmosphere of togetherness. They were a wonderful band, and it was a wonderful night which I will remember for evermore.

### MIKE CRAIG

Me and a mate drove down in an open top Triumph Spitfire. We didn't have tickets. My mate was in the army and had just got back. We went down and paid on the door. Coming out, the handbrake broke on the steep hill out of the venue, and I had to get out and hold the car while he got it back into gear and then jump in as he was moving.

### ROGER ROWE

My mates ransacked some poor sod's garden and sold the flowers in the car park because Morrissey had just been on *Top Of The Pops* with flowers in the back pocket of his Levi's.

### RACHEL SARA

I was in love with Johnny Marr and I took a photo and he saw the flash and waved at me!

## LEISURE CENTRE

### 18 OCTOBER 1986, GLOUCESTER, UK

### KATE ARNOLD

Still my best gig entrance ever. The drum intro to 'The Queen Is Dead' and Morrissey dancing in from stage left brandishing a placard with the title of the song on and – I think, although I might be making this up – a noose around his neck. I still see this every time I hear that intro. I enjoyed the gig, despite the fact that the acoustics in that hall were always – always! – piss poor, but the best thing was that their tour bus was blocked in in the car park and they hadn't been able to make a swift exit before we all poured out. The curtains stayed firmly closed for a while (and I don't blame them, because word got round pretty quick). But then Johnny Marr whipped back his curtain to wave and smile. He was with a lady – I guess it was his wife. Then he whipped back another curtain to show us a cowering – and unimpressed – Morrissey, with his glasses back on. I felt for him, I really did. Luckily for him, cars were moved and they were soon able to get away. He came back. I saw him there a few years later, around 1991.

### JUSTIN BURTON

I saw them a few times. Gloucester was amazing, and to this day I don't think there's a band lyrically that can beat them. Morrissey was a lyrical genius and Johnny Marr's guitar riffs are just amazing. I was

*Nick Byrne was there with his mate Hag*

14 or 15 the first time I saw them. Me and a great friend of mine, Andy Fox, went to several gigs, seeing The Smiths, The Cure and The Pogues. And U2 on the *Joshua Tree* tour at Wembley, with Chrissie Hynde and The Pretenders as the support.

# LEISURE CENTRE

## 19 OCTOBER 1986, NEWPORT, UK

### GREG ARCHER

This was memorable for all the wrong reasons. Some clown in the audience tried to pull Morrissey into the crowd. The band played a couple of instrumentals whilst Morrissey composed himself, but the announcement that he wouldn't be returning to the stage led to a riot inside the venue, ruining what should have been a magical night.

### DEBORAH PENHALLURICK, AGE 17

I got into The Smiths as an impressionable 16-year-old. I remember thinking how cool they looked on *Top Of The Pops* with Morrissey dancing around with bunches of flowers in his back pocket. It was just so different to all the pop in the charts at that time.

I bought the albums on cassette (I didn't get much pocket money). I'd spend hours in my bedroom listening to them. The tunes were so catchy, and the lyrics were so meaningful. I've still got *Hatful Of Hollow*. I don't know what happened to the others.

I had never been to a concert before, and my mum didn't want me to go. My older brother was a music fan and assured her there was never any trouble at concerts, so she agreed to let me go with my friend, Debbie Ascough. Well, the concert turned out to be pretty legendary as Morrissey was pulled off stage after a few songs, refused to come back on and a riot broke out.

I fixated on Johnny Marr. He was so cool – and still is! I can't remember how far on they got before Morrissey was pulled off but until then I was in awe of it all. The crowd was quite aggressive and intense. Halfway through 'The Boy With The Thorn In His Side', Morrissey shook hands with the crowd at the front and they yanked him in. He was down for a fair while before security got him out. He went off stage and the band kept playing. The crowd were chanting for Morrissey but after a while it became apparent that he wasn't coming back on. The aggression in the crowd intensified and all hell broke loose.

As a sensible 17-year-old girl I got myself out of there. I think we went home on the bus. I can remember being really disappointed that it finished early and didn't think much more of it. When I got home my poor mother was panic-stricken. There were no mobiles in those days and the news had reported 'a riot' there. I still love The Smiths music and still follow Johnny Marr. The highlight of my Glastonbury in 2019 was The Killers playing 'This Charming Man' on the Pyramid stage with Johnny. And, of course, Johnny's own set!

### TIM GAMLIN, AGE 21

I remember seeing them in 1983 at the Derby Assembly Rooms on an *Old Grey Whistle Test* special on TV. It was mad because the stage was full of fans. I had never heard of them so I thought I would check them out and after watching it that was it – I was hooked. I saw them live the following year in the student's union in Cardiff and again in 1986 on the *Queen Is Dead* tour in my hometown of Newport in Wales. After five or six songs, Morrissey was dragged off the stage. Then all hell broke loose.

### PHILIP HOLLEY

My wife and I stood at the back of the concert hall at the top of the stairs. We seemed to be waiting quite some time and then suddenly taped music began to build up and a bank of lights spun around to face the crowd. People started cheering and on came the band, followed by Morrissey. The band started playing and Morrissey began leaning out into the crowd, handing out flowers. Whether he lost his balance or was pulled, he tumbled into the crowd who immediately started crowd surfing him. The next thing I remember seeing is a roadie run across the stage and launch himself into the crowd. Unfortunately, he landed on top of Morrissey, and they both disappeared into the crowd. Several seconds later, Morrissey was thrown from the crowd back onto the stage. All this time the band continued to play. Morrissey was led from the stage by a roadie and the band played on and on and on.

An announcement was then made that Morrissey would not be returning to the stage and the band walked off. The crowd started booing and throwing things at the roadies as they unplugged the equipment, I'm not sure if the roadies retaliated but several of the crowd climbed onto the stage and started fighting with the roadies. Next thing I saw was the side doors open and police pouring in and moving people out of the auditorium. No refund was ever given.

Whatever happened to 'the show must go on' ethos? The big Jessie.

### DARREN JONES, AGE 20

I was really excited as my mate had seen them in Gloucester the night before and told me 'Meat Is Murder' was awesome. Legend has it that Morrissey was pulled off the stage as they came on and they refused to continue, but that's not true. They got a good few songs in before that happened – maybe 40 minutes – and then he was grabbed, there was a lot of argy bargy, and the lights went up and we realised that was it.

### RHYDDIAN LEWIS, AGE 20

I went with a few of my friends who unfortunately have passed away. The Smiths had not long come on when Morrissey slipped or was pulled off and fell into the crowd. He refused to come back on, and a riot then ensued, with speakers and drinks being thrown. That was when we left. The next day *The Sun* said the riot happened due to the name of the tour.

### ALLAN PETRIE

After Cardiff in 1984, I remember being on the dole for five months, playing darts in my bedroom and listening over and over to *Meat Is Murder* on vinyl on my little record player. Some of the lyrics inspired me to write poetry.

Around ten songs in, Morrissey was shaking people's hands whilst singing and was dragged to the floor and had to be carried off the stage. The band played an instrumental whilst we waited for Morrissey to return, and a guy came on stage to say Morrissey would be back on soon. Another announcement was made a short time after, and the gig was abandoned as Morrissey was taken to hospital.

I remember all hell breaking out. People starting throwing stuff and being jostled by the police, who were called as a mini-riot broke out. Later on, I met a girl from Gloucester who worked at a local hotel, and she got me each of the band's room cards with their names on them from when they stayed and played in Gloucester.

### MARCUS PONTING

The only time I got to see The Smiths the gig ended with a riot and with Morrissey in hospital. It was perfect until over enthusiasm on the front row caused a delay – they played The Fall during the break – and then cancellation. The riot then ensued. I bought a huge *The Queen Is Dead* poster and went home.

### JONATHAN JONES

He was touching hands with the crowd, and someone pulled him in. I think the riot started because of the announcements that were made saying the band would be back on shortly. I remember seeing a report in *The Sun* saying angry royalists had dragged Morrissey off stage and then rioted. They always have talked out of their arse. And it's still one of the best gigs I've been to!

### MATTHEW WILCE

Riot! Our love for The Smiths was gushing, like many at that time. Still is now, regardless of silly old Moz nowadays. Nice seat. No way am I going down the front for this one. I'm watching everything. Marr... jeez, you don't get this in Newport, Morrissey... the same. Rourke, Joyce? Wow. Take me back to dear ol' blighty... Drums kick in... fuck that, I'm off to the pit. 'Queen Is Dead', 'Frankly, Mr Shankly', 'Panic', etc., etc. Bliss.

Some dickhead pulled Morrissey in. Landed close by and looked a little bit shocked. Bouncers jumped in, got him out. Band played on. Three instrumentals, I think? Someone came out to tell us gig was over. Bottles flew, monitors were trashed. Newport was angry. We were done by some dickhead. It was still one of the greatest gigs I've seen and probably due to the notoriety, the most memorable. Long live The Smiths.

### ANDY WAINWRIGHT

I was there with my now wife. The band came on and played a stunning set for 20 to 30 minutes with Morrissey on top form. At the end of one number, he dived into the audience. The band seemed nonplussed, as if it was expected, and launched into an instrumental (possibly 'How Soon Is Now?'). Johnny Marr kept the band going with further instrumentals. After what seemed like an age but could have been just a short while, and with no sign of Morrissey, they left the stage. The lights came up and it was announced that Morrissey had been injured and the concert would not be continuing. I seem to recall a general feeling of deflation and there may have been some jeering.

Upon leaving, it was noticeable that there was a large police presence outside. I suspect they were expecting angry punters, but I can't recall anything untoward happening.

## 'ASK'

### RELEASED 20 OCTOBER 1986

*'Ask' reached number 14. Craig Gannon claimed credit for the chord structure.*

## ROYAL CONCERT HALL

### 21 OCTOBER 1986, NOTTINGHAM, UK

### JOHN GOODWIN

The sound was powerful with the addition of Gannon, but he was a supporting player and never a real member of The Smiths. I bought a peachy/pink t-shirt with a boy sucking on an ice-lolly.

### ADRIAN KEELING

After seeing them in Sheffield in January 1984, I bought everything – record, import, etc. – I could find and afford. I ended up at Nottingham Trent Poly and they were playing the Royal Concert

Hall there in my first week. A mate on the course asked if I wanted to try and get tickets, so we went on the day in the afternoon and got some returns. It was a great gig. The video is on YouTube, filmed from behind the stage so you can see a lot of the audience. A couple of girls danced on stage at the end and we saw them in town the next day and ended up spending most of the afternoon with them.

### JACKIE NUTTY

I had been obsessed with The Smiths for two years by the time I purchased tickets to see them. I'd seen a few other bands at the Royal Concert Hall in Nottingham, but it was an all-seater venue you wouldn't normally associate with a band like The Smiths. The atmosphere that night was what can only be described as charged, something I'd not experienced before.

Most of my friends were obsessed with Morrissey, but I'd always been more interested in the stylish guitarist Johnny Marr, and with my hero just a few feet in front of me I was transfixed in awe at both his musical ability and also his effortlessly cool style.

With the passionate performance from Morrissey and the steady heartbeat and pulse of the percussion of Mike Joyce and Andy Rourke, the melodic, euphoric riffs of Marr were just rapturous.

Towards the end, during 'The Boy With The Thorn In His Side', some people in the first few rows decide to invade the stage and I decided this was my only chance to share the stage with my heroes. What could possibly go wrong?

*Ask*

With trepidation, I put my foot on the chair in front of me, lost my balance and grabbed the nearest thing to me to break my fall. I looked up in horror as I saw the thing I had grabbed to stop my fall was – Johnny's foot! I swiftly let go and ended up in an ungainly heap on the floor. Not exactly the cool impression I'd intended to make.

It'd be 27 years before I came face to face with Johnny again. When the time came and I met my hero, I kept quiet about my failed attempt at a stage invasion.

# NATIONAL BALLROOM

### 23 OCTOBER 1986, KILBURN, LONDON, UK

### ANDREW MALTMAN, AGE 31

Suddenly they seemed to be all over television. On other shows such as *Top of the Pops* and the *Oxford Road Show* they had mimed early singles, but in 1984 *The Tube* featured The Smiths performing 'Hand In Glove', 'Still Ill' and 'Barbarism Begins At Home'. They played live and their true capabilities shone out bright and clear.

In 1985 I was lured into a London-based band on the promise of a gig at the famous Marquee Club. We settled on the name Black Cillas and began playing regularly at the Bull and Gate in Kentish Town. We got a couple of reviews in *Melody Maker* and *NME*. Our sound was heavily based on what is now termed jangle pop ('the sound of 86') and it was hardly surprising when we were compared with The Smiths, either favourably or unfavourably.

I used to go to gigs with our bass player, Ben Bartlett. We saw such bands as The Fall, The Cramps, Iggy Pop, etc. There was a bit of a rush for Smiths tickets when they played Kilburn National Ballroom in '86 but we somehow got lucky.

My diary records the venue as being 'grossly overcrowded and taking ages to get back out via inadequate stairs/exits'. The reward was seeing the five piece version of The Smiths going full tilt. The second guitar seemed to give them more of a huge wall of sound rather than any extra dimension but that probably had more to do with the acoustics and sound system at the venue. (Ben and I both thought the PA system looked a bit undersized.)

Morrissey surprised me when he first walked on stage. I'd expected him to politely mutter a few brief greetings, but he barked a very deep "ello" at the audience. They launched into a powerhouse set and played all their crowd pleaser numbers toward the end of an exhaustive 90 minutes. No one went home disappointed.

### STEVE BROWN

My mates Kev and Lee, the Haçienda members, now had a band together called Soil. Their drummer lived in Stretford and was friendly with a band from around there called Easterhouse, who were apparently friendly with Morrissey and/or Johnny Marr, so Soil ended up getting a gig supporting The Smiths at Kilburn Ballroom. Me and a couple of other mates jumped at the chance to be roadies, so we all went down to London in the archetypal battered Ford Transit. We were in the support band's little dressing room when we heard The Smiths were soundchecking. A couple of us went out to have a look.

It was a typical boring soundcheck – 'one two, one two' – and endless banging on the bass drum. Morrissey was stood in the hall a few yards in front of the stage, watching the rest of the band do their thing. I was in a band myself throughout the eighties and always carried a demo tape around. This was a chance I couldn't miss! I walked over, legs shaking, and said that we wanted to support The Smiths as well, and gave him the tape. I felt guilty about intruding on him, but he didn't seem bothered. He was exactly as he came across in TV interviews, a little bit inscrutable; he said, 'Well I'll certainly give it a listen,' in that polite, vaguely arch way, head slightly on one side. I don't think he recognised me from the Salford stage, but if he did he didn't say so!

I was desperate to tell him what a hero he was and all that, but I thought he'd probably have heard that stuff a million times before, and I didn't want to start gushing. When time came for Morrissey to soundcheck, a roadie politely told us to make ourselves scarce. We never heard anything back about the demo tape. I wonder if he's still got it or whether it went straight to landfill?

I was privileged to be given the job of operating Soil's slide projector on stage, projecting pictures of completely random things such as parsnips, Kev's cat (Henry), etc. onto the backdrop behind the drums. Before Soil went on, I crept onto the side of the stage, stooping and trying not to be noticed. I'd been going to gigs since I was 14 and always stared at the roadies doing whatever technical jobs, a little bit awestruck. Now I glanced around and realised that hundreds of people in this big, elegant theatre were looking up at me on this huge stage under the lights. I was desperate to just stand up and look back at all of them and take all of it in, but I had a job to do, and I was supposed to be inconspicuous, so I restrained myself. There were a load of BBC vans outside when we came out after the gig. They'd been recording it, and a few months later it was released as the live album, *Rank*.

We stayed the night at Soil's singers' parents' house in Essex. Driving there in the early hours, I was in the back, sandwiched between the amps. We were going round a roundabout somewhere east of London when one of the back doors of the old, knackered Transit flew open and the snare drum, which Soil had borrowed from another Stretford band called The Valentines, went rolling out into the road. I shouted, 'Whoaah – pull over!' Whoever was driving did a U-turn and as we were going back round the roundabout a car in front of us stopped, the door flew open and an arm reached out and pulled the upended snare drum into the car, and the car shot off! There was no way the Transit was catching up, so all we could do was swear loudly in profuse disbelief. I couldn't help stifling a laugh. Fortunately, I didn't have to pay to replace it.

I wasn't too surprised when The Smiths split up a few months later. As far as a fan like me could see, they always seemed too honest and true to themselves to be dragging the band on past its peak. I admit to feeling very slightly betrayed when they got a second guitarist in. Nothing against Craig Gannon, I actually became friendly with him a year or two later when Lee and Craig both joined a sort of Manchester super group called The Cradle, and then my band played on the same bill as Craig's next group, The Family Way. He was a really nice guy.

But you know how it is when you're young and a band you've grown up with, and feel very close to, changes the magic formula; you take it a little personally. Anyway, when *Strangeways* came out, although I thought I'd now left The Smiths behind, I couldn't hold myself back and I bought it out of a burning curiosity. I was glad I did; it's brilliant basically – the tunes, the savagely funny lyrics. I almost want to say it's better than the first album, but that first album occupied a magical moment in my life.

In my reckoning they went out on a high and left a fantastic and important legacy. It must have been '88 when I was in the Haçienda on one of those great Thursday student nights, the place now pretty full and on an upward curve. The mix of funk, hip-hop and indie halted for half an hour while the deejay played back-to-back Smiths. There was a crowd of younger people, the lads with hair shaved at the back and quiffs at the front, and wire-framed glasses, going mental. Apparently, it was some sort of organised trip to Manchester for Smiths fans, possibly from somewhere in Europe. I stopped dancing and just soaked up the music.

What made me really happy was about 25 years later, when my oldest son got into The Smiths at around the age of 15, totally unprompted by me. One of my younger sons also started listening to them a couple of years later; they were on their own journeys of discovery and I envied them; they were hearing all that stuff for the first time. Discussing the music with the two of them gave me quite a buzz, and made me remember how special that music was to me.

### STEVE CATTERALL

I had never been to the National Ballroom in Kilburn before, so I had no idea what to expect with security and hall layout. But I wanted to try and film all three of the London dates, so I brought my camera along anyway. I went up to Paul's place in Kentish Town first, and we went across to Kilburn together. The hall was on the High Road with the entrance on a corner. It looked like an old concert hall. We hung around outside on the street, watching as the people filed in to see what security was like. It didn't look good. Everyone was having to show their tickets as they first entered the building and then they were frisked. We waited for quite some time, hoping that somehow things might get a bit more lax as we got closer to show time. Eventually there was no time left, so we made our move. I handed in my ticket and flashed my out-of-date Access All Areas pass – and they waved me through without blinking. I'm starting to believe this pass will always work… I shouldn't worry so much about it.

But now there's not much time before the show starts and I've no idea where I can film from. I go upstairs – the balcony seems the best bet. It's a big D-shaped balcony, with seats all around. Most people are seated, but there are already a number of people loitering at the edge of the balcony. There's an aisle right down the middle and some space down at the front. The lights go down and the 'Romeo And Juliet' intro starts up. We dash down the aisle to the front and squeeze into a space. I'm almost dead centre and in a pretty much perfect position to film, although there's nowhere to easily rest the camera, and there's a fair bit of jostling. But there's no time to worry and out comes the camera and on it goes. I start filming just as the intro to 'The Queen Is Dead' starts up.

It's not a bad film. A bit shaky at the start and there's a lot more of just straight shots of Morrissey. The filming position I had gave me a great view, but wasn't ideal for handling the camera – it wasn't always easy to see the viewfinder without the picture shaking, so I tended to set up a shot and try and keep the camera steady for as long as I could. This meant that the film doesn't follow the action as well as some of the other ones.

The show itself was good. London dates are always a bit funny, as there's an element of 'come on, impress us' in the crowd, which you don't tend to get outside of the capital. So the crowd tend to hold back a little. But as Johnny said, there hasn't been a bad Smiths gig, and this one has its moments. Morrissey is on good form with his between-song comments and there's a great version of 'I Know It's Over'.

### ROBERTO FERDENZI

I saw The Smiths play live three times, all in '86. I saw them at the Kilburn National Ballroom, the following night at the Brixton Academy and finally their last ever live gig at the Brixton Academy. What more can l say other than that they were the best three live gigs l have ever seen – just magical. I couldn't believe l was seeing my musical icons and heroes in the flesh. The memory of those three shows will live with me forever, especially the first one, as this was the very first live gig l ever attended. The third one turned out to be their last ever gig, although, no one knew this at the time.

## BRIXTON ACADEMY

### 24 OCTOBER 1986, LONDON, UK

### ANDREW FURTEK

There was no support band, just what seemed like an eternity of George Formby. Then the band came on. I've been to many gigs, but this gig was – and still is – the best I've ever been to. They were incredible live, with such power, poise and passion. It was mesmerising. I'm so glad I saw them. They split soon after.

### KELVIN BILLING

I loved every minute, from 'Why Don't Women Like Me?' by George Formby and then the volume turned up for Prokofiev before they came on. It was just pure energy, with a writhing mass of bodies almost in one. At times you could take both feet of the floor and still be carried around in the mass. My only disappointment was that they didn't play 'Barbarism', but it is an evening I'll never forget. The year 1986 seems so long ago.

### TIM MARTIN

I still have the ticket stub. They came on to 'Take Me Back To Dear Old Blighty'. For 'Hang the DJ' ('Panic'), Morrissey had a noose spinning above his head. There were flowers in the back pocket. I think the album was a big influence over me. It changed my mood. For those two hours I really thought I was at the centre of the world.

### DAVID BEARDMORE

I saw them at the National in Kilburn, which was recorded as the *Rank* album, and two or three times at the Brixton Academy, including their last ever gig. I also saw them at the Hammersmith Palais and at the Free Trade Hall in Manchester. I remember seeing 'Hand In Glove' on *Top of the Pops*. It was like seeing David Bowie playing 'Starman' ten years earlier. That was a major moment.

I was 15 then. I think the first single I got was the seven inch 'Hand In Glove'.

I was going to loads of gigs. I probably went to a gig once a week ever since I was at college. I moved to London when I was 18 and spent all my working life in London. In Manchester I used to go to lots of gigs in the early seventies – some heavy rock stuff like Deep Purple, Wishbone Ash, Yes, Emerson, Lake and Palmer and all that kind of stuff. I saw David Bowie on the *Ziggy Stardust* tour at the Hardrock in Manchester before he 'killed himself' at Hammersmith, which was one of the most amazing gigs in my life.

I don't know what it was about The Smiths that attracted me to them. They just sounded great, you know? Great lyrics. I always found them very funny, and I liked all the artwork with all the northern aspect to it. Two or three of us used to go to gigs. We went to Brixton Academy and when we got inside the auditorium there was a guy selling spliffs quite openly for a quid: 'Do you want to buy a ready-rolled spliff?' They were always very raucous gigs. But never much more than an hour.

We had seats at the Free Trade Hall. That was a very bouncy gig. I was sat next to a younger couple and someone came on to do 'Hand In Glove' with them. The girl was saying, 'Who's that? Who's that?' And of course it was obvious to me. It was Sandie Shaw!

## LONDON PALLADIUM

### 26 OCTOBER 1986, LONDON, UK

### ALAN HAMMETT

The last time I saw them was at the London Palladium. They were now a five-piece with Craig Cannon joining. This seemed to give Johnny Marr even more confidence, as he seemed to be dancing and smoking more on stage. And Morrissey had his props – the rope for 'Hang The DJ' from 'Panic' and his 'The Queen Is Dead' placard. They both seemed to be having a lot of fun on stage, and they were sounding better than ever. But only nine months later they'd split up although they did leave us with another great album in *Strangeways, Here We Come*. It was a shame they didn't get to tour this live!

## PAUL WHITE

Sadly, my ticket has long since disappeared but not the memory of the gig. Nor the excitement of the first day of each single release to see what the cover pic was.

## PETER MARTIN

The final time I saw The Smiths. Obviously, I didn't realise this at the time. We drove down to London and spent most of the day trying to get tickets. We thought Johnny had let us down so managed to get tickets from the people hanging around all day. Then when the Palladium opened, we were told that there were four on the door for us. Much to their surprise and joy, we gave our tickets to the people we'd met during the day who hadn't managed to get sorted. An all-seater venue was never going to be the best, but Morrissey was on top-form, and it was good to actually watch the boys perform rather than spend the whole gig just trying to stand up and breathe, as a lot of the previous ones had been about.

After the curtailed performance at Newport in South Wales, the Preston Guild Hall gig saw the fans getting less than they'd bargained for.

## WILLIAM SMITH

It's the tail end of *The Queen Is Dead* tour and The Smiths, now a quintet, having added 20-year-old second guitarist, Craig Gannon, to their rank, are playing the last of three consecutive London shows at the home of variety entertainment. After Kilburn and Brixton (they started north and travelled south), the mouthiest (and best) group in the world have finally made it to the West End, treading the same boards as the Beatles and the Stones, Cilla Black and Gracie Fields, Jim Dale and Frankie Howerd, Cliff Richard and Tommy Steele. Morrissey and Marr. Rourke and Joyce. And what a song and dance act they've become.

Maybe The Smiths – dwarfed beneath the recumbent Alain Delon backdrop – are trying too hard to rise to the occasion. The recruitment of Gannon

*Peter Martin had to collect his tickets from the box office*

on additional guitar is a mixed blessing; he relieves maestro Marr of his more mundane rhythmic duties but also allows his superior a freedom to roam somewhat unchecked through the boisterous rallying cries of 'The Queen Is Dead' and 'Panic', almost throttling songs like a man possessed of the urge to thrill, kill, or just rock out. Morrissey hides behind shades and a Queen Is Dead placard before casually swinging a noose aloft.

There was always a tension at the heart of The Smiths, perhaps exemplified by 'I Want The One I Can't Have' and 'Vicar In A Tutu' where tragedy and comedy co-exist. Pathos and harmony win out as 'There Is A Light That Never Goes Out' soars like a comet to the stars. Morrissey, either still ill or choked up, says little but remains a teasing agent provocateur. He seems to have abandoned the sensitive, pitiful persona of a man in torment for a new, improved one of strength and defiance, probably fortified by the slings and arrows (or glasses and hearing aids of yore). His comic philandering with members of the crowd during 'Ask' - he bumps and grinds, hips and limbs oscillating wildly - causes some to swoon, and it's a wonder he's not consumed by the arms reaching for some sort of unholy communion. Is there something you'd like to try?

Hurriedly, 'Rusholme Ruffians' emerges like a demon child from the shadow of 'His Latest Flame', as Rourke, Joyce and the new kid play roughly along at the behest of their increasingly vociferous conductor, Marr. The devoted congregation relish their supportive vocal role throughout the joyous 'Boy With The Thorn In His Side' and the heart-stopping 'What She Said/ Rubber Ring' medley and it's only when the chilling intro to 'Meat Is Murder' and a crimson spot hits the stage, does an eerie quiet descend. A chilling protest song, as magnificent as it is melodramatic, The Smiths most eviscerating moment becomes a haunting echo chamber as ghastly squeals and heifer cries strike horror in our hearts. You can't say no to beauty and the beast.

Slowly, The Smiths carry 'I Know It's Over' to its glorious finale as the connection with their recorded glory is made. If sometimes tonight bears more relation to a battle for rock supremacy than is good for some songs' emotional heft, witness the coruscating encores, 'How Soon Is Now' and 'Bigmouth Strikes Again', and know The Smiths have the capacity to shock and shatter in equal measure, uniting hearts and minds, body and soul in one almighty spiritual experience. Sometimes you get an ecstatic, devotional exchange of hugs and flowers and sometimes it's an exorcism. Either way, it's thrilling. And we'll probably never see them again.

## GUILD HALL

### 27 OCTOBER 1986, PRESTON, UK

### MARCUS PARNELL, AGE 22

I got a call on the day of the gig at about five o'clock off a friend who's no longer with us, Gary Barton. His mother worked in the box office at

*Carl Hinde's London Palladium ticket*

the Guild Hall. His mum had sorted us out a couple of passes, in return for which we had to watch the fire escapes to make sure people weren't opening the doors to let their mates in. I'm pretty bloody sure it was sold out and that there were a lot of people milling around outside and trying to sneak in. And lo and behold they were on – and they were off and it was all over before it began.

I didn't see what had happened. People said it was a two pence coin that had been cut down. I am not 100 per cent whether he got hit by anything. There was a lot of confusion about whether he was going to come back on again. About 20 minutes later, we got the announcement that they wouldn't be coming back on and that was it. Everybody was up in arms. There was lots of booing, and fire extinguishers were let off. But the lights were all up and that was it. Gone. Finished. Done.

People went around picking up ticket stubs off the floor to get the money back. I've heard stories since that they'd been at the Guild Hall in the afternoon, then gone back to the Midland Hotel in Manchester and been signed up to do some big American tour, and they didn't want to do the Preston show after that.

## LEN KENNEDY, AGE 18

I was 18. The Smiths were, quite simply, everything to me. My clothes, my hair, my music, my films, my books – all on prescription from Morrissey. For some reason, Liverpool was omitted from *The Queen Is Dead* tour. This was odd as The Smiths had always had a great relationship with the

city. And it meant a trip to North Wales or Preston for me and my fellow Smiths acolyte, Kenny. Either way we were going to miss the last train home. But who cared? A night sleeping rough would be worth it for the euphoric evening of Smiths that lay ahead...

## MARK BICKERDIKE

Absolute madness ensued for at least a minute or so when the intro music stopped. The next thing we knew the band had walked off stage, never to return, Morrissey (apparently) being the victim of an item thrown from the crowd. I was absolutely gutted. It was made even more uncomfortable by having to suffer the support band Raymonde.

## CAROLINE ALLEN

Morrissey went off after the first song. This was a big deal for us because we were only 16. We didn't travel very far and we'd gone to Preston, which seemed like miles away to us at the time.

But we thought, 'We want to see them again', and we'd heard that this other gig had been cancelled so we didn't even know if it was going to go ahead.

We got front row position again, and it would have been just brilliant because, if he hadn't have gone off, it would have been the perfect gig. Because we had a brilliant spot and we weren't too crushed and we had just a brilliant view. I don't know to this day what it was that hit him. But he wasn't coming back on.

People say it was a coin. I don't know. When he went off, we thought, 'There's no way he's going to go away for good. He'll come back on.' And he just didn't, and we were absolutely devastated. We were absolutely gutted.

The crowd were really shouting and were getting quite angry. The atmosphere definitely took a turn for the worse when he didn't come back on.

### AJAY SAGGAR

Having seen the band perform live from the start of their career and grow artistically and in popularity, the feeling that was generated at shows was that of a gathering of the masses belonging to a cult. It was a not-so-secret-anymore society, but one that still strongly bonded the attendees, and who greeted each other with a knowing nod, acknowledging the fact that *they* knew!

The pubs around the Guildhall were filled with mostly lads (and a small smattering of lasses) who had come out of the woodwork from every part of the northwest. The Manchester crew were there, as were the Liverpool lads, the Burnley and Bolton lads and, of course, the Preston gang. But everyone was part of a larger whole, the northwest united by a northwest band. And not just any other northwest band. They were the truth, the way, the life.

Inside a packed Guildhall, as the pre-show music played, we all hustled for a place near the front of the stage. But that meant piling through hordes of people who had the same idea about where they wanted to stand. The whole crowd resembled a football crowd standing at the home end on old school terraces… swaying from one side to another. At about 8.45pm, the lights dimmed, and the crowd, already dizzy with anticipation verging on hysteria, erupted. A frenzied and passionate audience simply fell for the poetic touch of the 'Romeo & Juliet' theme (for the band were a band of poets) and shouted even harder for their heroes to appear.

Three minutes later the band walked onstage, with Morrissey brandishing a large billboard with 'The Queen Is Dead' written on it. The drums pounded in hard, and everyone knew that was the introduction to the album's title song, 'The Queen Is Dead'. Like a match being thrown into a barrel of kerosene, the audience exploded. WE ALL KNEW! We were a part of the whole! We sang along, we danced, we swayed within the football crowd. The rush was overwhelming. The power generated was intoxicating. And then suddenly the vocals stopped, as we continued singing.

The band played on. I looked up at the stage, and only a brief few minutes after the set had started, I couldn't see Morrissey! Bizarre. But we were swept along in a tidal wave of exuberance and assumed it was all okay. But then the band stopped. And they walked offstage. Confusion. The audience grasping for answers. The lights went up. People started booing. Before long the rumours went around that somebody had thrown something at Morrissey and it had hit him on his head, and he had been seen bleeding.

Woah! Smiths fans were passionate, but would it really go so far? It had, and after 20 minutes, an announcement was made that the show was over.

It felt like the Guildhall might be taken apart, or that a witch-hunt would ensue to look for the perpetrator. Everyone eyed each other suspiciously, but also with that feeling that a great night had been lost. We left the Guildhall and entered the autumnal Preston night, thinking of what could have been.

### EMILY KELLY

My friend Jane was at the gig with my sister Louisa (Whizz), who recalls the gig starting and people throwing items at the stage from the beginning. At one point someone threw a 50p at Morrissey (the press described it after as 'a sharpened 50p') which hit him in the face. He then walked off stage and didn't return. Preston Guild Hall told the audience that if they had their ticket stubs, they could get their money back. There was then a scramble on the floor for ticket stubs!

# FREE TRADE HALL

## 30 OCTOBER 1986, MANCHESTER, UK

### CAROLINE ALLEN

After the Preston gig was abandoned, there were rumours that this one might not go ahead so we were absolutely panicking. But it did. We were in the side circle, so we didn't have the best view of the stage. But we hung around outside the stage door before to see them arriving – we always used to do that – so we saw them all when they came in.

There was a lovely crowd of people outside the back door of the Free Trade Hall, some of whom didn't have tickets. We were chatting to these girls who didn't have tickets themselves. They were gutted that they didn't have tickets themselves, but they were saying, 'Have a brilliant time, we really hope you have a good time.' They'd never seen The Smiths live, but they weren't jealous. We bought Johnny Marr some socks as a birthday present and we managed to give them to him as he was walking in. I don't know what we were thinking.

We met Johnny a few weeks later, because the girls we were talking to at the gig had told us 'Johnny lives here' and 'Andy lives there'. They basically told us where they all lived. One Saturday a few weeks later, me and Nicky and Jenny decided to go to Altrincham hoping we might bump into one of the Smiths. By chance we bumped into those same girls, so they showed us where the band all lived, and the week after we went back to Johnny Marr's house.

We were naughty. We just sat outside, like teenage fans do. Mike Joyce pulled up in his car and went into Johnny's and Johnny came out and we spent ages chatting to Johnny and Mike. Johnny remembered the socks that we bought him and said they were a bit small. Because he's only quite small, we thought he had small feet as well.

The Free Trade Hall gig was absolutely brilliant. Nothing ever touched Salford, but that was a brilliant atmosphere. And I didn't realise that was the last time I'd ever see them live.

### CRAIG MULHERN, AGE 16

I couldn't believe my luck. I was staring at the poster in the shop window of EGS Records in Wakefield, which advertised gig tickets for sale. There it was: 'The Smiths'. From memory, the tickets were £12 each including £5 coach travel from The Spaniard pub in Wakefield. Or were they £12 plus £5 coach travel? I've slept since then.

It's my favourite time of the year, leading up to Bonfire Night – the clear starry skies and the smell. I love that smell; I can't explain it. I had to go in and check to see if they had any tickets still available.

I'd just come out of my many years of shyness, and had recently discovered girls. Up to that point I'd always been into football, climbing trees, playing conkers and doing other lad-type things that boys did at that age. I nearly wet myself with excitement when the shop assistant told me they had a few tickets left, though I felt shy as hell, but excited in anticipation at the same time asking them. 'I'll be right back,' I said, 'I need to go see how much money I can withdraw from my account. Please save two, I'll be five minutes.'

I had just enough money in my account to buy three. I was shaking when the bank machine gave me my money. I couldn't get back to EGS fast enough. 'Three tickets please,' I said. I cradled them like gold all the way back on the 485 bus to Ackworth.

I was sweet 16, still at school, and had got into The Smiths about a year before. My mum still reminds me that she was so pleased when I left home that she wouldn't have to listen to another Smiths song again, only then to pull her hair out when one of my younger brothers then started listening to them.

I guess Morrissey, along with several Leeds United football players, was my idol. I tried to dress like him. He was the coolest person on the planet when I saw a picture of him in a pair of white Levi 501s. I owned a long red woollen cardigan, which my friends affectionately called 'concert cardie', as I'd worn it to a few gigs. I thought it was the type of thing Morrissey would wear. I just knew that concert cardie would make an appearance on 30 October 1986.

My friend Juls jumped at the chance when I told him I had three tickets. Now, who was going to have the third, as my girlfriend, Andrea, didn't want to go? 'I'd rather stick pins in my eyes,' was her response. I had a very close-knit group of about half dozen friends. We played football together and did 'lads' things together. But none of the others were really into The Smiths.

Our next-door neighbour had two daughters, one a year older than I (she would later become Juls' girlfriend) and one a year younger. The older one was a stuck-up snob and seemed to look down on me, but the younger one, Leah, was lovely. I bumped into her by chance – I guess she really never left the house other than for school – and I couldn't resist telling her I was off to see The Smiths. Leah told me she was their biggest fan. That wasn't possible, I thought I was. But that was it. Leah was to have the third ticket.

I managed to sneak a pint at The Spaniard before jumping on

the coach for Manchester. I guess
I looked older than my 16 years
back then. I don't remember much
of the journey, until I looked out
of the window of the coach, and
everything in Manchester appeared
grey. It reminded me of seeing
*Coronation Street* on a small black
and white TV when I was younger.

Next thing, there was a crowd.
Mainly guys. And every single one
looked like Morrissey. There were
guys with National Health glasses,
flowery shirts and gladioli sticking
out of their back pockets. I thought
I'd gone to a Morrissey fancy dress
party.

Juls, Leah and I parked ourselves
right behind the mixing desk.
I'd read so much bad publicity
regarding this tour in the
newspapers, with outrage in
some parts of the national press
at Morrissey swinging a noose
on stage and holding a sign
proclaiming 'The Queen Is Dead'.

Before we knew it, the lights
dimmed and Prokofiev's 'Romeo and
Juliet, No 13 Dance Of The Knights'
started playing. It still makes the
hairs on the back of my neck stand
on end whenever I hear it now. And
there they were, The Smiths, right in
front of my very eyes.

I'd been so excited for weeks
knowing I was going to be there in
Manchester that night. And yet it
was over before I knew it. I knew it
was over, before it even began. The
most memorable songs that night
were 'The Queen Is Dead', 'How
Soon Is Now?', 'Rusholme Ruffians'
(Juls had to shout to tell me it was
kickstarted by '(Marie's The Name)
His Latest Flame'), 'What She Said'
(with 'Rubber Ring' as the intro)

and 'Meat Is Murder' with 'The
Headmaster Ritual' intro.

I bought a 'The Queen Is
Dead' t-shirt outside from some
scally, which I probably still own
somewhere in one of the many boxes
I've packed away. Likewise, I still
own the gig ticket and bus ticket,
which I'll never throw away. No
doubt my son will, when I'm gone.

I've been to so many memorable
gigs over the years: a disappointing
REM in Huddersfield (the acoustics
were shite; however, they made up
for it many years later at Lancashire
Cricket Ground when I thought
the bass was going to smash
right through my chest); Marilyn
Manson at Roundhay Park in Leeds;
Eminem a few times in the early
days; a totally off her face Amy
Winehouse in Manchester before
The Arctic Monkeys came on; and
the gig I waited nearly 30 years to
see, the one and only Ms Kate Bush.
But The Smiths, less than two weeks
before my seventeenth birthday,
remains without a shadow of a
doubt the best gig I've ever been to
in my life.

### THOMAS JONES

This was the swansong, although we
didn't know it at the time. Again,
we couldn't get stalls tickets due
to their popularity, so we 'gurgled
from the circle'. Morrissey took the
stage wielding a placard that read
'Two Light Ales Please'. I think there
had been some controversy about a
'Queen Is Dead' placard at previous
gigs, and a recent incident where
he'd been hit by a missile (again)
and refused to carry on. At those
later Smiths gigs, it seemed he was
occasionally sacrificing melody for

theatricality in the way he messed with the lines, and used a variety of daft voices to emphasise or undermine his own lyrics. This was certainly the least memorable of the four gigs I saw. In retrospect it was easy to see that the magic was fading.

### JAYNE O'CONNOR

My first proper gig. I took my sister for her 21st. I can still remember as plain as day Morrissey coming on to '(Marie's The Name) His Latest Flame' combined with 'The Last Night of the Fair' ('Rusholme Ruffians'). It was brilliant.

### VICKI MARES-PAGE

I lived in Old Trafford as a teenager, literally around the corner from where Morrissey lived on Kings Road. He went to the boys' Catholic school St Mary's, and I went to the sister school Cardinal Vaughan, albeit eleven years apart. I was the usual angst-ridden teenager so naturally gravitated to the music of The Smiths. My older sister by three years, Carole, was a huge music fan and had been to lots of gigs, including quite a few from that particular Smiths tour. We didn't have much money growing up but I really wanted to go to that gig and I begged my family for the money for a ticket, which Carole bought for me. It was a very exciting time looking forward to my very first gig.

As a seasoned gig-goer, Carole said we should go into town early to hang around the Britannia Hotel where the band were staying. After waiting there for a while, Morrissey and Marr arrived. They were very generous with their time and signed autographs and had photos taken. I was too starstruck. I stood with my mouth open the whole time.

We got to the Free Trade Hall early and were first in the queue – me, my sister and four of my sister's friends. We were at the front of the stage, and this was before barriers installed, so we were right against the stage.

They came onstage with Morrissey waving a placard which said 'The Queen Is Dead'. It was amazing and I was in my element but very quickly I was separated from my sister and her friends. I was now the only girl at the front, and I was terrified that if I got stuck in the crowd somewhere, my sister wouldn't know where I was. I clung onto the stage monitor for dear life.

There was a brilliant moment during 'How Soon Is Now?' where Morrissey knelt on the stage and held my hand. It was probably only a couple of seconds, but it felt like an age. I was only half enjoying this amazing gig as I was getting crushed against the stage. Then I was scared and probably in tears and the guy behind me realised I needed to get out and was shouting to the security, but they didn't hear or notice.

He shouted in my ear, 'Do you want to go on stage?' and I said 'no', but he said to other people to push me up because I was getting squashed. The next thing I knew, I was stood on the stage a few feet from Morrissey. I knew it was a once-in-a-lifetime moment, so I put my arm around the front of him and kissed him on the cheek! My sister said the crowd cheered but I didn't notice.

Then I walked off the left-hand side of the stage and Mike Joyce winked at me. I practically collapsed onto the security man who was very kind and took me for some water (I guess security then was very different to now). He asked me who I was with and I told him my sister and that she was still in the gig. He said I couldn't go back in but that I could stand at the side door to listen to the encore. I then had to wait with him until my sister came out and found me. He was a nice, kind man.

The song playing when I got onstage was 'I Know It's Over' and it's still one of my favourites. I never saw the man who pushed me on that stage but I'm eternally grateful to him, even if he was one of the ones crushing me. The front of the stage was a deep red colour. I realised after that I was wearing blue jeans and a blue floral shirt (very Morrissey) which I'd borrowed from a friend. Both were ruined by the red dye which had rubbed off on me and stained them.

Carole had gone to loads of Smiths gigs but never got close to getting on the stage or holding Morrissey's hand. I'd managed both at my first gig. When she finally found me after the gig, she gave me such a whack!

### CHRIS GREEN

We had no tickets and everyone was queuing up and mingling outside. They were building at the end of the Free Trade Hall, and they had big wooden sheets up surrounding the construction site inside. We were looking at how we could get in, going up to the door, how many bouncers are on and that sort of thing. Now this was down to me, and I'm not having anyone else claim this, but I went round the end of the building and got myself through the wood and there was a hole in the wall covered up with a bit of tarpaulin. I pulled the tarp open and there was a human-sized hole in it. I peered in and right in front of me was a yellow builder's ladder. I looked up and it went up and up and up for about three floors. It was all breeze block; there was all building stuff and cement and everything going on inside. I had a shufty up and it was really high.

Me, Dibs and Stan Bowen went in, had a scoot up and peered over. And, as we peered over, we could see it was just a corridor next to the bar on one of the upper floors. So we went back down and round to the front, gathered everyone together and said, 'Listen, come and have a look at this,' and we went in. Everyone just went up the ladder.

There must have been 25 of us – boom, boom, boom, boom, boom – we all came bowling over the top. Full of shit, full of dust everywhere. We were absolutely hanging. We went straight to the bar. We were proper mucky, proper hanging. People were looking at us.

We were waiting and as the gig started and they said you could go in, we just gathered en masse at the top of the stairs and we just – boom, boom, boom, boom, boom – again. It was just a case of dodging around the door staff to get in. That was an absolute belter.

I remember finding a little James Dean badge on the floor that this girl had lost and I gave it to her, thinking it would get me in with her. She wasn't interested. Because I was covered in dust and shit. I probably looked like a football thug.

### MANAMI NANRI, AGE 23

The Smiths never came to Japan, but I was extremely lucky to be studying in Wimbledon from September 1986 to July 1987 and so had the chance to see four gigs on the *Queen Is Dead* tour, at Kilburn National Ballroom, twice at Brixton Academy and at the Free Trade Hall in Manchester. I took a

National Express from Victoria Coach Station to Manchester, travelling up without a ticket, as I so desperately wanted to see them play on home turf.

In 1983 I had travelled to the UK for the first time, staying with an old couple for a month to take English lessons. I took a train to London every day and ended up bringing 20 or 30 records back to Japan. But Smiths records were not amongst them. A year later, I returned with my college mate for a month, booking a holiday flat in London. We travelled to Brighton – I wanted to go after watching *Quadrophenia* – and Dover, Oxford, Leicester where my pen friend lived and Scotland, where I went to see Simple Minds.

Again, I popped into record shops and bought 20 or 30 records, this time including *The Smiths*. When I first played it, I wasn't sure I liked it and didn't play it again for some months. However, the next time I was strangely struck by their sound and became interested in the lyrics. I bought *Hatful Of Hollow* from an import record shop, which got me more into both the lyrical world and the sound – the combination of those were what made The Smiths.

I was 23. Although I had graduated from college as a secretary and took all the available English subjects, I wasn't satisfied with my own English skills. So, in 1986 I flew to the UK again and worked in an office for two and a half years, staying with a family in Wimbledon. I had no people or friends around me who liked The Smiths. I remember once being asked if I became depressed or gloomy listening to their music. It was really mean to say such a thing, but I really didn't care about those people, people who didn't understand the world of The Smiths.

Arriving in Manchester on the day of the gig, I hurried to Tourist Information to book somewhere to stay for the night. There were other people there and we all were introduced to the same B&B and were recommended to share a taxi. An elderly lady, two teenage boys and me, a Japanese woman, all sat in a black cab. That was probably an odd sight! I sat next to the lady, and the two boys were in front of me, face to face. I could see the boys had many Smiths badges on their sacks. Although it was obvious, I asked them if they were going to the gig. They said 'yes!' in astonishment but with smiles. I said I was going too, and that I was a complete stranger from Japan. They kindly offered to guide me to the Free Trade Hall.

After we checked in at the B&B, they waited for me and we caught a bus to the city centre. They were a bit shy but kind and friendly and when we arrived at the Free Trade Hall, they introduced me to other friends. The other friends all kindly welcomed me and showed me their photographs of The Smiths. When they knew that I didn't have a ticket, they let me know where I could possibly get one and said to rejoin them after. Not long after I was successfully back with the ticket, a car arrived and Morrissey got out of it.

My mind went blank for a few seconds but, instinctively, I got close to Morrissey, holding a memo and a pen. I asked him for his autograph with my name, 'To Manami.' As it was an unfamiliar foreign name, Morrissey asked me to spell it out. As I did, he kindly wrote my name one letter at a time and then his name underneath. In my imagination, Morrissey was rather hard to approach and not snobbish but proud, a little reserved and possibly moody. It was a lovely surprise to find that he was gentle, mild-mannered and a tender-hearted person.

Morrissey chatted to some other people and then entered the venue via the stage door. Fans gathered around me and asked me what I was talking to Morrissey about. They were all happy for me and pleased I had been lucky enough to talk to him.

At the concert, the opening song was 'Ask' followed by 'The Queen Is Dead' and then 'Panic'. Then, Morrissey greeted the audience by saying 'Hello, nice to be back!'

I had another chance to see Morrissey at the 12 December gig at Brixton Academy, and he agreed to pose for a photograph with me. Standing next to him, I could feel his warmth and geniality, and I still have the memory of his pleasant fragrance.

Hearing Johnny had left the band in 1987 meant the end of The Smiths for me. I was devastated but hoped that whatever the problems were, they would be solved and they'd reunite. To me, Morrissey's lyrics and vocals, Johnny's song writing and the guitar and Andy's bass and Mike's drum all have to be there. Morrissey sings Smiths songs at his gigs but it's not the sound of The Smiths. Johnny sings and plays The Smiths too and the sound is almost The Smiths, but it still isn't the same. Their solo performances of Smiths songs make me think of the days when they were all together, and make me slightly sad that those days won't come back anymore.

### MICKO WESTMORELAND

When I was 16 years old, I was lucky enough to catch The Smiths live on *The Queen Is Dead* tour at Manchester's Free Trade Hall. It was the last but one show of the tour, and turned out to be almost their last as a band. I remember travelling over the Pennines on a National Express coach, listening to *Hatful Of Hollow* on my Sony Walkman, wondering if they would include 'How Soon Is Now?' in the set and if it could be replicated live. Its sound was so unique – different from any other Smiths song, different from any other song in existence.

There was always something about the track that felt other-worldly – right from the shimmering rotating-speaker intro Johnny Marr plays (a disguised Bohannon disco riff reinvented like no other). Then the drums and bass come in, and that extraordinary soaring guitar. On first hearing the

*Micko Westmoreland was at the Free Trade Hall*

song's opening line – 'I am the son and the heir' – my teenage brain thought it was 'I am the sun and the air'. It just seemed to fit with the spacious, elemental feel of the whole sonic landscape.

The title itself plays with temporality. *How soon is now?* Well, now is now. The apparent riddle can only be solved when viewed through an emotional lens. The overriding themes of the song are loneliness and yearning: the need for human connection, the desire for love. The 'now' becomes the pull that will never quite happen – the moment of release that will never arrive. When I used to sing along, I'd find myself going, 'I am human and I need to belong.' Another teenage malapropism that almost makes sense.

*There's a club if you'd like to go*
*You could meet somebody who really*
*loves you*
*So you go and you stand on your own*
*And you leave on your own*
*And you go home, and you cry and*
*you want to die.*

No fake romanticism there – emotion served up cold and hard as a Northern winter. My brother, who was three years older than me, was struggling at that time to come out as gay. He later told me how much these lyrics captured his early experiences on the scene – where young gay men would tentatively risk the ritual humiliation of rejection in search of a dreamed-of magical moment. I knew that feeling too. But that was part of Morrissey's genius: to take queerness and make it universal.

The track perversely became a dance-floor filler. The clubs 'you liked to go' to would play it quite often. I was working as a glass-collector at the time, every Friday night, at Leeds alternative nightspot The Warehouse. Whenever the song came on, the crowd would respond – Goths, New Romantics, students, Echo and the Bunnyboys, punks – all dancing together, a sea of hormonal confusion, everyone finding some kind of personal identification with the solitude of the lyrics. Or maybe they just liked the tune.

Arriving at the Free Trade Hall, we were greeted with an incredible opening run: 'Ask' followed by 'The Queen Is Dead' followed by 'Panic'. These were all very current songs, central to the mid-eighties zeitgeist. Morrissey was wearing a t-shirt with James Dean on it. Later, he stripped it off and threw it into the crowd, where fans ripped it to pieces like a pack of hyenas.

Then, after a pause, the fourth song began. The familiar rotating-speaker intro. I held my breath. Mike Joyce crashed in on the drums and the song sounded exactly like it did on the record. Better! I got goosebumps. We all did. The crowd went nuts. It was pure Mancunian transcendence. It was heaven.

'How Soon Is Now?' has stood the test of time (the dimension it so audaciously plays with). The production on the 2011 remaster sounds incredible when played through my Adam studio monitors, freed from the wow and flutter of my Walkman. And the poetry of the lyrics remains: the song endures because it refuses to resolve easily. No sentiment. No easy warmth. It understands that sometimes the most honest act is simply to ask the question – and allow it to remain unanswered.

## ROYAL ALBERT HALL


### 14 NOVEMBER 1986, LONDON, UK

### RICHARD BLANT, AGE 17

I was beside myself with excitement as I was going along to see The Smiths play an anti-apartheid gig with The Fall in support. To say The Smiths had been an obsession of mine would be to underplay it. Everyone who got it was great. Everyone who didn't was beneath contempt. Ever since I bought the first album and the twelve-inch of 'Heaven Knows I'm Miserable Now' with my fifteenth birthday money, there had been only one group.

I still remember where I was sat when I heard the terrible news: on the top floor of Longueville block in an A-level Sociology class. I felt like I had been stabbed. Others had heard the gig was cancelled – at first, I thought they were winding me up (I was not very reserved about my Smiths obsession) – and to add a touch of teenage hideousness, a few of them were laughing about this.

The night before (or possibly more) Johnny Marr had been drinking heavily and crashed his car. He was only slightly injured – it could have been far, far worse – but he was unable to pick up his guitar and play. Postponed.

The thought of a 17-year-old me sat in a lesson crying makes the 49-year-old me very sad. The thought of a group of them laughing at a 17-year-old me makes the 49-year-old me very angry.

The gig itself was to be rearranged just before Christmas on 12 December 1986 in Brixton. I chose to cash my ticket in – money being tight and Christmas presents to be bought. 'I'll go on the next tour,' I assured myself. Early in 1987, I saw an interview with Morrissey in – I think *Q* magazine – saying he didn't know whether he wanted The Smiths to tour any more. Alarm bells rang loudly.

For anyone who knows The Smiths mythology, 12 December 1986 was the last gig that The Smiths ever played in the UK. I missed it because of Christmas, and I have never regretted anything more. I would never make that choice again.

I am now 49 and my only regret in life was never seeing The Smiths play live. I have seen Morrissey in all his majesty (and some ropier gigs to be fair) and I have seen Johnny Marr in all of his brilliance. In 2018, I saw Morrissey and Marr play 'How Soon Is Now', albeit nine months apart. In my delusional way, I count that as a reunion.

## PEEL SESSION, MAIDA VALE STUDIOS
### 2 DECEMBER 1986, LONDON, UK

The band's fourth and final Peel Session saw them record four tracks – 'Is It Really So Strange?', 'London', 'Half A Person' and

Michael Farragher was on the guest list for several shows

Some of Michael Farragher's tickets

'Sweet And Tender Hooligan'. These were broadcast on 17 December 1986. 'Sweet And Tender Hooligan' and 'Is It Really So Strange?' were later released on the *Louder Than Bombs* album.

## BRIXTON ACADEMY

### 12 DECEMBER 1986, LONDON, UK

### SALLY WILLIAMS

My first Smiths gig turned out to be their last. It was the last day of my first term at uni, so we'd been in the bar all day. I went with my house mate who was from Manchester and really into The Smiths. I'm from Liverpool and was into the Bunnymen but I went along for the ride and – it was amazing!

I was surprised how energetic Morrissey was and I wasn't prepared for the level of showmanship – him swinging a noose around and holding up signs so I guess 'Panic' must have been on the set list. I made a short film for the BBC about Morrissey fans a few years ago and none of them had seen The Smiths, which made me feel even luckier to have been there.

### MICHAEL FARRAGHER

That show was stand out. Craig Gannon had done the previous tour with them. Their sound had changed. If you listen to something like *Rank*, they had this huge sound. The two guitars allowed Johnny to do lots of things that he couldn't do when he was on stage by himself. But when they did the Brixton gig, they were back to being a four piece

again and the set was completely different from what they'd done two months earlier. For so many songs you were thinking, 'That is a first.' They did 'This Night Has Opened My Eyes' for the first time in years. They did this fantastic segue from 'Miserable Lie' into 'London', which they'd never done before and obviously never got the chance to do again, and which was brilliant. They premiered 'Shoplifters'. They did a fantastic version of 'Hand In Glove'. It was incredible that that was the last song that they played.

There's a lovely moment in the video of that Brixton show where Johnny goes over to Andy and they're playing together and Morrissey comes and joins them. The three of them are on the side of the stage and they look like they're having a fantastic time. They're all smiling and it doesn't look like there's any kind of problem with the band. It's hard to believe that less than a year later they'd split up.

### JOHN DEOL

It was the only time I saw The Smiths.

I was twelve years old in 1982. I've got three older sisters and they're all really music mad. We were all music mad in our house. I'm from Birmingham and I'm Indian. We're British Asians.

My parents were Indian. They came over in 1968, and I was born the following year. My parents were educated so they could speak English, but we were all learning to embrace the popular culture and everyone including Mum and Dad loved music. These were my parents' first years in Britain and my earliest years, and we all loved *Top Of The Pops*.

My sister Sandy, who's three years older than me, was going on about this band who were playing at the Tower Ballroom, this little venue in Edgbaston. She was saying, 'There's a big buzz going around and some of the older kids at school are talking about this band, The Smiths,' and just around that time they appeared on *Top Of The Pops*. They looked other worldly. This guy had flowers in his pocket, and he just looked so cool. And the guitarist looked hip in his own way, with a really cool guitar.

You don't get much pocket money when you're eleven or twelve, but Sandy managed to get the money together to buy the first album and, in the weeks after getting that, we were all obsessed. We'd tape every *Top Of The Pops* appearance on our video recorder. And they were on a programme called *Riverside* on BBC2.

We all became hugely into them, but I was very young and so I couldn't get tickets when they played in Birmingham and Wolverhampton in '84 or '85. Then in 1986 Sandy was at the University of Surrey in Guildford. I'd just left school. I was an avid reader of the *NME* and *Melody Maker* and *Sounds* by then and I saw that The Smiths were playing an anti-apartheid gig in Brixton. I think it was a rearranged gig after Johnny Marr had his car accident.

The next time Sandy phoned home to see how we were all doing, I told her about this gig that The Smiths were playing in Brixton, and she headed down there and got two tickets. I remember her saying that it was nearly sold out.

I remember how excited I was just getting the coach down. That buzz never quite leaves until you walk into the building. London was all new and exciting to me. I remember walking into Brixton Academy, and we opened the doors downstairs. It's a great venue.

It's quite cavernous, and one of the biggest non-seated venues in London with a big dance floor that dips down. The whole room was absolutely rammed all the way back to the door. We looked at each other and just went, 'We're not going to get in there. Or we're not going to be able to see if we do.' We're both quite short. I'm five foot eight and she's five foot two. But Sandy said, 'I've been here before. There's an upstairs area,' so we went upstairs with just a handful of people and a really good view. Pete Shelley was already on, so we saw some of the Buzzcocks' set.

It was just rapturous when The Smiths came on. A lot of people think of The Smiths as having a similar audience to Morrissey, quite fey and a bit camp. It wasn't. It was a normal football crowd type of gig. I remember looking downstairs, seeing how it was absolutely rammed, and thinking – how can people breathe down there?

We now know it as The Smiths' final gig, but they certainly weren't breaking up at that point. They were all over each other, with loads of hugging, and it was so celebratory. Johnny and Andy, schoolmates, with their arms around each other's shoulders. Morrissey messing around with Johnny Marr. It was a very joyous gig.

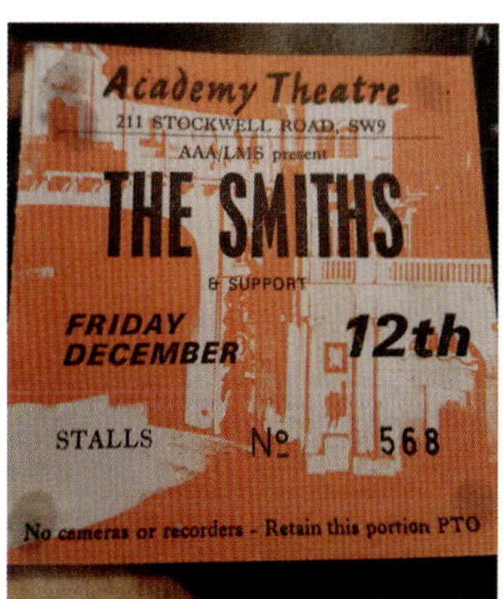

*Brixton Academy ticket (Alan McAdam)*

They played 'Shoplifters Of The World Unite' for the first and only time and, when he announced it, we didn't even know the song because it hadn't been released, but everybody cheered at what sounded like such an outrageous statement. There was quite a lot of banter with the crowd. The place went mad when they played 'Hand In Glove'. Then they went off and came back on for an encore. They didn't play for that long, about an hour and 15 minutes, but it was such a tight set.

With The Smiths, it always felt like you were in a club. You'd chosen to be in this club called 'The Smiths' that said 'no' to Wham!, Five Star and all that poppy stuff. You were in this clique.

I was 15 when *Meat Is Murder* came out. I'd see in the *Melody Maker* and the *NME* when they announced the album release dates, so I'd be ready. I was at HMV in Birmingham New Street that morning. I can't remember what excuse I used to go in late to school but I got away with it. So, I was there as it opened, got the first copy and when I took that record home and heard that final track, it was excruciating. You hear a cow dying. Like many fans I'd never connected the food on my plate to the animal.

A few days before the release The Smiths had been on *Whistle Test* with an album report. They'd been in the studio with them and Morrissey explained why eating meat is wrong. At that point, like many of us, I'd have done anything The Smiths told us to do. But that really just made sense. It was really tough. My mother didn't think I'd last a week as a vegetarian. And

here we are 30 odd years on. I haven't touched meat since that day.

After university, I ended up working for MTV for nine years. I've never met Morrissey, but I've met the other three Smiths. When I told Andy Rourke that I'd been a vegetarian since 1985, I remember him saying, 'Oh no mate, after a few months I was back on the meat because I missed it too much.' I was a bit downhearted at that. But then I met Mike Joyce, and Johnny Marr when he was doing Electronic, and I remember Johnny saying to me, 'I'm really proud that my music can have that effect. I'm really proud of you.' If my hero says that about me, I'll stick with it for the rest of my life.

### MICHAEL ROSE

I became a full-on fan of The Smiths in between the *Meat Is Murder* and *The Queen Is Dead* albums. 1986 was the first time I bought a Smiths album as a new release and *The Queen Is Dead* was played to death. I was relatively new to gig-going at the time but knew I wanted to see The Smiths when tour dates were announced. Three London dates were scheduled for October, all at different venues, and I was gutted at not being able to get tickets for any of them.

Fast forward to December 1986 and The Smiths are playing a one-off show at the Brixton Academy as a benefit for Artists Against Apartheid. Once again, with no ticket, I could only dream of seeing them at this stage. But a friend was gifted some money so that we could go and buy a ticket from a tout, something we'd never done before!

On 12th December we arrived at Brixton Tube station, buying tickets from the first seller we encountered on the platform.

Inside, excitement levels were off the scale, and we tried to get as far forward as possible. As the lights went down and the band came onto the stage, we fully expected to hear 'The Queen Is Dead', the opener for the album tour, but instead the band launched into recent single, 'Ask'. The pace was not to let up, with 'Bigmouth Strikes Again' and 'London' following. I'd only been to a handful of gigs at this point, but don't remember anywhere where the audience felt as wild. This was something different. We were treated to 'Some Girls Are Bigger Than Others' which hadn't been played on the recent tour, so it was now clear the band had mixed things up a bit for this gig. We also got to hear upcoming single 'Shoplifters Of The World Unite' as a new addition to the set list.

What happened next is my most overriding memory of the concert. When the familiar intro to 'There Is A Light That Never Goes Out' rang out, there was another massive surge forward from the crowd. I was now so wrapped up in the whole experience I decided to go with it and get nearer the stage.

Back then, Brixton Academy had a bottle neck created by raised sections either side of the floor and I was squeezed through it and in doing so fell to the ground. I was trampled, with people walking over me as they were forced forward with the momentum of the crowd. I panicked, feeling pain and claustrophobia, but with the help

of the adrenalin rush that followed, managed to right myself and get back up. The adulation from the crowd singing back at Morrissey was amazing: 'To die by your side' indeed! I remember thinking, 'What a way to have nearly gone!'

I was relieved when things calmed down at some point, and the band played a track I really never expected to hear, 'This Night Has Opened My Eyes'. The main set was wrapped up with 'Panic' and Morrissey swinging a noose around, and I recall feeling disappointed that they'd only played for about 45 minutes. When they came back on, I finally got to hear 'The Queen Is Dead'. The gig ended with 'Hand In Glove', and I pointed out to my friend on the way home that it was kind of amazing that they'd opened with their most current single and ended with their first.

What is amazing about this gig now, and which no one knew at the time, is that it was to be their last ever. How poignant that the closing song ended with, 'And I'll probably never see you again.' This also means it was the one and only time the band performed 'Some Girls Are Bigger Than Others' and 'Shoplifters', adding to how unique it was. I have since always felt privileged and incredibly lucky that I got to see The Smiths live.

I've gone on to see Morrissey over 20 times, but it's not the same, is it?

### MARK WATERS, AGE 16

I'd had a rough few years in my teens and The Smiths were always there for me. My mum surprised me with a ticket. I remember being scared of Brixton due to the riots the previous year. All I remember of the gig is how surreal it was and how different it was to the previous gigs I'd been to – Shakin' Stevens and Big Country. Unfortunately, it turned out to be their last gig. So very bittersweet…

### TIM MARTIN

What can I say? I still have the ticket stub. They came on to 'Take Me Back To Dear Old Blighty'. I remember 'Hang The DJ' ('Panic') with a noose spinning above his head and flowers in the back pocket. I think the album was a big influence over me. It changed my mood. Now I look for more positive, simpler sounding things. But that evening, I really thought I was at the centre of the world for those two hours.

### JOHN FEATHERSTONE

I would have loved to be in the audience for a Smiths show at Barrowlands. The Glasgow audiences were nuts and the energy in that place and I saw a ton of bands in there. I did a ton of shows myself later in my touring career. They were all great but those Smith shows in Barrowlands were really special. The first show we did on *Meat Is Murder* at the Aragon Ballroom in Chicago is memorable. Barrowlands and the Aragon Ballroom are sort of sister venues. The Aragon was where Al Capone used to 'entertain' people. The alley behind the Aragon has pockmarks in the brick from where people thought they were going to go have an audience with Mr Capone and ending up having an audience with Mr Capone's mobsters. For a bunch of kids from northern England it was like, 'Holy crap, this is like being in *Starsky & Hutch*.'

Irvine Meadows on *The Queen Is Dead* tour was great. A big show, southern California sunshine, cute girls, good-looking boys, everybody out for a good time and, again, it's a bunch of lads from northern England. We were like, 'Holy crap, there *is* a promised land!'

And I would love to go back to the last Brixton Academy show and experience it knowing it was going to be the last show. There was no such thing as a throwaway gig with The Smiths, but we were supposed to do it and then Johnny had his accident and it got pushed back. And so it felt like a one-off blip in the middle of the tipping point between *The Queen Is Dead* and *Strangeways*. I don't think any of us realised the gravitas of the occasion. And, in some ways, it might have not been such a great gig if we'd realised it, but I would love to relive that just so I could take those memories more clearly and put them in a little box and just kind of tuck them away.

I would not want them to reform. There's no need. The work stands for itself. But if they did, I wouldn't want to not be there. That sounds like having my cake and eating it. I haven't talked to Morrissey in a long time (although a good friend of mine is Morrissey's lighting designer) so I can only speak from my experience of being very good friends with Johnny. Our kids grew up together. Nile is in Hans Zimmer's band. Johnny and I see each other all the time. We talk regularly.

Even if hell did freeze over and

Johnny and Morrissey could be on a stage together and reconcile their differences, I don't know if it would ever be as good. Morrissey has his body of work and Johnny has his body of work. And I think they have both – and they've done this remarkably well – threaded the needle of not being has-beens, and doing the 'Morrissey of The Smiths featuring all the Smiths music' thing. Morrissey's got his own body of work. Some of it I like, some of it I like less. But some of Morrissey's songs are bangers. Obviously, I'm a sucker for Johnny's stuff. He's a dear friend of mine.

I think it would do a disservice to the body of work they've both done since the Smiths to go, 'All right, we need to rewind.' I would encourage people that want to have a sense of that to go and listen to some of the material that captured how it was in the moment and relish that as part of a continuum.

We're often looking to recreate experiences which we loved, and we're frequently disappointed with it. It's very hard to capture that moment because we're different people now to what we were then. The band members are different people.

## 'SHOPLIFTERS OF THE WORLD UNITE'

### RELEASED 26 JANUARY 1987

Released after the band decided to scrap the single release of their original A-side, 'You Just Haven't Earned It Yet, Baby'. A commercial success, reaching number twelve in the UK.

## CATHEDRAL CLUB

### 13 FEBRUARY 1987, DUBLIN, IRELAND

### DES FOLEY

We were approached on Grafton Street by a girl who asked if we would like tickets to see the band recording a TV appearance for a show called *TV Gaga*. It was an invite only audience and I remember we were all in the venue when the band came in and walked right past us all. Morrissey was wearing a denim jacket with a painting of Elvis on the back; they were recording 'Shoplifters Of The World Unite'. I managed to get a quick word with Mike Joyce and told him about us getting t-shirts off him at the Stadium gig. He was really friendly and we were so chuffed to get to meet one of the band. Back then, they were the most important band for me; everything they did was hugely relevant and we followed them avidly. I heard them first just at the right age. I was too young for punk, so The Smiths were my year zero for music.

## *LOUDER THAN BOMBS*

### RELEASED 30 MARCH 1987

*Louder Than Bombs* was initially a US-only compilation released on the Sire Records label which Rough Trade then released in the UK. *Rolling Stone* magazine has since rated the album at No. 365 on its *500 Greatest Albums Of All Time* list.

*Shoplifters Of The World Unite*

*Louder Than Bombs*

DAVID SCOTT

'Can you play 'Veronica's House'?'

'What?!'

"Veronica's House'?"

'Never heard of it, mate.'

But, of course, the DJ in Aqua Bar had never heard of the song a drunk teenager was begging him to play – it didn't exist. For months, I'd been singing, 'There is a light in Veronica's house' on a dance floor not knowing I'd got the words wrong and, even worse, being oblivious to the band themselves.

There is a scene in *The Godfather* where Michael Corleone is in hiding in Sicily. He's strolling across the countryside when he comes across a local girl and is dumbstruck. His protective bodyguards, Calo and the sly Fabrizio, say 'colpo di fulmine'. That he's been struck by lightning, an Italian proverb when someone has a sudden, intense overwhelming feeling of love.

The Smiths are my Apollonia Vitelli, and unlike the fate of Michael's true love (*that bastard Fabrizio*), no car explosives will take them away. As the compilation suggests, they are *Louder Than Bombs*. I was a double-A side of a younger man. On one side of my vinyl was Oasis, all that piss and vinegar, 'fuck the world' ethos that teenagers have. On the other was The Smiths. And next to no-one got to listen to that side. What you are being sensitive for, you soft git. Emotions, pah… ah the arrogance of youth.

I wonder if there was some alternative universe where I never knew The Smiths and how I would have turned out – because they showed me dimensions to being a human that weren't wholly on display. It's a reaffirmation of existence to hear someone who grew up in the same city as you giving you a shoulder to lean on. Tenderness wasn't a trait I was really comfortable showing off, let alone that I wrote poetry…*such bloody awful poetry.*

What's hilarious about all that, is that The Smiths are the greatest unveiling of machismo there ever was. The most manly of men will weep to any given song like a teenager at a Taylor Swift gig. I know, I've seen them. Let me tell you there's nothing tougher than a heartbroken man on a pub step wiping his eyes to 'Please, Please, Please Let Me Get What I Want'. Nothing. This but one of the many contradictions of Messrs Morrissey, Marr, Rourke and Joyce.

Take the music. Marr's guitar riffs are legging it like they're late for the bus, whilst Morrissey's elongated laments are a lad who can't go out tonight, 'cos existence is futile. It's that contrast, high-octane riffs mixed with the odes of an outsider that reflect the human experience.

When I found them, I bought *everything* they made. I was lost in a world of stories; it was as though I was being serenaded by Charles Dickens over the greatest guitar riffs that made me want to dance. Say what you will about Morrissey, but he's extended at least two generations' vocabulary more than any high school thesaurus.

It was like hearing your diary read back to you before you'd written it down. I never wrote to a buck-tooth girl in Luxembourg, but I'd written enough poems that I'd never sent – thankfully. *Christ.* I've never punctured my bike on the moors, but I've ended up arse over elbow on a moped wondering when is it I will grow up. Then there's the heartache, crying to your mum because another one's broke your ticker and you just need someone to toss the soil on for it to complete the job.

The Smiths weren't a cure. They were a belonging and explained that, in its own unique way, being miserable is also beautiful. And you weren't the only one feeling that way. Yet for all the gloom, they are hilarious records – 'Girlfriend In A Coma', 'Heaven Knows I'm Miserable Now'. This double A-side of a man has had more than enough dead-end jobs corroding my soul, and when I walked away from them – more times than I care to admit – I'd be marching out the door with 'Frankly, Mr Shankly' playing on my CD Walkman. My only regret was never writing the lyrics down as a resignation letter.

Still, there's time.

If I was to say The Smiths are the greatest of all time I will no doubt piss off a lot of scousers, but I'm a United fan so… The Smiths are the greatest of all time. This isn't to denigrate The Beatles or any other musicians. All the greats went through periods of change (for better and worse). The Smiths arrived fully formed, never shifted direction, and with every record they sound unmistakably themselves. They started and ended the same band: timeless. Drop the needle anywhere – 'Asleep', 'Girl Afraid', 'Hand In Glove', 'Still

Ill' - and it still feels like colpo di fulmine.

The Thunderbolt.

Every single time.

### BARRY PAGE

It was a great time to be a music fan in the eighties, and whether you were one of the pop kids or one of the slightly cooler indie enthusiasts, there was something for everyone in the hit parade, and every Sunday evening I'd enthusiastically tune into Radio 1 and record as many of the Top 40 hits as the space on a 90-minute cassette would allow.

My introduction to The Smiths would have been their playback performance of 'What Difference Does It Make?' on *Top Of The Pops*, but for a number of reasons it would be several years before I bought an album of theirs. Stop me if you think you've heard this one before, but the album was a luxury item then, and for a youngster who received only 50 pence in pocket money per week, there wasn't much change left after picking up a copy of the fortnightly *Smash Hits* (40p) or the weekly *No 1* (35p) magazines.

Asking either of my parents for money for an album was unthinkable, and I'd consider myself lucky if I was able to blag a Booty Bag (the ones with the Fruit Salads and ghastly Black Jacks) and a copy of *Look-In* during the weekly trip to the supermarket. And soon pocket money would be a thing of the past as my overbearing father would organise a paper round for me behind my back.

That's not to say my music collection was bare, since I could afford the odd single by Queen or

Marillion (especially if it was in Woolies' bargain bin) and on my birthday and at Christmas there was normally an album to enjoy (usually a *Now* compilation) or a pack of Memorex or TDK blank cassettes in which to record LPs from more financially resplendent mates. (One such friend showed me how to cut the tape in order to avoid there being a lengthy gap at the end of side one, something today's generation of entitled streamers with their instant music access would probably laugh at.) And at Christmas there were nice folks who generously tipped this freezing cold paperboy with the ridiculous balaclava, and the proceeds certainly weren't deposited in my Barclays Supersavers account.

By the winter of 1986 I had become a music obsessive, and one of the first bands I seriously got into was A-ha (not knowing then that years later I would write a book about them). The Smiths were very much on my radar then though, and I enjoyed all of the singles they released, and even my father – whose musical tastes were somewhat questionable – singled out 1984's 'Heaven Knows I'm Miserable Now' for praise. So what better entry point into the band's catalogue than a career-spanning double album that mopped up the majority of their singles and incredible B-sides that were arguably as good as the A-sides? It was the compilation *Louder Than Bombs*, an American release that came hot on the heels of UK retrospective *The World Won't Listen*, and I later learned it was designed to house all the tracks not included on their Stateside albums, with the added bonus of scrapped single 'You Just Haven't Earned It Yet, Baby'. This meant I dipped out on signature song 'How Soon Is Now?' as it had been appended to *Meat Is Murder*, though for some reason the compilation didn't include instrumental 'The Draize Train'.

It later got a more widespread release the following year, but my version was an imported cassette released in May 1987. It became my soundtrack for a school trip to Armentières in northern France that summer. I may have looked decidedly untrendy with my portable Saisho cassette player (the poor man's equivalent of the Sony Walkman), but I soon became a lifelong fan of one of the coolest bands around. (Little did I know then they'd played their last concert and were on the verge of breaking up.) I didn't need to press the fast-forward button once as every one of the 24 songs was brilliant (well, perhaps not the version of 'Golden Lights'), and I was blown away by Morrissey's witty wordplay and the band's superlative musicality. The Beatles may have had their mighty *Red* and *Blue* albums, but this social misfit had their little orange cassette, which would resonate far more deeply.

### ROBERT PLUMMER

Morrissey and Marr's finest are the same old songs, but with a different meaning now my youth has gone. Despite being a compilation, *Louder Than Bombs* was always my go-to Smiths album. I had a cassette copy that I played incessantly on one of the early Walkmans. Now, in a more modern CD edition, the music seems filtered through a veil – of irony, of age, of chronological distance – that makes it less relatable than it used to be.

It's not merely because the tunes are old. The pop music of the 1960s and the punk rock of the 1970s – The Beatles and the Stones, the Pistols and The Clash – still sound as urgent and as stirring as ever. Their primal connection kicks in every time. The Smiths, by contrast, feel hermetically sealed in their era, walled in by a big force-field of archness. Like Andrew Windsor, nothing ever breaks sweat.

The process starts with the album cover. 'Louder Than Bombs', it says in inverted commas, right under the picture of kitchen-sink dramatist Shelagh Delaney. In the CD booklet, all the song titles are in quotation marks too – an alienation effect that extends to the music itself.

For all of Johnny Marr's highly-prized instrumental prowess, it's the still enigmatic figure of Steven Morrissey who governs our attitude to these songs. 'How can someone so young sing words so sad?' he asks during 'Sheila Take A Bow'. It's a question that you immediately want to turn back on the questioner. Were his own sad words sincere? Was he really miserable then? How much was the Smiths singer playing a role and how much did he mean it, *maaaaaan*? Subsequent events and solo albums have not made that conundrum any easier to solve, they've just made him a harder person to love.

Frankly, and much as I hate talking about myself in reviews, it's impossible for me to divorce this music from the person I was at the time it came out. These songs found me at the start of my career in journalism, expected to exhibit all the wisdom of adulthood while being all too aware that I wasn't really grown-up enough: that I just hadn't earned it yet, baby. It's not pleasant to be reminded of a time when I could sing along with the words of 'Please Please Please Let Me Get What I Want' and be deadly serious about every single one of them.

Even now, however, some songs resonate more than others – especially the ones where Morrissey escapes the thrall of his carefully constructed persona, the ones where he surprises himself with his insights. 'Sweet And Tender Hooligan', with its satirical portrait of a sharp lawyer trying to get an irredeemable thug off the hook, is one such moment: 'Because he'll never never do it again (at least not until the next time).' That kicks off a thrilling sequence that takes in the brooding 'Half A Person' ('Call me morbid, call me pale/I've spent six years on your trail') and the hell-for-leather 'London' ('Do you think you've made the right decision this time?')

So if you're going to listen to The Smiths, why choose *Louder Than Bombs*? Well, it plays merry hell with the band's timeline, and that's one of its great charms. It has a lot of the right songs, but not necessarily in the right order. The sleeve credits are also endearingly ramshackle: they mention that the late and much-missed Kirsty MacColl sings on 'Ask', but not that she also features on the unfairly disparaged cover of Twinkle's 'Golden Lights'. The album has the feel of a compilation thrown together in haste for the US market, which it was, and as we know with pop music, the throwaway releases often outlast the ones that were ostensibly built for the ages.

In short, for all the personal challenges posed for me by The Smiths' music 40 years after the fact, *Louder Than Bombs* is as good a way as any to experience some of their finest work. It is a first-rate collection and I commend it to the House.

## *THE TUBE* CITY ROAD STUDIOS
### 10 APRIL 1987, NEWCASTLE-UPON-TYNE, UK

### CARL HINDE

Newcastle's only 15 miles from where I live, and *The Tube* was up on the Friday night, half five to half seven. I found out on the Friday morning that they were playing, and I thought, 'Right, I'll go through and see if I can get in.' Obviously, no tickets, but I thought, 'We'll just hang around outside and see if I can see them.' And as we walked towards the studio, we saw the bus passing with them all in. I thought, 'Oh shit, we've missed them, we've missed them.' So we thought, 'Right, we'll try and find out where the bus has gone.' So we were wandering around down Quayside and we found the bus parked up. The curtains were all

closed. So we hung around outside the bus and then eventually knocked on the door.

The driver came out and we asked, 'When will The Smiths come out? Can we have a word?' He went, 'No, no, it's not The Smiths.' I went, 'It is. We've just seen them.' He went, 'No, no, it's not The Smiths.' I went, 'I know it is, I know you're lying.' And he went back on the bus and he got his sheet, which showed what band he was transporting, and it wasn't them. We thought it was the same bus and it wasn't, so we legged it back up the studio.

It was about a quarter to five when they arrived. And as they got off the bus, they recognised us. I spoke to Mike and then I spoke to Johnny, and I said, 'Johnny, we haven't got tickets, can you get us in?' He said, 'Yeah, no problem.' So Johnny put my name and 'plus three' on the guest list.

As they came off stage afterwards, Johnny gave us a setlist and Mike gave us his drumsticks and his 'Sheila' t-shirt. I'm convinced that was the last ever live performance. They might have done something in Italy, an Italian TV show, but it wasn't live. That was Morrissey performing to background music.

## 'SHEILA TAKE A BOW'
### RELEASED 13 APRIL 1987

The band's joint highest charting UK single and final 'non-album' single, reaching the number ten spot.

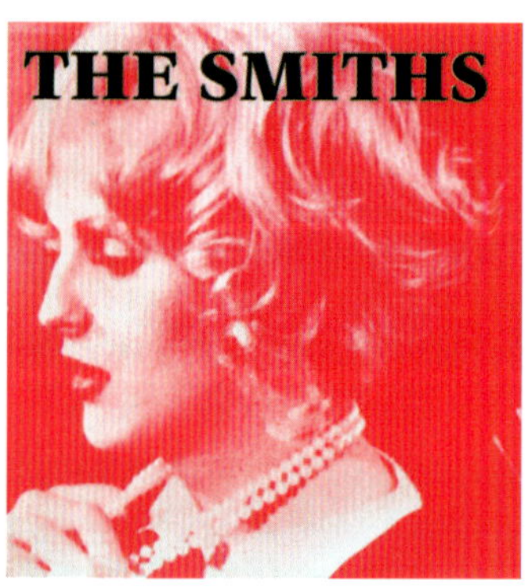

*Sheila Take A Bow*

## NEW MUSICAL EXPRESS

### JULY 1987, LONDON, UK

### SMITHS TO SPLIT

An article in the *New Musical Express* carried the story…

## BOX STUDIO

### AUGUST 1987, DENTON, MANCHESTER, UK

### IAN MOSS

In the early eighties I had fronted a couple of bands but now my forays into the world of music were infrequent and sporadic. I was being encouraged to re-engage by a friend, Simon Taylor (later a long-time road manager for The Fall). I played a couple of ad hoc gigs, borrowing from Marc Riley some members of his group The Creepers, and my appetite was whetted. I wanted to record some music and set about enlisting musicians. Simon and Marc Riley would play guitars, my brother Neil (ex-Frantic Elevators) would play bass… but I needed a drummer. Who I wondered might be suitable?

Carousing in the Haçienda one night I bumped into Smiths drummer Mike Joyce. Now I knew Mike pretty well from his stint as sticks man in The Hoax, an abysmal third-rate plastic punk band featuring one of my best friends, Steve Mardy, amongst their number. My distaste for their music hadn't stopped me liking young Mike and he had often expressed his admiration for my group, The Hamsters.

We chatted amiably and then I had one of those light bulb moments which I immediately vocalised. 'Do you fancy doing some drumming for me Mike? Help record a couple of songs?'

'I'd love to,' he responded but permission had to be sought from senior Smiths, Morrissey and Marr. I expected a refusal, but permission was granted, which I thought was very gracious. Box Studio in Denton was booked, a date was set and two songs were selected to record; a self-composed one entitled 'Digging In The Dirt' and Marc Bolan's 'Baby Strange'. I also played Mike The Flamin' Groovies' 'Slow Death' and proposed we record it at a later date, perhaps with Johnny Marr on guitar. 'He might do it,' Mike opined, 'because I know he'd love that track.'

We gathered with further performers added to round out the sound. We put the tracks down with a minimum of fuss. They were fine but rather spoilt

*Ian Moss put a band togehter whose line up briefly included Mike Joyce*

by my overindulgent whisky drinking, which turned my vocal performance into a hippopotamus-like bellow.

But the big news (after we promised it would go no further) was Mike telling us that Johnny Marr had walked out of The Smiths. Over the next few days, we were updated on the goings on as the band considered their options. A week later, Marc and Simon were back at the studio to mix the tracks. The surprising presence of a Smith in Denton had clearly excited interest and the studio was packed with people hoping for a meet with the music icon.

We stayed in regular contact over the next few months and after another chance encounter, this time at a Nico concert at the Library Theatre, I had recruited New Order bassist Peter Hook to play on some further recordings. The thought of a rhythm section comprising Hooky and Mike was exciting. I asked Mike if he would play. His circumstances had changed, he explained. His situation was insecure, and he said he would play but required a very modest session fee. I understood his position and was in no way unsympathetic towards him, but felt paying somebody to participate was against the spirit of the enterprise. I explained my position to Mike and without recriminations we moved on. I ultimately recruited Marc's ex-Fall colleague Paul Hanley for this session…

As a footnote, Marc was interviewed by Sounds magazine at around this point. Rumours of a supergroup forming with members from The Smiths, New Order and The Fall had reached the press, and Marc was quizzed about it. He explained it was just about helping out an old pal (ie. me), although the journalist suspected wrongly that there was a lot more to the story.

*Smiths split*

# GOODBYE, SMITHS

## GROUP SPLITS, MORRISSEY TO GO SOLO

**THE SMITHS** are dead. After weeks of speculation about a replacement for Johnny Marr, *NME* discovered at the weekend that Morrissey intends to record under his own name in the future.

His new songwriting partner is Stephen Street, the producer and engineer who has worked with The Smiths since the Sandie Shaw collaboration in March, 1984.

And it's now more than likely that the two remaining Smiths – drummer Mike Joyce and bass player Andy Rourke – will team up with Johnny Marr in his new band.

The news started to break on Friday when the *NME* received a statement from Joyce announcing his departure, saying he had "fulfilled his role" with The Smiths.

Rough Trade and The Smiths' office were unaware that Joyce intended to quit, as he had been approached by Morrissey to play on his solo material.

The full truth was revealed on Saturday by Pat Bellis, spokesperson for Morrissey: "It's end one era before beginning another.

"The Smiths were Morrissey, Johnny, Andy and Mike. Any other combination would not have been the same, so the auditions to replace Johnny were never taken really seriously. They just tried out a few people suggested by friends.

"There was a tremendous pressure on Morrissey when Johnny left, and he knew it would be a difficult task to replace him."

Morrissey has already recorded a couple of songs with Stephen Street in demo form and is said to be happy with the results. Product may be in the shops before the end of the year, on EMI.

Pat Bellis added that Morrissey will *not* be appearing in *Brookside*, as earlier suggested, although the thought of being Harry Cross's neighbour was very appealing.

Joyce's statement said he would be soon working with other musicians, and sources in Manchester say it is likely he will link up with Marr, and Rourke will he quit The Smiths will be out next month. He plays guitar on the new Bryan Ferry LP, as yet untitled, and has co-written one of the songs with the singer. Ferry has also recorded a vocal version of The Smiths' instrumental 'Money Changes Everything', which will not be on the album, but may surface as a B-side sooner or later.

So, the new Smiths album 'Strangeways Here We Come', released later this month, will be the last we hear from the band, unless negotiations by Rough Trade to release a live album are successful. The label wants to issue an LP from the Kilburn National Ballroom show last year, the tapes of which belong to the BBC.

Morrissey and Marr are still both signed to EMI as individuals, but the label will now never release a Smiths record.

Nick Gatfield, head of A&R at EMI, was not available for comment at the time of going to press. He was at the company's annual sales conference, the same conference here The


We were starting design and kicking ideas around for a tour to support *Strangeways*, talking about stage layout and venue size and what we were going to do and all of that kind of stuff. I still remember getting the call from Johnny saying, 'Hey, can you come over again? There's something I need to talk to you about,' and learning that he had decided to leave the band.

They did one ill-fated show without Johnny after he left. I don't know how it went. It was clear. It wasn't clear. It felt to me the right thing to do to stick with my mate. I always got on fine with Morrissey. He was always lovely and kind to me. But after Johnny left, I was like, 'I'm out. I'm not going to be involved with The Smiths without Johnny.'

There were many occasions, back in the day, when I was living with one of my good friends in Leicester, spending hours on the phone with Morrissey in great conversations talking about staging and theatrics and this series of iconic backdrops and how we were going to heighten the excitement of the opening of the show.

The band were very embracing of the notion that 'there's no such thing as a bad source for a good idea'. I remember Morrissey saying, 'I really want to have an iconic opening where the fans get to know that this is really when the show is starting.' And then he suggested Prokofiev's *Romeo And Juliet*. And I'm like, 'This would be great. Let's do searchlights over the audience.' Everybody was just spitballing ideas.

I bounce back and forth between the Smiths camp and the New Order camp. My friend Andy Little, who was the lighting designer for New Order, would help me with Smith shows and I'd help him with New Order shows. There were a lot of parallels between the two of them. There was a lot that we didn't know, but we liked that we didn't know what we didn't know because it was liberating. In dealing with bands now, there's a lot of, 'Well, you have to do this and you have to do that' and, 'You can't do this and you can't do that.' We're working with a couple of bands early in the arc of their career, and there's so much of a formulaic pattern. Back then, we were making shit up as we were going along!

The Smiths were always challenging from a management standpoint. With the possible exception of the Hans Zimmer Organisation, I don't think I've ever worked for a band where the band and the crew were so tight. I do the design for Hans Zimmer Live and when you go into catering, there's a truck driver, a bus driver, the guitarist, Hans and a roadie, all sitting around the same table. That's exactly how The Smiths were.

There wasn't a ton of organisation. The gang at Rough Trade did a

*Smiths split*

# MARR QUITS

JOHNNY MARR has left The Smiths — but Morrissey and the band plan to continue and are currently auditioning new guitarists.

That was the official version of events according to the band's record company Rough Trade this week. A statement issued by the label said that "although Johnny's departure is sad the band wish him happiness and success with his future projects."

Smith's PR Pat Bellis told the Maker that Marr's departure was entirely amicable but at the same time would be permanent. This effectively scotches rumours that the split was just a temporary bust-up caused by Morrissey and Marr being locked up in the studio for too long together while recording the new album "Strangeways, Here We Come". It's no secret that the pair's lifestyles differ and this has caused several arguments between them in the past.

"It isn't over one particular argument," Bellis said. "Johnny just wants to move in a completely different direction." She pointed out that the split had nothing to do with Marr's increasing amount of guest appearances on albums by the likes of Bryan Ferry and Talking Heads. She also said reports claiming Marr had interrupted Smith's sessions to work with the above artists and that he and Morrissey had not spoken for three months were completely fictitious.

Pat also denied that Morrissey was "unhappy" with the company Marr was keeping. "Half the time he doesn't even know who Johnny's seeing. Johnny keeps these things very private."

Although The Smiths are already auditioning new guitarists they say it will be a few months yet before any decision is made. Rumours that Craig Gannon, who joined the band as second guitarist in 1986 only to leave eight months later, would rejoin were also discounted.

"Craig's an extremely good guitarist but he hasn't done a lot of songwriting. I think he's a bit young for them," Bellis said. Indeed, Gannon said on his departure in December '86: "I knew they weren't happy with me personally. That's one of the reasons I left." Rumours circulate that Marr is now looking for musicians to form a new band. However, the man himself is keeping quiet. Meanwhile, the prospect of a Smiths tour to accompany "Strangeways" looks almost non-existent now.

"They did say at the start of this year that they wouldn't be playing in the UK," Bellis said. "However, a proposed tour has been on off for the last six months basically because the band's last agent's contract ran out at the end of last year."

EMI, who signed The Smiths last October are refusing to comment on the situation. But a spokeman said: "Nevertheless it is grounds for a certain amount of anxiety. Obviously we'd rather have a Smiths with Johnny Marr than one without but, if it is true, we'll be getting two for the price of one."

Under the terms of their deal The Smiths and individual members are contracted to EMI if they release further records. If nothing else EMI will definitely get a live album from the original line up. A number of shows on their winter tour last year were recorded with that thought in mind.

yeoman's task trying to keep us on track but there were times when we knew we were playing Leeds and we'd say, 'Let's get to Leeds and then find a poster to figure out where we're playing.'

I remember Phil Powell, Johnny's guitar roadie, jumping out of the bus and jumping in a cab to take the cab to go to the gig and saying to the cab driver, 'Go slow, there's a bus and a truck following me behind you.'

When you're 17, 18, 19, and you don't know any better, that's all a grand adventure and I wouldn't have not done it for all the money in the world.

Managers would come and go. 'We're going to get everything organised. It's going to be a whole different world,' and we would all be like, 'Uh-huh.' At one point, somebody who shall remain nameless walked into backstage and said, 'Oh, I've been hired as the new manager and I am…', and the much-missed Eddie Hallam, who was part of Oz PA, who were kind of the Manchester audio mafia and who did The Smiths and New Order,' said, 'No, no, no, don't tell me your name because then I'll just be sad when they fire you.'

Subsequently, I started to work with Johnny on The Pretenders and The The and some of his other ventures and started to spin out on my own and people were like, 'Here's an itinerary. This will tell you where you're going. Here's your confirmation numbers.' We were like, 'Whoa, these people are pretty organised,' and they're like, 'No, this is the way this stuff works.'

But I think that excitement and their newness came through in the shows, because there was an energy to it. It just felt like every new piece of music was so well received and so exciting. And the guys in the band, and especially Johnny and Morrissey, really were so focused on what they were going to do with the music and we knew that, so long as the music kept coming like the comet, we were super happy to be the tail to that comet.

We had a very narrow, tight stage and when we started to get into bigger gigs, we did the natural thing of spreading the band out more. And then the guys were like, 'We hate this. We want to be tight, physically as well as musically.'

So, we would do these big venues, especially in the States, and people would be like, 'You've got a 60-foot-wide stage, you're only using 30 feet of it.' And then they'd see the

*Smiths split*

show and they'd go, 'Oh, okay, that makes sense. Now I get that.' So we just kind of Forrest Gumped our way into doing all of these things because it felt like the right thing to do.

Grant Cunliffe (Showbiz), the sound guy, was really instrumental in helping guide the band, because he was kind of the seasoned old guy. He was probably the ripe old age of 30 and kind of like the elder statesman of our group. And I didn't realise it at the time, but he very kindly and very gently would nudge the band and the crew in the right direction when things were sort of at the point of chaos. Pieces were going to start flying off from the vortex of chaos. But we just were making shit up as we were going along, which I think was very much the way that band were with the music and in the studio: 'Let's try this, let's experiment, nobody's done that before so let's do it.'

I would travel with the crew. By default, I sort of filled the role of production manager even though I didn't realise it until we were figuring out credits for *Strangeways* and everyone was like, 'You're the production manager.' I am?

We would get to gigs at 10am or 11am for load in. The band would show up at four or five o'clock. It was a little earlier when we were doing shows in the States, just because we had to make allowances for union breaks and that kind of stuff.

We would we would show up mid-late morning, get everything loaded in, and get everything set. This was back in the days when bands would do proper sound checks. The band would show up late afternoon, sound check, and then we would batten down the hatches for the shows, especially when we were doing a stand-up gig in a traditional ballroom with a sprung dance floor like the Aragon Ballroom in Chicago, the Barrowlands in Glasgow or Manchester Free Trade Hall. We knew that the energy at these shows was going to be intense and we'd be like, 'Oh, it's going to be bonkers tonight.'

### MICHAEL FARRAGHER

Cathouse Studios in Streatham is where The Smiths ended up recording their last recording sessions. When they were doing the B-side for 'Girlfriend In A Coma', they recorded 'I Keep Mine Hidden' and 'Work Is A Four-Letter Word' there, in the studios across the road from where we lived. You could see that house from our front room. I was visiting a different sister up in north London, giving them a hand with mending their roof, when I got a call from my sister Rita. She was in Streatham and she said, 'You're never going to believe this, but I've just met Mike and Andy in the chip shop at the top of the road. I said, 'What are you doing in Streatham?" and they made up some story.' They didn't say, 'We're recording.'

So, after we knew that The Smiths were in town we were sitting at our front window watching people come and go into the studio. We never actually saw Morrissey or Johnny arrive, but we knew that there was something going on there. We wouldn't go over and knock on the door, and we weren't going to camp outside. We weren't that kind of fan. But we knew that they were likely to be over there. We did talk to Johnny about this. I've met Johnny since and had a good few chats with him. He told us that because they'd written to us and had our address and knew where we lived, they were considering coming over and knocking on the door. Can you imagine opening the door and Morrissey or Johnny Marr was there? You'd faint. That didn't happen, fortunately. But we saw Chrissie Hynde going in there, and Billy Bragg. We knew people would come to record. And it wasn't really until those B-sides appeared that we realised that that's what they were doing there.

When the split happened, there had been a rumour in the press that all was not well. Fred, the guy who lived with Grant Showbiz in the house across the road from us, was in a band called The Impossible Dreamers. He played drums with the band on one of the London gigs when they played 'Draize Train' at either Kilburn or Brixton when they had a second drummer come on. I think the house actually belonged to him. Rita had become friends with Fred, and he said to her in the July before the split had been announced, 'I've got an advance copy of the Smiths' new album. Do you want to come over and listen to it?' So she went over on her own – without me – to listen to *Strangeways* in his house two months before it came out. He hinted to her at that point that all wasn't well with the band.

Whether he knew they were splitting up at that point, I don't know. I don't think even the band knew that they were splitting up at that point. But he intimated to her that all wasn't well within the Smiths camp. And she came back and she had a copy of the tape which I still have. It has a slightly different mix of 'I Started Something'. We were listening to that for months before the album came out. And then we heard on John Peel that The Smiths had split. It was completely devastating. It was like, 'Is there any way this couldn't be true?' And then we were watching the music press

*Smiths split*

and, 'No, this looks like it's going to be permanent.'

I talked to Johnny afterwards. I met him at a The The gig in around '95 or '96 when they played at the Albert Hall. I went up during the day, and Johnny came outside and he was speaking to lots of people. It was a really lovely summer's day, and he sat down on the steps outside and just chatted to us for about an hour. We were talking to him about The Smiths and about other stuff.

I said to him, 'How long had you been wanting to leave The Smiths before you did?' He said, 'I wanted to leave after the first album.'

### MALCOLM GREENLEY

I remember opening the *NME* and seeing the story that they were splitting and thinking, 'Please don't let this be true.' They'd only been around for just about five years by then.

It was obviously between Morrissey and Marr, and the full truth has never yet come out. I've read several books about them, and I think Morrissey must be a very difficult person to work with. I think Marr had had enough.

I don't understand why they didn't get proper management. I remember reading that Johnny would come off stage and there'd be people there with cheque books waiting for him to sign. He was only 21 when that was happening. Morrissey wouldn't speak to people, and if Morrissey wanted rid of somebody out of the Smiths camp he would say 'he's gotta go' and then Johnny had to do all the dirty work. For someone who was 21 and who just wanted to play guitar and write music that must have been a nightmare. I just don't

*Kev Jones' Smiths tickets - he couldn't believe what he was reading in the NME*

think Morrissey trusted anybody. When you look at it in that light, it's amazing that they lasted as long as they did.

### CAROLINE ALLEN

I can remember it like it was yesterday. We were in the sixth form at school at the time, so we had a lot of free periods. I just happened to be at home one afternoon. *Granada Reports* came on and the woman reading the news said, 'And we're having reports that Johnny Marr has left Manchester band The Smiths.' I couldn't believe it. It was the worst thing to ever happen to me as a youngster.

### KEV JONES

Every Wednesday morning it was a bit of a joke at work. 'It's *NME* day, is it? There'll be no work for half an hour.' Before I'd opened my copy, someone else had got one

# SMITHS TO SPLIT

**THE SMITHS** look likely to call it a day after the release of their next album in September, and insiders are blaming a personality clash between Morrissey and Johnny Marr – the group's nucleus and songwriting partnership – for the split.

There's no official word from Rough Trade, apart from a rather flippant dismissal from Mozzer, but *NME* understands that relations between the two main men are so bad that they won't even enter the same studio together.

And promoters have been instructed not to arrange any live shows, either in Europe or America, to promote the new material, it is believed.

Morrissey, when approached through his press office for a comment, said: "Whoever says The Smiths have split shall be severely spanked by me with a wet plimsoll".

While *NME* newshounds await the arrival of young Steven armed with soggy footwear, sources in both London and Manchester continue to feed us with snippets which point towards the decline of the nation's top indie band:

● Marr has reportedly told friends in Manchester than he and Morrissey are no longer pals, and he is sick of the singer acting the self-centred star. He says the working relationship has also suffered considerably.

● Morrissey is not pleased with the company Marr is keeping, acting the guitar hero and playing on albums by Keith Richard, Bobby Womack and Bryan Ferry.

● The final straw was allegedly Marr interrupting Smiths recording sessions to fly to the States to record with Talking Heads, and using Rough Trade money to pay for the trip. Insiders say Morrissey blew his top and declared it was the end of The Smiths, and he never wanted to work with Marr again.

In Manchester last weekend, a friend of Johnny Marr's told an *NME* mole:

"I'm surprised that the press hadn't got hold of this earlier. It's been brewing for months, Marr and Morrissey haven't spoken to each other for three and a half months. There's a situation where they now see it as backing down to do so."

As mentioned earlier, Rough Trade have said next to nothing, and EMI – who are due to release Smiths material in 1988 – are none the wiser. But what about the secondary characters in the band? In/out bass player Andy Rourke could not be contacted, but a series of calls to drummer Mike Joyce hinted that all was not well.

The phone was answered by a young woman who, discovering it was the *NME* on the line, said Joyce wasn't in and wouldn't be back for a few days.

When told we wanted to ask Joyce about the break-up of the band, she said, "He doesn't want to comment on that. He has nothing to say". No surprised reaction, no flat denial.

Meanwhile, The Smiths' next single, 'Girlfriend In A Coma', will be released by Rough Trade on August 10. The album, 'Strangeways, Here We Come', follows on September 28.

The single is backed with 'Work Is A Four Letter Word', a cover of a Cilla Black song from the 1968 movie of the same name. The 12-inch features an extra Morrissey/Marr track, 'I Keep Mine Hidden'. Shelagh Delaney is the sleeve cover star.

'Strangeways, Here We Come' is The Smiths' last studio album for Rough Trade – and their last ever? – before the planned move to EMI. It was recorded in Bath, produced by Morrissey, Marr and Stephen Street, though not necessarily all at the same time.

The full track listing reads 'A Rush And A Push And The Land Is Ours', 'I Started Something I Couldn't Finish', 'Death Of A Disco Dancer', 'Girlfriend In A Coma', 'Stop Me If You Think You've Heard This One Before', 'Last Night I Dreamt That Somebody Loved Me', 'Unhappy Birthday', 'Paint A Vulgar Picture', 'Death At One's Elbow' and 'I Won't Share You'.

A *South Bank Show* on The Smiths, which could turn out to be their swansong, will be screened in the autumn.

*That NME headline*

*Rita & Michael Farragher were often in correspondence with Morrissey*

Dear Rita and Michael,
Your support shall always be remembered when we think of the tour. It was long and hard and not always enjoyable. But there were, for me, some joyously tearful moments.
The non-success of "Shakespeare's Sister" is hard to live with. That record meant so much to us. Our days with RT are certainly numbered. Have you done your second demo yet? The world is waiting.
love at least,
MORRISSEY
X X X

and one of the guys I worked with said, 'I think you'd better sit down, Kev. There's some news before you open that.' I remember the headline, 'Smiths to split', I was just a bit gutted, really. I don't think anybody really saw it coming.

### DAVID TIMLIN

When *Strangeways, Here We Come* came out, I wasn't, and I'm still not, a fan. It's my least favorite album. I thought Morrissey was running out of ideas, which is funny because The Smiths themselves think it's their best album. For me something had changed. The music was cleaner than tracks like 'Hand In Glove' and 'This Charming Man'. The way they'd dressed had changed too; towards the end they were smarter. They looked like a proper band rather than just people. Morrissey was vocal early on about never selling out

and doing music videos, and then Derek Jarman's stuff for *The Queen Is Dead* came along. They'd done a few videos for 'Bigmouth Strikes Again' and 'Sheila Take A Bow' and such. Things were changing. They weren't the band that I got into. But I still loved them.

There were all those rumours that that Morrissey and Johnny Marr weren't getting on. After the *Eurotube* thing, there were 'the lads' and then Morrissey at the back of the bus waiting to go… like 'I've done this, now it's time to leave.' I don't think Johnny was enjoying it.

I think I read the about the split. I'm not trying to be smart after the event, but I remember thinking, 'I bet Johnny Marr has got fed up with it.' He was doing the whole lot – general management, tour management stuff, the lot. I've read he'd lost loads of weight at the time because he was just so stressed out by it all.

### RITA FARRAGHER

People often asked us if we ever got bored seeing the same band over and over again and I can honestly say it was never boring. No matter how tired we were, as soon as The Smiths hit the stage we would be mesmerised. We couldn't wait for them to announce dates. They were a brilliant live band and when I have read about how difficult things were behind the scenes during those years, I am amazed, because they put on a great show.

We certainly did it the hard way. We were just students and pretty penniless, so we looked for the cheapest forms of transport – usually a coach – and collected vouchers to get discounts all the time. Mars Bars did a National Express offer, and we collected every wrapper we could to get free coach travel, saving us a fortune. We also hardly ever got a place to stay, sleeping in the coach station or trying to find somewhere open all night where we could safely hang out. We had a few sticky situations!

The last year of The Smiths was all a bit strange. Our dad died, so we missed some things. Then they turned up to record what turned out to be their final recording in the studio on our road. I met Andy and Mike in the chip shop, and they seemed very upbeat, but when I spoke to Fred, the studio owner, it was clear that all was not well. Shortly after that we heard about the split, and it was pretty devastating.

To be honest I thought at the time that it would just be a short break and that we would definitely see them as The Smiths again. But then, as the years went by and the court case came, it was clear that would never happen. I still hope for a Morrissey and Marr reunion at some point.

It was a great way to spend our late teens, and it was great to have my brother to share that time with – I would never have done it on my own. I fell out of love with music in general a bit after The Smiths. They remain unmatched for me.



## 'GIRLFRIEND IN A COMA'
### RELEASED 10 AUGUST 1987

The first single to promote forthcoming album *Strangeways, Here We Come*, allegedly inspired by Nina Simone's 'To Be Young, Gifted And Black'. The video received copious plays on ITV's *The Chart Show*.

### BEC MORRIS

It's 1998 in Blackburn, Lancashire. I'm seven years old, legs not quite touching the floor of the passenger seat, while my dad drives us around town with *The Smiths – The Singles* on repeat.

He'd been introduced to them by my Uncle Frank, who'd loved them since the start, and now they were just there – in the car, at home, on our camping trips. A reliable constant, and the soundtrack to everything. I had no idea who Morrissey was, what Salford Lads Club was, or in my innocence, what a coma was.

What I did know was that 'Girlfriend In A Coma' was my favourite song. I danced to it with pure joy, coming to the conclusion that 'coma' was probably a misspelling of comma. I pictured his girlfriend trapped inside a punctuation mark, folded awkwardly into a curve – it sounded inconvenient. No wonder he was worried about her. Still, the song was upbeat and bouncy, which was irresistible to seven-year-old me. Whatever the words meant, the rhythm felt happy – I didn't need to understand it to love it.

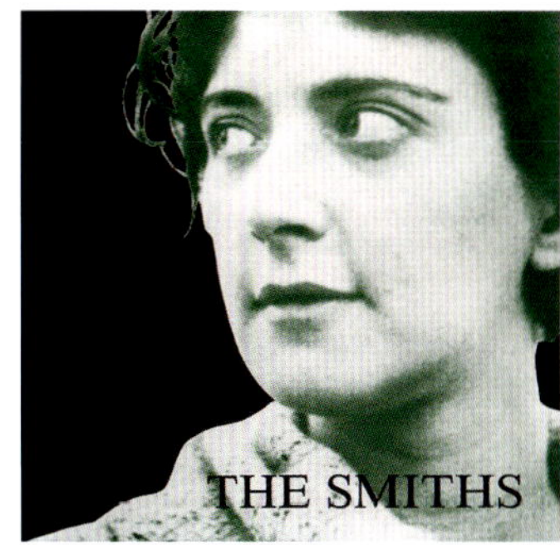


*Girlfriend In A Coma*

*Bec Morris with her dad's homemade Smiths compilation*

At school, I asked my teacher if she'd heard of The Smiths. She looked at me, puzzled, and said no. Years later, my mum told me the teacher had asked my parents about it, wondering what I was talking about. Nothing to worry about, we just listened to The Smiths.

My dad made me a cassette so that I could listen to the album on my Walkman, and I played it over and over. I loved how personal it felt – this was the era of the Macarena, the Spice Girls and Aqua singing about Barbie and her life in plastic. This was a little different… I felt like I'd discovered a secret that no one else knew, and this band made me different – they were mine. Only a few adults shared this secret with me, which made me feel grown up and special.

A few years passed and I was still listening, except now I was a teenager – earnest, morose and miserable in that way teenagers are when they haven't actually experienced much loss but feel the drama of life anyway, convinced they know it all. Suddenly the sadness made sense to me. I found a dark comfort in it, and I felt seen by lyrics written decades before I was born.

At home this felt safe, but at school I was considered a little strange. The music I loved didn't match what anyone else listened to, and no one else cared about jangly guitars or melancholy men with big feelings. I'd be mocked, but thankfully I growled back and stuck to my identity, still proud that I was different – I had this private world others knew nothing about and could never understand. Years later, that music has been revived in popular culture and those same people wear the t-shirts that I was singled out for.

For years, the only image I saw of the band was that photograph outside Salford Lads Club. From it, I invented entire worlds; I imagined seeing them live, hanging out with them, existing in some parallel present where they were still the young men from 1985, frozen in time.

When my dad passed away in 2021, I asked my mum to dig the old cassettes out of the attic, hoping it would still be there. It was – I bought a Walkman and played it again for the first time in years. It was an emotional moment, hearing that tape run again and wondering when it was last played. My dad's handwriting is still on the cassette, slightly faded but listing each track in blue ballpoint. It's become a treasured object, this cassette that impacted who I am from such a young age.

The Smiths have been there for almost my entire life. In childhood joy, teenage melancholy and adult reflection. Good times and bad, all looping back to that first misunderstanding, now driving my car alone listening – 'Girlfriend In A Comma'. (sic) A song I loved before I knew what it meant, and one I still love now that I do.

*Strangeways, Here We Come*

## STRANGEWAYS, HERE WE COME
### RELEASED 28 SEPTEMBER 1987

Reaching number 2 in the UK album charts, the band's final album was released after they had announced their split.

### IAIN KEY

While *The Queen Is Dead* was an instant hit, *Strangeways* for a long time felt like the black sheep of the band's canon. Maybe it's because the album was released after they split, the tracks never recorded for radio sessions or TV broadcasts or performed live in front of their passionate and loyal fanbase.

The Smiths sound had developed over their short career, and this album sees them at their most experimental, with tracks like 'Death Of A Disco Dancer' – a potential album closer at the midpoint on side one – going beyond your traditional indie fare and hinting at where they may have gone next.

As with The Beatles and *Abbey Road*, the recording sessions were reportedly cordial and productive despite the band being on the verge of falling apart, with Marr citing it as their masterpiece.

Although death and closure are constant companions throughout, there is a well-balanced mix of knowing humour ('Stop Me If You Think You've Heard This One Before'), yearning ('Last Night I Dreamt That Someone Loved Me') and the most accurate and damning portrayal of the music industry ('Paint A Vulgar Picture'), the latter predicting the reissuing, repackaging and re-evaluation that was to come. Not just for The Smiths or 'dead stars' but practically every artist.

Five years into their career, *Strangeways, Here We Come* saw Morrissey and Marr in almost perfect harmony with the final 'I Won't Share You' the perfect way on which to sign off.

### MOLLY VULPYNE

The Smiths are one of those bands capable of raising goosebumps in the first bar of a song. My connection to their music is deeply emotional. They soothe me and make me feel excited about music again whenever I crave inspiration. I wasn't fortunate enough to be born during their era, but that has never diminished my reverence and obsession for every note and lyric in their legacy.

Morrissey's lyrics are astonishing. I envy his gift for phrasing and his ability to express feeling with such sincerity, wit and nuance. That authenticity is unmistakable, and every Smiths song title feels instantly recognisable and etched into culture. The Smiths have shaped generations of artists, but they are still impossible to imitate, their brilliance lies in how unique they are. Morrissey and Marr will always be my Lennon and McCartney. I've tried to adopt the brutally honest way Morrissey delivers lines and you know what… he makes it look so easy, but it's not. And I love him for that.

Choosing a favourite Smiths song feels impossible, but the opening chords of 'Stop Me If You Think You've Heard This One Before' (on *Strangeways*) fill me with joy every time. And the lyric, 'Nothing's changed, I still love you, Oh I still love you, only slightly less than I used to, my love,' is perfection in its bite and its everyday phrasing. Devastatingly simple and utterly human.

### ROB LEVY

I was a freshman in college when

*Iain Key with Phil Brett*

*The Smiths' music & lyrics have inspired Molly Vulpyne as a singer-songwriter*

*Rob & Kelly bonded over The Smiths in an astromony class*

this album came out. It has the distinction of being the first album of theirs where I played their music on my radio show in real time. Yes, there were a ton of other singles, but it was great to play something from them that was fresh and new.

Everyone at the station played a different cut from it. Some of the disc jockeys who wanted smoke breaks put 'Death of a Disco Dancer' or 'Last Night I Dreamt That Somebody Loved Me' on and then stepped outside for a quick cigarette.

I bought the album the day it came out. I went with my friend John and we each bought copies before going back to my house and sequestered ourselves in my room and played it. This was the first time I ever listened to an album that just came out with a friend. John was way more into The Smiths than anyone I knew. His perspective was invaluable.

We sat there, me a straight fan of theirs and John a gay one, and listened to the album. Back then I didn't think of it as anything other than two fans of a band listening to music. But as years have gone by, I am glad this happened. It speaks to the power of music to bring people together.

*Strangeways, Here We Come* also brought me together with Kelly who was in my college astronomy class. As someone who was interested in the subject, I took the class as an elective without knowing it would be math heavy. I am rubbish at math.

The second week of class the professor put us into pairs for a project. I was not sure who I would end up with until this girl with spiky bleached-blonde hair introduced herself to me, She said she dug my shirt. I owned a few different shirts with The Smiths on them but on that day, I had donned my blue *Hatful of Hollow* shirt. This led to an immediate conversation about The Smiths and our project didn't get finished. Luckily, at the next class we got our act together and got it finished.

### JOHN PARKES

I don't think I was that concerned when I heard they were splitting. I didn't like *Strangeways, Here We Come*. It's not a record I play a lot. I was already coming out of my love affair with The Smiths and reverting back to the other music that I was progressing with – John Coltrane, Miles Davis, Wayne Shorter. I moved to London round about the same time, and it was a renaissance of the jazz scene. The Smiths went on the back burner.

I worked at Tooting Bec hospital. As much as I'd moved on from The Smiths, I still had a few Smiths t-shirts. One day I came out of Tooting Bec hospital to go on the Tube into London. I got up to Tooting Bec station and this guy walked past me and gave me this really nice smile. It was Mike Joyce. I didn't think anything else of it, but this was '87 and it turns out The Smiths were recording in Streatham, ten minutes away from Tooting Bec.

## THE SOUTH BANK SHOW

18 OCTOBER 1987,
LONDON, UK

### STEVE WILLIAMS

*The South Bank Show* was a big
thing for anybody arty at the time,
particularly if you were into music
or into punk. It was coming up on
the Sunday night, and I was really
excited to be seeing it, right up
to the death of The Smiths. And
in the week leading up to it, the
announcement came that they were
splitting up. I'll always remember,
on the introduction, Melvyn Bragg
saying, 'We've filmed this show but
since we've filmed it they've split, so
we've had to edit it and change it.' I
was shocked. I thought, 'This can't
really be happening.'

It seemed such a strange thing to
split up just before they got on the
programme when it was all about
them. I can't remember how I heard
about the split. I can remember
friends saying, 'It can't be true.
They're the biggest thing around in
indie music at the moment. Surely
they can't just disappear like that?'
But that's what happened.

### BEN WILLMOTT

*The South Bank Show* was the start
of my real education. It explored
the inspirations of the band as well
as their history and opened up a
treasure trove of culture, from Oscar
Wilde and Joe Orton to kitchen sink
dramas like *Saturday Night And
Sunday Morning* and *The L-Shaped
Room*. I was getting into Public
Enemy and Coldcut and, although
they might not seem similar on the
surface, the way Morrissey 'sampled'
(sometimes literally, sometimes
by stealing specific lines) was very
similar, leaving clues which could be
followed up on and explored more
deeply when you came across them.

## 'I STARTED SOMETHING I COULDN'T FINISH'
### RELEASED 2 NOVEMBER 1987

Released after planned single,
'Stop Me If You Think You've
Heard This One Before', was
banned by the BBC in the wake of
the Hungerford Massacre. Despite
the group breaking up, the video
features Morrissey and fans with
quiffs and glasses riding around
Salford on bikes.

## 'LAST NIGHT I DREAMT SOMEBODY LOVED ME'
### RELEASED 7 DECEMBER 1987

Billed on promo posters as 'The
Final Single' the seven-inch
version removes the two-minute
intro which had consisting of
piano playing against a backdrop
of crowd noises from the miners'
strike of 1984–85. It reached
number 30 on the UK chart.

## VIVA HATE
### RELEASED 14 MARCH 1988

After much speculation in the
music press about whether the
Smiths split was permanent,

*I Started Something I Couldn't Finish*

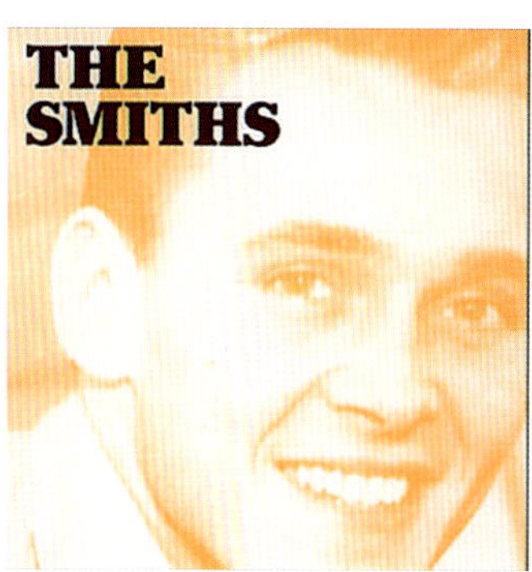

*Last Night I Dreamt Somebody Loved Me*

Morrissey unveiled *Viva Hate*, his debut solo album.

### ROCHELLE D WEISKOPF

I slept in someone's yard for about ten to twelve hours and about half a mile from the record store where Morrissey was doing a signing. This was when *Viva Hate* came out. We had to get wrist bands showing we were first in line before they would let us in. I'm six people away from the door and so excited. Next thing I know, Morrissey is being hurried out the door because someone ahead of me was talking about The Smiths. I was devastated.

*Rank*

# *RANK*

### RELEASED 5 SEPTEMBER 1988

Almost two years after their last live performance, and following the band announcing they were splitting, the live album *Rank* was released. It captured the October 1986 performance at Kilburn's National Ballroom. One title suggestion for the album was *The Smiths In Heat*. The band's 21 song setlist was trimmed to 14 numbers, with 'There Is A Light That Never Goes Out' and 'How Soon Is Now?' amongst those failing to make the cut. It was a poor memento of an illustrious live career.

### MARK REZZANO

Like all great stories, this one begins at a bus stop in Stockport. It was 1993 and I was 18. Alighting from the 192 bus I ran into an old school friend, Stephen. He greeted me with the words, 'Who is she?' Perceptively, he had read my gloomy expression to be the result of a romantic infatuation that was consuming me. As we walked home, he told me that he was going through a similar predicament. It was an encounter that rekindled our friendship and helped me navigate my way through this first taste of teenage heartache.

Amidst this emotional turmoil, The Smiths entered my life. One song in particular encapsulated everything I was feeling at the time, 'I Want The One I Can't Have', and the lines, 'I want the one I can't have / And it's driving me mad / It's all over / All over / All over my face.' A lyrical sleight of hand that conveyed the desperation I was feeling at the time, while in the next breath hitting you with the double meaning.

I was only twelve when The Smiths broke up, and never got to see them live. However, I have been in close proximity to all four on occasion (Morrissey at the Festival Hall for the New York Dolls' *Meltdown* concert, Johnny at Manchester City games, Andy sashaying down Whitworth Street and Mike at Borders).

Eventually I met someone and my torment dissipated. Nevertheless, it softened my heart and taught me more about myself than just about anything else in the interim. The trivial things that once meant so much before suddenly lost their significance. You feel everything so intensely as a teenager, especially affairs of the heart. 'I Want The One I Can't Have' was the soundtrack to that.

# LEGACY

### RICHARD PREECE

The Smiths changed everything for us, as of course they did for so many.

I first heard them on the school bus in 1984 and I knew then that, for once, there was the possibility that things could get better. It was the same for my future best friend, Keith, although he was even more obsessive than me, collecting many rare records, writing about (and to) The Smiths in fanzines and even meeting Morrissey a couple of times at Smiths concerts. When Keith and I got to know each other years later, it was our shared history of loving The Smiths that brought us closer. He'd recently finished with his Smiths-influenced band, Blueboy, and their various side projects, but he still held a creative spark and desire, at least part inspired by Morrissey's poetic playfulness.

We approached our then record label and persuaded them to compile and release a tribute to The Smiths, *Romantic And Square Is Hip And Aware*, the title stolen from a Smiths run out groove. This was 2003 but the album didn't see the light of day until 2004. We'd missed our self-imposed deadline of the twentieth anniversary of 'Hand In Glove'.

We recorded two songs for the album – one was a version of 'Girlfriend In A Coma', the other a faked 'live' recording of 'Bigmouth Strikes Again' which was one of Keith's last vocal recordings (he very sadly died in 2007) – but it was a belter. And, with Morrissey-like attention to detail, he lifted crowd noise from an actual Smiths 1983 concert bootleg tape to enhance our 'live' performance. This came complete with cheers, claps and whoops and also the prominent and emphatic comment from a female audience member: 'This band are fucking crap!'

The irony that The Smiths would go on to become one of the greatest bands ever doesn't detract from the fact that they were always also a little divisive, to say the least. But if such feedback was good enough for The Smiths, it was good enough for us. And Keith was of course the cover star, in a picture taken 20-ish years previously, dressed as Morrissey and posing as if in preparation for a future album cover. Poetry.

### RICHARD BOWES

Born in 1981, I was too young to experience The Smiths while they were active. But I learned…

Like many people, Oasis were my gateway drug. Noel Gallagher often spoke about his love for The Smiths, and as a devoted Oasis fan, I felt compelled to investigate why. At first, I'll admit, it didn't immediately click. There are no obvious anthems, and they lack the pulsating Mod power of The Jam or The Who. The Smiths possess an elegance and deftness that most other seminal bands don't, and that took some work.

But 'How Soon Is Now?' made an instant impression, because it's one of the most remarkable pieces of music ever recorded. Then, as I entered my late teens and angst began to take full control, Morrissey's lyrics started to resonate. As one does at that age,

*Richard Preece's 'Romantic' album cover*

I felt no one suffered as much as I, and that Morrissey was speaking directly to me on 'I Know It's Over'. (Little did I know I was simply the latest in a long line of thousands who felt exactly the same.)

I have a theory that the reason The Smiths have endured so well is that each member speaks to you at different stages of life. Morrissey taps into the melodrama of your teenage years. Later, you come to appreciate the wizardry of Johnny Marr's guitar work, taking the slinkiness of Nile Rodgers and turning it into something entirely his own. Then there's the marauding barricade of Mike Joyce; understated, but never anything less than vital to the song. And has there ever been a more under-appreciated bass player than Andy Rourke?

The songs themselves are so textured and diverse that it's almost impossible to have a single favourite. For years, 'The Draize Train' had passed me by, but when I listened to *Rank* recently, it hit me like, well, a train. It's a glorious slice of action-funk and a band flexing their muscles, knowing just how good they are. Franz Ferdinand built a career out of it.

Their catalogue truly is the gift that keeps on giving. Not only that, but it's full of life lessons too. Is there a more inspiring lyric than: 'Shyness can stop you from doing all the things in life you'd like to'?

I interviewed Mike Joyce in 2022, and he summed it up perfectly: 'We were slap-bang in the middle of the 1980s, but we were nothing to do with the 1980s. I think that's testament to the kind of music we made and the sounds that we made.'

## CRAIG WALKER

I can remember the first time I heard The Smiths, aged twelve in my parents' house in Walkinstown, Dublin in 1983. It was 'Hand In Glove' booming out of my five-years-older brother's bedroom, on heavy rotation. He always had excellent taste in music.

When he finally went out, I snuck into his room and saw my first ever Smiths' single sleeve. 'Hand In Glove' was the beginning of a lifelong fascination with the band and the record sleeves.

More singles on twelve-inch came out. The B-sides were each their own little kitchen sink drama, vignettes of lyrical brilliance allowing us to get more insight into the brain of Morrissey. He spoke about subjects that as a near teenager I didn't fully grasp, but as I grew into my teens and bought each album on the day of release, they spoke more clearly and moved me in a way that no other music had done before.

I still measure the years of my adolescence by the Smiths album releases. I was 13 when their debut album came out and 16 when *Strangeways, Here We Come* was released and they split. The lyrics spoke to me at a time when I needed to hear them. It was okay to feel weird and lonely because Morrissey made it sound almost glamorous. My hair during those years was mostly a large quiff, and the clothes of Johnny Marr were a big influence on how I dressed. I was all in.

Retrospectively, it's easy to say The Smiths came out of the blocks fully formed, but to have lived through that glorious run of singles and albums in five masterpiece-filled years? The pleasure the privilege is and was mine.

More than 40 years after discovering them, I have had a second chance through my teenage son finding and loving them as much as I do. He blasts out The Smiths at home, in the shower, in the car, and I never once tell him to turn it down.

He tells me that Gen Zs love The Smiths more than any band from the eighties. They still speak to teenagers, and they will as long as teenagers exist.

## STEPHEN CANAVAN

Some bands just *mean* more to you, don't they?

Even now, years after their dissolution, their songs still stirring the soul and making you feel mighty, evoking memories that even merciless time cannot diminish. The Smiths are one of those bands…

Creating songs that you did not merely listen to …You *lived*…

Johnny Marr reinventing the Rickenbacker for a modern audience and creating rock alchemy in the process, with Morrissey, a genuine Northern poet, his startlingly original lyrics, alternatively aching with the pain of loneliness and isolation, yet also gleaming within the gloom with warmth and humanity. Morrissey crafted lyrics that could make you laugh and cry, sometimes making you do both within the same sentence. Rourke and Joyce, the rhythmic bone and sinew and pulsing blood of the band, an invaluable duo. Yes…The Smiths,

for me at least, *mean* more…

But I have a confession to make. I was too young to really appreciate the Smiths when they were in their glory. By the time I truly understood and appreciated their genius they had split. At least, that's what I always *thought*…

For growing up as kid in the eighties, The Smiths were hard to ignore, making an impression even if I didn't quite understand at first the brilliance and significance of what I was seeing and hearing. So when I hear 'This Charming Man' I'm a nine-year-old boy again, kneeling in front of the TV with a Wham bar in one hand and a small plastic microphone precariously attached to the side of a wheezing tape recorder in the other. I'm pointing it directly at the screen, trying to record *Top Of The Pops* for my sister. This was as high tech as it got in our house, it being years before we, and most people, could afford a video machine.

I recall being utterly baffled, but oddly entranced, not only by Marr's chiming, propulsive, Byrds-ian guitars, but by the appearance of the remarkable, charismatic lead singer with the striking voice, hair like a black surfboard jutting out the top of his head. I didn't really know what the song was about but – as always with me – the words pulled me into a narrative I didn't understand but which I still found utterly compelling.

The fact that Morrissey was twirling a rather starved-looking bunch of gladioli around his head like they were swords only added to the bizarre atmosphere. The moment was only slightly spoiled by my dad heading out to the pub, but sticking his head around the lounge door to enquire, 'What's that gangly drip doing, swinging a load of bloody flowers about?'

Similarly, when I hear the propulsive charge of 'Stop Me If You Think You've Heard This One Before' now, I'm back on a bus ploughing through West Germany on an school trip, while the glam pop stomp of 'Sheila Take a Bow' throws me back in time to a sun-dappled Old Trafford in the summer of 1987, watching spectacularly hirsute Perry boys in pristine Adidas Gazelles and expensive multi-coloured Lacoste jumpers, their designer jeans already beginning to show signs of nascent flaring at hems, clambering down from the cheaper wooden seats of E stand into the Streford End. It was a rather odd choice of pre-match song that stadium announcer Tom Tyrell, not exactly the Graham Park of football DJs, had taken a fancy to playing before each home game, along with the dolorous sway of 'Shoplifters Of The World Unite'.

Isn't memory strange?

But as I got older my love for The Smiths grew… Their music, as I moved from adolescent to manhood, taking on not only a greater depth, but also greater meaning, for as I said earlier, these were songs that you *lived*….

Words you felt had been written almost for *you*…for you *alone*….

Each album was a glorious treasure to be discovered, the wonderous single and album sleeve designs being nearly as anticipated and debated as the music and only

adding to the band's intoxicating allure. These were all factors that made me mourn the fact that I was too young to have seen them live…

By what memories The Smiths have made, and I have no doubt, will still make for me?

And what are great bands if they are not touchstones for memory? For listening to The Smiths is like opening a time capsule is it not?

So now it's 1993, and I'm reeling round a cold kitchen in Tree Court A in Owens Park, trying to cook cold sausages and beans in a tin on a mini stove, after a session on the ale in The Queen of Hearts, Fallowfield. I'm bellowing along to Morrissey's plaintive cry for understanding and empathy on 'The Boy With The Thorn In His Side', a plea warmly cocooned in Marr's gloriously warm Rickenbacker, and cracking up at the lyrics to 'Ask', singing along heartily with its doleful, but delightful chorus…

But now it's 2026 and I'm remembering old friends taken too soon, as the glacial stum of 'I Won't Share You' aches across my room, as now, aged 51 years, I try to put some order into these reminisces…

Oh Manchester… So much to answer for….

The squabbling between Morrissey and Marr in recent years has been an unpleasant and unedifying spectacle. But the great bands that are no longer with us are like our lost loves. While there may be pain in remembering the bitter ending, we should feel a greater joy in remembering the pleasure that they once gave us… and which they continue to do…

I still love the Smiths… I always

will… And, as someone once sang,

*And if not love, then it's the
bomb… then it's the bomb…
That will bring us together*

### TIM BAIGENT

Leading up to The Smith's 1987 album, *Strangeways Here We Come*, I started to have my head turned by Big Audio Dynamite, That Petrol Emotion, Beastie Boys, Schooly D and other early rap bods – when it was still a creative environment.

I didn't buy the singles released at the time such as 'Shoplifters Of The World Unite', 'Sheila Take A Bow' or 'I Started Something I Just Couldn't Finish'. They were good, but didn't have the crackle of the earlier risk-taking singles, just more of the same, good though it was. I wasn't prepared to part with my hard-earned YTS cash for it. Was it me? Was it the records? Then I heard 'Death Of A Disco Dancer' on John Peel show. I bought the album and regretted it. It was more of the same. Was I being unfaithful when purchasing The Wedding Present's George Best?

I had been working at the local printers for three and a half years, hopping off my Vespa every Wednesday morning and into the newsagents in the town square of Ilminster to buy my copy of the NME, as I had done for what seemed years.

'SMITHS SPLIT!' read the headline.

WHAT!?

I felt a wee bit of panic… and the sense of bereavement in my tum that I had when The Jam split five years earlier. No! This was my band. I hadn't been 'mentally present' for those first two or three Jam years, but I had been there for most of The Smiths. The singles, albums, the interviews, press cuttings… and now it was gone.

Reflecting that later that week at work, it felt right somehow, finish at the top, just like The Jam. Class. Things were moving on. When you are hot, you are hot… and then you are not.

Things started to move on for me too. I decided to pack in my job at the printers and blag my way on the local art foundation course. The band I had formed with best friend Stew was catching light too.  Within two years we were on the John Peel show, and I was on my art degree in Central London, blagging time off to support the Inspiral Carpets on tour, then off to Germany and Switzerland, my college mates covering my non-attendance tracks like ruthless KGB agents. My Smiths LPs made the trip to London with all my other records, first to halls of residence in Battersea, then to £25-a-week rentals in Peckham, Camberwell and Brixton.

By then The Smiths had been tucked away at the back and not left out in plain sight when 'entertaining' in my room. Was I embarrassed? Not really. How could I be, they were such a big part of me. But there they stayed, unplayed.

In 2024 I bought a long metal army ammo box from the local tip to house all my 45s. Transferring them to their new home I came across 'Shakespeare's Sister'. I popped it on the Dansette my lovely wife Bethan had purchased for me for Christmas so I could 'Play all that lovely vinyl you have'.

*Tim Baigent could be found busking in Taunton, inspired by The Smiths*

*Keeley Moss with her Smiths mural*

What a record. Such ballsy chaos to deliver to Thatcher's Britain and a treat for me and my mates living via Top Of The Pops or The Tube for our musical kicks. It took a slightly sweating me by surprise and right back and has kicked it all off again. Distance from a loved one can release an over emotional outpouring.

That out is still pouring as I type… Thanks lads.

### KEELEY MOSS, ARTIST

The glistening guitar sounds, the pulsating bass lines, the military mastery of those drum parts. The production too. The songs, absolutely. But those words... that world view. Through these words I was suddenly privy to a lyrical landscape that was at once familiar and yet unprecedented, unique and unknown:

*I left my bag in Newport Pagnell...*
*Well there's panic on the streets*
*of Carlisle, Dublin, Dundee,*
*Humberside...*
*The Leeds side streets that you slip*
*down*
*It took a tattooed boy from*
*Birkenhead to really, really open her*
*eyes...*
*Smoke lingers 'round your fingers...*
*Trains heave on to Euston...*
*Do you think you've made the right*
*decision this time?*
*What do we get for our trouble and*
*pain but a rented room in Whalley*
*Range?*

Each of these lines referenced ordinary, everyday, specific places. To a kid who had grown up on the mean streets of Dublin, this was so unexpected, so odd, so off-kilter. And so bloody brave and brilliant. This was Morrissey's genius writ large, the shining of a spotlight on provincial life, real life, without any real equivalent in music.

Here was a band, and a frontman, daring to dispense with those standard reference points that visuals that I have ever experienced. And I wasn't watching it in a cinema, or on television. I was seeing it from a car window. My own private movie soundtrack of sorts, 'Some Girls Are Bigger Than Others' juxtaposed to real-time footage of the streets of Anglesey passing by before me. Houses, shops, pubs and roads, a hodgepodge of homes housing sleeping humans who I would never know, behind every door a story, under every floor a secret. And there I was privy to this unfolding film in the back seat of a car, my mind on fire at the cosmic collision of it all. That song made more sense to me in that moment and in that environment than anywhere else I would ever hear it. The sparkling tapestry of delay-drenched arpeggios and echo-laden vocal and guitar effects awash throughout 'Some Girls Are Bigger Than Others' was so reflective of the atmosphere around me. A sight so full of night, ghostly, dreamy and lonely, it's moonlit magnificence possessing a magical essence.

Nowadays, I live in my beloved 'Dear old Blighty' that I fell in love with through The Smiths' songs. Every home I've had since I left home at 18 has featured a giant Smiths mural that I painstakingly rebuild every time I have to move.

The mural features every record the band ever released, every single, every album, every import release, a giant sprawl of Smithsness that serves as a vast collage, a musical map and a patch quilt of pure perfection.

### ROB ALLEN

I dreamt of meeting a Smith, a member of Morrissey's band or Morrissey himself. But would that chance encounter ever happen? The first missed opportunity – a thrillingly violent, sweaty and loud gig – was at Aston Villa Leisure Centre in February 1995, as Morrissey was already in the habit of leaving before the final note of 'Shoplifters Of The World Unite' had rung out.

Then came Chester's Northgate Arena in December 1997, a strange yet wonderful show in another soulless sports hall venue with a live rendition of 'Paint A Vulgar Picture'. But, again, no face-to-face with the man himself. A ring of security, a waiting Ford Granada and not even a wave from Morrissey or his drummer, Spencer Cobrin, as they sped out of the car park.

It was early 1998, at Ten Bar on Tariff Street for a gig by The Pavement Family, that my first encounter with Johnny Marr happened. Did I know he'd be there? Yeah, it was likely. With a slip of receipt paper and a pen from the bar staff, first the autograph and then: 'Have you seen the latest issue of *The Word* with Morrissey on the cover?'

Johnny: 'No, anything good in there?'

Me: 'It's got a lot in it about his relationships with people and how he's quite difficult to understand.'

Johnny: 'I wish I could understand him.'

Fast forward to 1999 and a bar on Manchester's Oxford Road. A group walked in and one amongst them was instantly recognisable as Andy Rourke. My hero. Another slip of paper and a pen from the bar staff, a gushing word about the brilliant bass line of 'Barbarism Begins At Home' and a second dream had come true.

October 1999 and I agreed to go to Maine Road to watch Manchester City take on Ipswich Town. Heading up the stairs of the lower Platt Lane Stand for a half-time pint was Mike Joyce. A borrowed pen and the folded match ticket, an autograph and a 'nice one, Mike!' That was three members of The Smiths. Where could the fourth be found?

Time passed and Andy Rourke and Mike Joyce continued to play regularly in Manchester, with a band called Spector and long-standing songwriting luminary, Vinny Peculiar. A show by the latter, at Manchester's long-gone Bierkeller, would also include Craig Gannon (another slip of paper from the bar staff and a borrowed pen…), so that was three and a half Smiths! Mike became someone to talk to regularly. Johnny Marr was around more and more at gigs, emerging from his rehearsal room beneath the Night and Day Café. The Smiths were all around us. Apart from one.

Salisbury City Hall on Monday 27 November 1999 and Morrissey pulled me onto the stage during the guitar break of 'Now My Heart Is

Full', which was always the strategic point to try and beat security. We didn't speak, but we'd finally met. Sort of.

After the show, the dressing rooms were opened up to waiting fans by the wonderfully friendly guitarist, Alain Whyte. Meeting Morrissey's band, the players on *Vauxhall And I* and *Your Arsenal*, was such a thrill. Boz Boorer. Gary Day. Spencer was by that time no longer in favour, but the short-lived drummer, Spike T Smith, was a genial and welcoming Welshman.

That tour was a big one, trips away to Hamburg, Aylesbury, Leeds and loads more, funded by a job in Selfridges in the Trafford Centre. One late afternoon a colleague called on the internal phone network from a neighbouring section of the menswear department: 'Can you just come here a second? This guy looks so much like Morrissey.'

There he was. A slip of A4 paper, which we used for folding jumpers and shirts neatly, a ballpoint pen and then…

'Morrissey.'

'Yes?'

'It had to happen.'

Morrissey laughed and agreed: 'Yes, it did,' and Linder Sterling asked: 'Oh, have you been waiting a long time?'

Only around six years, as it happens. But a lot of water had passed under the bridge in that time. Growing up stuff, to the sound of Morrissey and The Smiths.

He signed an autograph 'To Rob' and then more eyes were on him, more autographs and fuss, so it was time to go. His shirt shopping interrupted, and *Bona Drag* playing entirely coincidentally on the stereo in the casual menswear section, he and Linder wandered, trying to ignore everyone staring, and choose to disappear into the modern, Romanesque hulk of the Trafford Centre.

That's four (and a half) members of The Smiths. It was the first time and the last, but we both knew it had to happen. Some day.

### DANIEL ASH

It's 1992. A spotty nineteen-year old me pulls into the last available car parking space at an angle so wonky I could be the lead role in a Specsavers advert. From my car stereo, the magical noise of Johnny Marr's shimmering guitar casts it spell over the fade-out of my beloved 'The Boy With The Thorn In His Side'. I know you'll understand why it's imperative that I stay until the very end.

Today is the day. The interview for my first 'grown up' job. Up until then I had spent my life either singing on a stage working towards that teenage dream of world domination, lying on my bed listening to records, or slumped behind the counter at Blockbuster Video. I was a cripplingly shy and nervous teenager, rarely comfortable in the company of others. Especially strangers. Back then, I'd sooner jump out of the nearest window than engage in polite small talk. I guess you could say I was born to be a Smiths fan.

How I got the interview was, in itself, something of a miracle. Especially considering the main skill required to do the job was an

*Daniel Ash is a literary soul*

understanding of numbers. Not a strength of mine. '1-2-3-4'ing the band into a song was the closest thing I had to experience with numbers. I was never entirely sure what came after '4', but I know there's a '7' in there somewhere.

A kind friend had naively put my name forward as someone that might be a good fit for the company (Lord knows why! Sympathy? A prank?), so out of respect to him, I put on my best tie, ironed my tweed trousers and tried to make sure there wasn't any McDonalds down my top. Beef, I'm afraid. Sorry, Morrissey.

I entered the room and nervously shook the hand of the man who might lead my quiet life into some terrible new chapter. Doomsday. The day the dream died. The very moment I hang up the guitar, start working for the man and begin to spend my weekends gathered around a pub table talking enthusiastically about Excel shortcuts. Eugh. That's not very rock and roll. Somewhere I can feel Keith Richards shaking his head. I feel fear and anxiety spread throughout my entire body. I am an imposter. I really shouldn't be there. I can't do numbers. I can't even do the seven times table without booking a fortnight off. Why am I playing along with this silly charade?

'Would you like a glass of water?' the well-spoken man in a suit asks.

'Yes, please,' I respond, remembering from an interview tips blog that this ol' chestnut will buy me a little time. I want to add, 'And could you knock me up a sandwich too? Crescent of crisps?'

He briefly leaves the room. My mouth goes dry and the panic hits a new level. A million thoughts tumble around my mind. None of them helpful. Thirty seconds later, the man in the suit returns and sits opposite me. He places a glass of water in front of me, and I take an enthusiastic swig, killing as much time as I possibly can. I try to think of something to say, but there's nothing. Just a long, awkward silence. I don't know much about job interviews, but I'm pretty sure this isn't what you're supposed to do.

'How are you today?' he eventually begins. Ahh, small talk. We meet again. I look around for the nearest window.

'Yeah, not bad,' I nervously respond, giving him absolutely nothing. Very 'on brand' for me.

'Ahh, well you'll have to excuse me if I seem a little tired. I went to a concert last night,' he smiles.

What? My brain slows down a little as a small percentage of panic seems to magically subside. Music small talk I can do.

'Ahh, who did you see?'

'A Smiths tribute.'

*Annnd relax.* He's only gone and bloody said it. With those three words, my mind is suddenly at ease. Talk about common ground. At nineteen, he's genuinely just picked my *Mastermind* specialist subject out of the sky and thrown it down on the table. (The Smiths. Not Smiths tribute bands!) It's my move and I've never been more ready for a chinwag. Maybe I could do this job after all. We end up chatting The Smiths for around thirty minutes. We speak of favourite songs, favourite versions of songs, we try to come up with a solid answer for what is the best studio album (*The Queen Is Dead*… but only just).

We talk solo projects, vegetarianism (me, tried it but smelt some KFC popcorn chicken, and blew it), him (a strict veggie since first buying *Meat Is Murder*) and how this magical band seem to be singing about and for us. They soundtracked both of our lives.

Heartbreak, sadness, good times, formative years. No matter what shit was going down in our personal lives, The Smiths were *always* there. At the end of the interview, the man in a suit finally snapped back to reality and asked me what relevant skills I had for the job. I'm calm, collected and honest. I tell him that ultimately, I'm rubbish at numbers, but good at discussing The Smiths B-sides. I know my parents are going to flip their lids.

Three weeks later I receive note that on this occasion, I haven't in fact got the job. Well, there's a surprise. There is, however, an extra comment attached to the letter explaining what a nice time the interviewer had chatting to me. He felt that despite the clear lack of experience required for the job, I was a very pleasant and vibrant person to chat to. I feel a great sense of relief and an even greater sense of contentment and comfort in the person that I am and will always be. Maybe strangers aren't so scary.

Maybe there is a place in the world for little old me after all. 'Hello, my name is Daniel Ash. I like The Smiths and I don't like numbers'. And most importantly, despite my brain often trying to convince me otherwise, I think everything is going to be just fine.

### JOHN DENTON, AGE 16

I was eight or nine and had been playing guitar for about a year, listening to bands like Oasis, the Rolling Stones and Guns N' Roses, when I stumbled across this completely random song. It was 'I Know It's Over'. I found myself listening to something based purely around lyrics that were original and brutally honest. I began digging into the catalogue of The Smiths. After two weeks they had become my favourite band.

They're just a gift that keeps on giving. Morrissey, aside from the stage presence and being such an interesting and funny character, has a God-given talent to be able to cover all areas of people's emotions and life experiences through his lyrics. He's able to say what everybody's thinking, but in a way that nobody else can really articulate. The only person I can really link this to is Bob Dylan. But Dylan's lyrics relate to specific time periods. Morrisey's lyrics are

*John Denton met Johnny at Piccadilly Records*

timeless, and I honestly think will continue to help people until the world stops spinning.

And Johnny Marr? I just love his style. It's a really over complicated and weird way of playing, almost as if he's a Premier League midfielder covering every blade of grass. I would rather listen to that than any other guitarist across history. But he knows how to capture a feeling, and I assume that that's always in his mind when writing a riff.

My relationship with Johnny began when I was eleven. I waited outside Piccadilly Records for three hours on the day his solo album Fe*ver Dreams Part 1-4* to meet him. We had a chat about guitars, starting a band (in which he talked me through meeting Andy Rourke and seeing Morrissey's poster advert in a local shop when he himself was looking for a band), and music in general. A year later, Johnny published an application form in partnership with Salford Foundation Trust with the prize for the winner (who had to be from Salford) of a year's funding from the man himself, along with the big headline, The Johnny Marr Award. Long story short, I won and appeared all over the country, and some of the world's biggest newspapers and channels (most notably ITV and the *NME*) to talk about my story and the award. And I was invited backstage at Johnny's show at the Piece Hall in Halifax, where we had a long chat and jam together.



### COUNCILWOMAN MONICA RODRIGUEZ

Growing up in California, I was always surrounded by music. My grandfather was a professional mariachi, and my parents, immigrants from Mexico, filled our home with everything from Motown to Chicano oldies. By the time I reached Pacoima Junior High, I began to gravitate toward music I could truly call my own.

I found my voice and fashion sense in the alternative scene. From my bob to my Docs, it was the first time I felt a sense of ownership over who I was. For me, and for so many Angelenos, The Smiths and Morrissey were more than just music. They were a sanctuary and blunt observers of political and human condition. There is a deep and almost spiritual connection between this British alternative sound and the Latino community. I have always believed it comes from the raw, unvarnished truth in Morrissey's lyrics, which mirrors the heart of rancheras. It is music that speaks to the outsider and gives voice to alienation and heartache in a way that resonates across languages and cultures.

I was elected to the Los Angeles

*Councilwoman Monica Rodriguez & Moz putting the M in Moz Angeles*

City Council in 2017, and it was always my intention to use my platform to celebrate the cultural icons who helped shape our city's identity. Early in my first term, I chose to honour the man that 'put the M in Moz Angeles' and declared November 10th as 'Morrissey Day' in Los Angeles. Presenting him with that certificate at the Hollywood Bowl was a full circle moment but seeing the joy it brought him was special because I know that's the sentiment fans feel at every show (that's not cancelled).

### JOHNNY MARR

Everything that I was doing in The Smiths I can do now; but there's things that I do now that I wouldn't have had the skill or the mindset to do in The Smiths. I would never have been able to stand in front of a 70-piece orchestra and play to thousands of people, for example. So it's all good. I'm happy with how things have turned out.

### MORRISSEY

I would rather eat my own testicles than reform The Smiths, and that's saying something for a vegetarian.

*Salford Lads Club is a place of pilgrimage for fans young and old*

# SPECIAL THANKS

Ann Nazario, Guy Burke, Mags Burke, Abigail Dawson, Ahmet Dervish, Alan Ewart, Andrew Greaves, Andrew Hann, Andrew Johnson, Andrew Meagher, Andy Dawson, Arjen van Reenen, Aspi Tantra, Bec Morris, Ben Prior, Bill Mather, Bri Lally, Callan Broughton, Carl Mann, Chris George, Chris Henry, Chris L Curnow, Christopher Hannaford, Christopher Quinn, Claire Melville, Colin Plank, Craig B Mulhern, Dameon Priestly, David Beardmore, David Brazendale, Donna Goodall, Emily Stark, Emmanuel Foricher, George Bray, Graham Love, Greg Cotmore, Helen Hulston, Ian Mcelhinney, Imran Hassan, Isaac Johnson-Caddell, Jamie Reid-Sinclair, Joe Bryant, John Baxter, John McMahon, John Opolski, John Welsh, Juanita Mantz, Julie Callaghan, Kieran Tanswell, Lana Menges, Laurence Byrne, Leah Callahan, Linzy Shaw-Case, Lisa Collins, Malcolm Goode, Manuel Parra Serrada, Mark Quinn, Michael Hamm, Mike Nettleton, Monica Rodriguez, Nalinee Darmrong, Pam Lawson, Paul Asplin, Paul Howard, Peter Martin, Philip Brett, Phill Gatenby, Rachel Evans, Richard Blant, Richard Del Rio, Richard Preece, Rick Lanning, Robert Middleton, Robert Plummer, Ross Kennerell-Walters, Russell Harper, Sean Koepenick, Sergey Kachanovskiy, Stephan Krueger, Stephanie Snyder, Stephen Canavan, Stephen Jackson, Stephen Reid, Steve Cutter, Steve James, Steven Sidebottom, Stuart Douglas, Theo Louki, Tim Naylor, Tony Heald, William Smith, Wouter Hiltrop

# STEPHEN WRIGHT

Signed photographs of The Smiths and other
iconic musicians available from:

www.smithsphotos.com

thesmithsphotographs